The Hostile City of Love and Antibodies of Hate

Global Populisms

The titles published in this series are listed at *brill.com/gpop*

The Hostile City of Love and Antibodies of Hate

Urban Contestations of Identity and Belonging

By

Ipek Demirsu

BRILL

LEIDEN | BOSTON

Originally published in hardback in 2024.

Cover illustration: Verona, Piazza Brà with the Municipality and the Roman amphitheater Arena di Verona. © Ipek Demirsu, 2019.

The Library of Congress has cataloged the hardcover edition as follows:

Names: Demirsu, Ipek, author.
Title: The hostile city of love and antibodies of hate : urban
  contestations of identity and belonging / by Ipek Demirsu.
Description: Leiden; Boston: Brill, [2024] | Series: Global populisms,
  2666-2280; volume 5 | Includes bibliographical references and index. |
  Identifiers: LCCN 2024020438 (print) | LCCN 2024020439 (ebook) |
  ISBN 9789004692893 (hardback) | ISBN 9789004692909 (ebook)
Subjects: LCSH: Verona (Italy)–Social conditions. | Verona
  (Italy)–Politics and government. | Group identity–Italy–Verona. |
  Right-wing extremists–Italy–Verona.
Classification: LCC HN488.V44 D46 2024 (print) | LCC HN488.V44 (ebook) |
  DDC 307.76/20945–dc23/eng/20240502
LC record available at https://lccn.loc.gov/2024020438
LC ebook record available at https://lccn.loc.gov/2024020439

Typeface for the Latin, Greek, and Cyrillic scripts: "Brill". See and download: brill.com/brill-typeface.

ISSN 2666-2280
ISBN 978-90-04-73840-9 (paperback, 2025)
ISBN 978-90-04-69289-3 (hardback)
ISBN 978-90-04-69290-9 (e-book)
DOI 10.1163/9789004692909

Per gli anticorpi dell'odio,
ovunque siano ...

∵

Contents

Preface

> The ache for home lives in all of us, the safe place where we can go
> as we are and not be questioned.
>
> MAYA ANGELOU, *All God's Children Need Travelling Shoes*

∙∙
∙

I started this research as a doctoral student in Sociology at a perturbing time of rising right-wing populism and far-right politics: With the Trump administration at its zenith, Bolsonaro's success in Brazil threatening indigenous communities, the negotiations of Brexit commencing, an anti-gender wave taking over much of eastern Europe, and a far-right alliance consolidating its political victory in Italy. As a Turkish migrant woman living in the mid-sized city of Verona, I was watching the winds of far-right and populist influence change the course of politics in myriad different settings, including my own country of origin which had already been going down the road of democratic backsliding for almost a decade. However, I was utterly unaware of what was going on in my immediate vicinity in Verona, where I had been living for over two years. My impression of Verona as a resident was, at first, that it was the quintessential touristic city where you could wander the streets of the historical center in fascination. I lived the everyday as a tourist and was comforted by my distance from local politics at a moment when I was overwhelmed by the socio-political tension in my hometown of Istanbul. Such carefree attachment of a flaneuse was bluntly interrupted when I first started to observe overtly racist and neofascist markings hidden within this impeccable touristscape. I perfectly remember the time I was waiting for the bus across from the world-famous Arena when I noticed a writing using a racist slur for black people in a call to 'send them all to Africa', lucidly communicating the type of racism that assigns a 'territory' to every racial or ethnic group which is not to be trespassed, especially in the case of Fortress Europe. Initially, I could not ascertain any individual in the historical center corresponding to the typical image of an extreme right figure in outfit and appearance (since they mostly sport an elegant middle-class outfit in Verona), yet their presence was rendered visible through inscriptions on urban materialities. Eventually, I realized that this city has been a harbinger of the rise of the populist and the far-right due to its geopolitical as well as historical positioning not only in Italy per se, but in Europe at large. Such a realization more or less coincided with my discovery of the cosmos of Veronetta, where I found an unexpected cosmopolitan air in an imperfect urban backdrop. This part of Verona reminded me of the neighborhood of Taksim in Istanbul that used to unite everyday struggles with the plurality of actors and the diversity they conveyed as part of this social space, offering conducive grounds from which the remarkable Gezi movement had blossomed, named after a public park whilst conveying a much more transversal justice claim. It was at that moment when I finally ceased to be a tourist-migrant wandering aimlessly and became a city-zen of Verona, as the protracted struggles of an assemblage of civil society actors located in Veronetta rekindled the sort of activist citizenship that is nourished from an attachment to place. This new attachment allowed me to pursue once again the claims of justice which I had withdrawn from in my old hometown.

In this sense, this research has been the perfect opportunity to 'integrate' into the city I have nominated as my new home. Understanding the perspectives of the locals (not only the friendly ones but also those that are unwelcoming, hostile, and even threatening), how they view their own territorial identities, how they perceive and perform the so-called *Veronesità*, and the counterposed spatial belonging of Veronetta, allowed me to comprehend the boundaries of identity which were historically shaped. Every single interview, every meeting I attended, every social media post was a window to the stories of these individuals inhabiting the same social space and a chance to make sense of this space through their thoughts, experiences, and feelings. These situated constructs have been intimately imbued in broader struggles of identity while being clearly manifested in everyday urban spaces if one were to employ a curious and informed eye. Understanding those all-too-relevant historical and cultural signposts revealed throughout the research enabled me to make sense of competing identity constructs inescapably forged along the time-space axis and to notice shared themes that incessantly travel across borders, uniting like-minded actors. Most importantly, by the end of my research, I had the chance to witness the unexpected victory of a progressive left alliance in the city administration of Verona after decades, owing to their collaboration with grassroots actors that have been authoring the protracted struggle against nativist closure. Such a political victory, pointed out in the book, doubtlessly offers hope for hostile settings elsewhere.

In this journey, I was lucky to have brilliant scholars by my side who were fundamental in shaping the final outcome presented in this book. I want to extend my most sincere gratitude first of all to my doctoral supervisor Prof. Annalisa Frisina, whose guidance has been and continues to be invaluable in helping me realize my full potential as a social researcher. I would like to thank my co-supervisors, Prof. Luca Trappolin, for pointing out the strengths of my work when I got lost, and Prof. Michela Semprebon, for providing me with the right suggestions at the right moments. I must also mention my gratefulness for Prof. Devi Sacchetto, who was always willing to offer support, especially during the devastating COVID-19 pandemic in Italy, when an essential part of this research was conducted. My special thanks go to Prof. Camilla Hawthorne for her warm hospitality during my stay at the University of California Santa Cruz Sociology Department, where I had the opportunity to acquire a deeper understanding of racism and racialization in Europe in her classes. I would also like to thank Prof. Manuela Caiani for welcoming me to her doctoral course on radical right in Europe at Scuola Normale Superiore, which provided me with the necessary theoretical background on far-right movements. I want to thank Prof. Pietro Saitta and Prof. Andrea Brighenti for their fair and constructive reflections on an earlier version of this monograph.

I want to express my gratitude to all the participants who showed great interest in taking part in this research, enthusiastically telling me their account of Verona and what it means to be a part of this city, for better or for worse.

Lastly, I would like to thank my husband for his extensive support throughout this process, and my dearest son for teaching me the value of persistence.

Figures and Tables

Figures

Tables

Abbreviations

AN	Alleanza Nazionale
ANED	L'Associazione Nazionale Ex Deportati nei Campi Nazisti
ANPI	Associazione Nazionale Partigiani d'Italia
B&B	Bed and Breakfast
CAS	Centri d'accoglienza straordinaria
Cestim	Centro Studio Immigrazione
GAP	Gruppo di azione patriottica
GasP!	Gruppo di Acquisto Sociale Piccoli
MSI	Movimento Sociale Italiano
MS-FT	Movimento Sociale-Fiamma Tricolore
NUDM	Non Una di Meno
Palazzo INA	Palazzo Istituto Nazionale Assicurazioni
PoliTeSse	Politiche e Teorie della Sessualità
RSI	Repubblica Sociale Italiana
UAAR	Unione Atei Agnostici Razionalisti
UDU	L'associazione Unione degli Universitari
VFS	Veneto Fronte Skinheads
WCF	World Congress of Families
WWI	World War 1
WWII	World War 2

Introduction: Cartographies of Belonging in a Mid-sized Italian City

> Is it not possible for a sense of place to be progressive; not self-closing and defensive, but outward-looking?
>
> MASSEY, 1994: 147

∙∙

On 26th of July 2018, the city council of Verona witnessed a peculiar controversy during the discussion of a motion proposing to proclaim Verona 'a pro-life city', when a councilor rose from the benches to pose the fascist salute against the silent protest of a feminist group dressed as handmaids after the TV series *The Handmaid's Tale*.[1] The motion itself was defended by its creator from the populist right *Lega* party as an opportunity to encourage Italian births against the threat of being "invaded by Muslims" and the subsequent "imposition of the Islamic law on the native population".[2] While the motion eventually passed paving the way for other cities to follow suit, the same year a local far-right group declared 'ethnic resistance' in a multiethnic neighborhood of Verona against an impending 'ethnic replacement' in their city. These concerns that reverberate in different settings are part of a so-called 'Great Replacement' theory claiming white populations risk being replaced through immigration, a demographic anxiety that was overtly articulated in 2023 by the Italian Agriculture Minister from the far-right *Fratelli d'Italia* party.[3]

The last decade has been marked by a steady rise of populist right and far-right actors around the world, promoting defensive and reactionary outlooks in various localities. At this critical historical conjuncture, the UK had chosen the sovereignist Brexit path, the Trump administration left its mark in the US with some of the most drastic anti-immigration measures, while Bolsonaro's

---

1   For more information on this incident, see: https://www.repubblica.it/politica/2018/07/27 /news/saluto_romano_destra_verona_consiglio_comunale-202795134.
2   Interview with the Verona city councillor Alberto Zelger: https://video.repubblica.it/polit ica/verona-il-leghista-della-mozione-anti-aborto-senza-bimbi-italiani-saremo-invasi-dagli -islamici/316126/316755.
3   The statement can be accessed at: https://www.bbc.com/news/world-europe-65324319.

presidency existentially threatened indigenous communities in Brazil. In much of Europe, we witnessed nativist and far-right discourses becoming ever more mainstream, the issue of immigration being securitized, with governments in Eastern Europe pioneering policies against the sexual rights of women and LGBTQ+ individuals. In Italy, the post-fascist party Fratelli d'Italia together with the populist Lega has been pledging to bring back traditional Christian values and to prioritize native Italians over ethnic minorities. Both the political rhetoric and the subsequent policies they have in common underline the principle of *sovereignty* reinterpreted as taking back control in the 'homeland', coupled with re-inserting an *identity* that is defined through primordial ties to this place, emphasizing local traditions, cultures, and values.

The loud volume of these arguments struck me profoundly in the city of Verona where I had been living as a Turkish migrant woman for a couple of years, when I discovered that such themes had already been the order of the day in this city preceding its global take. The case of Verona attests to how a defense of one's territory and local identity could easily transform into everyday expressions of hate toward any form of difference and even into ritualized micro-violence. Yet, on a closer examination, one discovers that the setting of Verona not only foreshadows these political trends as a privileged laboratory of exclusionary localist pride, but more importantly, offers glimpses into possibilities of bottom-up community-building practices and everyday struggles to create democratic spaces undertaken by an assemblage of local actors. It is at this point that the study took off to unearth the dynamics that made the city of Verona such an attractive location for far-right and rightwing populist actors on the one hand, and to understand the prospects of social inclusion and pluralist membership in this hostile social setting on the other hand, with the objective of finding hope for local struggles elsewhere.

The mid-sized touristic city of Verona in the north-east of Italy has thus been taken as a stimulating setting from which to comparatively analyze contending efforts to define belonging in and through urban space. The case selection reflects upon the rise of reactionary nationalisms taking place not only in Italy but in Europe at large and in the Americas (Akkerman et al., 2016; Greven, 2016; Hochschild, 2016; Duyvendak et al., 2022; Barbosa & Casarões, 2023), as well as novel forms of resistance in different contexts seeking to rewrite scripts of belonging in everyday exchanges (Roth, 2018; Hall, 2019; Rygiel & Baban, 2019). Verona has been at the forefront as the fortress of far-right which has become institutionalized through its alliance with the populist right, partly owing to its historical imprints, and partly due to a modern reinterpretation of such historical belonging with reference to a construction of territorial identity that is shared with nativist actors operating in different settings. As a matter of fact, the recent success of far-right discourses in the Italian peninsula has been dubbed by some experts as the 'Veronification' of Italian politics (De Medico quoted in Torrisi, 2019; Bernini, 2022).

As a tourism hub, the marketed face of Verona is the city of 'Romeo and Juliet', with a long and rich history that has been perfectly preserved since Roman times, making the historical center seem like an open-air museum. Concomitantly, the city is the migration capital of the region of Veneto,[4] despite the prevalence of anti-immigrant sentiments that also find expression in the local administration. Previously a bastion of the Christian Democrats, in the last couple of years, the city has been pioneering in Italy what is considered a 'return to the traditional family',[5] accompanied by identitarian motifs that shelter xenophobic and even supremacist tendencies. The municipality on the one hand, and far-right groups with both formal and informal ties to the city administration on the other hand, have been actively involved in making Verona become a trademark in this global trend, visible for instance in the organization of events such as the World Congress of Families, pro-life demonstrations, sponsored nazirock concerts, and the hosting European counterparts from various far-right backgrounds. Such mainstream representation of the city goes hand in hand with the marketing of 'heritage' for touristic consumption, explicitly embodied in the historical center as the official face of Verona and what it means to be 'Veronese'.

This is until one crosses the Adige River to wander into the streets of *Veronetta*, a neighborhood at the heart of the city where the first human settlement took place, pre-dating even the early Romans. Separated from the main *piazzas* by the river, the neighborhood is adjacent to and partly overlapping with the historical center. At an initial glance, it seems like any other 'multiethnic' quarter that has become commonplace in the periphery of the Italian landscape, being associated with migration and urban degeneration for decades, notwithstanding its central location. Echoing the conceptualization of urban marginality by Wacquant, the area is associated by an external gaze with 'undesired' migrants, 'dishonored' minorities, and working-class families (Wacquant, 2016: 29). Over time, its proximity to tourist attraction sites led to rising housing prices alongside 'revanchist policies' that seek to reconquer this central area of the city, cleansing it from 'unwanted' elements (Semprebon, 2011).

Yet, on a closer and more informed look, one can observe in *Veronetta* a contending representation of the cityscape that breathes a cosmopolitan air,

---

4 For more information see: http://dati.istat.it/Index.aspx?QueryId=19106.
5 For more information, see: https://www.veronasera.it/attualita/verona-congresso-mondi ale-famiglie-polemiche-critiche-arci-contro-manifestazione-10-marzo-2019-.html.

composed of colors, sounds, and sights that contrast representations prevalent in the historical center. The neighborhood articulates a different way of being 'Veronese', an alternative membership in a community that is based on an inclusive understanding of belonging, co-created by migrants, non-migrants, and other minority groups. In this sense, the area has become an object of citizen mobilization over the years owing to the extraordinary collocation of diverse progressive actors, transforming the existing multiethnic social fabric into everyday intercultural practices, thereby offering an outward-looking social space that reaches out to places beyond. Hence, solidarity among local grassroots movements in Veronetta who refer to themselves as 'the antibodies of hate'[6] contest the type of exclusionary territorial identity in the official representation of the city, negotiating instead for a dynamic alternative that incorporates local experiences with global themes of social justice. The protracted struggles and successful mobilization of this network of actors have been one of the primary factors leading to the 2022 victory of a progressive city administration after decades, which went on to introduce a groundbreaking new approach to local governance underlining social inclusion and pluralism.

Given the wider socio-political conjuncture that the case of Verona is positioned in, this research is an inquiry into the relationship between identity politics, social movements, and urban spaces, seeking to illustrate the spatiality of global themes in everyday movement-countermovement dynamics across urban landscapes. Therefore, the book has undertaken to explore the following questions: What were the mechanisms behind the success of populist right and far-right actors in Verona's sociopolitical space? What forms of progressive resistance have been possible in a hostile urban setting? How do such movement/countermovement dynamics unfold in everyday landscapes? What is the relationship between belonging, mobilization, and cityspace? And finally, in what ways do (trans)national themes of identity politics translate into city life, and how do local struggles in turn connect with global struggles of belonging?

While Verona presents itself as an interesting case foreshadowing larger political trends, urban struggles of belonging that characterize its everyday can be traced in myriad different contexts: including populist local politics in Messina, Italy (Saitta, 2022) or in Toronto, Canada often considered as a bastion

---

6 It must be noted that the biological metaphor here chosen by the actors in question is not taken uncritically by the researcher, as biological lexicon in politics can carry extremist meanings. That being said, a critical reflection on the choice of this term by these actors themselves reveals its connotation signifying 'hope', 'a solution', or 'a way out' to what is considered an environment of exclusionary intolerance.

of liberal democracy (Silver et al., 2020), anti-immigrant sentiments in Athens, Greece (Papatzani, 2021), anti-Roma mobilization in Timişoara, Romania (Creţan & O'Brien, 2019), nationalist heteronormativity in Çanakkale, Turkey (Gezgin, 2023), and urban conflict among far-right and anti-racist groups in Berlin, Germany (Shoshan, 2019), which are then posed against bottom-up forms of resistance to this growing tide of urban populisms seeking to rewrite citizenship by localized practices of belonging (Misgav, 2016; Turam, 2019; Harald & Jonathan, 2019). The *extended case* approach (Burawoy, 2009) to study these social processes in Verona, therefore, is employed to revisit the nexus of collective identities and attachment to social space, investigating constructions of place and place-based belongings of antagonistic social actors with the aim of providing novel analytical tools to study urban dynamics of identity politics applicable beyond the case study.

This has been done by borrowing from the timeless insights offered by Doreen Massey (1992, 1994, 1999, 2004, 2005) on a conceptualization of space that is not merely taken as a surface or container, but instead an unfixed product of multiple social relations, thereby highlighting the mutually constitutive nature of space and politics (Featherstone & Painter, 2013). As a result, the restructuring of theory that the extended case method foresees (Burawoy et al., 1991; Burawoy, 2009) has been undertaken with the dual concepts 'identity of place' and 'place-based identities' in the field of collective action to help expand this avenue of research by accentuating the role of 'place' as an affective configuration in shaping political possibilities and collective identifications (Wills, 2013; Grossberg, 2013; Featherstone & Painter, 2013). Identity of place is used to capture material and symbolic characteristics attributed to space, its representation, and its historical memory that turn it into an affective 'place'. Place-based identity, on the other hand, is employed to connote shared outlooks, feelings, and values derived from inhabiting the same social space. A comparative investigation of antagonistic actors that operate in the same city reveals the interplay between these dual concepts, their impact on collective identity and collective action, as well as how these in turn convey constructions of 'city-zenship' (*cittadinanza*). The latter is utilized here to connote participation in everyday urban life, equal recognition as a member of the city as a polity, and a sense of belonging thereof. As such, the research explores the intersection of urban space and sense of belonging on the one hand, collective identity and collective action on the other hand, whilst investigating how local articulations of city-zenship are influenced by, and in turn reverberate in broader struggles of belonging.

The field of social movements has been primarily focused on macro-level cross-national comparisons of political and economic contexts shaping organizational behavior and its outcomes, represented by the predominance of opportunity structures approach (McAdam et al., 1996; Tarrow, 1994; Meyer, 2004), and the employment of resource mobilization theory (McCarthy & Zald, 1977; Jenkins, 1983; Mayer, 1991). Here, 'space' usually stands for external conditions setting opportunity structures, the availability of resources, or networking opportunities (Diani & McAdam, 2003), including strategic action fields (Fligstein & McAdam, 2012). On the other hand, micro-level analyses of social movements usually employ a rational choice approach in understanding motivations behind activists' participation, interpreted through sociodemographic factors such as education level, gender, and socioeconomic conditions (Johnston et al., 1994; Klandermans, 2004; Klandermans & Mayer, 2006; Caiani, 2019), which extends the same treatment of space over the individual unit of analysis. Instead, meso-level sociological analyses of mobilization have been increasingly employing constructivist perspectives in understanding social movements, ranging from the conceptualization of 'collective identity' (Melucci, 1980; Johnston et al., 1994; Polletta & Jasper, 2001; Van Stekelenburg, 2013), to the process of 'symbolic framing' (Benford & Snow, 2000; Snow, 2013) in claims-making. Hence, in response to the over-reliance on instrumental motivations based on economic action, identity struggles, symbolic production, and affective solidarity have eventually gained visibility in explaining political mobilization (Della Porta & Diani, 2006; Eder, 2015). These have included studies that point out the role played by a sense of place in shaping collective identity and collective action (Melucci, 1984; Routledge, 2010; Routledge, 2013; Nicholls, 2008; Nicholls et al., 2013; Della Porta & Diani, 2006).

The subfield of urban social movements, famously known as the 'right to the city' movements (Dikeç, 2002; Harvey, 2012; Mayer, 2009; Soja, 2010; Domaradzka, 2018), has developed relatively independent from the mainstream social movements theorizing (for a detailed treatment this argument, see Pickvance, 2003), and focused primarily on local movements seeking to influence decision-making on urban policies or resources (Nel·lo, 2016; Mayer et al., 2016; Domaradzka, 2018). Manuel Castells's canonical work *The City and Grassroots* (1983) has been a milestone for the study of urban social movements, emphasizing the centrality of socio-spatial relations in the study of mobilization and the latter's impact on the city. These forms of situated collective action have material claims to urban life, responding to the devastating effects of neoliberal policies with a vision of spatial justice (Castells, 1983; Soja, 2010; Harvey, 2012) that "not only takes the city as its stage but also its motivation and subject." (Nel·lo, 2016: 2)

It is at this juncture that the present study seeks to contribute to this thriving field in an attempt to restructure theory by operationalizing the city and its various neighborhoods as 'social spaces' with their own characteristics and types of attachments that translate into the collective identity of movements and hence impact the forms of collective action aimed at transforming the (material or immaterial) experience of city-zenship. These analytical lenses can be employed in similar contexts of urban hostility for unearthing spatialized forms of populism and nativism, as well as for highlighting situated forms of resistance by progressive actors. This is made possible by the diachronic socio-spatial analysis of contentious movements that the book offers, conferring space an agency of its own. This point is systematically drawn out in the beginning of Chapters 4 and 5 dedicated to the analysis of antagonistic groups, their relationship to social space, and their constructions of city-zenship, as well as Chapter 6 which explores the nexus of collective action and identity of place.

As such, the book offers a novel approach in several ways. Firstly, it highlights the interactive and relational dynamics involved in the evolution of two opposing movements in shared everyday spaces (Işın, 2008; Van Stekelenburg, 2013; Nicholls et al., 2013; Fillieule & Broqua, 2020), thereby uncovering those situated mechanisms and micro-conflicts that echo wider trends, which cannot be sufficiently addressed in a multiple case cross-national analysis. There is a pending need for longitudinal analyses demonstrating everyday spatial processes in movement formation and the impact of movement-countermovement dynamics on collective identity to "move away from synchronic mechanisms toward diachronic variations with regard to context change." (Fillieule & Neveu, 2019: 14) Such undertaking was made possible through 3-year long ethnographic fieldwork involving participant and non-participant observation, qualitative interviews, online ethnography, and archival research, capturing personal accounts alongside historical processes. Secondly, by focusing on the everyday practices of competing social actors, the study offers a systematic investigation of contentious collective action in urban realities, whereby struggles of belonging that do not solely pertain to access to resources or material deprivation become entwined with other urban processes such as touristification and gentrification. These everyday aspects of movement/countermovement dynamics upon material, cognitive, and lived spaces (Miller, 2013) are explored through the utilization of participant visual methods that view shared spaces from the point of view of those who inhabit them, and the employment of online ethnography alongside traditional fieldwork in capturing the online/offline continuum of social space.

Therefore, the book first explores the ways in which far-right and populist right actors gain the upper hand in the local, as well as bottom-up progressive responses thereof, as their interaction unravels in urban exchanges.
Furthermore, mechanisms from which situated struggles find expression
beyond the locality are elucidated, alongside global themes that are translated
into such local struggles, manifested in everyday struggles of city-zenship conveying wider themes of identity politics that travel across space. As such, the
study contributes to the burgeoning literature on spatiality and belonging in
social movements (Agnew & Brusa, 1999; Herb & Kaplan, 1999; Nicholls, 2008;
McFarlane, 2009; Dochartaigh & Bosi 2010; Nicholls et al., 2013; Routledge,
2010; Routledge, 2013; Cumbers & Routledge, 2013; Miller, 2013; Sbicca &
Perdue, 2013; Bruttomesso, 2018; Yuen, 2018), through an understanding of
space as both the author and the product of social ties. As each chapter will
demonstrate in great detail, such an approach helps to unearth mobilization
around place-based belongings and the construction of collective identity situated in a given space, which goes beyond a mere 'space as a resource' or 'space
as a container' approach.

In what follows, Chapter 1 sets out the theoretical foundations of the book,
revisiting the intersection of space, identity, and social movements grounded
in existing literature, whilst taking a step further to offer a new analytical angle
to studying spatial identities and practices of territorialization in social movement research. Chapter 2 goes on to explain the research design and the choice
of Verona from an extended case method approach, delineating the triangulation of complementary qualitative methods, discussing my positionality in
the field, and subsequent limitations this has posed. Chapter 3 provides a historical analysis of the social space of Verona, investigating historical episodes
that have played an indispensable role in the construction of the identity of
place, and the so-called *Veronesità* (place-based identity), also exploring the
particular history of the neighborhood of Veronetta. Chapter 4 and Chapter 5
offer an investigation of the two competing movements that operate in Verona
cityspace, their evolution, their roots, their alliances, as well as their relationship to urban space, the city administration, and one another, by utilizing the
reformulation of collective identity and collective action through the lenses
of social space. The former examines the alliance of far-right, populist right,
and ultra-Catholic elements that unite around sovereignist identitarianism
and promote a territorial identity that seeks exclusive city-zenship, while the
latter analyses the formation of the assemblage of local actors constituting
the 'antibodies of hate' who promote an alternative expansive place-based
belonging with a vision of an inclusive pluralist city-zenship in Verona. Lastly,
Chapter 6 investigates movement/countermovement dynamics through the

identity of place across two adjacent neighborhoods: (a) the historical center as an inward-looking touristscape with local symbolisms of heritage for identitarian actors, and (b) Veronetta as an outward-looking intercultural space undergoing gentrification, tied to the collective identity of the antibodies. The chapter thus highlights the manifestations of social conflict in urban realities and the everyday aspect of identity politics, which includes practices of territorialization and alternative representations of the city in connecting with similar causes in distant contexts. The book concludes with a discussion of the findings of the extended case of Verona for places beyond, reflecting on the analytical power of the categories 'identity of place' and 'place-based identities' for a spatial exploration of struggles of city-zenship in hostile cities.

CHAPTER 1

Social Space, Belonging, and Mobilization: The Role of Spatial Identities in Social Movements

> Human beings do not inhabit only a physical or geometric space;
> they simultaneously live in emotional, aesthetic, social, and histori-
> cal spaces, spaces of signification in general.
>
> LÉVY, 1997:144

∴

The conception of space as a social construct plays a fundamental yet long-
overlooked role in social movements, forging spatial collective identities and
shaping translocal struggles over belonging. The city is a particular socio-
spatial unit that produces and is produced by intersubjective engagements
among its inhabitants, whether it is marked by mutual indifference, civic
awareness, a sense of community, or antagonism. It is constituted by a constellation of everyday interactions of social actors whose paths cross in its various
streets and districts. The city is home to exclusionary practices of territorialization and a restorative nostalgia of a glorified past, as well as counterspaces
that resist timeless singular identities and seek to foster alternative forms of
belonging. It is this setting that has historically witnessed some of the most
important claims-making episodes and subsequent negotiations of membership in a given community. The city itself can also become the object of such
struggles, bringing themes and perspectives that travel across borders into
the proximity of urban life. Hence, to analyze the relationship between social
space and social movements, this chapter will delve into cityspace, elaborat-
ing on the identity of place and place-based belongings, and finally spatially
defined collective action. Following Lefebvre's (1991 [1974]) timeless insight
that social relations can only come into existence through space, this chapter
offers a constructivist conceptualization of urban space and the workings of
social movements therein, in order to respatialize collective identity, and as an
extension, the conceptualization of 'city-zenship'.

© IPEK DEMIRSU, 2024 | DOI:10.1163/9789004692909_003

1 Space, Territory, and Place-Based Identities

This study borrows from Massey's (2005) threefold conceptualization of space, taken first and foremost as an artifact of social relations. It is a product of exchanges between identities that take up space and are rewritten in every encounter. Moreover, social space is a sphere of 'coexisting heterogeneity' in the sense that it allows multiple modes of existence and a multiplicity of identities contemporaneously. As an outcome of interrelations, space is also understood as a process that is constantly in the making and never static or fixed: "In this open interactional space there are always connections yet to be made, juxtapositions yet to flower into interaction ... relations which may or may not be accomplished." (2005: 11). With an operationalization of space not merely understood as a surface, a container, or resources, but instead a product of social relations, Massey's insights help understand the mutually constitutive relationship between space and politics, and how different imaginings of space can translate into different, even antagonistic, constructions of political agency (Featherstone & Painter, 2013). As such, space is taken here as a socially constructed entity that not only accommodates a plurality of actors conveying different stories of the place they live but also plays a role in the production of such social actors and their identities, whilst being shaped by them.

Space becomes *place* through lived human experiences that confer meaning to this entity through acts of naming, imagining, and creating emotional attachments with a given space (Hubbard, 2005). As put by Lofland, places are 'especially meaningful spaces' that are enriched with associations and sentiments (Lofland, 1998: 64). A sense of belonging is an emotional state in which one feels 'at home', in a safe space constituted by everyday experiences, social ties, and situated memories. Massey (1994), similarly argues that place is a space that intersects with time, defined through interaction among living beings. It is an affective reality which involves "different ways of living in already socially determined locations, different possibilities of the forms and configurations of belonging and identification ... subjectification and agency." (Grossberg, 2013: 37). In fact, the situatedness of human society is one of its foundational characteristics, whereby those that inhabit the same location are presumed to convey sociocultural homogeneity over attributes such as language, traditions, education level, or income (Soja, 1971).

It is based on this understanding of human activity that *territoriality* is defined as "a behavioral phenomenon associated with the organization of space into spheres of influence or clearly demarcated territories which are made distinctive and considered at least partially exclusive by their occupants or definers." (Soja, 1971: 19). Brighenti (2014) suggests that territories are 'constitutively imagined' entities, created by expressive work and acts of coexistence, which render them living carriers of meaning. They are to be understood as relational processes composed of practices or acts rather than simply physical space. Therefore, understood not only as a setting for social relations, but also as a form of social relation itself, territories operate on the assumption of pre-announced ownership, marking hierarchies of belonging (Brighenti, 2010). Thus, the territory does not only involve access to resources but is also an indispensable resource for identity formation (Brighenti, 2010). For instance, the notion of autochthonism linking belonging and space conveys a sense of 'we were here first', and thereby assigns a sense of naturalized righteous belonging to a category of people, while deeming others unfit (Yuval-Davis et al., 2018).

The concept of identity, consequently, acquires substance through situated social processes and relations that are spatially defined, whilst attributing meaning to the territory where such human interaction takes place. Specific historical contexts produce particular identity types that help us orient ourselves in everyday life (Berger & Luckmann, 1966; Mead, 1934). In this regard, the spatial experiences of an individual play an indispensable role in their identity by providing the social setting and social relations necessary for its formation (de Certeau, 1984). The inextricable relationship between place and identity has been eloquently underlined by Kevin Lynch (1981):

> The simplest form of a sense of identity, in the narrow meaning of that common term: 'sense of place'. Identity is the extent to which a person can recognize or recall a place as being distinct from other places – as having a vivid, or unique, or at least particular character of its own ... Place identity is closely linked to personal identity. 'I am here' supports 'I am'.
>
> KEVIN LYNCH, 1981: 131–132

This much-overlooked spatial dimension in the construction of identity can be understood as a mutually constitutive process, wherein individuals shape the identity of the place they inhabit and in turn are characterized by this very socio-spatial entity (Massey, 1994).

This twofold process is aptly captured by Banini (2017), who differentiates between identity of place (*identità di luogo*), connoting "subjective perceptions, feelings and attitudes towards both the territory people inhabit and the local collectivity" (Ibid.: 20), and identity of the place (*identità del luogo*) found in material or symbolic elements that undergird representations/narratives pertaining to a place, its historical memory, and its current state. While the former signifies the forms of belonging that flourish in a given space, the latter indicates the representation of space itself, those physical, historical, and cognitive characteristics that make it what it is today. It is at this juncture that 'place' plays an indispensable role in the formation of collective identification and political inclinations (Wills, 2013). Moving from this theoretical foundation on the relationship between collectivities and the territory they inhabit (Banini & Pollice, 2015), the study opts to articulate a more refined terminology by differentiating the mutually constitutive categories of *identity of place* coming to signify those material and immaterial characteristics that make space become place, and *place-based identities* defined by the shared outlook and values of subjects derived from occupying the same social space. From this perspective, place is not only a container of territorial identities premised on collective memories, but also a constitutive part of this identity as it conveys tangible signs of its transformation through time (Aru, 2015: 71). Lived space is a point of reference for identities and histories, encapsulating symbols and cultures (Ibid.: 72).

As bounded space, *territoriality* begets geographical exclusiveness to human interaction; and therefore, harbors the tension between power and identity (Soja, 1971; Herb & Kaplan, 1999). Contending sets of social actors engage in acts of territorialization, deterritorialization, and reterritorialization through social space in everyday practices, with material and immaterial repercussions of belonging. These practices involve processes of boundary-drawing as the kernel of territory-making, which is a visible and public endeavor (Brighenti, 2010a; Brighenti 2010b; Halvorsen, 2015). Lefebvre (1991 [1974]) illustrates how boundary drawing of social space can involve natural boundaries such as mountains and rivers, as well as artificial boundaries such as city walls, or conceptual boundaries marked by discourse and signs. As the 'skeleton' of everyday life (Raffestin, 2012), territoriality comes to denote "sociospatial power relations that are shaping (and shaped by) everyday life" (Klauser, 2012: 113). Territoriality, therefore, encapsulates 'everyday bordering practices' (Yuval-Davis et al., 2018) that redefine the political constructions of belonging, and as a result, that of identity and citizenship.

The appropriation of a territory can also take place on the semantic plane through its selective representation, constituting a form of territorialization impacting social practices and the forms of place-based identities (Banini & Ilovan, 2021). Discourses of places, or what some have referred to as 'place-framing' (Martin, 2003), can unite people around a particular understanding of space and even guide collective action. This dynamic has been accentuated also by Schwarz and Streule (2022) who argue that spatial contestation among social actors is manifested in urban imaginaries and representations of territories as a collective endeavor in shaping social relations within. In this way, spatial identities are formed and crystalized through the association not only with the material, but also symbolic identifiers of a territory (Soja, 1971; Kaplan, 1994). A significant mechanism linking places with identities is the practice of *naming*, which can reflect power hierarchies through gendered, racial, and colonial characteristics, or bourgeoise values. In turn, the naming of places and landscapes yields an impact on meanings individuals attribute to space, and shape their self-defined group identity (Berg & Kearns, 1996). Thus, "naming place is also an act of naming the self and self-histories," in other words, assigning a certain type of belonging to the place in question (McKittrick, 2007: xxii).

In short, a geographical territory is inextricably linked to a feeling of belonging to a certain group, who is in turn identified by the social space that they inhabit and its historical legacy that render cultural characteristics concrete (Herb & Kaplan, 1999). Within this process, certain settings come to operate as 'nodal points' in the cognitive mapping of shared places and social relations that define them, which can include piazzas, buildings, museums, parks, or other artifacts. In the construction of identities through landscapes, collective memory plays an irrefutable role in a world of constant flux, "shaping discourses on preservation, development, and how heritage is defined and represented" (Moore, 2007: 97). The enactment of spatial identities through "powerful local territorial mechanisms" is also visible in the modern city most notably so in the urban territoriality of neighborhoods that accommodate human integration which is often segregated along race, ethnicity, class, and religion (Soja, 1971: 36).

2   The Configuration of the City and Belonging in Cityspace

The city is famously defined by Park et al. as:

> a state of mind, a body of customs and traditions, and of the organized attitudes and sentiments that inhere in these customs and are transmitted with this tradition. The city is not, in other words, merely a physical mechanism and an artificial construction. It is involved in the vital processes of the people who compose it; it is a product of nature, and particularly of human nature.
>
> PARK ET AL., 1967 [1926]: 1

In their canonical work on city life, Park and Burgess have argued that the city is constituted by the habits and customs of its inhabitants, which reflect not only on urban morphology, but also on its particular culture, or one might say on the 'identity of place'. The elementary units that make up city life are its constituent neighborhoods, which are the gradual materialization of particular sentiments, traditions, and history of the locals into a concrete neighborhood. Hence, the past of the neighborhood that has conferred its distinctive characteristics is carried onto the present as it continues to assert local traditions, attitudes, social rituals, and other signifiers. Neighborhoods marked by proximity and face-to-face everyday contact provide the basis of political participation for its residents, in addition to functioning as an object of political control. The neighborhood is the 'time-geography' where individuals' paths converge, and therefore, they are 'socio-spatial' structures where shared interests and values can thrive (Kearns, 1995: 166). As the character of each neighborhood develops historically over time, it is embedded in a cobweb of relationships, hence the aphorism: "Neighborhood relationships do not grow overnight" (Ware, 1994: 86).

Everyday encounters in the neighborhood also have the potential to create a sense of antagonism over perceived differences, shaped by conceptions of race, class, and gender (Massey, 1994; McKittrick, 2007; Frisina, 2020). In this sense, interpersonal exchanges at the neighborhood level can culminate in exclusionary practices for those who do not conform to the social profile or value system of a majority; therefore, social cohesion can succumb to social conflict (Kearns & Forest, 2000: 1013). The characterization of a neighborhood is based on the perceptions of external actors as much as its residents, culminating in the 'cognitive map' of the city that assigns reputation to each neighborhood (Ibid.). These constitutive elements of urban life, as famously suggested by Park and Burgess, "make the city a mosaic of little worlds which touch but do not interpenetrate" (Park et al., 1967 [1926]: 40).

Within city space, some neighborhoods are marked conceptually as well as physically different than others. Certain neighborhoods and districts can work as borders/boundaries, marking urban segregation as tools of territorialization (Brighenti, 2014). On the one hand, urban décor and safety are maintained in the city center by keeping to a minimum the visibility of the poor, the marginalized, and the immigrant, since their presence disturbs the elegance of historical centers and their shopping streets (Mazzei, 2018). Thus, urban marginality is contained in stigmatized neighborhoods, represented in a disproportionately negative light by the media, local administrators, as well as government officials, associated with various social problems, labeled as 'no-go zones' inhabited by 'undesired' migrants, 'dishonored' minorities, and working-class families (Wacquant, 2016: 29). These are the places that formed as a result of physically banishing strangers from the orderly world and confining them in ghettos: "In the postmodern city, the strangers mean one thing to those for whom 'no go' areas (the 'mean streets', the 'rough district') means 'no go in', and those to whom 'no go' means 'no go out'" (Bauman, 1995: 10). In other words, those districts in the city marked as districts to be avoided can act as a confinement for such marginalized groups in the city. In this way, racial, sexual, and economic differences also become spatial matters manifested in the social production of space through processes of concealment, stigmatization, and territorialization (McKittrick, 2007; Brighenti, 2014; Saitta, 2015).

Today, ghettoized neighborhoods near the city center that lost their value over time are subject to heavy reinvestments and gentrification projects to redeem them for middle-class interests. Once exhibiting distinctive characteristics of the city, these neighborhoods are being transformed into 'boutique' quarters (Zukin, 2015) with universal characteristics easily recognized by consumers that are identical around the globe and that promote the same type of transformation. As a result, they end up losing their character and their unique appeal. Whether it is called regeneration, requalification, improvement, or restoration, the process of gentrification involves the penetration of commercial interest and the 'back-to-the-city' movement of the middle-class (Semi, 2015). This results in soaring housing prices and exclusive residencies, thereby slowly replacing previous inhabitants who come from low-income, immigrant, and other minority backgrounds, with those of middle and upper-middle classes who are leaving their suburbia lives to reconquer the city (Smith, 1996; Semprebon, 2011; Semi, 2015).

In his theory of 'the revanchist city' Neil Smith (1996) argues that the process of gentrification is ultimately a reclaiming of the city in defense of privileges, imbued in a discourse of morality, family values, and security. Thus, it is to be understood as a 'revenge' directed towards minorities, the homeless, immigrants, LGBTQ+ individuals, women, and the working-class: "[R]evanchist city expresses a race/class/gender terror felt by middle-and ruling-class whites who are suddenly stuck in place by a ravaged property market, the threat and reality of unemployment, the decimation of social services, and the emergence of minority and immigrant groups, as well as women, as powerful urban actors." (Smith, 1996: 207) Such socioeconomic transformation also translates into cultural dispossession corroding the multicultural identity of place by reproducing ethnic and racial boundaries (Polat, 2020). As a result, 'white spaces' are produced in the intersection of racism and urban identity, premised on 'hostile privatism' and 'defensive localism': "Because of practices that racialize space and spatialize race, whiteness is learned and legitimated, perceived as natural, necessary and inevitable" (Lipsitz, 2011: 6).

Racialized spaces are an indispensable element of urban life, giving way to privilege as well as discrimination and social exclusion by the self-proclaimed right to determine who belongs where and who is simply 'out of place'. Merrill (2014) utilizes the concept of 'relational place' to capture how everyday material and symbolic practices of racialization undergone by certain categories of people assign them to a sub-human status of social invisibility in shared places. Yet, concomitantly, racialized spaces allow for practices of resistance through acts of respatialization and remapping (McKittrick, 2007). Frisina (2020) points out how territorial conflicts can manifest themselves either as a defensive response on the part of those who consider themselves 'natives' against others that they view as responsible for urban degeneration, or as an undertaking by segregated and racialized groups to solve problems of stigmatized neighborhoods (2020: 116–117).

Everyday lived experiences of marginalization and exclusion in urban spaces also have a sexual dimension. Spaces and places play a crucial role in the creation of sexual subjects, be it through sexual identities or desires and practices, by drawing the boundaries of appropriate sexual behavior and policing of sexual relations or representations (Hubbard, 2000; Brown & Browne, 2016). Hence, heterosexuality can come to be territorialized in the city (Hubbard, 2000; Gezgin, 2023), where urban public spaces are underwritten by heteronormative scripts of appropriateness. Those who defy these normalized markers of accepted sexuality are punished verbally or physically. Such everyday forms of discrimination endured by sexual others can also work as a resource for creating alternative constructions of belonging in space and mobilizing collective action (Brown & Browne, 2016: 3). This can involve the appropriation or transgression of heterosexual spaces by sexual minorities as a tactic to overcome moral oppression (Hubbard, 2000).

2.1   Public Space, Contending Identities, and Everyday Struggles of City-zenship

It is in the urban context that the term 'public space' comes to the fore as the cradle of identity formation and political orientations (Mitchell, 2000). Public spaces accommodate processes of inclusion and exclusion, demarcating belonging by setting standards of 'appropriateness'. Given their significance in forging collective identities, public spaces witness struggles over the representations of space and collective memory pertaining to it (Ibid.). They can come to harbor coherent and homogenous identities based on defensive reactionary sentiments against perceived uncertainty and fragmentation, which romanticize heritage and demonize newcomers. A 'sense of place' might therefore come to constitute stability and rootedness amidst sweeping change and incessant movement in our societies, taken to signify the preservation of a singular timeless identity, as a source of perceived 'authenticity' and boundedness (Massey, 1994). This tendency can also be traced in cultural centers that employ local nostalgia, or other landmarks that offer a 'sanitized' feeling of urban space founded on essentialist conceptions (Mitchell, 2000: 446).

Preservation of 'cultural capitals' as safe and clean landscapes of touristic consumption aims to transform 'competitive localism' into profit (Massey, 1994; Zukin, 1998; Moore, 2007). As succinctly put by Winchester and others: "In the process of place marketing, history and landscape are commodified into saleable chunks" (2003: 135). Memorialization of places involves a selective reconstruction of the identity of place, as desired aspects of the collective memory are accentuated while undesired aspects are trivialized and calculatedly forgotten, which might differ according to the group that undertakes the narration (Moore, 2007). The marketing of 'heritage' in urban centers follows the same course, as desirable aspects of local history, culture, and urban life are embellished, such as museums, theatres, or festivals; whilst those elements found to be uninviting (what can be categorized as urban decay, poverty, and immigration) are avoided (Moore, 2007: 97–99). In this way, the presupposed authenticity of the city and its timeless identity is not only employed to forge ideal protagonists of city life but also to proactively market this traditionalist identity on the global scene.

That being said, against a reactive imagining of the city, alternative re-imaginings challenge taken-for-granted identifications and exclusionary territorializations in lived spaces. What comes into play is a rethinking of place not in terms of what *it is* in a static timeless nostalgia (Massey, 1994), but opening room to discuss and fantasize about what it *could be*. As argued by Castells, "locally based identities intersect with other sources of meaning and social recognition, in a highly diversified pattern that allows for alternative interpretations." (Castells, 2010: 63) Thus, landscapes are also sites of resistance to dominant identity constructs (Winchester et al., 2003). These bottom-up initiatives are indispensable in unsettling essentialist claims to authenticity that have become ever more pronounced under processes of globalization, working to exclude certain groups while prioritizing others (Massey, 1994). For instance, against the 'Disneyification' of urban space (Zukin, 1998; Semi, 2015) which construes a given locality as frozen in space-time, therefore inexorably 'authoritarian' (Mitchell, 2000), a search for progressive spaces arises, one that negates existing hegemonic narratives of a glorious past and a fixed future.

Such 'counterspaces' (Mitchell, 2000: 447) or 'subaltern counter-publics' (Fraser, 1990) within the city foresee an alternative construction of the landscape and thereby, an alternative construction of the self. This is possible through "parallel discursive arenas where members of subordinated social groups invent and circulate counterdiscourses," that work to "formulate oppositional interpretations of their identities, interests, and needs" (Fraser, 1990: 67). Everyday lived spatial practices of difference and their interpretation by social agents, thus, create spaces of resistance that challenge dominant representations in public spaces (Semi et al., 2009). Such contextualized experiences are not isolated occurrences, but instead have a wider resonance beyond their locality and can only be fully explained by placing them within a broader setting (Massey, 1994; Semi et al., 2009). As succinctly put by Massey: "It is a sense of place, an understanding of 'its character', which can only be constructed by linking that place to places beyond. A progressive sense of place would recognize that, without being threatened by it." (Massey, 1994: 156). These alternative imaginations of urban spaces beckon alternative construction of place-based belongings that can fuel collective identity and collective action in the struggle to define the city and the experience of lived city-zenship.

The city with its shared public spaces and contested identities is a conducive platform for rescaling and respatializing struggles over membership rights. Historically speaking, the city became the fertile ground from which active citizenship and democracy could flourish, notwithstanding its disciplinary practices for non-citizens (Işın, 2013: 9–11). Işın suggests that the city "may no longer be the milieu where citizens learn civic virtue, but the public spaces of the city, from streets to squares, are still where citizens enact their public selves" (Ibid.: 12). It is not a coincidence that the Italian word connoting citizenship (*cittadinanza*) also comes to signify the aggregation of the inhabitants of a city, and the 'citizen' (*cittadino/a*) as the individual that belongs to a city and takes part in its social life. Moving from this historical and etymological foundation, the study utilizes the term 'city-zenship' to correspond to the Italian *cittadinanza*, not defined through political entitlement through residency (De-Shalit, 2020; Barak, 2020; van Zeben, 2020) as might be suggested by the notion of 'urban citizenship' (Bauböck, 2003) connoting the decentralization of state power; nor an abstract universal notion soliciting inherent rights (Oomen, 2020). Instead, I propose a conceptualization of city-zenship in the practice of residing, that signifies everyday participation in city life, recognition as equal members, civic involvement in local affairs, and a sense of belonging towards this social space, with or without legal status. Not an endpoint or entitlement, but taken rather as a social process, city-zenship, therefore, connotes a "contested process of negotiation through which various agents can make claims on, for, and through urban space" (Gawlewicz & Yiftachel, 2022). This respatialization of the term is particularly helpful in investigating social movements that undertake claims-making in lived urban spaces, thereby providing content to struggles over belonging in the city, which simultaneously convey themes that travel across different settings. Once again, the practice of city-zenship can encompass an inclusive and pluralist vision, or advocate localist privileges to certain groups considered as 'natives', thereby excluding 'non-native' or unwanted groups (Gargiulo & Piccoli, 2020; Gawlewicz & Yiftachel, 2022).

This conceptualization of 'city-zenship' is therefore "a form of identification with the city, the construction of which through political struggle is enabled by the right to difference and collective resistance" (Routledge, 2010: 1167). Actors embedded in socio-spatial contexts can 'act out' (Işın, 2009), intentionally or not, citizenship in everyday politics and participation in community life, which resonate beyond their particular localities and reach the transnational scale "precisely because they are nodes within highly complex and overlapping networks rather than self-contained and isolated territories" (Işın, 2013: 4). From this perspective, those who do not have the legal citizenship status can still undertake such acts, whereas those that do possess the status of citizenship may be unable to do so: "We define acts of citizenship as those acts that transform forms (orientations, strategies, technologies) and modes (citizens, strangers, outsiders, aliens) of being political by bringing into being new actors as activist citizens (claimants of rights and responsibilities) through creating new sites and scales of struggle." (Işın, 2008: 38). These new sites of struggle are typically located in the everyday life of urban spaces, where claims and counter-claims on identities meet one another (Ibid.). A similar conceptualization is offered by Holston and Appadurai (1996), captured by the term 'insurgent urban citizenship' to signify those everyday struggles of subaltern groups in the city to negotiate membership and rights through active participation: "It is an insurgence that begins with the struggle for the right to have a daily life in the city worthy of a citizen's dignity" (Holston, 2009: 246). It is this perspective that the book utilizes in its employment of the term 'city-zenship', connoting everyday acts of rewriting belonging and identity, which ultimately interacts with and play into (trans)national struggles of citizenship rights (Hawthorne, 2022) as the main objective of much social movement mobilization.

3   Social Movements in Social Space: Identity of Place and Place-
       Based Identities in Collective Action

Social movements are defined by Kriesi as "a group of people involved in a conflict with clearly identified opponents, sharing a common identity, a unifying
belief or a common programme, and acting collectively." (2011: 293). Tracing
the convergence on different approaches to social movements literature, Diani
provides a similar yet more comprehensive definition: "Social movements are
defined as networks of informal interaction between a plurality of individuals, groups and/or organizations, engaged in political or cultural conflicts on
the basis of shared collective identities." (1992:1). Coming to represent contentious politics in sociological research (Leitner et al., 2008: 157), social movements have been characterized by (1) *conflictual* collective action with a clearly
defined opponent, (2) situated in dense and informal *networks*, (3) sharing an
identity and common goals (Della Porta & Diani, 2006; Kriesi, 2011). Social
movement actors engage in cultural, social, or political conflicts defined
through historical processes and socio-political settings in an attempt to provoke or prevent social change, which involves claim-making against elites,
authorities, or opponents (Tarrow, 2011). Shared values, outlooks, and a common goal define collective action in movements, binding actors together and
building trust by evoking deep-rooted feelings (Ibid.). They do not operate in
isolation, but rather reach out to other actors to join struggles, foster solidarity,
and exchange valuable material and non-material resources. In this endeavor,
the role of transnational networking and mobilization, especially through the
Internet has become one of the salient features of various movements around
the world (Della Porta & Diani, 2006; Tarrow, 2011).

The growing field of social movement scholarship has applied a rich supply of theories and methodological approaches to explain the emergence,
success, and impact of social movements (McAdam et al., 1996; Goodwin &
Jasper, 2003; Della Porta & Diani, 2006; Snow & Soule, 2009; Della Porta &
Diani, 2015; Tarrow, 1994; Tilly et al., 2019) Much scholarship has focused on
what has been called as 'new social movements' since the 1960s, bringing up
new issues, articulating new frames, and devising new repertoires of action,
thereby distinguishing themselves from traditional working-class movements
of the past (Melucci, 1980; Della Porta & Diani, 2015). These movements do not
seek to change the political system *per se*, but instead to render certain issues
more salient in public debate and political discussion whilst forging collective identities around them: "'Success' for some movements may consist more
of establishing a collective identity than of achieving policy success. It may
also consist of placing issues on the political agenda that would not get there

without the movement's efforts." (Tarrow, 2011: 217). Hence, it can be argued that the goal of so-called new social movements has been related to the production of meaning and systems of interpretation, in which the construction of a common identity becomes fundamental for the mobilization (Snow & McAdam, 2000), whilst the object of claims-making tends to revolve around the politics of identity (Aronowitz, 1992).

3.1   *Collective Identity and Identity Politics*

The constructivist turn in the social movement scholarship offers a vantage point different than the dominant rational choice or structural explanations manifested in dynamics such as the political opportunity structure model, economic determinants, and psychological factors. This approach has contributed to the concept of *collective identity* borrowed from social psychology in recasting the centrality of identity in social movement participation, involving the cognitive, moral, and emotional connections (Polletta & Jasper, 2001). As a critique of the over-reliance on rational motivations based on economic action, identity struggles and symbolic production have gained prominence in explaining political mobilization, pointing out emotional motives for symbolic action and affective solidarity (Della Porta & Diani, 2006; Eder, 2015). Understood as an interrelational concept, collective identity is the product of ongoing processes of interaction, communication, and negotiation, in other words, the process of meaning-making (Van Stekelenburg, 2013). It involves a sense of belonging by establishing boundaries of social groups that share definitions of membership, issue frames, and an outlook for collective action (Johnston et al., 1994). Collective identities that undergird social movements can be inclusive, pluralistic, and open to a multiplicity of belongings as found in progressive movements, but they can also be exclusive and particularistic as we observe in nativist, far-right, or religious movements (Ibid.).

The construction of a collective identity within a movement relies on shared symbols, practices, rituals, and narratives as a sign of differentiation from the rest of the public and other adversary movements in the same socio-political space (Della Porta & Diani, 2006: 108). Certain styles and rituals function as 'identifiers' that communicate membership in a given movement or network and its distinctiveness. These might include clothing and appearance, various objects and artifacts, reverence to certain historical figures directly or indirectly associated with the movement or significant historical events that have been turned into ritual practices, which work to cultivate feelings of a shared identity and belonging to the group. As suggested by Della Porta and Diani, "These elements are merged into stories or narratives which circulate among members of a movement, reflecting their vision of the world and reinforcing solidarity." (2006: 109). Some identifiers can also function as everyday forms of protest, for example in the case of graffiti, music, or outfits, or the act of renaming objects or places with different symbolism (Tarrow, 2011).

From this perspective, the emergence of social movements is explained by *situated socio-political conflicts* that are imbued in structural and cultural cleavages, giving rise to opposing identities. The more salient the cleavage, the more pronounced will be the supply and demand for mobilization around organized identities (Johnston et al., 1994). Collective action comes to signify a struggle between social actors competing over social values and resources, who share with fellow members the collective memory of the group's identity and objectives (Melucci, 1980). Opposing movements keep each other alive by highlighting distinctive collective identities and interests in a movement-counter movement dynamic, such as the pro-life versus pro-choice movements. This also involves issue-framing wherein what one group reckons 'class' conflict might be defined by the opposing group as a matter of 'ethnicity' (Dillard, 2013). It is argued that the mutually reinforcing contestation between opposing movements that diverge from single movement demands from the state, is becoming ever more visible in various socio-political contexts despite an inadequate academic focus, most notably embodied in Europe in the neofascist nationalist versus antifascist struggles (Meyer & Staggenborg, 1996).

More importantly, these cleavages that culminate in socio-political conflict take place in shared spaces, and are inextricably embedded in them: "A place is a metaphorical expression and concerns people's social embeddedness, that is the networks, organizations, associations, groups, and categories of which they are members." (Van Stekelenburg, 2013: 222). Thus, the lived experience of shared places, whether physical or metaphorical, is essential not only in organizing mobilization but also in the realization of a collective identity. Hence, today social movements seek to rewrite the meanings attributed to everyday life and focus on quotidian interactions, as new cleavages and grievances are adjoined to existing traditional cleavages of class, religion, and region (Melucci, 1980; Van Stekelenburg, 2013). As such, a "collective search for identity" or a "defense of identity" tends to mobilize masses into collective action (Ibid.: 10).

Whether they aim to democratize the spaces of everyday life or accentuate ethnonationalist entitlements, social movements uphold a sense of belonging that is underscored by shared meanings, values, beliefs, and symbols, where 'identity' is understood both in *being* (normative, idealized and stored in memory) and *doing* (lived and experienced) (Melucci, 1980: 16–17). In this sense, it is argued that the objective of contemporary collective action has been "the reappropriation of time, of space, and of relationships in the individual's daily existence" (Melucci, 1980: 219). It is the setting of everyday life where identities are summoned when they are openly challenged with respect to our social status and social location. The *body* occupies a particularly important space both for the system of domination and new forms of resistance, as an extension of nature, as an object of desire, and as a locus of interpersonal relations (Melucci, 1980; Johnston et al., 1994). These might include a wide array of issues such as our sexual and bodily presence, our food, our leisure, our choice of career, our consumption patterns, our health, or our parenting preferences (Melucci, 1980; Johnston et al., 1994).

3.2   *Social Movements, Spatialized Belongings, and Urban Mobilization*

Social movements, like all political and social mechanisms, are inherently spatial and inevitably extend across different spatialities (Tilly, 2000; Miller, 2013; Routledge, 2013). The vast literature on urban mobilization introduced the centrality of space and place in social movement dynamics, (Castells, 1983; Pickvance, 2003; Harvey, 2012; Mayer, 2009; Soja, 2010; Nel·lo, 2016; Dikeç, 2017; Domaradzka, 2018), focusing on collective action that not only takes place in the city, but also takes the city as its object in spatial claims to justice. In fact, Niall Dochartaigh and Lorenzo Bosi argue that "territory is both the site and the object of social movement mobilization" (2010, 405). The so-called 'spatial turn' in social sciences in general has ever since extended into the social movement literature giving way to scholarship that has deepened our understanding of the relationship between space, spatial belongings, and forms of collective action (Agnew & Brusa, 1999; McFarlane, 2009; Routledge, 2010; Cumbers & Routledge, 2013; Nicholls et al., 2013; Işın, 2013).

It has been suggested that movements mobilize *on* space, *use* local resources, and *create* space for political participation and solidarity (Routledge, 2013). In a similar vein, Miller (2013) argues that social movements operate in three overlapping spaces, namely: (1) *material space* connoting the concrete urban realities and resources, (2) *conceptual space* of signification composed of shared identities, values, and collective memories as the basis for collective action, and (3) *lived space* that mark the everyday setting social actors operate in, where the existing order is legitimized. One example that can illustrate this tripartite schema is *street art* as the lasting medium of micropolitics in urban life, firstly taking place in material urban surface, secondly reflecting conceptual space in conveying messages that can be deciphered through shared meaning and values that resonate on different scales, and lastly constituting a background of lived space in everyday encounters. Different forms of street art such as graffiti, stickers, posters, and murals are particularly prominent in areas characterized by competing social movements and contending identities (Pavoni et al., 2021). The city offers a conducive setting for these forms of mediated interactions that can evolve into prolonged dialogues, as city walls offer visible surfaces that can be 'written' over by actors seeking public attention (Brighenti, 2010b). Some of these writings on urban space are every-day visible attempts of boundary-drawing, in which walls become territorial devices (Ibid.).

Social space does not merely constitute a surface/container in which mobi-lization takes place, or the material and immaterial resources activists resort to. Spatiality is much more intrinsic to collective action, as it comes to define the values, outlooks, emotions, experiences, and memories that constitute the collective identity of a group, whilst tending to be the primary object of action in trying to transform social relations of the place the latter is embed-ded in (Routledge, 2010), even if globally resonating themes are employed in the mobilization. Mobilization around spatial belongings and the subsequent attachment of the collective identity to a given space is largely overlooked or relegated to a matter of resource mobilization (Agnew & Brusa, 1999). Yet, geo-graphical determinants of insiders and outsiders, even in the sub-state, sub-region, and sub-city level, are indispensable in laying out politicized identities. It has been argued that for many grassroots activists, "it is their own locality and sense of community that remain the most important source of collective and individual identities" (Cumbers & Routledge, 2013: 217). As social actors mobilize in space, they also construct and crystallize their collective identity in relation to it.

Different social actors assign different meanings to a given space, which in turn become sites of social conflict rewritten with competing memories and identities. Previous work has demonstrated how collective action undertaken by social movements, benefiting from physical proximity in forging social ties, often capitalizes on cultural codes that are also spatially defined (Cumbers & Routledge, 2013; Routledge, 2010, 2013). These might include myths, stories, songs, poems, metaphors, or other symbols that prompt feelings of solidar-ity and reinforce a sense of place, becoming part of the repertoire of place-based resistance. New meanings attributed to the city socially reproduce the cityspace, as contending visions of different groups are negotiated, contested, and bargained in urban settings. The impact of meaning-production by local movements in the urban context constitutes "an essential component of cities, throughout history, as the built environment, and its meaning, is constructed through a conflictive process between the interests and values of opposing social actors." (Castells, 2010: 64). Given the dialectical character of spatial struggles, rather than concentrating exclusively on one particular group, a bird's eye view of the whole panorama of 'conflict' involving different social actors can convey a deeper understanding of the movement-space-identity nexus: "Identities and interests are not established prior to power struggles with multiple others (near and far) but through these struggles, with relational exchanges through struggles becoming the driving force for shaping the dispositions and outlooks of different subjects." (Nicholls et al., 2013).

This study seeks to take a step further in exploring the heuristic power of social space in the nexus of spatial identities and collective action, by arguing that the persistent conflict among opposing movements today manifests itself in a competition to represent a territory (Martin, 2003; Banini & Ilovan, 2021; Schwarz & Streule, 2022), and the form of identities that are associated with it (Banini, 2017), thereby fueling collective action in this 'space/identity' axis (Massey, 1994). Hence, in the proximity of shared urban spaces, contending social actors mobilize around competing collective identities based on different visions of the shared space, whether it is a sanitized white exclusionary space harboring restorative nostalgia, or an outward-looking inclusive space seeking new possibilities. Today, we witness discourses on 'sovereignty' and 'identitarianism' being interlaced, proliferating among far-right and ring-wing populist groups. Their unison indicates a sense of 'being the patrons of the homeland' one feels entitled to, no matter how large or small it might be, from which one derives the comfort of a homogenous identity. Especially in the Italian context, such a sense of territorial entitlement and identification is accentuated more on the regional and even subregional levels (Paasi, 2011), giving way to a particular form of local pride, an attachment to one's city, its traditions, and its unique identity, in what has been dubbed 'campanilismo' (Nevola, 2010; Mielke, 2005). On the opposite end, we see progressive groups undertaking a bottom-up transformation of urban settings to create open spaces that enrich through new connections and new subjectivities. This prolific imagining of an alternative pluralist space nourishes a sense of place that is always in becoming, authoring an inclusive place-based identity connecting with places beyond.

As depicted in Figure 1, in employing social space as a heuristic category in social movement research, I argue that alternative representations of space foresee different forms of belonging to such space and a different set of relations shaping the practice of city-zenship. While collective identity and collective action can be defined in and through social space with place-based belongings, it must be reiterated that this is a mutual process in which social actors can also transform the identity of the space. Local struggles are not only carried in and through places but are also shaped by the identity of the place perceived by its residents, and the social ties enabled by it (i.e., place-based identities), which are sources of collective identity guiding collective action to define city-zenship. This is not to argue that social movements are limited to

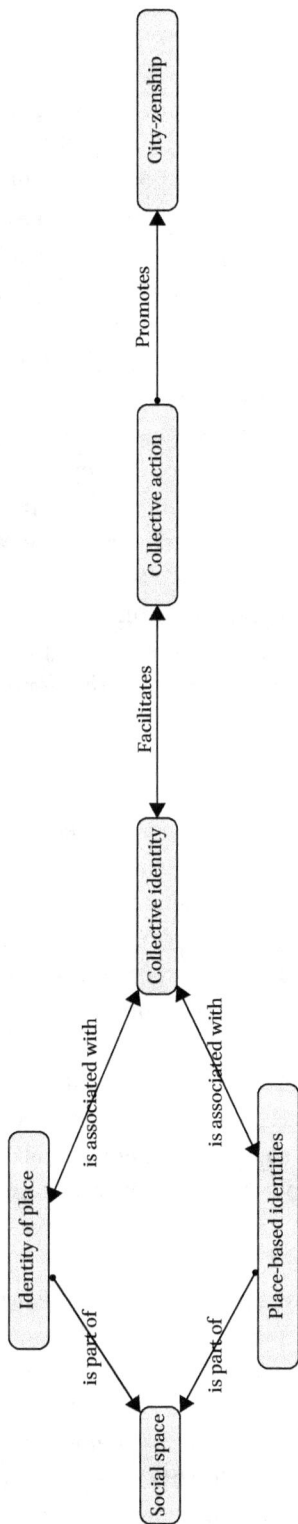

FIGURE 1   The relationship between space, identity, and collective action

the immediate locality in their operations or self-identifications, nor is it a contention that claims-making pertains to local politics. Instead, it is an attempt to contribute to the burgeoning literature on spatialities of social movements by proposing to zoom in on social conflict over city-zenship in shared urban spaces, to unravel the relationship between the social construction of space, a sense of attachment to that place, and everyday struggles over belonging, which provide us a glimpse into the microcosmos in which to make sense of global trends across borders. While the link between place-based identities and mobilization has been accentuated in previous work (Sbicca & Perdue, 2013; Bruttomesso, 2018; Yuen, 2018), this was done so in relation to ad hoc events such as protests and temporary occupy events, thereby, overlooking elongated everyday place-based dynamics of the politics of belongings and their manifestations of territorialization in cityspace. When we operationalize space as 'an unfolding of interactions' (Massey, 1992), it becomes clear why and how everyday struggles to represent the city and therefore belonging to it can give way to antagonistic social actors with contrasting city-zenship ideals, despite emanating from and reflecting upon the same city.

3.3   *Progressive Movements and Transformative Placemaking: Expansive Place-Based Identities*

It has been previously argued that city life can help foster mobilization around a tolerant identity that promotes principles of diversity and inclusiveness as opposed to exclusionary territorial identities. This environment also makes it easier to form networks and facilitate cooperation among various actors who might uphold different ideologies or focus on diverse issue-areas, yet come together in their joint struggle to create open and inclusive spaces in the city (Nicholls, 2008). When such a network forges common frames employed in collective action, it can create a 'culture of resistance' that is tied to the place it is situated in, underwritten with a collective memory of shared struggles (Ibid.: 848). An analysis of social movement organizations operating in civil society at the local level allows the researcher to trace the historical evolution of the movement, the relational interactive dynamics that unite a network of actors, and their exchanges with local authorities (Diani, 2015). Struggles in one locality with their own contextual characteristics often are not isolated instances but are instead part of 'translocal assemblages' as place-based social movements that "exchange ideas, knowledge, practices, materials, and resources," (McFarlane, 2009: 562) with other sites and actors.

The way progressive social movements operate across space can be through spectacular events such as protests, strikes, demonstrations, or flash mobs, as well as everyday ordinary acts such as placing stickers around urban artifacts

or choosing to frequent one particular locality over another for political reasons. The vibrant field of protest and urban spaces has demonstrated well how
material spaces have an intricate relationship with claims-making, as they
partake in the construction of identities and symbolism of social movements
(Carmo, 2012; Reiss, 2007; Della Porta & Mattoni, 2014; Gunning & Baron, 2014;
Hatuka, 2018). Whether it is the act of occupying, reappropriating, or attributing new meaning to place, being embedded in the local while producing global
frames, the protest itself comes to construe a sense of place (Della Porta et al.,
2013). That being said, there continues to be insufficient academic interest in
everyday struggles and protracted practices of progressive resistance by city
dwellers. Scholars have previously pointed out the fact that the civic square
is not the only urban space where an alternative construction of citizenship
emerges, but the realm of everyday mundane life in the peripheries of the
city where the urban dispossessed operate far from the elite centers (Holston,
2009: 246).

   In the social life of the city, social justice movements can come to be associated with a specific urban area or neighborhood, or vice versa, in which space
functions as the locus of collective action and/or organizational practices,
where simply partaking in everyday cultural activities can be a form of activism
(Melucci, 1984; Della Porta & Diani, 2006). Socialization within a movement
does not only occur through engagement with organizational activities but
also through participating in the cultural life of local communities, referred to
as 'movement areas' or 'social movement scenes', where physical space is associated with a subculture or counterculture (Ibid.). This might involve frequent-
ing particular cafés, bars, bookstores, or local shops of a given neighborhood:

> [I]ndividuals do not create connections solely through organizational
> memberships, but also through their participation in various types of
> social and cultural activities (music festivals, communities of taste, read-
> ing groups, alternative cafes, cinemas, theatres, etc.). By doing so they
> reproduce specific subcultural or countercultural milieus that offer both
> opportunities for protest activities and for the maintenance and transfor-
> mation of critical orientations even when protest is not vibrant.
> DELLA PORTA & DIANI, 2006

Thus, urban subcultures or countercultures can come to be called after the
cityspace it operates in, or the neighborhood might be marked as the 'territory' of such movement by the rest of the inhabitants, most importantly by
oppositional groups. Nevertheless, it must also be noted that urban spaces
characterized by a subculture of resistance are increasingly appropriated by

market and political interests in the process of gentrification, re-branded to convey the 'diversity' of the city in an attempt to boost tourism and investment (Domaradzka, 2018).

Usually associated with the slogan 'right to the city' (Dikeç, 2002; Harvey, 2012; Mayer, 2009; Soja, 2010; Domaradzka, 2018), movements operating in urban spaces not only seek greater access to local resources, but also right to change and reinvent oneself by transforming the city (Harvey: 2008: 24). From this perspective, the question: "What kind of city do we want to live in?" does not only address issues of redistribution, access to services and public spaces, affordable housing, local governance or urban social justice in general, but expands to the semantic field of representations of such space and its character, the constructions of alternative forms of belonging within and through everyday urban practices, and the resonance of global struggles of identity in the microcosmos of city life. In this sense, urban mobilization does not merely pertain to claims to urbanism (Desai & Sanyal, 2011), but also to struggles over the definition of city-zenship and the boundaries of belonging in everyday encounters that harbor far-reaching themes of social conflict. The city offers a cosmos in which grassroots initiatives can envision a more 'humane public sphere', cultivating urban conviviality of difference and complexity, and thereby recreating a collective identification with the city that is grounded in local cosmopolitanism acquired through "face-to-face cross-cultural encounters of strangers in a physical space" (Boym, 2001: 76).

Approached from this vantage point, the contestation and reformulation of the boundaries of belonging give rise to participatory politics of citizenship (Yuval-Davis, 2006), linking local struggles with (trans)national claims-making. In turn, situated contestations have a bearing on the spaces they occupy: "[Everyday acts of conviviality and community building] are massively underappreciated. But they have significant potential to make places, and worlds, beyond murderous logics of securitization, privatization and territorialization that characterize our current context of racial and colonial capitalism." (Bacchetta et al., 2019: 168). Particularly for those groups who experience a sense of 'not belonging' to the nation, the family, or the local community, the socio-political setting of the city allows them to re-inscribe urban spaces as a strategy of 'transformative placemaking' (Bacchetta et al., 2019). It is through the practices of transformative placemaking that social actors can realize alternative imaginings of space, taking concrete action in creating open, breathable, democratic, and inclusive spaces with porous borders that are not static or homogenizing. I would like to go further in arguing that such spaces, in turn, can nourish *expansive place-based identities* carrying global themes of pluralism, thereby converting the sense of 'non-belonging' into an alternative form of belonging that is enriched through multiple connections.

3.4 Sovereignist Identitarianism and Far-Right Movements: The Defense of Territory, Tradition, and the 'Native' Identity

In recent years with the wave of populist right and far-right mobilizations across and beyond Europe, overt expressions of racism, sexism, and xenophobia have become ever more salient in everyday urban spaces. An investigation of the far-right social movement and the populist right from a spatio-temporal perspective is possible by focusing on the interplay between territory and identity. While much of the literature has sought to shed light on far-right political parties and their constituents, the non-party dimension of far-right movements is yet a growing field (Rydgren, 2005; Caiani, Della Porta & Wagemann, 2012; Ruzza, 2017; Rydgren 2018; Gattinara & Pirro, 2018), which helps to uncover grassroots actors and their ties with institutional figures operating on various levels (Caiani, Della Porta & Wagemann, 2012; Caiani & Della Porta, 2018; Rydgren 2018), with repercussions on city life. The term 'far-right' has been used in the field as an umbrella term that encompasses both radical groups that operate within the democratic framework and extreme groups that defy existing institutions (Mudde, 2007; Ravndal & Bjorgo, 2018). It is for this reason that the study uses the term *far-right* to denote the panoply of social actors operating in the Veronese social space to capture the diversity of outlook and operations, from nativist expressions to neofascist orientations, and to trace their connections with similar actors in different contexts. Yet, further differentiation needs to be made between far-right and right-wing populist tendencies in order to analyze the alliances between these two political orientations in local settings, and how they impact the everyday.

To begin with, the differentiation of far-right groups from other orientations on the right scale of politics lies along the territory/identity nexus, characterized by the 'nativist' branch of nationalism (Mudde, 2007; Duyvendak et al., 2022). While nationalism is taken as an umbrella political doctrine that advocates cultural unity through internal homogenization, the nativist form of nationalism is distinct in that it comes to underwrite 'anti-immigrant' attitudes in the European context by arguing that states should be inhabited exclusively by the 'natives', i.e., the perceived 'nation' (Ibid.). Such an exclusionary understanding of citizenship is premised on ethnonationalism rooted in historical myths, championing the slogan 'our people first', where 'non-native' elements are considered to jeopardize the unity of the nation-state (Mudde, 2007; Rydgren, 2018; Muis & Immerzeel, 2017; Duyvendak et al., 2022). On a transnational scale, these groups unite and cooperate under a shared white-European identity, fighting for their ascribed privileges and common heritage (Caiani, 2018). The far-right also engages in sociocultural authoritarianism[1] emphasizing public order and family values, welfare chauvinism, and traditional ethics (Mudde, 2000; Rydgren, 2018; Caiani, 2019). Fear of losing one's status, economic standing, and cultural traditions is usually attributed to the presence of 'foreigners' in the country, which are not only considered an economic burden but also a threat to public order. Within this framework, women are portrayed as the biological and symbolic reproducers of the native community (Yuval-Davis, 1999), against the fear of being replaced by non-white minorities in their own lands.

From a similar vantage point, the right-wing variant of populism usually works in binary oppositions of the 'pure' or common people as the true champions of democracy that have been neglected or undermined by the conceptualization of an 'elite'. The depiction of society is premised on an antagonism between hard-working, authentic, and homogenous 'people' versus corrupt and immoral elites (Rydgren, 2018; Rucht, 2019). In contrast to leftist versions of populism, a right-wing interpretation of this political ideology similarly defines the 'people' through exclusionary, nativist, and ethnocultural contours (De Spiegeleire et al., 2017), thereby drawing to its orbit actors from the far-right who share a desire of ethnic homogeneity. The perceived ills of contemporary society include economic globalization embodied by multinational corporations, the corruption of established parties, the growing prevalence of supranational bodies such as the EU in the political arena, and finally, cultural pluralism that is seen to erode traditional values. The sociocultural left and cosmopolitan values such 'elite' groups espouse are targeted for introducing new 'unwanted' cultures, religions, and even gender roles (Rydgren, 2018; Rucht, 2019).

Distrust towards the forces of globalization and international institutions shared by far-right and populist right actors is captured by the ever more salient discourse on 'sovereignty', referred to in the Italian political context as *sovranismo* (sovereignism) connoting a particular political outlook. Traditionally coming to signify the nation-state's unfettered authority over its own territory, it is argued that Westphalian sovereignty has, since its inception, held a deep-seated assumption on the homogeneity of the nation, seeking to assign difference outside national borders as a source of threat (Demirsu, 2017: 19–21). The recent surge in the rhetoric of 'sovereignism' as a political position has come

---

1 *Authoritarianism* is taken as a belief in an adamant law and order in society and not necessarily an undemocratic political system (Mudde, 2007).

to the fore with the rise of the populist right and their far-right allies, based on the postulation of 'mutually exclusive territories' and 'reterritorializing state power' (Basile & Mazzoleni, 2020), against the intrusive politics of supranational institutions and the processes of globalization (Basile et al., 2020). While there is a growing interest in exploring the relationship between populism and sovereignism from a comparative perspective on the national level (Baldini et al., 2020; Mueller & Heidelberger, 2020; Heinisch et al., 2020), there is an evident lacuna in the field when it comes to how the sovereignist rhetoric resonates at the local level. One study that does point out the connection between "state and street" is offered by Suzanne Hall (2021), who argues that racialized migrant communities are not only placed on the outskirts of the 'nation', but also relegated to peripheral space in city life. The book, therefore, addresses this void by tracing how Lega's slogan *'Prima gli italiani!'* (Italians First!) translates into *Verona ai Veronesi* (Verona to Veronesi), and the mechanisms through which actors on the extreme end of the political spectrum are drawn to its orbit through nativist discourses with repercussions in everyday life.

Today, globalization and the unprecedented movement of people, goods, and ideas have been perceived by the ever more dispossessed masses as uncertainty in their everyday lives, culminating in a drive to go 'back to basics' in recalibrating the sense of belonging to the immediate social and material realities: "Suddenly defenseless against a global whirlwind, people stuck to themselves: whatever they had and whatever they were, became their identity" (Castells, 2010: 65). At this juncture, some scholars have pointed out to a comeback of regional loyalties nourishing a sense of community and being part of a shared identity that is distinct from a national feeling (Paasi, 2011). With the failure of established political parties and institutions to aid citizens' grievances in the face of economic hardship, and a perceived loss of identity, people opted "to react on the basis of the most immediate source of self-recognition and autonomous organization: their locality" (Castells, 2010: 64). As a result, scholars have pointed out localized manifestations of far-right and populist sentiments in urban and regional settings (Silver et al., 2020; Papatzani, 2021; Saitta, 2022), where the conception of a people bounded by cultural and regional homogeneity is treated as a bulwark against the perceived perils of larger multicultural and open-border policies (Lamour, 2022). It is, therefore, no coincidence that scholars have been calling attention to urban ramifications of nativist sentiments: "[W]e call for recognizing neo-nationalism as a key driving force in the emergence of urban hostile environments. This factor has been largely ignored in urban studies literature." (Gawlewicz & Yiftachel, 2022: 351).

In this perspective, a 'natural' primordial attachment to the land exists by a group of people who claim to be the pre-announced owners thereof (Brighenti, 2010; Brighenti, 2010b). This new orientation is undergirded by a parochial version of belonging that offers to remedy the lost sense of community in symmetrical opposition to the universal conceptualization of citizenship and plurality that cross-cut particularistic identities and affiliations (Işın & Wood, 1999). Duyvendak and others (2022) have demonstrated in their work the global rise of the nativist logic in different contexts by highlighting the perception of an essentialist relationship between a social group and geography. Such 'territorialized' conceptualizations of identity posit a hierarchical separation of natives and migrants from a chronological point of view with respect to their presence in such territory, where newcomers are seen to threaten 'the natives' in 'their own lands' (Duyvendak et al., 2022: 3).

The spatial claim to take back control of a territory is accompanied by a temporal claim to 'restore' an imagined order of the past that is believed to have existed in this space with the underlying postulation 'we were here first' (Freeden, 2017: 4). According to fascist philosopher Julius Evola, the rediscovery of *tradition*, located at the intersection of a golden age and the native land, is the cure for the ills of modern society (Valencia-Garcia, 2020). The populist right finds another common ground with far-right movements in the glorification and romanticizing of the past, whilst problematizing the present and the future. Such 'invented tradition' (Hobsbawm, 1990), conveying a set of rules and rituals, entails continuity with a 'suitable' past seen as a safe harbor in an endlessly changing world. In the rewriting of 'the glory days' of a people, identified through their similarities as well as their quasi-biological tie to the land, slogans claiming to reinstall 'greatness *again*' assume a form of restorative nostalgia. A restorative nostalgia (Boym, 2001) projects a romanticized social cohesion based on the exclusion of difference and upholds *historical revisionism* in rejecting the history written by the liberal democratic order, insisting instead on a reinterpretation of the past from the point of view of the 'losers' of World War II (hereafter WWII). Yet, such reinterpretations of a "guilt-free homecoming" (Boym, 2001: XIV) can drag along legitimations of ethnonationalist, racist, sexist, homophobic, and classist tendencies under the banner of 'tradition' and 'identity' (Valencia-Garcia, 2020).

As a matter of fact, in defense of local tradition and traditional values, the so-called 'anti-gender' position (Stoeckl 2016; Garbagnoli & Prearo, 2018; Trappolin, 2022) has also been a common thread that ties far-right and right-wing populist movements. According to this perspective, feminist and LGBTQ+ rights movements that constitute the 'gender ideology' have been perceived as a threat to traditional values and the future of the nation, as they erode public morality and lead to low birth rates. The latter finds much resonance in western settings underpinned by a 'demographic anxiety' of white European populations being replaced by non-white and/or non-Christian immigrants (Gökarıksel et al., 2019), in the Italian context being capitalized on in relation to the country's aging population. Hence, the *traditional natural family* is celebrated against the perceived 'indoctrination' of sexual minorities (Trappolin, 2022), and a panacea against the so-called 'The Great Replacement'.[2] In this sense, the defense provided by the traditional family is posed against feminist and LGBTQ+ movements that challenge the white patriarchal outlook (Frisina, 2020: 78), as well as against the threat of becoming an ethnic minority in what is considered the native land.

A more recent rebranding of far-right movements that encapsulates nativism together with traditionalist nostalgia and moral conservatism has been *identitarianism* (Handler, 2019): a new mantra that has allowed the institutionalization of some otherwise unconstitutional political outlooks. As put by Šima, "[i]dentity politics is now facing an identitarian counterattack" (2021: 78). Also considered as the ideology of the 'New Right' (*Nouvelle Droite, Neue Rechte, Nueva Derecha*) that differentiates itself from fascism, nationalism, and traditionalism, identitarianism advocates 'authentic' identities grounded in ethnic, racial, and cultural characteristics that are tied to a 'fatherland' and a shared history. Premised on the works of figures such as Julius Evola, Pierre Krebs, and Alain de Benoist, identitarianism is a revolt against the perceived 'forced sameness' that lies at the core of the universalist approach, instead promoting 'particular belongings' that might manifest itself in subnational, regional, and local belongings with a 'small fatherland', as well as larger ethnic and cultural unities such as White Europeans with a 'great fatherland' (Tudor, 2014).

With a conceptualization of identity understood not as "an abstraction or a simple social construction but felt as something more profound, primordial, tied to space, territory, memory, and ethnicity, that *must* be revitalized today" (Zúquete, 2018), identitarianism converges with sovereignism in a shared sense of lost control over one's own land, adding the desire to restore an imagined golden age. In this narration, the identitarian is the one who is in defense of this identity under threat by foreign peoples and cultures, undertaking the role of guarding the homeland, its traditions, and its native culture. The use of seemingly innocuous terminology, such as defending one's identity, tradition, and homeland, is heavily imbued with hues of white supremacy and the

---

2 For more information on this theory shared by transnational far-right actors, see: https://www.bbc.com/news/world-europe-65324319.

fear of being replaced by non-white immigrants (Murdoch & Murhall, 2019). European identitarians, whilst being anchored in their own locality capitalizing on localized issues, are concomitantly ever more interconnected with transnational counterparts today in defense of European borders and a nativist identity (Creţan & O'Brien, 2019; Lamour, 2022). In this narrative, place-based historical and cultural stereotypes alongside myths play a significant role in the cultural defense of an identity rooted in a given territory (Šima, 2021).

Contemporary forms of racism are highly visible in the discourses of far-right movements, including in their identitarian rebranding. In his formulation of the term, Balibar (1991) argues that racism today can manifest itself as protection of one's identity against invasion or contamination, premised on the stigmatization of otherness by names, skin color, or religion. For instance, anti-Muslim racism is usually based on the belief that the Islamic lifestyle is uncivilized, incompatible with European values, and unwanted, rather than being biologically inferior (Anthias & Yuval-Davis, 1992). Signifiers of hate and fear of difference have replaced the 'biological' thesis into what has become in the age of decolonization a 'racism without races', as people from former colonies are moving into the old metropolises to share the same socio-political space with their ex-colonizers: "The functioning of the category of *immigration* as a substitute for the notion of race and a solvent of 'class consciousness' provides us with a first clue" (*Original emphasis*, Balibar, 1991: 20). For greater resonance and success, far-right groups in countries where immigration levels are high, tend to shift their focus from 'losers' in economic terms to 'losers' in cultural terms, thereby capitalizing on feelings of intolerance, xenophobia, anti-establishment, anti-immigration, and opposition to leftist organizations promoting multiculturalism (Prowe, 2004; Kriesi et al., 2008; Caiani, 2019; Rucht, 2019).

Hence, it is no longer a claim of racial hierarchy that is at play, but rather a cultural difference so stark that it does not permit the co-existence in the same geographical as well as socio-political space (Tudor, 2014). Unlike the old hierarchical conceptualization of racism, it is argued that this new form of 'ethnopluralism' posits different cultures as 'incompatible' and 'insurmountable' rather than 'superior' or 'inferior', where integration is considered as the invasion of the immigrant culture (Rydgren, 2018). It is precisely this understanding of 'culture' which underlies the calls to 'protect Europe' from such perceived invasion, where white communities lament being the real subject of contemporary racism inflicted by the 'Other' who disrespects and threatens western values (Balibar, 1991; Lentin & Karayakali, 2016). As a result, culture assumes a 'quasi-biological' disposition, and 'Fortress Europe' is defended as the cradle of civilization against the invasion of immigrants portrayed as "lazy, parasitic, dirty, violent, criminal, diseased, or libidinous" (MacMaster, 2001: 217–218). 'Europe' understood in this way is the home of whiteness and Christianity, where racial others whose heritage does not lie in Europe (i.e., people of color and non-Christians) are constantly sought to be kept as distinctive, 'non-Europeans' (Goldberg, 2006), or *extracommunitari* as they are referred to in the Italian language. On the transnational scale, networking initiatives by far-right actors tend to be construed around a 'global white identity' (Caiani, 2018) with racial-nationalist hues or Pan-European ideals that demonstrate the continuity of pre-war and post-war racism in Europe (MacMaster, 2001), today masquerading in the form of 'anti-immigration'.

4 Conclusion

This interdisciplinary theoretical framework at the intersection of urban sociology, critical geography, and social movements allows us to investigate the nexus of social space, spatial identities, collective action, and claims to city-zenship. Urban topographies, through their material realities, cognitive imaginations, and lived everyday exchanges, play an indispensable role in forming situated identities as products of contestation over who belongs and who is out of place, thereby respatializing the notions of collective identity and collective action which, ultimately reverberate beyond the particular locality. Moving on from these theoretical insights, the book argues that feelings of attachment to and identification with a place can take the form of an *exclusionary territorial identity* ingrained in sovereignist identitarian discourses, looking inward in defense of what was, or it can beget an *expansive place-based identity* that espouses opening to new possibilities, new forms of belonging through the creation of outward-looking inclusive spaces. Lived spaces, especially cityspace with its multiplicity of social relations, are fundamental in the creation of shared corporeal experiences, exchange of values, symbolism, culture (or counterculture), and collective memory that animate various forms of mobilization in a claim for rights not merely as legal entitlements or access to resources, but as benchmarks of social relatedness and a sense of 'home'.

By utilizing the heuristic categories of 'identity of place' and 'place-based identities' from a social space perspective, the study thus seeks to expand this avenue of research. This is done so by a comparative investigation of actors who constitute two antagonistic movements that operate in the same cityspace, conveying globally resonating ideas and themes in their local conflicts and shaping the direction of everyday struggles of representation, territorialization, and boundary-drawing (or erasing). The proximity of the city can offer a new sense of belonging and identity in the type of everyday exchanges that allow face-to-face interaction and tangible ties as the basis of mobilization, alongside their extension on virtual online spaces. In this endeavor, the focus on movement/countermovement dynamics in the online/offline continuum reveals global themes of identity struggles and transnational ties of local groups on both ends of the political spectrum.

CHAPTER 2

One City, Two Movements, and Contending Constructions of City-zenship: A Multimethod Qualitative Research

> Un luogo non è mai solo 'quel luogo': quel luogo siamo un po' anche
> noi. In qualche modo, senza saperlo, ce lo portavamo dentro e un
> giorno, per caso, ci siamo arrivati.[1]
>
> ANTONIO TABUCCHI

∴

Qualitative research is conducive to a wide variety of different theoretical approaches, yet is defined by the unifying assumption that social phenomena are contingent and contextualized processes, where the aim of the researcher is to acquire the point of view of social actors being studied (Frisina, 2013). As such, it is a work of bricolage that requires a skillful interweaving of various tools, methods, and techniques of representation and interpretation (Denzin & Lincoln, 2017). This research is premised on a structured multi-method qualitative investigation in which different data sources and methodological tools complement one another to strengthen the validity of the arguments presented and enhance theory building (Flick, 2017). The employment of such *methodological pluralism* (Della Porta, 2014) is interwoven with a historical dimension, providing a solid ground for the ethnographic research and depth to the analysis by integrating a temporal dimension to the spatial approach that underwrites the study. Such a time-space axis not only allows the researcher to trace historical continuities in the construction of identities and representations of space, but also sheds light on the subjective perceptions of change and future expectations by different social actors (Ayoub et al., 2014).

The triangulation of methods utilized in this study premised on the extended case method is composed of: (1) three years of *ethnographic field research* in

---

1 A place is never only that place: We are also somehow that place. In some way, without being aware of it, we carry it within us. And one day, by chance, we arrive there.

shared urban settings producing fieldnotes as well as photos capturing every-day manifestations of collective action; (2) more than one year of *online eth-nography* focusing on the outlooks, constructions of collective identity, and motivations of collective action by various far-right groups; (3) *semi-structured qualitative interviews* with activists, members of local associations, and other city-zens of Verona to acquire their perspectives on social conflict and identity politics, as well as their conceptualizations of belonging; (4) *archival research* on key historical episodes in the city and spatio-temporal evolution of antag-onistic movements; and, lastly, (5) the visual method of participant-generated *photo-elicitation interviews* to visually map out acts of territorialization as well as everyday practices of transformative place-making. This rich corpus of data has been analyzed with the help of the qualitative research software ATLAS.ti through an approach of thematic coding to reveal cross-cutting patterns and themes. The following section will elaborate on the extended case method approach and the choice of Verona for the study, followed by an account of each qualitative method employed, and finally, offering a final word on reflexivity.

1   Extended Case Method and the City of Verona

1.1   *The Extended Case Method*

The distinguishing feature of ethnography among other social research meth-ods is the opportunity to study social actors in their everyday lives, in other words, "in their own time and space" (Burawoy et al., 1991: 2). Here, the primary objective does not reside solely on the observation of individuals' actions, but also on the meaning they attribute to such actions. Notwithstanding criti-cisms raised regarding participant observation over its validity, objectivity, and generalizability, Burawoy (2009) in his canonical work on the extended case method, responds with what he calls the 'paradigmatic' approach of fieldwork that encapsulates two constitutive attributes of social science, namely *under-standing* and *explanation*. The former is realized through dialogue between the participant and the observed, while the latter is attained through a dia-logue between data and theory in an attempt to turn observation into explana-tion. The extended case method accomplishes both goals of social research by demonstrating how the macro "shapes and in turn is shaped and conditioned by the micro world, the everyday world of face-to-face interaction." (Burawoy et al., 1991: 6).

This is done with the aim of restructuring existing theory, differentiating from the grounded theory approach seeking the construction of new the-ories or the positivist endeavor of verifying 'good' and 'bad' theories. The manifestations of 'macro' upon the 'micro' are sought through 'interesting' or 'surprising' cases which might present themselves as abnormalities, issues that existing theory failed to address or has remained inconsistent about with the purpose of enhancing the explanatory credentials of the chosen theoretical lense(s) (Burawoy et al., 1991: 9). From this vantage point, the case is therefore a means to analyze the larger society it is embedded in, rather than a population of similar cases (Small, 2009). This approach valorizes the historical and contextual determinants of social phenomena, while linking it to broader mechanisms that are at work on a macro level, therefore, beyond particularism towards the 'general'. This approach starts off with "dialogue, virtual or real, between observer and participants, then embeds such dialogue within a second dialogue between local processes and extralocal forces that in turn can be comprehended only through a third, expanding dialogue of theory with itself." (Burawoy, 2009: 20).

As such, the extended case method is premised on four interlocking *extensions* that invite dialogue: (1) the extension of the observer into the lives of the observed, (2) the extension of the observation across time and space, (3) the extension of micro-processes into macro forces, and (4) the extension of theory (Burawoy, 2009). The first extension stresses the need to be cognizant that the line defining the ethnographer and the participant is always blurry. The second extension indicates how the ethnographer conducts fieldwork for an elongated period and in different social spaces. The temporal dimension also entails what Burawoy (2009) refers to as 'revisits' that involve a historical extension of the same place to uncover continuity and change. This extension combines sociological and historical approaches into the ethnographic work, allowing the researcher to discern multiple processes, interests, and identities that define the site. The third extension states that ethnographic case studies should seek to reveal linkages between micro-processes of everyday life and macro forces that reach beyond the site. The investigation of the everyday is to demonstrate how it is shaped by and, in turn, impacts larger processes. Last but not least, the extended case foresees the reconstruction and revising of theory as the starting point and the primary goal of research by engaging it with data alongside other theories (Ibid.).

The process begins with pinpointing what is surprising or interesting and then turning to a set of theories that might explain different characteristics of the social phenomenon at hand. The researcher gradually narrows down the theoretical framework to choose an existing theory worthy of reconstruction. The selected case is significant for "what it tells us about the world it is embedded in," with respect to the insights it offers about the society as a whole and not just other similar cases (Burawoy, 1991: 281). From this perspective, the city is taken as an intersection of institutions and actors situated in space and time (Burawoy, 1991: 281). Thus, the task of the researcher is to uncover mechanisms and trace processes that lead a certain state of affairs to come into existence by tracking a concatenation of events undertaken by the same social actors across a long duration of time (Small, 2009: 22). By doing so, the extended case method illustrates how such events are linked to one another and so are competing social actors. The merit of the case lies in the fact that "one good case can illuminate the working of a social system in a way that a series of morphological statements cannot achieve" (Gluckman, 1961: 9).

These insights, alongside the four points of extension proposed by the extended case method, have been adopted in this research and reflected in the case selection. The extension of the observer into the lives of the observed has been discussed in the section on reflexivity which explicates the positioning of the researcher as a Turkish migrant woman living in the urban area she is studying, and how this factor has impacted the research process. The extension over time and space, on the other hand, has been given particular attention in the research design. The study offers a diachronic socio-spatial investigation of the evolution and interaction of two antagonistic movements through urban space. The ethnographic study has been carried out in multiple spatialities, firstly in the complementary online and offline spaces that these actors operate in, and secondly across the contending spaces of the touristic historical center and the multicultural neighborhood of Veronetta. The third extension looking into the linkages between micro-processes and macro forces is sought through the investigation of everyday urban life and how broader political trends that reverberate at the regional, national, and transnational levels are carried out in daily local struggles, which in turn leave an imprint on the macro forces they refer to. The triangulation of online and offline ethnography has been rather fruitful in this respect by unraveling transnational connections of local actors. And lastly, the extension of theory is sought by introducing insights from critical geography alongside urban sociology to the field of social movements by activating 'social space', manifested in the dual concepts of identity of place and place-based identities, in reinterpreting collective identities and spatially reformulating our understanding of movement/countermovement dynamics. The restructuring of theory that the extended case method undertakes has been applied in the analysis of the empirical data, whose summaries with the novel analytical tools are presented in the introduction of Chapters 4, 5, and 6 in the form of figures and tables. The restructuring of the theory of collective identities in social movements with the categories of social space is then revisited in the Conclusion.

1.2 The Case of Verona and the Comparative Analysis of Competing Movements

The case of Verona was chosen for this study because, put simply, it is an 'interesting' case that has foreshadowed the growing salience of populist right and far-right politics, which today has come to mark Italian society, much of Europe, and other extra-European contexts. I first arrived in Verona in 2016, at the height of reactionary nationalisms and nativism around the world. The initial impression I had was that of a beautiful Italian tourist destination, with a perfectly maintained history, clean and ordered streets, fancy restaurants, high culture events such as the opera festival, and elegantly dressed individuals strolling in its streets. Later on, I came to discover that this elite and sterile touristic city was in fact well-known in the Italian society for another reason, namely as the fortress of far-right movements in all its different shades, where intolerance of difference was given free rein, taken as a rightful defense of native identities and control over the 'fatherland' (Tudor, 2014). The populist right Lega party (by then, it was still Lega Nord espousing a 'northern' identity) gained success in this mid-sized city way before its nationwide success and established informal as well as formal ties to far-right groups, leading to their institutionalization in the city administration. This alliance has pursued an anti-immigrant and anti-gender stance in the city council, with various forms of 'urban populisms' (Saitta, 2022) on the streets. The city was already establishing itself as a world brand in the identitarian turn when the populist right Lega dropped its northern emphasis and became a powerful partner in the national coalition government, bringing far-right themes in the Italian parliament together with the post-fascist party *Fratelli d'Italia*. It is at this conjuncture that experts commented on such political trend as the 'Veronification' of Italian politics (Del Medico quoted in Torrisi, 2019; Bernini, 2022) to describe the rising prominence of nativist and traditionalist orientations. As such, the city of Verona has presented itself as a conducive field to study the rise of territorial belongings premised on a sovereignist identitarian discourse and the cultivation of exclusive city-zenship, in order to contextualize and make sense of macro-level political trends.

As I pursued my academic curiosity regarding the sociopolitical setting of Verona and the local actors, I further discovered the existence of the neighborhood of *Veronetta* within the dominant conservative realm of Verona, offering a different social space. Despite being part of the historical center, this neighborhood in the common imagery was associated with urban decay, immigration, and sexual minorities, in stark contrast with the sterile touristic area. Although it is not the neighborhood with the highest number of immigrants, the fact that it was an extension of the touristic center rendered unwanted difference more 'visible' due to its proximity. When I first moved to Verona and was in search of housing, I was warned by several local acquaintances to avoid Veronetta as it was not a place for 'families'. Two years later, through various grassroots initiatives I became involved in, I discovered that behind the façade of a multiethnic neighborhood lay a political reality, an informal but deep-rooted network of antifascist/anti-racist/feminist/LGBTQ+ associations, cultural organizations, student movements, counterspaces and social collectives which engage in cultural, social, educational, artistic, sportive, or openly political initiatives in the city to create an alternative democratic space where one could breathe a cosmopolitan air. Through decades of everyday struggles, enduring violence, discrimination, and negation from sanitized and guarded spaces of the historical center, they have been realizing an alternative way of belonging and a pluralistic version of city-zenship in lived spaces for those who do not feel part of the prevailing reactionary local culture.

Unlike the argument that this sort of urban resistance emerges in the peripheries of the city by racial, ethnic, or religious minorities (Holston & Appadurai, 1996; Bachetta et al., 2019), the case of Veronetta demonstrates how old Veronesi and new Veronesi side by side from varying socioeconomic as well as cultural backgrounds, united in their distaste for the exclusive and homogenizing forms of belonging in Verona. These progressive groups have been gradually pushed away from the city center to eventually find refuge in this neighborhood, and continue to be pushed further east due to ongoing gentrification and touristification efforts. This gradual move was due to two forces, namely a centrifugal force implemented by far-right boundary-drawing in the touristic heart of the historical center, and secondly, a centripetal force of low housing prices coupled with an indifferent multiculturalism and the legacy of old left movements. This air of relative freedom in a working-class neighborhood with an atmosphere of tolerance for different migrant communities provided them the ideal social space for establishing solidarity, sharing spaces and stories, recruiting new members and supporting newcomers, finding new issues of social conflict, turning such tolerance into intercultural exchange, and merging justice struggles to form a place-based collective identity.

These two discoveries, namely Verona as the stronghold of the far-right who reigns the city center capitalizing on symbolisms of heritage, and Veronetta as an imperfect oasis nourishing an inclusive pluralist form of city-zenship, together provided the impetus to address the need to respatialize theories on collective identity and collective action, and to revisit movement-countermovement dynamics from an everyday spatio-temporal angle. The actors that are involved in the rewriting of the boundaries of belonging in everyday situated practices are thus antagonistic social movements operating in the vicinity of urban spaces, whose interaction, conflict, and negotiation with each other, as well as with the city administration, determine the possibilities of city-zenship and identification with the territory one inhabits. This contestation is not only marked by local dynamics, but also borrows from and contributes to extra-local struggles in places beyond.

The case of Verona, therefore, presented itself as the perfect choice for the extended case method as it allows a comparative analysis of opposing social movements who operate in the same setting, the everyday manifestation of collective action on urban realities through movement/countermovement dynamics, the relationship between identity, place, and collective action translating into claims to city-zenship which extend beyond the confines of Verona. This does not equate to relegating collective action to a circumscribed geography, but on the contrary, it offers an opportunity to observe the materialization of wider identity claims in the everyday life of the city.

2   Doing Ethnographic Research, Offline

Ethnographic research is utilized when the research questions intend to understand the nature of a social phenomenon, rather than setting out to test a hypothesis about it, and therefore involves a detailed analysis of a small number of cases (Flick, 2009: 233). While Geertz (1973) sets 'thickness' as a criterion to evaluate ethnographic fieldwork, Becker (1996) argues in favor of 'breadth', that is trying to understand multiple dynamics that touch upon the phenomenon under investigation. At the heart of ethnographic research lies participant observation to study social interaction in which the researcher does not undertake a passive and external role, but one that lives with and lives as the people that s/he studies (Frisina, 2013: 11). Participant observation is ultimately a performance requiring the negotiation of the researcher's role in different settings in establishing and maintaining a relationship with the group whose interactions and social relations are the object of study. The situated experiences of here and now, everyday settings and situations constitute the bedrock of this approach (Flick, 2009).

Although ethnographic research has not constituted a cornerstone in social movements research, it has been argued that it has nonetheless produced significant paradigm changes in the field (Balsiger & Lambelet, 2014). This method has provided valuable insights into different membership dynamics and heterogeneity within groups, while challenging standardized self-evident categorizations and homogenizing tendencies. Moreover, participant observation allows the researcher to observe what happens before and after public protests or demonstrations, thereby providing an insight of what goes on 'offstage' beyond a simple reaction to external factors (Balsiger & Lambelet, 2014: 149). As a result, participant observation is useful to go beyond public statements of social movements and to take part in their everyday operations. The field is 'mobile' in the sense of being constituted by several localities, events, as well as online activities of social actors that take part in these movements, which the researcher follows across different settings (Ibid.: 152).

Participant observation foresees that a reliable rapport is established with the field, requiring the researcher to perform interpersonal skills to build a relationship based on trust, especially with the gatekeepers who can grant access to the field. The access is also based on how the researcher presents themselves and how they negotiate their role. In this study, access was first achieved by taking part in the Italian courses offered to migrants living in Verona by the cultural association *Veronetta 129*. Working on the themes of migration and intercultural relations in the city, this association invited me to take part in a number of projects as a 'Turkish migrant woman' living in Verona. I first took part in the project called *Indovina Chi Viene a Cena* by hosting four Italians at my home and cooking them a Turkish dinner to talk about my culture, which was a means for establishing one-on-one relations between locals and newcomers. This night was also televised on a local TV channel called *TG Verona Telenuovo* as a 'good practice of integration', a terminology that the organizers did not necessarily agree with. Later on, I was asked to present a film about my hometown, Istanbul, and also to take part in a book project involving local recipes of migrants from different countries living in Verona. As a result, a mutual trust was established as the association also helped me discover and contact other important collectives in Verona that made up the antibodies of hate. I gradually started to explore this rich network constituted by informal ties among various organizations, associations, collectives, and initiatives, which, at times of social conflict, manage to assemble and act as a single entity. My positionality in the field as a woman migrant interested in learning about 'the other face of Verona' facilitated my entry, as most of the people I've encountered were eager to talk about the history of Verona, its social fabric, the protracted struggles of progressive actors, points of contestation with antagonistic groups, and even its local dialect.

In addition to participant observation with much of the assemblage of activists present in Veronetta, *non-participant observation* (Flick, 2009) during the same period was conducted where direct participation was deemed inaccessible or unsafe. Distance was maintained as an observer in public spaces to follow the flow of events without disturbing the ongoing social relations at the site (Flick, 2009: 222–223). These have typically included public demonstrations, conferences, celebrations, and recruitment events of far-right, Veneto nativist, or Catholic fundamentalist groups, where observation was made and recorded, public speeches were registered and later transcribed along with any ethnographic interview that was possible to conduct. On some occasions, when public speeches were being delivered or particular media attention was given to an event, approaching participants to ask questions was rendered relatively easier. In other instances, such as a social event of far-right youth branches or the local hooligan fans meeting, I tried to be part of the backdrop, avoiding any attention. On one occasion, during a stand in the historical center for a far-right recruiting event, my greeting and friendly introduction were deliberately ignored due to my distinctive positionality.

The bulk of the ethnographic fieldwork lasted from July 2018 until July 2019, which involved regular visits to Veronetta and the historical center several days of the week. After this main phase of fieldwork, the field was revisited regularly yet less frequently in 2020 until the beginning of 2022, as much as the situation with the pandemic would permit. A substantial part of the fieldnotes were gathered through moments of conflict or significant social, cultural, or political events, such as the World Congress of Families, anti-abortion rallies, Verona Pride, 8th of March demonstrations, the local carnival, events on the issue of migration, sit-ins, protests, clashes between opposing groups in public spaces, conferences, flash mobs, and the like. In a relatively small provincial city like Verona, one would expect the socio-political environment to be calm, yet on the contrary, it seemed like tension never ceased to exist with the agenda rapidly changing. The same set of issues manifesting in different guises seemed to circulate over and over again, revolving primarily on the issue of migration, sexual rights, and political positioning over WWII.

Apart from these key events, I have participated in the regular meetings of the movement operating in and from Veronetta, involving cultural, social, and political realities such as *Veronetta 129, Social Street, La Sobilla, Gigi Piccoli, Paratodos, NUDM,* and *Pink.* Since I was well-recognized by a majority of activists by the winter of 2018–2019, I did not face any issues visiting their locales, stopping by, and chitchatting. Moreover, I would also spend free time in Veronetta and the historical center to observe both neighborhoods in their daily flow of crowds and the usual routines. During these free visits, I spent time in bars (the Italian version of the French notion of café) and tried to strike up random conversations with locals, paying attention to the profile of buildings, stores, bars, restaurants, streets, and people that characterized both neighborhoods. Walking around the city, I paid particular attention to urban graffiti and stickers dispersed around material urban realities, which provided additional insights about the territorialization practices in these neighborhoods and the bridges extending over the Adige River connecting the two areas. Hence, these free visits have also constituted an important part of the ethnographic fieldwork.

Against the understanding of ethnographic writing reflecting 'reality', this research holds that every form of writing is a construction of social processes that the writer opts to depict through the choice of what to write and what to leave out, use of wording, and the creative description of a given neutral event. Hence, it "functions more as a filter, than a 'mirror' reflecting the reality of events" (Emerson et al., 2011: 211). The unavoidable selectivity in taking field notes is mitigated by photo and video documentation of the site, where possible, to help recall the flow of events (Flick, 2009: 298), which also proved to be an indispensable part of the fieldwork in capturing material manifestations of social conflict over urban spaces. These observations were, in turn, organized according to their dates, places, occasion, and the social actors that they involved and archived accordingly for the analysis.

3   Doing Ethnographic Research, Online

While our cultural experiences have become more and more mediated by digital technologies, online spaces in turn, have become embedded in and continuous with lived spaces. The impact of the Internet on social relations and interaction has been fundamentally ingrained, thereby becoming an ordinary part of our everyday rituals (Markham, 2017). It has even been suggested that it is not plausible any longer to conduct ethnography without taking into account online spaces. Online ethnography is carried out by applying ethnographic methods and insights to online spaces, while concomitantly requiring reflexivity and communication with offline fieldwork (Airoldi, 2018). As put by Hine: "Rather than transcending time and space, the Internet can be shown to have multiple temporal and spatial orderings which crisscross the online/offline boundary" (2000: 11). Digital platforms are performative spaces continuing through conventional identity categories such as race, gender, and sexuality, instead of fading away in the anonymity offered on the Internet (Hine, 2000: 12). What we observe online is a collection of texts representing users' perception of reality, which are readily available also outside of their immediate production, unlike the forms of verbal communication that constitute much of conventional ethnography. The ethnographer's task is to understand the meaning attributed to these textual communicative cues (Hine, 2000).

Conducting ethnography in online spaces subsequently entails 'reading' online material which is paramount to participant observation in an online space, where we are already active participants by the mere act of reading content, since reciprocated interaction is not necessary as it would be in offline research: "[R]eading is its own form of interaction, and posting, submitting, and publishing one's text online invites readership in an audience, if not a community" (Gatson, 2012: 251). These texts also include other linguistic devices such as emojis, hashtags, and other inside codes that partake in the meaning-making in online spaces (Hine, 2000). The researcher is often a 'disguised' reader in online ethnography, but such a position does not necessarily lead to an ethical ambiguity since publicly accessible online material presupposes being observed without having control over the observer's intentions (Gatson, 2012). It has been argued that online ethnography can provide the same depth and content as that of interview or offline field research, since the researcher undertakes the task of reading hundreds of posts produced over a long period of time, pertaining to a particular topic usually by the same set of online participants. It can also provide a similar form of rich archival insights as that of a historical analysis where the text to be analyzed is elicited from archival sources (Gatson, 2012: 250). The type of new communication technologies make interaction possible for both the informant and the ethnographer to be absent in the interaction but present in the ethnography, in what Hine refers to as "ethnography in, of, and through the virtual" (Hine, 2000: 65) .

Especially when it comes to social network sites, these platforms have become intertwined in the everyday and political lives in Europe and North America, giving way to new forms of cultural and political participation (Johan, 2018). Scholars of social movements concur on the centrality of social media in the last two decades (Postill & Pink, 2012; Caiani, Della Porta & Wagemann, 2012; Mosca, 2014; Johan, 2018), as online activities of organizing, disseminating frames of claims-making, and recruiting new members have become an indispensable part of the movement as much as offline mobilization. Unlike previous forms of online output, these platforms usually convey transient newsfeeds and posts that are composed of the everyday practices of individual users (Airoldi, 2018), and are immersed in a visually stimulated digital environment (Hjorth & Pink, 2014). By treating online spaces as an extension of offline social spaces (Hjorth & Pink, 2014; Airoldi, 2018), this research has conducted online ethnography by following official media accounts of social movements in Verona, as well as the public accounts of their members. These posts were followed and documented both by screenshots of posts with images and the manual copy-pasting of the texts (Airoldi, 2018), archived according to the actor, the topic, and the date. This 'microarchiving' undertaken by the researcher is done through *purposive sampling* in line with the research interests based on offline knowledge of the field (Mosca, 2014).

The period of online ethnography undertaken in this study started around December 2019 and lasted until August 2020, with regular visits to social media accounts on Facebook, Twitter, and Instagram and other relevant websites of social actors who are active in Verona, later continuing into 2021 with occasional visits. This method has focused on social media posts of personal and official accounts of the local groups, initiatives, associations and collectives under study, including national and transnational accounts that they repost and refer to. For ethical reasons, it is important to note that only open-access public accounts and public websites have been utilized throughout the study, which involved key political actors in Verona, local far-right organizations, identitarian groups, accounts related to the local branch of populist Lega party and Fratelli d'Italia party, social and cultural organizations, ultra-conservative religious groups, and social media accounts dedicated to the hooligans of the local football team. These social media accounts and websites constituted the 'home bases' (Postill & Pink, 2012: 127) for the online ethnography, from which transnational accounts and other organizational pages have been reached, thereby revealing themes and arguments that travel across borders beyond the locality.

A significant part of the research focusing on far-right groups has therefore relied mainly on online ethnography, complementing non-participant observation at public events and the few interviews conducted with far-right actors, in order to bridge the gap of participant observation and qualitative interviews that were possible with the progressive movements. This was due to the difficulty of gaining access, given firstly the suspicion of academic work in general among this circle of political groups (Pirro & Gattinara, 2018), and secondly, the researcher's positionality in the field as a Turkish migrant woman. At this point, the Internet has provided an invaluable platform from which to access and systematically collect precious data. The anonymity and low entry barriers that online presence offers are not only conducive for the researcher to freely investigate commonly shared arguments, values, and beliefs among far-right circles, but also for the latter to express freely their anger and resentment in the company of like-minded others without fear of legal persecution, thereby offering unfiltered data (Caiani & Kröll, 2014; Rydgren, 2018).

The centrality of the Internet for the mobilization of far-right social movements has been underlined in the literature in recent years (Caiani, Della Porta & Wagemann, 2012; Caiani, 2019; Klein & Muis, 2018; Rydgren, 2018). As succinctly put by Caiani: "Instead of a formal organization and leadership, face-to-face interactions and identities in the real world, the Web, and the technological potentialities it offers, is becoming the main organizational element for radical right-wing groups, providing potential activists with the feeling of 'being at home' and no longer marginalized by society" (2019: 924). Activists with no contact in the offline world can get in touch, share ideas, foster a collective identity, and mobilize online. Such mobilization also includes transnational networking activities as local groups seek to unite in a common 'European' cause (Caiani, 2018). It is also suggested that much of the violent actions of far-right groups either take place online, or are instigated by exchanges online (Rydgren, 2018).

4   Qualitative Interviews

In qualitative research, interviews are "conversations conducted for a purpose, which frames the interaction" (Brinkmann, 2017: 991). They are particularly fruitful means of collecting data to grasp the point of view of the respondent, to understand everyday the workings of a setting, to make sense of actions in their social context, and to underline time and process (Della Porta, 2014a). While conducting qualitative interviews, it is important to establish a communicative platform in which the interviewee feels that they have the flexibility to ask questions or express their concerns in their own words from their own perspective. Attention must be given to how to get the interviewees involved actively in the conversation, how not to overuse social science categories, and how to stimulate the conversation respectfully to draw out contrasting views (Brinkmann, 2017). Three types of qualitative interviews have been utilized in this research, including 23 semi-structured interviews, 7 ethnographic interviews as part of the fieldwork, and 13 photo-elicitation interviews. The latter will be explained in detail under the section of Visual Methods.

Semi-structured interviews were undertaken with activists, volunteers, members of key associations/organizations and other individuals from diverse backgrounds living in Verona, who agreed to meet with me and talk about topics of interest for the research. The aim has been to understand their opinion on identity politics that have been unfolding within shared urban spaces, their perception of the city, its various neighborhoods, how they define belonging to Verona and the concept of *'cittadinanza'*. These interviews have ensured that the interviewer can channel the flow of the conversation, and concurrently, that the interviewee is seen as a knowledge-producing participant in the conversation with a comfortable room to express themselves freely (Brinkmann, 2017). Hence, while being open-ended, the interviews were guided by "a general script" and covered "a list of topics" (Bernard, 2006: 210). Semi-structured interviews have also allowed room for the discovery of unaccounted perspectives and the multiple processes involved in a social phenomenon (Galletta, 2013: 9).

In addition to semi-structured interviews, *ethnographic interviews* (Flick, 2009: 169) were conducted during the fieldwork on the site, usually at key events such as the World Congress of Families, the opening of Forza Nuova's new office in the neighborhood of Veronetta, or community building events by the network of activists. These relatively shorter impromptu interviews were conducted by approaching social actors present at the site, introducing myself and the study, and asking for their take on what was going on. These short conversations were recorded with the permission of the respondent, later transcribed, and incorporated into the relevant field note instead of being analyzed separately.

Hence, through qualitative interviews, the study sought to capture the reality from the social actors' eyes, using their own vocabulary and their own narration (Frisina, 2013: 13). During each interview, the role of a 'good listener' was sought as much as possible and comments were kept at a minimum. With old Veronesi and other Italian respondents, the interview proceeded in a way that, as a migrant studying Veronese territory, I was explained the historical context of Verona and social relations in this city. With migrants and refugees, on the other hand, my position as a fellow newcomer in a challenging city created a feeling of mutual empathy and eased the conversation flow. The interviewees were given room for maneuver (Frisina, 2013: 15) to present their story in their own words and order of precedence that they preferred. An informed consent was sought from all interviewees before the interview, who were guaranteed that they would remain anonymous and that the interview will be used exclusively for research purposes. Where possible, a written informed consent was signed; nevertheless, in cases where signing an official document generated a suspicion, consent was asked verbally and audio-recorded.

5   Documents and Archival Data

Documents in qualitative research are categorized as *primary* or *secondary documents*. The meanings they convey, their credibility, and their representativeness are considered part of the analysis. A corpus of documents has been constructed purposively for this study, guided by research interests (Flick, 2009: 257). The research utilized a variety of primary documents ranging

from official documents produced by the city administration (such as proposals submitted and/or passed at the city council, press statements of the
Municipality of Verona, and announcements made by the mayor), to unofficial documents produced by activists and members of various organizations
that reflect the organization's outlook and agenda (including pamphlets, flyers, activity reports, and public declarations). These are also accompanied by
secondary sources such as academic works on Verona and its history, alongside local newspaper articles in the city of Verona (which were not treated as
objective sources of unbiased information) reporting key events, moments of
conflict, or declarations by important figures.

Archival documents help evaluate the representativeness, credibility, and
continuity or changes in the meaning conveyed by fieldwork. This is done so
by juxtaposing documents, artifacts, or images from the past alongside contemporary events and actors being investigated. As put by Bosi and Reiter,
"by exposing researchers to aspects of process, context, sequence, and tim-
ing, archival work can make important contributions to theory building, data
collection, and hypothesis testing" (2014: 118). While most frequently utilized
archival sources in qualitative research usually involve state archives, new
social movements also tend to generate nonstate archives with a pregiven
political disposition. These initiatives seeking to create social documentation
of the collective memory of movements, preserve valuable materials pertaining to 'politics from below' (Bosi & Reiter, 2014). Despite the fact that most
new social movement archives tend to be free, access can still be guarded and
requires the establishment of trust.

This study has made use of historical archives produced by the activist
network in Verona in the course of the last 30 years of local struggles, sustained by different associations/collectives throughout the years. Obtaining
access to what they call 'dossiers' covering key historical episodes, moments
of tension, as well as systematic documentation of far-right militancy and
their allies, has been a gradual process. This was enabled by the establishment
of mutual trust, first with a historical LGBTQ+ activist and later with an ex-
member of *La Chimica* who has been devoting himself to the documentation
and archiving of every political and social episode in Verona since his early
activist years in the 1980s. He also plays a crucial role in the establishment
of the archival association *InfoSpazio 161* that offers an online blog where the
documentation is uploaded regularly, notification is provided on all ongoing
mobilizations in the surrounding area, and historical information with primary sources is available.

6   Visual Methods

The visual occupies a privileged position in our contemporary societies, especially when it comes to our social lives. Visuality influences our emotions, identifications, memories, and aspirations in life. No matter the distinct form of
visual technology, whether it is a photograph, a video, or a digital graphic, they
are taken as vessels of meaning (Rose, 2023). Visual artifacts, whilst offering
an interpretation of a neutral occurrence, also invite a particular positioning
of the viewer in relation to the object, embedded in the social context of the
viewing (Ibid.). Visual methods have gained momentum in social sciences
with a new focus on practices of everyday life and their spatial aspects, creating routes through which "people's understandings, experiences, and ways of
doing things can become 'visible'" (Pink, 2011: 446). These new methods render
visible the materiality and sociality of lived settings from the eyes of those who
experienced them (Pink, 2011; Frisina, 2013).

It has been argued that visual tools and approaches can reinvigorate the
discipline of Sociology that is becoming "increasingly abstract and distant
from the world it seeks to understand," by "opening the eyes" of the discipline to the richness of the perceptual world that lays ahead (Harper, 2012: 4).
This research has utilized three sources of visual material which have been
incorporated into the study as 'primary data' (Pauwels, 2016) to be analyzed
alongside other forms of written or verbal data: (1) images accompanying
the ethnographic fieldwork, including a collection of urban graffiti and stickers, (2) social media images gathered through online ethnography (which is
handled in the previous section), and finally (3) photo-elicitation technique
where the respondents are invited to participate actively in the research process. While ethnographic research seeks to observe macrosocial phenomena
by studying the microsocial level, the camera is utilized to produce visual
descriptions of the details of everyday life that are usually treated as insignif-
icant (Frisina, 2013: 27–28). The principal visual material utilized in this study
has been photographic images, which included imagery that was produced by
the *researcher* and the *respondents* as participants in the fieldwork, alongside
images available on social media.

These artifacts have not been taken to offer a 'mirror image' of the world; on
the contrary, they are considered selective representations or 'constructions' of
the social world, much like discourses. As lucidly put by Rose: "These images
are never transparent windows onto the world. They interpret the world; they
display it in very particular ways" (2023: 17). Moreover, visual data is not treated
as self-sufficient objects but must always be considered in the context in which
they have been produced and the social practices of signification that define

such context (Frisina, 2016). As argued by Chalfen (2011), there is a growing field of using pictures to support ethnographic fieldwork, linking 'site' to 'sight', with particular attention to the researcher's positionality as an observer and producer of imagery in the field. In this study, the researcher-generated images of the field have captured interactions in the spaces of various associations and grassroots movements, far-right organizations and their operations, performative events such as protests, demonstrations, festivals, celebrations, and lastly, moments of social conflict spread across cityspace. Moreover, regular urban walks around the touristic historical center and its neighboring Veronetta have led to a collection of street art conveying political messages. Referred to by the respondents as 'urban dialogue', these artifacts embodying social conflict in and through shared spaces by opposing actors have been an invaluable source of data for tracing practices of territorialization upon urban realities.

On the other hand, the participant approach of respondent generated imagery has allowed me to see the same spaces through the eyes of those who inhabit them and take part in everyday rituals. This participant visual method allows the researchers and the respondents to 'see' social reality together (Frisina, 2016). The incorporation of respondents as participants by generating their own photography, or in other words "stimulating the field to produce its own imagery" (Pauwels, 2015: 95), has been adopted in different fields: research on migration and racial studies (Martiniello, 2017), youth perceptions of multiculturalism (Johansen & Le, 2014), older people's perceptions of urban social inclusion (Ronzi et al., 2016), lived realities of migrant women (Sutherland & Cheng, 2009), and mental health research (Glaw et al., 2017). Also known as *photo-elicitation*, this method is a form of data gathering whereby respondents are asked to generate photos of their daily routines, their surroundings, or any other focus of the research questions. Participant methods can help emphasize the positioning of the individual as a social actor in creating representations as well as counter-representations of the world around them, which often go beyond dominant narratives (Frisina, 2016).

The researcher has limited control over the production of these images, aside from offering some guiding questions or themes, as respondents produce their own visual representations (Pauwels, 2010; Glaw et al., 2017). These images are then elaborated and reflected on to create narrative accounts of the images through semi-structured interviews, thereby capturing their interpretation by the participants who took them and avoiding a 'pictures-speaks-for-themselves' approach (Chalfen, 2011a: 192). The juxtaposition of visual material produced by the participant alongside their narrative depiction enriches the interview by providing a multi-dimensional account that brings to light deeper layers of meaning which might not be available in a conventional verbal interview (Johansen & Le, 2014; Pauwels, 2015; Ronzi et al., 2016; Glaw et al., 2017). As suggested by Frisina (2016), visual qualitative methods allow us to recognize the plurality of gazes and provide the chance of self-representation, generating in the context of Verona visual accounts of material and immaterial borders in cityspace narrated by residents of different backgrounds.

In the investigation of cityspace as a "multi-authored communicative space" (Pauwels, 2016: 1325), the visual dimension of places and everyday life substantially deepened the narration of the lived territory. In fact, it has been primarily through the narration of respondent-generated images that have elicited the role played by 'vernacular landscapes' (Krase, 2009) of conviviality, pointing out how space impacts social relations. The landscape defined by social relations can be analyzed through visual cues that are 'read' politically. Especially when it comes to the processes of territorialization, visual methods can help grasp the intertwined nature of the material and the immaterial (Brighenti, 2010a).

For this purpose, individuals who live, work, or frequent the neighborhood of Veronetta have been chosen for the photo-elicitation technique on the basis of their membership in local associations ranging from informal neighborhood committees to politically oriented collectives. The aim has been to acquire an insider view of life in Veronetta beyond dominant representations, to understand why and how this neighborhood has come to represent citizen mobilization, and everyday identity struggles within it. Participants had varying backgrounds with respect to gender, age, place of origin, and citizenship status, which provided different vantage points of the same social space. Before the invitation to participate, confidentiality was assured, and informed consent was duly sought from the respondents who volunteered to take part. Thus, there was a shared awareness that the photos they generated would be used for research purposes and published in academic outlets. Participants were asked if they were in possession of any photographic camera, also the type that was present in smartphones, since "camera phone photography has become part of the everyday reality and visuality of people whose experiences they describe" (Hjorth & Pink, 2014: 43). If they preferred, they were offered single-use cameras provided by the researcher. The guiding questions involved practices and places that make them feel at home or out of place, spaces of mobilization in the neighborhood, and finally, positive or negative changes they have observed in time.

The subsequent phase was to ask the participant to send all the photos taken and set an interview date. During the interview the respondents were asked to elaborate and contextualize the photos they have produced, which of the question(s) each photo responded to and what it signified for them. These visual cues have kindled rich conversations that superseded the questions presented by the researcher, extending onto matters of everyday urban life, neighborhood issues, personal stories, feelings of attachment to Veronetta, and memorialization of social conflict and resistance in Verona. In this way, the photo-elicitation technique has deepened personal narratives with respect to place-bound experiences.

7   Data Analysis

According to Clifford Geertz, analysis of ethnographic data is "sorting out the structures of signification" (1973: 9). In this study, data analysis has involved a systematic re-organizing of data in light of the research questions. This final process sought to interpret "meanings, functions, and consequences of human action and institutional practices and how these are implicated in local, and perhaps also wider, contexts" (Atkinson & Hammersley, 2007: 3). This has involved a recursive process in which the researcher moves from the fieldwork to the analysis, and from the analysis back to the fieldwork to develop and refine the theory. It is through this process that the initial research questions become more specific, and the sampling is finalized as the existing categories are saturated and no new themes emerge from the analysis (Frisina, 2013: 9).

The primary phase in the analysis has been coding, where the "data has been broken down, conceptualized, and put back together in new ways" (Flick, 2009: 307). Through coding, this corpus is organized into meaningful codes and categories in light of the theoretical framework by the employment of repetitive comparison of single instances with others. Codes are understood as labels or tags that classify together similar ideas, topics, perspectives, or other social phenomena. They are usually accompanied by memos that clarify the former and elaborate underlying assumptions (Lofland et al., 2006). These codes are then sorted on a higher level of abstraction and tied to more general categories with a complex web of relations between each code. This study has utilized *thematic coding* wherein social actors and groups are defined a priori in light of the research interests, and their perspectives on a given issue are analyzed comparatively. As put by Flick, under thematic coding, "[t]he research issue is the social distribution of perspectives on a phenomenon or process" (Flick, 2009: 318). Unlike grounded theory coding, theoretical sampling is employed to circumscribe the groups to be studied and compared, whilst the collection of data follows the same approach to accumulate data that can convey each group's perspectives (Ibid.). As a result, correspondences and differences are identified and analyzed in each respective group, with the objective of uncovering how the analytical themes are manifested in antagonistic groups through the distribution of codes and categories (Flick, 2009: 320–323).

Thematic coding entails tracing patterns and critical moments of a phenomenon as manifested in the data to develop recurrent themes by moving up from single instances. Thus, following the initial phase of *systematization* of the data, the *thematization* phase seeks to discover *thematic threads* that connect the data whilst refining existing codes and new angles (Boellstorff et al., 2012). Towards the final phase of the analysis, key themes have become concretized and lead to the *narrative building* phase that crafts a narrative of the phenomenon in conversation with the literature. In this study, all the data gathered through triangulation are treated as 'texts' to be analyzed, including visual and written material, which are then categorized. The thematic coding was conducted with the help of the qualitative research software ATLAS.ti.

8　　A Final Note on Reflexivity and Limitations of the Research Design

It is important to reflect on my positioning in the field as a Turkish migrant woman living in Verona who had arrived in Italy only two years ago at the beginning of fieldwork. The usual power-laden relationship inherent in most ethnographic studies involves a European or North American researcher who studies various groups of interest in 'developing' countries or minority groups such as migrants in their own societies (Bejarano, 2019). Such hierarchical positionality has been inverted in this study, which ultimately shaped the flow of the research in significant ways. To begin with, the researcher being 'visibly' a migrant due to physical traits, qualifying in Italy as an *extracomunitaria* (non-European foreigner) whilst studying the host European society (without a particular focus on specific migrant categories) is quite novel in terms of one's location in the field. On the one hand, with respect to the assemblage of progressive groups in Veronetta, my positionality in the field eased the access for two reasons. Firstly, the latter consider themselves as a minority in a city perceived to be dominated by an alliance of sovereignist identitarian actors, and thus seek to expand participation by welcoming individuals interested in the alternative social reality they propose. Secondly, despite working on issues of anti-racism, migration, and social inclusion, the antibodies are primarily constituted by Italian nationals with few exceptions; therefore, they appreciate any involvement by migrants or refugees, in other words 'new Veronesi', to partake in their struggles of city-zenship.

On the other hand, my positionality has limited the same level of rapport with far-right, nativist, and openly racist groups with whom an 'awkward relationship' (Snow, 2006) was expected. In conducting research with so-called 'ugly movements', an emic approach was sought to understand the point of view of the members and their internal dynamics (Avanza, 2018) and to try to understand their emotions and motivations (Hochschild, 2016), including the sense of loss of control and/or identity that underlie the deep-seated hostility towards difference. In order to contextualize the nativist logic and provide depth to the analysis, Chapter 3 offers a detailed historical account of various epochs marked by war, foreign invasion, and poverty that the city and its residents have endured, leading to widespread diffidence and defensive localism in shaping *Veronesità*. That being said, when it came to elongated periods of personal contact with these groups, my identity as a migrant woman from a Muslim country has impeded the type of access I could establish with progressive movements. At one instance, my attempt to strike up a casual conversation with a group of young far-right activists was completely ignored as I was deemed invisible due to my looks and my accent.

Another attempt to interview a member of one of the far-right movements in Verona resulted in the respondent seeking to infringe my privacy, thereby putting me in an ethically compromised position. Moreover, a respondent reached through a common contact made it clear that without such personal reference, he would have refused to be interviewed and so would other members of this group far-right, notwithstanding my academic credentials and affiliation. The reason for such diffidence towards academic or journalistic interest was the fear of being misrepresented: "The concern we have in our circle is that ... although we take pleasure in sharing our opinion and seeking to answer questions as much as possible, they end up being manipulated. The useful part is always extracted, and only this passage is projected or emphasized. Our message ends up being misrepresented" (L.P., 8 July 2020). Moreover, the experience of this interview has demonstrated that, even if a far-right member does agree to sit down with a migrant for an interview, they tend to excessively soften certain aspects in their answers in line with the positioning of the researcher, leading to a rather tangible 'social desirability bias' (Bergen & Labonte, 2019). This tendency became even more visible when the interview was compared with the content of posts shared by fellow members of the same group on social media.

For these reasons, beyond the instances of non-participant observation and rather few face-to-face interactions with actors of the far-right, the solution offered by online ethnography yielding a rich and unfiltered body of data, together with archival research on the chronology of conduct by these groups has been jointly utilized to bridge this gap. The results were more positive than anticipated, leading to access not only to more candid testimonies online, but also allowing the researcher to track diachronically movement evolution and synchronically to trace links with other national or transnational movements. This was made possible by triangulating ethnographic data both online and offline, together with archival data and visual data. Despite the fact that the type of data utilized to compare opposing movements have not been identical, the systematic analysis nevertheless has produced invaluable insights and a cogent comparison.

Thus, it is important to address three limitations of the study with respect to the research design and the comparative analysis. Like any other single case study, the decision to focus on one single case in trying to understand the workings of a larger phenomenon limits the generalizability of the findings. This limitation is lengthily addressed by the extended case method, where a unique case is chosen to shed light on the society at large and to restructure theory regarding the spatiality of social movements by introducing the categories of identity of place and place-based identities. By design, the single case is valuable as it offers a detailed historical analysis in investigating the complexity of socio-political dynamics and the competing actors that impact the local whilst extending to the extralocal, which is difficult to achieve in multiple cases. Moreover, the study offers a systematic comparative analysis with respect to the two different sets of social actors, their competing constructions of place-based belonging, and the two distinct social spaces cultivating the collective identity and fueling collective action of these antagonistic actors. Thus, two opposing social movements that operate in Verona are investigated comparatively in order to understand the everyday mechanism of wider themes that resonate in struggles of identity.

The second limitation is related to the way in which different forms of data have been utilized in the analysis of different groups. On the one hand, the analysis of progressive movements has been premised primarily on qualitative interviews and on-site fieldwork; on the other hand, the analysis of far-right groups for reasons explicated above is limited to face-to-face encounters with members and is therefore largely based either on online ethnography, non-participant observation, or archival documents. That being said, the triangulation of data has nonetheless resulted in invaluable insights into movement/countermovement dynamics in and through shared spaces. I, therefore, believe it is important to emphasize that the research design was formulated with full awareness of this inbuilt limitation. The insistence on carrying out comparative research of opposing movements despite different sources of

data has been to help overcome the theoretical consequences of not studying 'awkward movements' difficult to investigate. The over-representation of
'popular movements' tends to perpetuate a theoretical bias in the social movements literature and a consequent failure to understand the internal dynamics
of 'unpleasant' movements (Snow, 2004: 497).

'Veronesi Tuti Mati': A Historical Analysis of Social Processes Shaping Identity of Place and Place-Based Identities

> The past of the city ... is not entirely legible; it is irreducible to any anachronistic language; it suggests other dimensions of the lived experience and haunts the city like a ghost.
>
> BOYM, 2001: 76

∴

A historical perspective allows one to situate and contextualize contemporary struggles in public spaces and to make sense of how the identity of these places has been shaped alongside the place-based identities that they cultivate, with their own version of collective memories echoing in urban realities. Despite being a medium-sized city, owing to its geostrategic position Verona boasts a long and rich history marked by a line of alternating rulers, skillfully preserved and compartmentalized today in the marketing of heritage for touristic consumption, turning 'competitive localism' into profit (Massey, 1994; Zukin, 1998; Moore, 2007). These historical events, figures, and legacies that continue to leave an imprint on urban life are reappropriated by local groups to define the identity of place (Lynch, 1981; Banini, 2017) and the borders of belongings that are shaped by everyday encounters (Soja, 1971; Herb & Kaplan, 1999; Brighenti, 2014; Yuval-Davis et al., 2018). Hence, in order to comprehend and contextualize present struggles that characterize shared urban spaces, this chapter will explore the historical course of Verona drawing on critical junctures.

1   A Brief Historical Account of Verona and the Making of *Veronesità*

The city of Verona reflects a 'city-museum' model whereby historical texture is perfectly preserved giving the visitor a sense of travelling back in time as one wanders in the touristic center. Not surprisingly, the city has been granted the status of UNESCO World Heritage Site owing to this impeccable display of shifting historical epochs in its architectural and urbanistic landscape. Nevertheless, a subsequent 'Disneyification' (Zukin, 1998; Semi, 2015) of the city center for touristic consumption has led to its portrayal as frozen in space and time, with the ideal protagonist being the white middle-class heteronormative European. Two of the most visible cultural assets that have contributed to the city becoming a desired tourist destination have been the Roman *Arena di Verona* located in *Piazza Brà,* which is still functional today hosting the internationally-famed Opera Festival every summer, and the marketing of Shakespeare's play *Romeo and Juliet.* These two remarkable features that have today become an indispensable trademark of the identity of Verona are capitalized to attract thousands of tourists every day. This type of mass marketing of heritage (Mitchell, 2000; Boym, 2001) and heavy 'touristification' of the historical center (Pixova & Sladek, 2016; Sequera & Nofre, 2018, 2019) have led to what is considered by some as a 'monocultural' touristic experience, including a false archaeology of Romeo and Juliet, leading to the main city squares to turn into souvenir markets (Chelidonio, 2009: 45). Today, the historical center is exhibited in a showcase, with nothing new to be lived: "Probably it will continue to produce wealth and income for its inhabitants, it can feel alive by the only way granted to the dying: by taking refuge in memories, searching a sense of the self in the past" (Gastaldo, 1987: 110).

The urban center of Verona has a 2100-year history that hosted different cultures in different epochs, owing to its strategic location easily accessible by land and by water. The Adige River itself has been a medium of contact between trans-alpine populations and Adriatic-Mediterranean populations for over 10,000 years (Chelidonio, 2009: 39). The city has a long history of invasion by various groups, including the Ostrogoths under Theodoric the Great, the Lombards under King Alboin, the Franks under Pepin the Short, the Visconti of Milan, the Venetians, the Austrian Empire, the French under Napoleon, and Nazi Germany (Delibori, 2009). The first human settlement in Verona dates back to the Bronze Age with the establishment of a village on the San Pietro Hill, today part of the neighborhood of *Veronetta,* overlooking River Adige. During the Iron Age, the city had become a meeting point for the exchange of different cultures between Euganei, Raetians, Celtic, and Etruscan peoples. In 3rd century BC, the city was occupied by Romans and took on an increasingly strategic role at the intersection of the main Roman roads *Via Postumia,* connecting the Tyrrhenian Sea to the Adriatic Sea, and *Via Claudia Augusta,* connecting the Bavarian region of present-day Germany across the Alps to the Po Valley in northern Italy. As the city became a Roman Municipality and the inhabitants becoming Roman citizens, urban planning was redrawn in typical Roman style with a *Cardus Maximus* from north to south (*via Leone*), and a

Decumanus Maximus from east to west (*via Porta Borsari*) (Girolami, 2000), marked by city gates at each end, and at their intersection laid the Roman forum where today *Piazza Erbe* stands as one of the most important 'nodal points' (Moore, 2007) in the touristic center.

Given the long line of rulers that left their imprint on the city, the *Scaliger dynasty* (also referred to as *Della Scala*) ruling in the 13th and 14th centuries has undeniably come to be considered the true patrons of the city as reflected on its 'topographic map' (Berg & Kearns, 1996) as well as in the symbolism of the *scala* (stairs) as their coat of arms. This symbol profusely embellishes the city, not only engraved in ancient medieval structures but also utilized in modern depictions to represent the identity of Verona and of its inhabitants. It is used as the logo of sports teams, including the most popular football club Hellas, at times being appropriated by neofascist or neo-Nazi groups who promote defensive localism (Lipsitz, 2011) to mark an exclusionary territorial identity reflecting a sovereignist identitarian outlook. One of the reasons for the glorification of the Scaliger era was the fact that it had been the only period of independence lasting for 125 years, considered as the golden age of Verona where the city prospered and expanded its territory from Brescia to the West

FIGURE 2   Verona at the crossroads since Roman times
ILLUSTRATION: VERONISSIMA. IMAGE AVAILABLE AT: HTTP://WWW.VERO
NISSIMA.COM/SITO_ITALIANO/HTML/STORIA-DI-VERONA-ROMANA.HTML
(ACCESSED 15 SEPTEMBER 2023)

until Treviso to the East, all the way to Lucca to the south. The Scala family were wool merchants who were given the city's *podesteria* (highest civil office in the city administration during the medieval era) after the tyrannical rule of Ezzelino the 3rd, undertaken first by *Mastino Della Scala* referred to as 'the captain of the people' (Girolami, 2000). Notwithstanding the fame of the latter, Cangrande the 1st comes to the fore as one of the most beloved rulers from the Scala, who had hosted important names during his rule, such as Dante, Petrarch, and Giotto, contributing to the esteem and the wellbeing of the city. The short history of the Scala dynasty, despite its fame among the locals, was in fact tainted with fratricide, intrigue, and tyranny (Allen, 1910).

As a result, among the numerous successive rulers of the city, today Veronese territorial identity draws heavily on the heritage and legacy of the Scaliger, together with the *Republic of Venice* that ruled the city from the 15th until the 18th century, also embraced as a native ruler whose richness and success is still a source of local pride. During the 18th and early 19th century, the city of Verona became a playground of powerful actors operating in the region once again, including France, Austria, and the Republic of Venice. French forces first entered the city peacefully in 1796 as Napoleon took accommodation in *Palazzo Forti* in the historical center. With his military campaign towards the west of Verona, the city was transformed into a giant hospital hosting around 4000 sick or injured French soldiers accommodated in the houses, the churches, and even the stables of the local Veronesi (Romagnani, 2009). The following year, with the leadership of the local elite, the inhabitants staged an uprising against the oppressive French occupation. The revolt began the second day of Easter, thereby coming to be known as *Pasque Veronesi* (Veronese Easters) and constituted one of the most important anti-Jacobin episodes in Europe.

The first instance of the uprising took place after the morning mass on the 16th of April 1797 when a group of locals attacked the Jewish ghetto considered as a 'Jacobin enclave'. The following day, a fake letter fabricated by the French calling Veronesi to revolt signed by the Republic of Venice succeeded in mobilizing a local rebellion, as the locals started executing French soldiers, thereby giving the latter an excuse for a ruthless response under the rubric of self-defense. The uprisings took place when Napoleon was fighting in Austria, and in his absence, Veronesi managed to drive the French out of the center who took refuge at the outskirts of the city. Yet, on the 25th of April, the French forces received an enforcement of 15,000 soldiers, owing to which the city was recaptured and the local population brutally punished. This episode also marked the end of The Republic of Venice whose territory was taken over by the Austrians as agreed in a secret article in the Treaty of Leoben in 1797, concretized with the Treaty of Campo Formio the same year. This treaty also saw the city being divided between the French and the Austrians until the bloody Battle of Verona in 1805, when the former reoccupied the city (Romagnani, 2009).

Hence, *Pasque Veronesi* revolts have been a fundamental historical episode in reinforcing a localist pride that is willing to exert its own will and its own traditions against foreign invaders with morals alien to the native land, in a period when the *Serenissima* (Republic of Venice) was considered to be the rightful ruler. This episode is reinterpreted today to become quintessentially ritualized as an 'invented tradition' (Hobsbawm, 1990) in breeding a local 'territorial nationalism' (Soja, 1971) in Verona and its province, coming to be annually celebrated with historical soldier uniforms and the San Marco flag by groups ranging from ultra-Catholics, right-wing populists, Veneto separatists, and local skinheads. The episode has even come to mark the topography of the city with a square next to Castelvecchio named *Piazza delle Pasque Veronesi*, an act of naming that assigns a certain type of territorial belonging upon shared urban spaces (Berg & Kearns, 1996; McKittrick, 2007). Moreover, the commemoration of this anti-Jacobin uprising is organized every 25 April, the same day as the celebration of the Liberation Day from the Nazi-fascist occupation of Italy, to counterpose the latter antifascist memorialization with an 'authentic' Veronese uprising harboring defensive reactionary identities.

As the city came to be divided by two foreign powers in the aftermath of the Republic of Venice's demise, the western bank of Adige corresponding to the heart of the historical center was officially given to the French Cisalpine Republic, whereas the east coast was granted to the Austrians (Massignan, 2020). The bridges connecting the two coasts of the Adige River were blocked, the riverbank was fortified, and communication was cut off. Border gates were placed on the bridges of *Ponte Navi, Ponte Pietra,* and *Ponte Nuovo*, painted yellow and black on the Austrian side, blue, red and white on the French side. This division of the city center had social, political, and economic ramifications for the local population as the everyday simple act of crossing one of the many bridges over the Adige was paramount to crossing interstate borders. It is noted that social order on the Austrian side was under rigid control and conscription was held mandatory, which did not please the young Veronese who were not accustomed to military discipline, leading them to flee to the French side (Massignan, 2020). The French applied the principles of the Revolution, namely equal citizenship and equal rights to all, including the Jewish community, while noble titles and religious functions were abolished. Notwithstanding their egalitarian rule, they had devastated historical architecture and desecrated places of worship. The zone under Austrian rule came to be referred to as *Veronette* in a degrading way by the French to signify 'little Verona', in which the *Church of San Nazaro e Celso* served as the Cathedral for this side of the city (Ibid.). The nickname lingered for years, albeit losing its negative connotation, and gave birth to the neighborhood that is today known as Veronetta, with its own 'identity of the place' (Banini, 2017) continuing to be a contested space in the modern city.

Following the Congress of Vienna, a series of international congresses and conventions started in 1814, forecasting the establishment of the Concert of Europe and consequently the downfall of the Napoleonic Republic of Italy. The Congress transferred much of northern Italy, which was politically organized as the Kingdom of Lombardo-Venetia, to the *Austrian Empire*, including the Veronese territory. This series of international meetings that reshuffled the balance of power in Europe also took place in Verona in 1822, coming to be known as the Congress of Verona. The unfettered Austrian authority in the city was characterized by a strong military socio-political as well as urbanistic imprint until 1866, when Verona finally became part of United Italy (Bozzetto, 1996). Undertaking the role of a military stronghold for the Austrian Empire, such transformation was also manifested in the material realities of the cityspace and changed the urban scenery, including the fortification of city walls established by the Republic of Venice, construction of the ex-Arsenal and Castel San Pietro overlooking the city on the San Pietro Hill, and the military bakery of Santa Marta in Figure 3 which today functions as one of the campuses of the University of Verona (Ibid.). During this period, in a city with 50,000 inhabitants, all the possible urban resources were mobilized to sustain an overwhelming army of 100,000 (Ferrari, 2018).

These historical periods marked by war, invasion and destruction in the city owing to its central position in the Italian peninsula, alongside the changing rulers, each leaving their own architectural and social imprint on the collective memory, have shaped the local identity and the imagination of its inhabitants, nurturing mistrust towards social change and those perceived as 'foreign'. The city's function as a military base and a fortress throughout different rulers, but most notably under the Austrian Empire, generated a collective social trauma on the part of its residents (Chelidonio, 2009: 51). As noted by a local: "Verona has a history that makes it what it is today. When there were the Austrians, there were more soldiers than civilians in the city; therefore, starting from this point a mechanism of order and discipline was initiated." (Interview with A.A., 5 August 2019). The city came to be known as the 'fortress-city', due to the city walls, fortifications, and other characteristic military architecture, holding a strategic geopolitical position throughout the ages as the resources of the city were put to the service of foreign armies. Hence, notwithstanding its worldwide fame as the city of love based on the story of Romeo and Juliet, Verona in fact has been *the city of war*: "Due to its strategic position that was conducive

FIGURE 3   The military bakery of Santa Marta built during Austrian rule, today reconstructed
             to be part of the University campus
             PHOTOGRAPH: IPEK DEMIRSU

for trade, other cities and rulers wanted to conquer Verona. The Veronesi
wanted to remain independent, so they defended themselves by building walls
around their city." (Interview with M.G., 6 April 2019).

As a form of place-based identity, the particularities of the Veronesi identity have been a matter of interest, not only to outsiders visiting this fascinat-
ing city but also to the Veronesi themselves. The famous saying in the Veneto
region goes: "*Veneziani gran signori, Padovani gran dottori, Vicentini magna
gatti, Veronesi tutti matti!*" (Venetians great lords, Paduans great scholars,
Vicentini cat-eaters, Veronesi all mad!). The particular characteristics, traditions, and lifestyles of the inhabitants of this city have been a topic of discussion so much so that the term *Veronesità* (the condition of being Veronesi)
has become a common nomenclature referring to this population and their
defining traits. It is argued that this local identity has also been shaped by the
physical realities of its inhabitants, such as the long tradition of agricultural
lifestyle and the memory of poverty that still echoes today despite the wealth
the city has come to enjoy (Gamberoni, 2009). As noted by a local tourist
guide, Veronese territory was transformed into a mass agricultural land under

the rule of the Republic of Venice that hitherto relied on external sources of food overseas (interview with M.G., 6 April 2019). The prevalence of agricultural production in Verona has led to a low level of education felt until the post-war years, since families preferred to keep their offspring as labor force in the fields (Gamberoni, 2009: 32–34). As blatantly put by Bonatelli, "wellbeing and consumerism arrived after centuries of *polenta* [a local dish made out of corn wheat] and *pellagra* [disease caused by malnutrition]" (Bonatelli, 2007). Following the economic boom of the 1960s, as put by an old Veronese activist, "money started to circulate, but without any culture to accompany it … as the local saying goes *tanti schei manca un libro* [lots of money not a single book]." (Interview with A.A., 5 August 2019). The agricultural lifestyle in which the aim was to perpetuate the yearly routine has left a *weltanshauung* whereby change and difference were perceived as threats, "whether it was a new idea, new bodies, new instruments, or new food." (Interview with M.G., 6 April 2019).

In order to understand today the resonance of the slogan *Verona ai Veronesi* (Verona to Veronesi) harboring local notions of 'sovereignism' (Basile & Mazzoleni, 2020; De Spiegeleire et al., 2017) articulated by identitarian actors, one must see past myopic lenses of the present and better comprehend the collective memory of the locals and the reminders of a long history still visible in the lived spaces of the city. For these reasons, it is argued that socioeconomic conditions coupled with the political vestiges of war and invasion have worked in tandem to curtail cultural growth, thereby culminating in a fertile ground for breeding reactionary, conservative, and even racist tendencies (Tutino & Verza, 2013). It is this setting that regional belonging (Paasi, 2011) in *Padano* nativism imbued in a form of localist pride (Nevola, 2010; Mielke, 2005) gives way to the contemporary exclusionary territorial identity that is often capitalized on by far-right movements and right-wing populist groups to address the sense of loss of identity in the immediate locality (Castells, 2010). Nevertheless, this is not the only form of spatial identity present and active in the Veronese landscape, there is another competing form of *Veronesità* rewritten by old and new Veronesi through the creation of an outward-looking space. The cognitive borders of this space overlap with the neighborhood of Veronetta, with its own historical course and its own identity of the place.

2   A Different Neighborhood, a Different Spatial Identity: The Evolution of Veronetta

The neighborhood of Veronetta holds an important place in the history of the city and is a continuation of the historical center rather than being merely adjacent to it. It is the neighborhood where the first human settlement took place on the San Pietro hill to the north, hosting the open-air Archaeological Museum as well as other landmark sites such as *Giardino Giusti* and various university buildings to the south. Being connected to the touristic center by a number of bridges that cross over the Adige River towards the west, the neighborhood extends all the way to *Porta Vescovo* on its eastern border alongside the city walls surrounding it. The lively everyday life of the neighborhood has been a constant throughout the years notwithstanding social change and the changing demographic profile of its inhabitants, allowing for ripe conditions of a real-life laboratory of city-zenship. Despite being physically and culturally part of the historical center, the neighborhood has been perceived as "a container of subjects alien to the city" (Di Nicola, 2018), offering clear boundaries of 'inside/outside'. Hence, in the conservative context of Verona where defensive localism reigns, the neighborhood of Veronetta came to be considered as the 'periphery' par excellence, not due to its geographic distance but rather because of the socio-political space it occupied in the locals' cognitive map of the city (De Vita & de Cordova, 2018).

The neighborhood is divided into four territorially homogenous zones with different socioeconomic characteristics: San Paolo, center of Veronetta, San Giovanni in Valle, and Santo Stefano. Today, the center of Veronetta came to be associated with a high presence of migrant communities and a multiethnic social fabric, while most of the university campus and student life revolves around San Paolo. The other two zones are known for their religious associations and private housing of individuals who come from a higher socioeconomic status (Ferrari, 2018; Di Nicola, 2018). On the one hand, the neighborhood is being transformed today by the process of gentrification manifested in luxurious reconstructed palazzi and the spill-over of touristification from the historical center reflected in the mushrooming of B&Bs. On the other hand, those structures that were once luxurious but today are left to wear out and decay are sites where urban poverty still lingers in this once working-class neighborhood. Another visible characteristic that has come to shape the identity of Veronetta has been the strong presence of military structures and personnel since the Austrian rule, including the military artillery Campo Marzo, military bakery Santa Marta, the Porta Vescovo city walls, and finally the military base Passalacqua which hosted 6000 American soldiers in the post-war period (Magagnotti, 2005).

Since antiquity, Veronetta has been a point of passage and commerce, not only connecting the periphery and the mountain range of Lessinia to the city center but also the city of Verona to neighboring cities and most importantly to Venice through to the Roman road *Via Postumia* that passes through Veronetta.

It is historically characterized by a high density of parishes and religious institutions, artisan workshops, local stores, and taverns, partly due to its strategic position overlapping the city center and also thanks to the canals of the river Adige which has allowed for a rich economic life to flourish in the area (Cevese, 2005; Magagnotti, 2005). Hence, during early medieval times, the neighborhood became a center of artisanal manufacturing undertaken by numerous families working primarily on wool, paper, timber, and dye by utilizing one of the branches of the Adige River known as *Aqua Morta* to power mills and other mechanism of the time. In the 15th century, Veronetta underwent an economic boom, giving way to most of the important mansions, churches, and monasteries that to this day characterize the neighborhood, including San Nazaro e Celso, San Giovanni in Valle, Santa Maria in Organo, and Santo Stefano.

Following the devastating flood of Adige in 1882, the channels and branches of the river, including *Aqua Morta* that gave life to much of the manufacturing, were placed underground. This led to the demise of economic activity in Veronetta and the deterioration of social life in the neighborhood, lasting until much of the 20th century. As described by a local inhabitant: "Veronetta was a neighborhood that was economically vibrant because it was located in an area with canals and streams. All commercial activity used to be born out of and prospered from water. Later, due to security reasons following a great flood of the Adige River in 1882, they constructed the riverbanks and eliminated all the canals. Verona became safer, but Veronetta died because all the economic activity relied on the water that was now gone. So, from there onwards, it became a poor working-class neighborhood for many years and when I came to live here, it was a neighborhood of elderly residents." (Interview with A.V., 15 February 2019).

After a long part of its history harboring urban poverty and marginalization, with the initiative taken by the city administration in 1973, an urbanistic plan of revalorization was undertaken. The plan foresaw the promotion of economic and cultural activities in Veronetta so that the area could become once again a part of the historical center (Ferrari, 2018: 19). The insertion of the university and its various departments, starting with the Faculty of Economy and Commerce and gradually including Humanities and Literature, was part of this revalorization that brought a flow of university professors, students, administrative and technical personnel to the neighborhood creating a new social reality. The university also undertook demilitarization of the neighborhood, absorbing the ex-Austrian military bakery Santa Marta and a part of the military barracks Passalacqua into the university campus. Notwithstanding the new presence of university life, the population of Veronetta had been decreasing significantly since the 1950s and was mainly composed of elderly inhabitants. From 1951, a population of 25,000 went down to approximately

15,500 in 1971, and plummeted to 10,000 in 2011 due to bad housing conditions and scarcity of work opportunities. Moreover, only 17% of the residents in Veronetta were young individuals compared to the 23% average of the Verona municipality, and 13% of which were above 65 compared to 10% in the rest of the city. During the same period, the level of education was also quite low, with 45.9% of the residents being elementary school graduates and only 1.7% with a university degree (Ferrari, 2018).

Since the 1990s, Verona started receiving an unprecedented wave of migration wherein the area of Veronetta came to be identified as the 'multiethnic' neighborhood of the city. This process saw the arrival of various migrant communities and the proliferation of the so-called 'ethnic stores' run by migrant owners. The ethnicity and religious makeup among the newcomers in the neighborhood are multifarious, with a statistically higher presence observed among residents arriving from Romania, Sri Lanka, Moldova, Morocco, Nigeria, Albania, China, and Ghana (De Vita & de Cordova, 2013: 9). The majority of the newcomers chose housing in the central part of Veronetta where old buildings were not modernized, and thus more affordable, particularly along the main streets of *via XX Settembre, via San Nazaro*, and *via Cantarane*. Over time, the neighborhood started to be perceived as a racialized space from an outside gaze, pejoratively referred to as *'Negronetta'* (Ferrari, 2018). Although the percentage of the migrant population is superseded in other more peripheral neighborhoods today, Veronetta still continues to be recognized as 'the immigrant neighborhood', due to the fact of being the only multicultural space as part of the historical center (Gamberoni & Savi, 2016).

A parallel yet by and large unexplored reality that exerts its presence in the neighborhood since the late 1990s is the high intensity of grassroots activism of local associations and collectives that contribute to the social life of the area. It was exactly this setting that prepared the conducive ground for 'insurgent urban citizenship' (Holston & Appadurai, 1996) to be born, drawing in its orbit new and old social actors that dreamed of a different place-based identity in Verona and a different understanding of city-zenship. Veronetta has become an object of citizen mobilization over the years (De Vita, 2008), authoring a different set of 'neighborhood sentiments' (Parks & Burgess, 1967 [1926]) premised on plurality and inclusiveness as opposed to particularistic loyalties. The neighborhood articulates a different way of belonging to the city, an alternative mode of membership co-created by migrants, non-migrants, and other minority groups, which will be elaborated in detail further ahead. To acquire a comprehensive understanding of the identity-space nexus in the making of competing spatial identities in Verona, we must go on to explore the modern history of fascism and the antifascist resistance that left a substantial imprint

FIGURE 4   A meme depicting via XX Settembre of Veronetta refusing the Veneto Contarina
             flag in favor of the Sri Lankan flag, capturing the diverse identity of place
             IMAGE FROM THE SATIRICAL FACEBOOK PAGE 'VERONA DEEP PEARÀ', 30
             MARCH 2021

on the collective memory still felt intensely in city life, continuing to shape
social movement dynamics today.

3   The Legacy of Fascism and Antifascist Resistance in Verona

3.1   *The Imprints of Nazi-Fascism on Urban Space*

Verona had been on the frontlines during the First and Second World Wars,
with the latter exerting an elongated sway both in the material and cognitive
realities of the city. In the interwar years, Verona was considered a proletariat
city with socialists and anarchists in the city administration (interview with
M.S., 6 April 2019). It was first with the 16th of October 1920 elections that

fascists entered the city administration in the local elections as a minority in a city which was until then considered 'red' under the majority of socialists in local politics. On the 4th of November, for the National Unification and Armed Forces Day celebrations marking the end of WWI and the finalization of the unification of Italy, socialist with the leadership of Policarpo Scarabello hung a red flag in the municipality building. At the same time, the fascist group was celebrating with their own pennant, which ensued in a violent clash between the two groups inside *Palazzo Barbieri,* which continues to serve as the main municipality building today (Zangarini, 1993). The clash resulted in the death of Scarabello with the accidental explosion of a grenade in his hand, that was intended to be aimed at the fascists. According to Zangarini (1993), this unfortunate event marked the turn of events for fascism in Verona, which capitalized on the role of the 'victim' in attracting followers to their political cause and growing their sphere of influence gradually.

The fascist political movement in Verona took off firstly as an urban elite initiative and included the local nobility who were used instrumentally by the fascist party when support from the traditional ruling class was required (Zangarini, 1993). In 1938, Mussolini arrived in Verona and greeted the city by describing it as "Black shirt of Verona [referring to the black fascist outfit], the Roman Verona ... fascist in spirit since the very beginning" (quoted in Zangarini, 1993: 27). As fascism took hold of city life in the 1930s, it was propagated through the weekly newsletter *Audacia* (Audacity) which gave life and substance to this ideology in Verona for five years, ceasing its publications when *L'Arena* officially took over the task of propaganda "as the official organ of the Veronese fascist federation" (Zangarini, 1993: 17). The local newspaper *L'Arena* had been the most read newspaper in the city of Verona before taking on this task and continues to be so to this day, known to side with right-wing populist politics and far-right political figures in their news coverage.

On September 8, 1943, an armistice was signed between Italy and the Allied forces, leading to the disarmament of the Italian army with the backing of King Vittorio Emanuele III, following the military defeats in the colonies and Mussolini's worsening health. The vestiges of the fascist regime, with the assistance of German troops, were moved to the small town of Salò on Lake Garda in an attempt to revise and reinstall fascism. As Mussolini was liberated by the Nazis following the government's decree ordering his arrest, he established the Italian Social Republic (*Repubblica Sociale Italiana,* hereafter RSI) in Salò and elaborated a revision of the fascist doctrine. The RSI marked the second episode of fascism which would leave a far more decisive legacy in the territory of Verona (Rocca, 2004). Hence, while the war was over in 1943 in the south of Italy, it continued in the north until the Anglo-American troops entered Milano on the 25th of April 1945 (Milesi et al., 2005).

The proximity of RSI and the attribution of its main functions to the city of Verona, such as the use of prisons and political executions, left an undeniable imprint on the identity of the city and its inhabitants as it became an epicenter in the battle to continue the fascist doctrine. The most controversial proceeding of the RSI took place in Verona by the extraordinary tribunals (*Il Tribunale speciale per la difesa dello Stato della RSI*), where members of the Grand Council of Fascism were condemned for treason for having voted in favor of *l'ordine del giorno* (political directive of parliamentarians addressing the government) presented by Dino Grandi on 25th of July 1943, ending Mussolini's mandate. The political agenda of the succeeding new fascist formation written by Mussolini in 1943 was enshrined in the *Manifesto of Verona* (Cammelli, 2018), formulated following a series of meetings at the Scaliger castle of *Castelvecchio*. The Manifesto of Verona foresaw the abolishment of the monarchy, recast the fascist party as the protector of the revolutionary principles, restated Catholicism as the state religion and the Jewish people as foreign enemy, envisioned a national economy strictly controlled by the state, ensuring fair wages for workers, and the introduction of public housing (Pugliese, 2004: 307–309). This new interpretation of fascism attracted important figures in its orbit, among which was the famous American poet Ezra Pound for whom the city of Verona was a 'sacred love', known for his admiration of the new republican fascism (Pantano, 2016).

Under the RSI, the German forces took control of Verona on the 9th of September with the help of the Republican National Guards. It is argued that during this period, Verona became the most 'Nazified' city in the Italian peninsula (Rocca, 2004: 12). The commander in charge of German police forces (including the SS, Gestapo, Sipo, and Kripo), Wilhelm Harster was stationed in *Palazzo INA* (*Istituto Nazionale Assicurazioni*, National Institute of Insurance) in the city center, which also hosted the IV B4 department of the SS under the leadership of Theodor Dannecker, in charge of the antisemitic struggle in the whole Italian territory. After the war, around 20 cells were discovered underneath Palazzo INA which were used to interrogate and torture antifascists that were captured. This building located on *Corso Porta Nuova* leading to the main square of Piazza Brà, is also in close proximity to the *Porta Nuova* train station where deportation of Jews, partisans, and those that were deemed 'different' was carried out, together with the *Porta Vescovo* station (Rocca, 2004; Biguzzi et al., 2015). Consequently, the horrors of WWII have left an immense mark on the identity of the historical center, with its material and symbolic elements, resonating to this day in the 'cognitive map' (Kearns & Forest, 2000) of the residents. In the urban landscapes where German troops marched alongside RSI soldiers, today thousands of tourists visit every day as the 'city of love'.

Other 'nodal points' (Moore, 2007) in the cognitive map of the RSI rule were a number of hotels in the historical center used as accommodation for the German military or the RSI forces, including Hotel Gabbia in *Corso Porta Borsari* and Hotel Torcolo in *Vicolo Liston*, in addition to private mansions that were confiscated in the middle-class neighborhoods of *Borgo Trento* and *Valdonega* (Rossi et al., 2019). The city fortifications on the outer ring of the center, either built or modernized under the military rule of the Austrians, were used by German forces as places of detention, torture, and later execution or deportation, including the forts of *San Leonardo, Santa Sofia*, and *San Mattia*. Lastly, *Scalzi* and *Montorio* prisons in Verona detained not only members of the antifascist resistance composed of various orientations including the communists, socialists, anarchists, Catholics, and American forces but also ex-officials of the fascist regime found guilty of treason during the Republican Fascist Party Congress held at Castelvecchio, for having signed *l'ordine del giorno Grandi* (Biguzzi et al., 2015).

FIGURE 5   A mural inside Palazzo INA, depicting legends of Verona
              PHOTOGRAPH: IPEK DEMIRSU

This fascist legacy left a strong impact on the socio-political fabric of the city and territorial identity, with lingering memories of occupation and Nazi violence embodied in the materiality of urban places echoing until today. Thus, for those who had placed their loyalties in the stillbirth of a second attempt at the fascist doctrine, this political legacy was passed on to the next generations with a sense of 'victimhood' for losing their rightful lands to antifascists backed by 'foreign powers', thereby cultivating radical movements in the post-war era imbued in antidemocratic and antimodern sentiments with a defensive locality (Milesi et al., 2005; Franzina, 2010; Tutino & Verza, 2013). In a city like Verona, devastated by successive invasions, violence, and destruction during both world wars, an exclusionary territorial identity found a fertile ground to materialize and lay roots. The backdrop of World War II and its aftermath contributed greatly to the city of Verona coming to be known as 'the laboratory of the far-right' in Italian society (Franzina, 2010), as a social space closing upon itself steered by the symbiosis between populism, reactionary conservatism, far-right groups, and more recently identitarians. As indicated by one of the respondents, "The Republic of Salò was lived here in Verona and this fact has moved things in a direction where we still feel it today. The social makeup of Verona continues to be of a far-right city, of a rich city, of a city that wants to maintain its privileges." (Interview with G.P., 10 February 2021). That being said, it is equally important to look into the legacy of local antifascist resistance that is honored and memorialized today by progressive local groups seeking to create alternative democratic spaces and congruently an alternative Veronese identity that is 'open to the world'.

3.2   *Local Resistance and the Legacy of Anti-fascism*

Given the socio-political imprint left by the fascist era observable in the variety of post-fascist actors operating in Verona urban space today, one part of the population has memorialized this historical period by taking pride in and seeking to carry on the antifascist resistance fought during WWII. Civil war intensified after 1943 in Verona and its province due to the newly established Republic of Salò. In this stage, it was not possible to speak about a single organization of antifascist resistance, as the partisan movement in the Veronese territory was not concentrated in a single locality, but rather extended from the lowlands to Baldo Mountain to the northwest, reaching east until Vicenza, with brigades and partisan divisions receiving substantial solidarity from the civil population in their endeavor to hinder Nazi-fascist activities (Zangarini, 1993). The movement included members from different walks of life, bringing together middle-class intellectuals and urban artists with priests, workers, farmers, and foreign detainees who happened to end up in Verona with the ongoing war. The movement was likely composed of a multitude of political inclinations, including socialists, communists, anarchists, liberals, monarchists, and Catholics (Rocca, 2004; Zangarini, 2012).

Initially, these various groups held meetings with the intellectual leadership of the professors Vittorio Zorzi and Francesco Viviani, the lawyer Giuseppe Tommasi, and accountant Tullio Tommasini in an attempt to set the foundations of the political formation *Partito d'azione* (Action Party). The principles discussed in the meetings included the need to change the common perception that politics was a business of the few in order to realize a form of government that was an expression of society as a whole and to the benefit of all. The individual was to be valued as opposed to what they believed was the 'massification' effect of fascism, which was to be guaranteed by a dignified level of education for all and strict control of private property whilst acknowledging its necessity. The result was a non-Marxist socialist vision, with a solid secular outlook that resonated with the principles pioneered by the Italian Unification (Zangarini, 2012). Thus, while the vestiges of fascism took on a heavy toll in the city, a relatively overlooked but important dynamic was the substantial influence of antifascist resistance in the collective memory of Verona which has also come to shape 'collective identity' of the antibodies of hate (Melucci, 1980; Johnston et al., 1994; Polletta & Jasper, 2001; Tarrow, 2011; Van Stekelenburg, 2013), with its own historical figures and historical events that are today invoked to reinforce solidarity among different social actors.

Later into the civil war, Giuseppe Tommasi among the leadership of the local resistance gathered a group of antifascists to realize the first *Comitato di liberazione nazionale provinciale* (Committee of national provincial liberation) in Verona, despite lacking an adequate structure in its organization. This local formation once again included figures from various backgrounds, such as the liberal Giuseppe Pollorini, communist Giuseppe Deambrogi and Guglielmo Bravo, socialist Giuseppe Marconcini and Angelo Buttutini, and anarchist Giovanni Domaschi, as well as military delegates Paolo Rossi and Arturo Zenorini (Rocca, 2004). During the same period, a local branch of *Gruppo di azione patriottica* (Group of Patriotic Action, hereafter GAP) was established in the autumn of 1943 with the initiative of the newly found *Comitato federale del Partito comunista italiano* (Federal Committee of the Italian Communist Party), which was primarily constituted by young artists from Accademia Cignaroli of Verona. Organized by the sculptor Berto Zampieri and with the membership of important names in the Veronese resistance, such as Vittorio Ugolini, Brigette Loewenthal, Antonia Zaccotelli, and Vittorio Avesani, GAP carried out a number of activities aimed to sabotage the infrastructure and military ranks of Nazi-fascist forces in 1944 (Ibid.). These dispersed partisan groups who often operated in the Lessinia mountain range overlooking the city went on to receive new recruits from men who fought to flee forced labor in Germany or forced army requirement of RSI, foreigners who escaped concentration camps, and soldiers who were disbanded after 8th of September. Therefore, the local resistance was not only composed of dissenting local Veronesi but also involved other actors, including foreigners who ended up in this territory during the war and even had a branch dedicated to them named *Brigata Stranieri* (Foreigner's Brigade). Concurrently, the task of antifascist propaganda through publications was undertaken by another citizen initiative called *Stampa e propaganda* (Print and Propaganda) under the leadership of Giovanni Faccoli and Berto Perotti with communist proclivities. These various groups worked in tandem in the absence of a centralized organizing body, carrying out different tasks that served the common cause of resisting Nazi invasion that was enabled with the help of RSI (Rocca, 2004).

Hence, the constellation of different groups and political outlooks that made up the antifascist resistance in Verona managed to carry out missions from 1943 until 1945 that interrupted the activities of German troops with the few resources they had at their disposal. The first act of resistance was carried out by Colonel Eugenio Spiazzi, a pro-monarchy antifascist and the commander of the military barrack in *Campofiore*, an urban area inside the neighborhood of Veronetta. Spiazzi, who was ironically an ex-fascist and the father of Amos Spiazzi involved in far-right political violence in the 1960s and 1970s, refused to send arms or soldiers to the Germans that had invaded the city on the 9th of September. That morning, he later ordered to fire against the approaching German tanks with the artillery at his disposition, managing to halt their advance for a couple of hours that allowed his officials and soldiers to flee at night (Rocca, 2004). The second significant episode took place in front of *Palazzo delle Poste*, today named *Piazza Francesco Viviani* after the intellectual father of the local antifascist resistance. This building, located in the historical center between Piazza Erbe and Porta Leoni, was the communication center to the outside world as the primary postal office. It was held by a number of antifascists by barricades in an attempt to resist German Tiger tanks. The former managed to hold several German soldiers as prisoners but were eventually defeated by night (Ibid.).

The most critical mission carried out by the antifascists took place on 17 July 1944 with the liberation of Giovanni Roveda by GAP members from the Scalzi prison, where many political prisoners were kept. Roveda was an important name in the national antifascist movement as a trade unionist and one of the founders of the Communist Party, who later went on to become the first governor of Torino after the war. This secret mission to liberate Roveda, which is believed to have earned Veronese resistance a military golden medal in the aftermath of WWII, was described as an 'audacious' move given the setting of Verona as the locus of Nazi-fascist activities in 1944 (Zangarini, 2012). The mission was undertaken by six local members of the GAP, who with limited resources at their disposal had dressed as German soldiers carrying out the transfer of political inmates (Ibid.).

These historical events are commemorated every year in Verona, not only by institutional actors, but also by antifascist grassroots movements of different forms and content, from social collectives to LGBTQ+ activists, serving as the marker of a collective identity with a shared collective history (Melucci, 1980; Johnston et al., 1994; Polletta & Jasper, 2001; Nicholls, 2008). These groups take pride in the local resistance initiated by the partisans who had risked, and in some cases sacrificed, their lives for a society premised on social justice and civil rights, which is a fight they deem continues to this day: "We shall never think that the fight is over, let's imagine the future and mobilize to change it." (Facebook post of *Potere al Popolo Verona* in commemoration

FIGURE 6   Commemorating Plaque on Scalzi Prison for the local antifascist resistance
PHOTO FROM THE FACEBOOK PAGE OF ANPI VERONA, 16 JULY 2022

of the Scalzi operation, 17 July 2020). Safeguarding the heritage of this alternative history of the city through local mobilization is taken on by these self-defined 'militants of memory' (Facebook post by *Libre!* on 17 July 2020, a local bookshop in the neighborhood of Veronetta), in an attempt to construe a different identity of place in the memorialization of local history. This involves commemorating the local figures that gave shape to the resistance against Nazi-fascism and actions taken by them in an attempt to mobilize for present causes around this alternative place-based belonging. One such example is the library *Biblioteca Giovanni Domaschi*, located in Veronetta and named after the anarchist partisan, first founded as part of the local anarchist collective Pecora Nera, currently finding its home as part of the cultural association *La Sobilla*.

The legacy of antifascist local resistance is thus taken as an indispensable part of collective memory that energizes local movements today in their struggle for rights and liberties. To this end, the Verona branch of the *Associazione Nazionale Partigiani d'Italia* (National Association of Partisans in Italy, hereafter ANPI) located in Veronetta, hosts *Istituto Veronese per la Storia della Resistenza e dell'Età Contemporanea* (Veronese Institute for the History of Resistance and the Modern Age) which meticulously documents WWII and its aftermath in the Veronese territory with a rich historical archive. The leading partisan figures are commemorated in public demonstrations for various occasions, underlining how the city is not only the fortress of the far-right, but also a city that has earned 15 gold medals for military valor thanks to the antifascist resistance it undertook.[1]

In short, the legacy of the antifascist resistance led by the partisans of different political orientations constitutes the cornerstone of an alternative Veronese city-zenship for the assemblage of translocal actors (McFarlane, 2009) tied to this particular social space and memories of past struggles that took place in it (Melucci, 1980; Nicholls, 2008; Van Stekelenburg, 2013). In this alternative representation of the city, collective action is directed at transformative placemaking (Bacchetta et al., 2019), where boundaries of belonging are rewritten with greater emphasis on inclusiveness and plurality against a fixed static understanding of membership (Massey, 1994, 2005). The everyday struggles in shared urban spaces as acts of city-zenship (Işın, 2008, 2009) are therefore seen as a continuation of the Veronese antifascist struggle of the WWII setting, which is highlighted as one of the defining characteristics of

---

1 ANPI Verona, *Medaglie al Valor Militare*, available online at: https://www.anpiverona.it /medaglie-al-valor-militare.

the alternative place-based identity in Verona, contrary to the predominant exclusionary territorial identity nested in the modern vestiges of fascism. Just like the antifascist partisans during the civil war, these individuals believe that change ought to start from one's locality and unite with other struggles in solidarity for a common future.

CHAPTER 4

'We Hate Everyone': Exclusionary Territorial Identity in the Making of a Laboratory of Intolerance

> When time stops, it becomes place.
>
> CHAWKI ABDELAMIR

∴

Verona is deemed the perfect tourist destination as the city of 'Romeo and Juliet', with a Roman Arena older than the Colosseum in Rome that still operates today hosting opera festivals and musicals. It is a city with a long and rich history that is perfectly preserved, rendering the historical center an open-air museum that seems to be frozen in time. What is not so much known by its thousands of visitors every day is the city's reputation as the stronghold of the Italian far-right in all its shades, described as 'the city at the furthest end of the Italian right' (Cazzullo, 2012) or 'the ideal space for the extreme right' (Paradiso, 2019). Even within the region of Veneto, where the elevated presence of nativist and conservative elements ingrained in the imagined land of Padania embraces a 'northern' identity, Verona strikes out with respect to the level of social tolerance towards neofascism in everyday life and local politics. As described by a leading activist, "people who are considered different for some reason are subjected to marginalization and intolerance, whether they are immigrants, homosexuals, democrats, young individuals with a left orientation etc., in which the aim is to create a model city that is safe, clean, and as white as possible in every sense of the term."[1] This section will offer an analysis of the evolution of different far-right actors and their alliances from a diachronic socio-spatial perspective, operating on a two-way mechanism of top-down and bottom-up everyday exclusion of certain categories of people in

---

1 Open letter by Gianni Zardini from Circolo Pink, *La Cittadinanza Va Scritta: Manifestazione Nazionale per l'affermazione della piena cittadinanza degli orientamenti sessuali, delle differenze e di tutte le minoranze religiose, etniche e culturali*, 9 June 2001, Verona.

the city of Verona, setting the boundaries for who belongs and who is simply out of place.

The analysis thus sheds light on the mainstreaming of extremist outlooks into institutional politics of the city administration. This is partly owing to the political magnetism of a nativist Padania identity that draws to its orbit far-right groups proclaiming ownership over the territory and seeking a historical rereading of it, together with ultra-Catholic groups upholding the Catholic tradition of an imagined fatherland and the family model it foresees. The municipality and other important local administrative bodies partake in the *top-down* policies of boundary-drawing with the institutionalization of far-right elements. The conceptual distinction between institutionalized populist parties and far-right movements is imperative in understanding the success of the identitarian logic, the instrumental use of sovereignism, the ways legitimacy is sought, and the mechanisms that unite them in tactical alliances with far-reaching consequences on national and transnational levels (De Spiegeleire et al., 2017; Rydgren, 2018; Rucht, 2019; Basile & Mazzoleni, 2020; Duyvendak et al., 2022). On the other hand, the wide range of far-right social movements present in Verona engages in *bottom-up* practices of boundary-drawing as a form of collective action by inscribing exclusive membership in city life through acts of territorialization (Brighenti, 2010, 2014; Halvorsen, 2015), that reflect the sovereignist logic in the everyday. Thus, the book argues that a 'sovereignist identitarian' cause unites different nativist actors as part of their collective identity (Melucci, 1980; Johnston et al., 1994; Polletta & Jasper), defending old privileges in a territory and an identity primordially tied to such space, whilst connecting with transnational counterparts.

As such, the chapter examines the process in which far-right groups have come to function as "incubators of new political and organizational ideas" (Caiani, 2019: 919), especially with respect to claims of 'native' identity (Tudor, 2014; Handler, 2019; Zúquete, 2018; Murdoch & Murhall, 2019), against minority groups, various forms difference, and newcomers (Muis & Immerzeel, 2017; Garbagnoli & Prearo, 2018). In so doing, it aims to contribute to this avenue of research by systematically addressing how such alliances are formed on the local level and how they are carried into the everyday life of the locality in which it takes place as shown in Figure 7, whilst connecting with similar causes of defending territorial identities in other contexts. This is a particularly pressing need given that these actors primarily operate in small local communities and set clear boundaries of membership, translating global themes upon the cognitive and material spaces of the city, while their struggles resonate in places beyond.

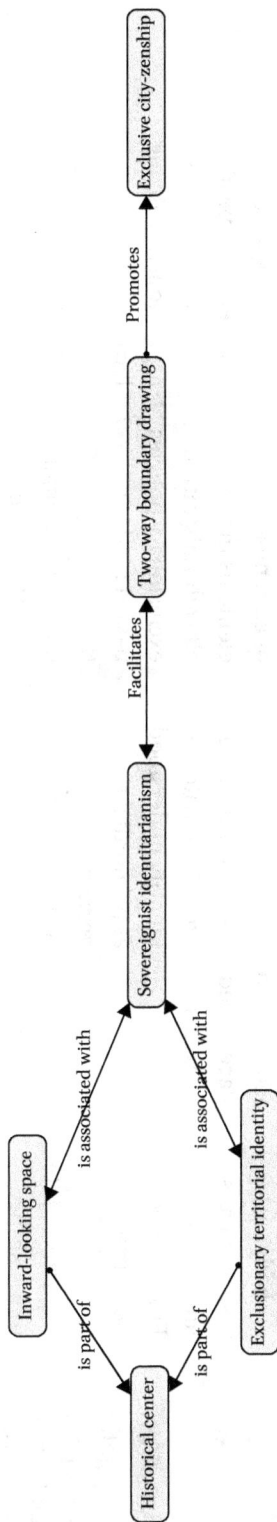

FIGURE 7   A socio-spatial analysis of the alliance of sovereignist identitarianism in Verona

TABLE 1   A socio-spatial analysis of the alliance of far-right, right-wing populist, and ultra-conservative actors in Verona

	Identity of place	Place-based identity	Collective identity	Collective action	Veronese city-zenship
	Inward-looking space of the historical center	*Exclusionary territorial identity*	*Sovereignist identitarianism*	*Two-way Boundary-drawing*	*Exclusive membership*
Alliance of far-right, right-wing populist, and ultra-conservative actors	Symbolic space embodying local history, myths, and symbols. Fixed timeless homogenous identity. Sanitized white touristscape, marketing of heritage. 'Model city' for the transnational identitarian network.	Nativist belonging to place, based on exclusion.	Nativist feeling of ownership over homeland, mutually exclusive territories. Identity understood as primordial ties to territory. Historical revisionism. 'Anti-gender' approach to sexual rights, promoting traditional family. Anti-globalization and anti-immigration.	Institutionalization of extremist elements in the city administration, exclusionary policies passed rendering the city a 'model' on a transnational level (*top-down boundary-drawing*). Everyday guarding of cognitive borders, ethnic resistance, and other acts of territorialization upon urban space (*bottom-up boundary-drawing*).	Whiteness of mittel-Europa as against Southern European identity, middle-class aspirations, idealizing local symbols and myths, use of local dialect in symbolizing privilege in one's homeland, heteronormative traditional Christian moral values, shared territorial culture and outlook.

1   The Vestiges of Fascism and the Birth of Far-Right Movements in Verona

1.1   *Post-war Fascism in Italy and the Years of Lead in Verona*

Following WWII, legitimacy was granted only to the political forces that joined the liberation war against Nazi-fascism as the Constitution of the new Republic was premised on antifascist principles. This was the context in which old elements of the fascist regime sought to continue their political legacy in various formations, with a sense of stigmatization and 'victimhood' as the losers of war. In the post-war era, the first party to carry on the fascist legacy was *Movimento Sociale Italiano* (Italian Social Movement, hereafter MSI), proclaiming to be the 'heirs of fascism' or 'post-fascists' (Milesi et al., 2005: 68). In this new political framework after the war, the party endured decades of marginality at the peripheries of the Italian political landscape, until the *Tangentopoli* scandal which revealed the network of corruption among the mainstream parties of the antifascist First Republic (Milesi et al., 2005). In order to acquire political legitimacy at this opportunistic conjuncture, the party leader of the time, Gianfranco Fini, declared that MSI would transform into *Alleanza Nazionale* (National Alliance, hereafter AN) during a national congress at Fiuggi in 1995. This move amounted to a rebranding of old loyalties with a more moderated façade to compete in national elections and win conservative votes, which carried them to the government as partners in the alliance with center-right Forza Italia of Berlusconi. In fact, the 2023 national elections in Italy have seen the victory of *Fratelli d'Italia* coming from this political legacy, becoming the first 'post-fascist' party to come to power in alliance with the populist right *Lega*.

Going back to the Fiuggi-turn and the establishment of AN, the decision to moderate the image of the party was not welcomed by all members and led to internal schisms that gradually bred into new movements. The most influential of which was the founding of *Movimento Sociale-Fiamma Tricolore* (Social Movement, the Tricolored Flame, hereafter MS-FT) by Pino Rauti, who was concomitantly the founder of *Ordine Nuovo*, a movement that was at the center of far-right-political violence during the years of lead (*anni di piombo*) where political tension was sought as a strategy to prevent communist influence over the Italian peninsula (Milesi et al., 2005; Tutino & Verza, 2013). Another fraction that transformed into a new movement with the passage from MSI to AN was *Movimento Fascismo e Libertà* (Fascism and Freedom Movement) under the leadership of Giorgio Pisanò. What these new movements had in common was a disillusionment with the Fiuggi-turn and sought to preserve fascist ideals, which signified safety for them, the comfort of the known, and social order in a changing world considered to bring immorality and chaos (Milesi et al., 2005).

An important factor that has led to a diversification of far-right political formations and their penetration into civil society in the form of social movements have been the youth and student branches of neofascist political parties in the post-WWII context. One of the most active of these groups, *Fronte della Gioventu'* was formed in 1971 as the youth branch of MSI. With a neofascist orientation, this youth organization was known to organize 'Hobbit Camps', influenced by the canonical work of J. R. R. Tolkien, which was reinterpreted as a reference to their understanding of 'the defense of race' as well as a symbology of events taking place in the 70s. It is in this context that the Celtic Cross came to be used as a symbol of Italian neofascist groups (Parlato, 2017). Another key organization, *Azione Giovani*, was founded in 1996 as the youth branch of AN and continued its activities until 2009, when it merged with the youth group *Giovane Italia*, led by Giorgia Meloni, the current prime minister and leader of the far-right political party *Fratelli d'Italia* (Griffin, 1996; Roversi, 1999).

Within the Italian post-war context, Verona became a playground for what some have referred to as a 'plurality' of right-wing institutional and non-institutional actors (Bonatelli, 2007), with a strong sense of territorial identity anchored in ethnonationalist, nativist, traditionalist, and white Catholic belongings. The constellation of these movements from the right end of the political spectrum who came from different social, political, or cultural positionings have united in their common aspiration to defend the material and symbolic 'territory' which they feel entitled to against the modern globalizing world forcing upon them unwanted social change (Castells, 2010). These actors could carry out their operations in the heart of the city, while having regular meetings at the popular locales of *Bar Motto* and *Forst Brewery* in Piazza Brà (Farina, 2020). These spatial nodes (Moore, 2007) in the historical center have tied together some of the most notorious far-right organizations involved in political violence during *anni di piombo*, who could operate with ease in the bustling streets of Verona, where much of urban life went on. It is in this context that a defense of what *was* (Boym, 2001), including ascribed privileges, takes the form of everyday border-drawing against all signs of visible divergence from the dominant 'Veronese' identity, including unconventional outfits or hairstyles. As put by Del Medico: "The privileged observatory of Verona allows one to monitor the progressive legitimation of words of hatred which give life and substance to those who translate into action the surreptitiously diffuse sentiment of intolerance" (2009: 74). In this re-formulation of 'race' an overt biological hierarchy thesis is dropped in favor of the 'difference' thesis, claiming that God has assigned every population their own *territory* that is to be defended from foreign invasion to prevent cultural and demographic contamination (Balibar, 1991; Del Medico, 2009; Tudor, 2014). This outlook, therefore, perfectly reflects the 'sovereignist' outlook (Basile & Mazzoleni, 2020; Freeden, 2017; De Spiegeleire et al., 2017).

In the city of Verona and its province, MSI emerging from the vestiges of the fascist party and its moderated successor AN both enjoyed substantive influence (Franzina, 2010). This period referred to as 'fascism after the fascism' saw media outlets, such as the Veronese journal *Carattere* with the leadership of Primo Siena, aim to incorporate Christian traditionalism in the fascist ideology of the MSI. In fact, Primo Siena himself was both the *capogruppo* (group leader) of MSI in Verona city council as well as a member of the religious group *Alleanza Cattolica Tradizionista* (Traditionalist Catholic Alliance) (Del Medico, 2004). Among the neofascist youth branches that operated in Verona, the most active were *Fronte della Gioventu* and *Azione Giovani* coming to be associated with the Hellas hooligan group *Brigate Gialloblù*, the most popular football team of Verona and a school of radicalization for the far-right (Griffin, 1996; Roversi, 1999). Another active organization in Verona was *Ordine Nuovo*, which adhered to the Manifesto of Verona formulated during the RSI as a guiding doctrine, whose Verona branch is believed to be involved in the 1974 *Piazza della Loggia* bombing in Brescia (Del Medico, 2004; Tutino & Verza, 2013). Among the leaders of the latter, Franco Freda later founded *Fronte Nazionale* in the 1990s with an anti-globalization and anti-immigrant stance.[2] He was the ideological father of *Terza Posizione* (the Third Position), espousing a traditionalist and ethnically homogenous society against the ills of the modern world, namely international finance, capitalism, and a 'multiracial' society. This new ideological stance was later taken on by contemporary movements such as Forza Nuova, playing a fundamental role in shaping their activities (Del Medico, 2009).

Far-right violence in Veronese urban space in the 1970s and the 1980s even involved a mysterious homegrown killer duo called *Ludwig*, who had a vision of eliminating unwanted elements from white Christian social spaces. This criminal neo-Nazi group was constituted by Wolfgang Abel and Marco Furlan in 1977, both upper-middle-class Veronesi. The two met in high school and realized that they shared the same ideals of 'cleansing' the world from what they deemed as the problem, which included pornographic cinemas, nightclubs, sinful priests, prostitutes, the homeless, homosexuals, and drug addicts. Ludwig was involved in numerous murders, not only in Italy but also in the Netherlands and Germany. In their crime scenes, they left a note stating the reason for the murder with Nazi symbolism, such as the Nazi eagle accompanied by the slogan of the Third Reich, '*Gott Mit Uns*' (God with us), written

---

2   Archival dossier by Kollektivo Porkospino, *Alarmi Sono Fascisti,* available online at: https://movimentandociaverona.files.wordpress.com/2017/04/allarmi-son-fascisti.pdf.

in German (Evangelisti, 2009). The sociopolitical imprint of violence towards difference that this homegrown neo-Nazi duo left on the collective memory in Verona is testified by a local activist: "These two guys murdered several people of color, it seemed like a serial killer thing, but it opened up a politics of intolerance towards difference. Later, such politics was carried inside the city administration after the '70s." (Interview with D.P., 4 February 2012). As a result, with a complicated past entangled in fascism and Nazism, the post-war setting in the Veronese territory saw the continuation of the vestiges of extreme ideologies unfold, embracing a particularly aggressive political culture that sought to 'defend' the territory against leftist influence whilst seeking to cleanse the urban decorum from those elements that do not belong to the white middle-class urban identity.

1.2 *Proliferation of Far-Right Groups in the Veronese Urban Space*

The 1980s and 1990s in Verona and its surrounding territory were marked by a proliferation of far-right social movements in the social and cultural life of the city, exerting its presence in everyday practices. The most influential group that came to the fore at this juncture was *Veneto Fronte Skinheads* (hereafter VFS), active in the region of Veneto as the largest neo-Nazi skinhead movement in Italy, founded by Piero Puschiavo mid-1980s, pre-dating its metropolitan counterparts in Rome or Milano (Del Medico, 2004; Fasanella & Zornetta, 2008). This movement has enjoyed a substantial presence among both the leadership and fandom of the Hellas football team in Verona, with a particular overlap of membership with *Brigate Gialloblù* hooligans named after the yellow and blue colors representing the city's flag. Although the group has been known to collaborate with MS-FT on the political scene, today it continues its political activities independently under the name *Progetto Nazionale* with important figures from Verona.

The members of VFS have been frequently subjected to legal investigations and, at times, found guilty under the *Mancino law*, criminalizing the incitement to hate and violence on the basis of racial, ethnic, religious, or national characteristics. One episode that led to legal action against the group was a written manifesto that appeared in Piazza Brà which made the following claim: "We are a neofascist executioner group who is reclaiming our *territoriality* being put to hard test by the arrival of black dogs who contaminate our land and bring their drugs into Italian blood" (quoted in Del Medico, 2004: 139, *emphasis added*). As depicted vividly in this extract, the native land which the regional movement feels entitled to is the spatial signifier of the ethnic bloodline and the local culture that are deemed endangered with the arrival of non-white immigrant groups. Not only does this demonstrate a revanchist reclaim of urban space (Smith, 1996), but a defense of homogenous exclusive identities exemplifying continuity of pre-war and post-war racism in Europe that takes the form of anti-immigration (MacMaster, 2001).

As its name suggests, the VFS was very active in the nazirock music scene in northern Italy, with some of its constituent active members of nazirock bands from Verona and its province, such as *Acciaio Vincente, i Nativi, 1903, Sumbu Brothers*, and *Gesta Bellica*, known for their overtly racist and homophobic lyrics.[3] In 2017, VFS organized an 'Arian' Christmas party in Verona called White Xmas, with the participation of the abovementioned bands and their songs, some of which openly espousing white supremacy.[4] One ludic example is a song by Gesta Bellica called *Società Multirazziale* (Multiracial Society), explicitly depicting this outlook:

One race for one history, one ancestry for civilization,	*Una razza per una storia, una stirpe per la civiltà*
One Europe unites itself: the desire for liberty.	*Un'Europa ci accomuna: desiderio di libertà.*
Thousands of peoples from all over the world, thousands of faces without dignity,	*Mille genti da tutto il mondo, mille facce senza dignità,*
And Europe shatters itself into thousands of little societies!	*E l'Europa si frantuma in mille piccole società!*
White, white power!	*Bianco, potere bianco!*
White, white power!	*Bianco, potere bianco!*
White, white power!	*Bianco, potere bianco!*
White for liberty!	*Bianco per la libertà!*
They say I need to submit myself, that a new age has begun,	*Dicon che mi devo rassegnare, che è l'inizio di una nuova età,*
Theft, drugs, black faces, all this does not work for me.	*Furti, droga, musi neri, ma tutto questo non mi va.*
Multiracial society, encampments for my city,	*Società multirazziale: accampamenti per la mia città,*
They want a house and a job, but all this will end!	*Voglion casa ed il lavoro, ma tutto questo finirà!*

---

3 From the archival dossier *Allarmi Sono Fascisti* compiled by Kollektivo Porkospino and Coordinamento Cesar K., 25 November 2000, Verona. Available online at: https://movime ntandociaverona.files.wordpress.com/2017/04/allarmi-son-fascisti.pdf.

4 Huffington Post, 30 November 2017. Available online at: https://www.huffingtonpost.it/2017 /11/30/a-verona-gli-skinhead-organizzano-il-concerto-di-natale-ariano-white-christmas_a_2 3293190.

This song, written by a local Veronese band, lucidly illustrates cross-cutting themes articulated by far-right groups that operate in different settings and societies in Europe. Firstly, a transnational European white identity based on a perceived common history and civilization is deemed under threat (Lentin & Karayakalı, 2016; Caiani, 2018) by the coming of a 'new age' that brings along uncivilized foreigners through immigration (Balibar, 1991; Anthias & Yuval-Davis, 1992, Rucht, 2019). In this sense, as foreseen by MacMaster (2001), the culture and civilization of Fortress Europe are assigned a quasi-biological character to be defended against the social ills and insecurity that non-native people have begotten in the homeland (Mudde, 2007; Zùquete, 2018; Murdoch & Murhall, 2019). Interestingly, this racist-nationalist defense (Caiani, 2018) of a transnational white identity, as depicted in the lyrics, is called to be carried out from the immediate locality of one's city, representing the territoriality of belonging and non-belonging (Lynch, 1981). It is exactly this conjuncture that makes room for the identitarian logic to come into play.

In the first decade of the 2000s, both old and new far-right social movements carried out everyday violence in shared urban spaces of Verona against 'racialized others' (Frisina, 2020), involving bottom-up boundary-drawing against a long list of groups who did not fit well with the white Christian urbanite Veronese identity. The militants undertaking acts of everyday chauvinism (Saitta, 2021) usually involved the same membership that connects Hellas hooliganism to far-right movements such as VFS, Forza Nuova, and later on Casa Pound. With the motto of "defend who's similar to you, destroy the rest,"[5] this unofficial network had declared the whole city as their rightful territory as part of their collective identity (Melucci, 1980; Johnston et al., 1994; Polletta & Jasper) and enjoyed the privilege of defining who constituted the 'other', where maintaining 'urban décor' became a form of collective action. The subjects that were racialized and targeted by these groups included the Jewish community, the Roma and Sinti community, and even southern Italians usually referred to as *terroni* in a racialized manner (Demirsu, 2023). Hence, similarity was defined through a territorial identity which has come to constitute a union based on exclusion (Boym, 2001).

---

5 "Difendi il tuo simile … distruggi il resto," from the archival dossier *A Verona tutta l'erba e uno (s)fascio,* available at: https://movimentandociaverona.files.wordpress.com/2018/03/dossier-verona-corretto.pdf.

On the 8th of July 2008, a neo-Nazi raid was carried out in the Jewish ceme-
tery which was left desacralized with swastika signs and writings against Jews,
nomads, and local antifascist social collectives. The following year, Hellas fans
stormed a birthday party in the historical center and started to chant Nazi
slogans and insults against women and southern Italians, which resulted in a
brawl. The subsequent police investigation demonstrated that those who conducted the assault were complicit in a previous series of violent harassments
around the city center.[6] One striking instance that exemplified Islamophobic
tendencies among these groups (Anthias & Yuval-Davis, 1992; Goldberg, 2006)
was the raiding of the local TV channel *Telenuovo*'s program that was hosting
the national president of the Union of Muslims in Italy Adel Smith, forcefully
ending the program in live broadcast.[7]

Those groups that were on the radar of far-right actors were not only constituted by racialized others, but also local leftist and progressive movements
considered to be the successors of the antifascist partisan legacy in Verona
and the supporters of multicultural society seen as the culprits of modern ills
(Prowe, 2004; Kriesi et al., 2008; Basile et al., 2020). This positioning is captured
in an interview of the national leader of Forza Nuova in the local newspaper
L'Arena on the 26th of September 2000, stating that the 'identity' characterizing the city has been first and foremost Christian traditionalism harboring
anti-communist values: "Verona deserves a defense because it is under attack
for its Catholic and anti-communist values, the city is a symbol that traditionally reserves miserable percentages for the Italian Communist Party and its
heirs" (quoted in Del Medico, 2009: 85). Throughout the early 2000s, a wide
panoply of antifascist grassroots movements in Verona, including anarchists,
communists, socialists, feminists and LGBTQ+ activists, were subject to aggressive attacks, whose members were followed and assaulted, offices and hangout
places were 'paid visits' by far-right figures in violent acts of territorialization
(Brighenti, 2010, 2014; Raffestin, 2012; Halvorsen, 2015). On one occasion in
2005, the social center *La Chimica* was singled out and assaulted with an arson
attempt, followed by rock throwing, and a year later, by Molotov cocktails.
Following these bottom-up acts of everyday chauvinism (Saitta, 2021), ultimately, in 2007, the collective was evacuated by a top-down boundary-drawing

---

6 For a detailed chronology of events see: *Verona Citta dell'Amore e dell'Odio*, available
   at: https://movimentandociaverona.files.wordpress.com/2019/04/verona-cittc3ao-dellamore
   -dellodio-2019.pdf.
7 From the archival dossier *Verona Citta dell'Amore e dell'Odio*, available at: https://movime
   ntandociaverona.files.wordpress.com/2019/04/verona-cittc3ao-dellamore-dellodio-2019.pdf.

FIGURE 8   Commemorative Plaque dedicated to Nicola Tommasoli's death at Corticella
Leoni, next to the Roman city gate *Porta Leoni*
PHOTOGRAPH: IPEK DEMIRSU

of the city administration under Flavio Tosi from Lega Nord, who had vowed to clean the city from 'undesirable elements'.

Everyday violence against subjects identified as non-native or non-decorative (Mazzei, 2018) became so pronounced in city life between 2006 and 2007 that it came to include people eating kebab on the street, men with long hair, young people considered to have an 'alternative' outfit. These everyday bodily representations of difference (Melucci, 1980; Johnston et al., 1994) being targeted on a regular basis culminated in the poignant murder of Nicola Tommasoli on the night of 30th of April 2008. Tommasoli was singled out at *Corticella Leoni* near the Roman gate due to his 'alternative' look and assaulted physically by a group of young men because he refused to give them a cigarette (Demirsu, 2023). Five individuals were investigated for this incident with ties both to Hellas fan group and various far-right movements, two of which were later claimed to have been assisted by Forza Nuova to escape to London,[8] just

---

8 From the archival dossier *A Verona tutta l'erba e uno (s)fascio,* available at: https://movime ntandociaverona.files.wordpress.com/2018/03/dossier-verona-corretto.pdf.

as the national leader of the movement in the 1990s when he was under legal investigation. As vividly demonstrated by these episodes, 'otherness' in the cityspace of Verona has come to be defined not only through ethnic and religious differences, but also non-conforming lifestyles, outfits, public behavior as public spaces came to be governed by what Del Medico defines as 'hyperfascism of the everyday' (*iperfascismo del quotidiano*) (Del Medico, 2009: 73). As such, far-right militants have taken on the self-proclaimed role of ensuring 'appropriateness' in the Veronese public space and define the boundaries of inclusion and exclusion (Mitchell, 2000; Merrill, 2014), promoting a timeless singular identity of cityspace.

1.3   *Competition to Territorialize the City: Extreme Right Groups Today*

The most active groups with a neofascist orientation operating in Verona today are Forza Nuova and CasaPound. Both groups portray characteristics of movement-party organization style (Pirro & Gattinara, 2018), whilst being active mostly in the civil society sphere, also running for elections and coming to occupy seats in local city councils in alliance with more institutional far-right parties such as Lega or Fratelli d'Italia. Both share the same origins as schisms from MS-FT, with Forza Nuova upholding the ideology of *Terza Posizione* (Third Position) (Adinolfi & Fiore, 2015), CasaPound instead coming to be recognized as *fascisti del terzo millenio* (third millennium fascists) (Cammelli, 2015). Among the two, Forza Nuova came into the social scene of Verona in the 90s and had been the dominant group, especially amongst Hellas fandom. The entrance of CasaPound in the early 2000s, therefore, led to a competition to recruit followers and to territorialize cityspace, which has at times turned into violent episodes between the two groups.

As mentioned previously, the leadership of *Forza Nuova* has its roots in the 'Third Position' ideology elaborated by Roberto Fiore and Gabriele Adinolfi at the end of the 1970s with the withdrawal of *Ordine Nuovo* and *Avanguardia Nazionale* from the Italian sociopolitical scene. After it was found to be involved in the Bologna bomb attack of 1980, the group was abolished as a subversive armed organization, and its leaders fled to the UK. There, they joined the leader of the British National Party, Nick Griffin, with whom they became the leaders of the International Third Position based in London, attracting youth groups such as *boneheads* (Del Medico, 2004: 57–60). During their exile in the UK, the leaders established Forza Nuova in Italy as a grassroots movement of the Fiamma Tricolore, while making lucrative business investments in London, including their own clothing brand (*Three-Stroke*) and a travel agency that also operated as a real estate and work agency, called *Easy London* (Ibid.).

In 1998, the group established itself as an independent movement that competed with Fiamma Tricolore in far-right activism, infiltrating the hooligan and the skinhead music scene. In 2008, the group started to run its own candidates in local and national elections without much success, continuing to be mostly active in movement politics (Gattinara, 2019).

Unlike much of the post-fascist movements, Forza Nuova distinguishes itself with its strong adherence to the Catholic tradition and ultra-conservative values (Ibid.), which leads to close collaborations with religious fundamentalist groups on sociocultural issues such as anti-abortion and the traditional family model to revitalize demographic growth. Considering themselves as the vanguards of the 'sovereign people', with an understanding of sovereignism to signify taking back control in one's homeland (Freeden, 2017; Basile & Mazzoleni, 2020), the outlook of Forza Nuova perfectly exemplifies the 'cultural difference' thesis (Balibar, 1991; Lentin & Karayakali, 2016; Frisina, 2020) seeing immigration as a threat to co-existence, public order (Gattinara, 2019), and by extension the native 'identity' understood with white supremacist undertones.

Ever since the group first opened its office in Verona in 2000, the city has been a bastion for the movement as a model city. The group has been involved in some of the most violent episodes the city has witnessed, which included physical assaults against leftist activists and political figures, social centers, LGBTQ+ activists, local Muslim associations, and immigrants.[9] The leader of the Forza Nuova Verona branch, who also served as the head of the local hooligan group for Hellas, was implicated in a scandalous case during the celebrations of the football team in 2017. Here, he was filmed thanking 'Adolf Hitler' for financing and sponsoring the celebrations in question, due to which he later faced a lawsuit.[10] The group's primary office is located near to the football stadium *Marcantonio Bentegodi*, operating as a clothing store called *The Firm*, selling products of fashion brands alongside clothing for the Hellas fandom of a local brand called *Movimento Verona*. These clothing items are usually embellished with the traditional local symbols of Verona that are merged with fascist symbology, such as the *Wolfsangel* sign also used by *Terza Posizione*. The

---

9   A chronology of violent episodes inflicted by Forza Nuova members in Verona can be found in the dossier *A Verona tutta erba e uno (s)fascio: Dossier sugli accadimenti Veronesi dal 2001 al 2014*, available at: https://movimentandociaverona.files.wordpress.com/2018 /03/dossier-verona-corretto.pdf.

10   For more information on this episode, see: https://www.veronasera.it/cronaca/festa -curva-sud-video-virale-pagato-tutto-adolf-hitler-10-luglio-2017.html.

FIGURE 9   Scarfs for Hellas fans, with the Scala coat
of arms merged together with the neo-Nazi
symbol of Wolfsangel
PHOTO FROM THE FACEBOOK PAGE OF
MOVIMENTO VERONA, 23 SEPTEMBER 2014

Firm was also used as a concert venue for local nazirock bands with wide followers among Hellas fans.[11]

On 22nd of December 2018, Forza Nuova inaugurated their new office called
Casa dei Patrioti (House of the Patriots) in the multiethnic neighborhood of
Veronetta with the participation of their national leader, as part of their identitarian mobilization *'resistenza etnica'* (ethnic resistance) against migrant
communities living in this area at close proximity to the historical center
(Fieldnotes, 22 December 2018). In celebration of the new office, a *Gesta Bellica*
concert was held at the original office, *The Firm*. Interestingly, on the very same
day, CasaPound organized a celebration for the anniversary of their office in
Veronetta which was inaugurated a year ago in 2017, with the participation
of their national leader. As such, the two leading movements of the Veronese
far-right are deeply involved in a competition of territorialization (Soja, 1971;
Brighenti, 2010, 2014; Halvorsen, 2015), not only over Hellas fandom but also
in the neighborhood of Veronetta considered to symbolize a different form of
belonging and different sets of social relations.

CasaPound Italia first came into being in 2003, mainly through squatting
activities in Rome undertaken by the youth branch of Fiamma Tricolore, from
which they split as a separate organization named after the famous American
writer Ezra Pound in 2008. Establishing itself as 'third millennium fascists' that
openly embraces the Manifesto of Verona, CasaPound's first significant action
marking the movement was the occupation of a building in the multiethnic

---

11   For more information, *A Verona tutta erba e uno (s)fascio: Dossier sugli accadimenti
Veronesi dal 2001 al 2014*, available at: https://movimentandociaverona.files.wordpr
ess.com/2018/03/dossier-verona-corretto.pdf.

FIGURE 10   Forza Nuova office in Veronetta 'Casa dei Patrioti': "The natural home
             of Veronese patriots that consider the militant and spontaneous
             identitarian fight as the frontline against ethnic substitution. You
             welcome the stranger? We welcome the patriot".
             FROM THE INSTAGRAM ACCOUNT 'CASA DEI PATRIOTI VERONA', 13
             JANUARY 2019

Esquilino district of Rome (Cammelli, 2018). The movement evolved into what Pirro and Gattinara (2018) call a 'movement party' and ran for elections in 2013, winning seats in local elections and forming alliances with Lega Nord under Matteo Salvini. In the 2014 European Parliament elections, CasaPound helped elect a Lega Nord candidate in the parliament, while securing its own members' election to local councils in 2015 and 2016. In the 2017 local elections, it received more than 5% of the votes, ensuring council members in different municipalities (Pirro & Gattinara, 2018). Most members are active in their extraparliamentary activities and grassroots initiatives considered as 'direct social action', including charity work and housing (Ibid.).

The movement initially gave priority to socioeconomic issues with a particular focus on housing, which is symbolized in their turtle logo carrying its house on its back. This position is also reflected in the references given to the Manifesto of Verona by its members, offering social housing schemes as a solution to overcome what is considered the usury of private banks and international financial institutions, in line with the legacy of Ezra Pound (Cammelli, 2018). Moreover, the movement has updated articles pertaining to a biological racial hierarchy as articulated in the Manifesto of Verona, instead proposing the 'cultural difference' thesis that reflects the sovereignist identitarian outlook: claiming different nations convey insurmountable cultural differences, and hence ought to occupy separate geographical spaces. Such differences in language, religion, and lifestyles are taken to hinder co-existence in the everyday lives of different ethnic groups, who ought to uphold and protect their particular identity against contamination from other cultures (Cammelli, 2018). The movement regularly organizes community-building events, such as rock concerts of their band *Zeta Zero Alfa* whose lead singer is also the national leader of the organization. Young members are drawn to the image of a 'rock star leader', alongside physical outlets for community building and the subculture of squadrism. Their youth branch, *Blocco Studentesco* (Student Bloc), pursues the recruitment of new members in high schools and universities (Ibid.)

It is no coincidence that CasaPound became active in Verona, given that Ezra Pound himself was a great admirer of the city and the Manifesto of Verona, spending some time in the historical center and around Garda Lake, where RSI was established (Pantano, 2016). CasaPound made its first appearance in Verona in 2008 through its youth branch *Blocco Studentesco*, with followers from high schools and the university. In the historical center, the group opened a pub called *Cutty Sark*, where experiences of *Fronte della Gioventù* were being shared by older militants of the Veronese far-right, now occupying administrative positions, with the younger generation (interview with C.P., 8 July 2020). The first move of CasaPound Verona was to open a stand in front of the football stadium with the hope of recruiting new members. This was, of course, a strategic move since it was a well-known fact that the stadium was a breeding ground for far-right and openly fascist orientations among the Hellas fans.

Such an entrance to the football scene drew antagonism from Forza Nuova, who had been enjoying a predominance over the fan circle and did not intend on sharing their political influence among the followers. As the tension rose, CasaPound's pub Cutty Sark was assaulted in 2012 by what was later discovered to be Forza Nuova members, although no complaints were made, and the matter was closed.[12] A rare episode marking collaboration between these competing groups was during an academic conference to be held at the University of Verona in 2013 by the writer Alessandra Kervesan on the controversial topic of *foibe* that involves accounts of mass killings of Italian fascists by Yugoslavian partisans during WWII and in its aftermath. The student groups of both movements, namely *Lotta Studentesca* of Forza Nuova and *Blocco Studentesco* of CasaPound, staged a joint attack during the conference, which resulted in some of the participants getting hurt.[13]

The themes evoked by these two dominant movements in Verona, despite their competition among themselves, are underwritten by a common collective identity understood through a sovereignist defense of the 'native homeland', defined through the attachment with a social space and a native identity tied to such space, constructed in the act of excluding difference. A form of nostalgic future projection of homogeneity and social cohesion made possible only through exclusion, such defense foresees the reinstatement of an ethno-cultural identity and tradition (Tudor, 2014; Goldberg, 2006; De Spiegeleire et al., 2017; Murdoch & Murhall, 2019).

2   Territorial Belongings and Right-Wing Populism of Lega Nord

So far, this section has explored the multitude of social actors in the far-right universe of Verona and their evolution over time. It is equally important to

---

12   For more information on this incident, see: https://www.ilfattoquotidiano.it/2012/12/24/estrema-destra-a-verona-assalti-tra-rivali-casapound-e-forza-nuova/454659.
13   For more information on this episode, see: https://www.bresciatoday.it/cronaca/universita-verona-convegno-foibe-fascisti-casa-pound-kersevan-mazzucco.html.

understand how extremist ideas have become ever more mainstreamed in present-day Italy (and Europe at large) through alliances between far-right and populist right actors starting from the locality. Verona offers us the perfect laboratory for this investigation, with everyday ramifications in city life. A major factor has been the political magnetism of *Lega Nord* (Northern League) in the early 1990s, with its undeniable appeal among Italian voters especially in the region of Veneto. The party managed to attract not only local nativist groups, such as the Veneto secessionists, but also myriad other actors of the far-right as well as ultra-Catholics, united in an exclusionary territorial understanding of belonging articulated with a sovereignist discourse (De Spiegeleire et al., 2017; Freeden, 2017; Basile & Mazzoleni, 2020), an identitarian outlook (Tudor, 2014; Zùquete, 2018; Šima, 2021), and conservative moral values (Mudde, 2000; Rydgren, 2018; Rucht, 2019). In order to understand their political success and the alliances they managed to forge, we must look into how geographical imagination has worked to construct the Padania territorial identity in mobilizing diverse actors.

Lega Nord achieved political significance in northern Italy by the 19990s with narratives of local folklore and northern identity. Its success in the northern regions of Lombardy and Veneto, which are considered the motors of the Italian economy, was premised on the construction of an imaginary geography and spatial identity attached to it, namely by drawing the borders of what came to be known as 'Padania', from the Po River basin going all the way north to the Italian Alps (Agnew & Brusa, 1999; Merrill, 2014). This so-called 'Deep North', likened to the American 'Deep South', has so far been the main stronghold of the movement. The claim to 'northernness' also conveys economic undertones, as the party claims independence from the national government in Rome not only on identitarian grounds but also in rejecting to pay taxes that are to be redistributed to the south of Italy. As Agnew and Brusa define it, "[t]he Northern League may be the first authentic post-modernist territorial political movement in its manipulation of territorial imagery to create a self-conscious sense of cultural/economic difference an existing state of which it is part" (1999: 123). In this sense, it is argued that Lega's politics has been novel in delineating a geographic entity to justify historical claims rather than the more common strategy of making historical claims over a geographical territory.

Such remapping of the area went hand in hand with the construction of a monolithic Padania identity associated with 'continental Europe' (*mittel-Europa*) belonging to the Celtic-Germanic culture, in stark opposition to what is characterized in the south of Italy as a devalued Greek-Latin culture (Merrill, 2014). The racialization of southern Italy was succinctly captured in the slogan of the party's historical leader Umberto Bossi, "Africa begins at Rome," which associated southern Italians with the 'backwardness' attributed to African populations for being 'primitive', 'unruly', and 'savage' (Pugliese, 2002: 156). This racial imagery was coupled with the stigmatization of the southern Italian for being *mafioso* and corrupt. Lega Nord later on turned its attention to incoming migrants first from Eastern Europe and later from Africa, the Middle East, as well as South Asia, who came to be projected as potential criminals. As put by Merrill, "The party uses criminalizing images and discourses against Africans, Muslims and other newcomers to promote its parochialist fixation on the purity of the Northern cultural space" (2014: 277). Thus, whilst the southerner was bequeathed 'proximate whiteness', non-European *extracommunitari* were assigned the role of the 'absolute other' and left outside the racially drawn borders of the national community (Pugliese, 2008). The xenophobia against the new non-European immigration was therefore underscored by a propagated paranoia of becoming a minority group as an endangered white race in their own lands (Ibid.). This theme found great resonance among far-right circles in distant contexts under the US-born 'Great Replacement' theory, epitomized in Hungary with the slogan 'procreation, not immigration', and documented to inspire racist mass shootings in Christchurch, New Zealand in 2019 and Buffalo, US in 2022.[14]

Given the diversity not only among the regions in northern Italy but also within them, the creation of a homogenous Padania identity with its own myths, distinctive culture, and moral values required some work. Common threads amidst such diversity included: (1) a shared contempt for the central government in Rome, (2) the political legacy of the Republic of Venice when the north was independent, and lastly, (3) an articulation of 'northern values' such as being hard-working, rule-following, and honest, as opposed to the stereotype of the lazy, free-rider, and deceitful southerner (Agnew & Brusa, 1999). Such communitarian imagination of belonging to a 'pure and homogenous culture as family', embellished by local myths and symbols (Boym, 2001), resonated in the north that was disenchanted by the centrist national parties, serving extant regionalist loyalties that predate the Italian Unification. This is plainly visible today in the differentiation championed by locals based on their local dialects, local cuisines, customs, and traditions (Merrill, 2014). In an environment where 'localist pride' (Nevola, 2010; Mielke, 2005) and 'regionalism' (Paasi, 2011) triumphed, by the end of the 1990s, populist rhetoric exerted itself

---

14   For a detailed account of this transnational conspiracy theory, see Steve Rose, "A deadly ideology: how the 'great replacement theory' went mainstream," in *The Guardian* (8 June 2022), available at: https://www.theguardian.com/world/2022/jun/08/a-deadly-ideol ogy-how-the-great-replacement-theory-went-mainstream.

by depicting multiculturalism, brought about by globalization and imposed by supranational institutions, as the primary threat to local communities (De Spiegeleire et al., 2017; Rucht, 2019; Basile et al., 2020). The centrality assigned to the 'native territory' in defining one's belonging and identity, and hence the necessity to protect this imagined space, is succinctly captured in a manifesto-style document written by Giorgio Mussa from Lega Nord in 1998: "The Apostles of extra-European immigration want therefore to negate the existence of people and nations, advocating an individualistic mass cosmopolitanism that crumbles identities and feelings of territorial belonging, all to the advantage of the global market" (quoted in Del Medico, 2004: 72). While the party dropped the 'north' from its name with the aim of expanding its political sway in the national elections of 2018, its members have also expanded the scope of the sovereignist discourse from regional to national borders notwithstanding the lingering sense of northern pride.

Such identitarian loyalties to the territory with nativist motifs are accentuated in Veneto and find expression through the *Liga Veneta* branch of Lega Nord as one of its constitutive and fundamental elements. Upholding an ideology which in Italian is referred to as *Venetismo* that presupposes an ethnic identity for people inhabiting the region of Veneto, with its separate history, tradition, and local dialect, Liga Veneta first came into the political scene on the 9th of December 1979 in the small mountain town of Recoaro Terme (Mutto, 2019). Its federalist political agenda sought to "defend the ethnic and linguistic character of the Veneta nation ... as part of a united Europe of peoples."[15] The political movement within Lega Nord, while sharing an anti-establishment outlook against mainstream politics and a localist distrust towards the central government, has accentuated the concept of 'territory' and accompanying symbols of local identity in the political arena as a form of collective identity (Melucci, 1980; Johnston et al., 1994). Hence, an ethno-regionalist primordial construction of the Veneto identity that belonged to *mittel-Europa* instead of south Europe was transformed into political mobilization by actors who considered themselves victims of Italianization and a loss of control over their own homeland. Such victimization at times equated to 'genocide', and in turn, has called for the safeguarding of a perceived ethnicity along with the local economy (Mutto, 2019: 32–33), once again a theme that travels across borders which will be revisited later.

---

15   The original text of the Constitutive Act of Liga Veneta, found at: https://www.ilgaz zettino.it/nordest/primopiano/atto_costitutivo_liga_veneta_notaio_todeschini_rocche tta-380201.html.

PER UN VENETO GOVERNATO DAI VENETI NON PIU' DISSANGUATO
DALLE TASSE DA UN POTERE A NOI ESTRANEO E OSTILE
affinchè drammi come quelli di San Bernardino (prostituzione, droga,
scippi, violenza) non si ripetino più
PER UNA VERONA PULITA E SICURA
PER VERONA CITTA' VENETA E MITTELEUROPEA
NON DA TERZO MONDO

FIRMA

LE PROPOSTE DELLA LEGA VENETA - REPUBLICA VENETA

Sezione di Verona. Coordinatore GRASSI Maurizio

FIGURE 11   Liga Veneta flyer in Verona from 1995, advocating an independent Veneto,
a secure and clean Verona that is part of *mittel-Europa* (central Europe)
and not the 'Third World', with the symbol of the Republic of Venice
ORIGINAL FLYER FROM DEL MEDICO, 2004

The dual themes of 'sovereignism' and 'identitarianism' on a regional scale
come to the fore in *Venetismo*, providing conducive grounds for an alliance
between the populist Lega with a variety of actors: (1) local neofascist groups
such as VFS, (2) other far-right movements waging 'ethnic resistance' in the
face of so-called 'white people's genocide' due to migration, as well as (3) reactionary ultra-Catholic circles seeking to defend the Christian tradition against
the threat of Islam in continuing the legacy of Lepanto: "The Republic of
Venice, being the ideal continuator of the Veneto State that has been there for
centuries, the most coherent and insurmountable bulwark against the incessant attempts on part of Islam to invade the West, offers itself once again with
the benediction of God and San Marco, its protector, for the glorious defense
of our land."[16]

---

16   Original Liga Veneta flyer with the title "Extra-communitarian Invasion and the Threat of
Islam: Two Faces of the Same Medallion," found in Del Medico, 2009, p. 184.

3   City Administration and the Institutionalization of Far-Right
      Movements since the 1990s

Over time, adherents of far-right political configurations have established
themselves in the Verona city council by siding with center-right and populist right parties. This alliance was bound by localistic resentment of losing
privileges enjoyed in their own territory (Del Medico, 2009). The political success of Lega since the early 2000s hastened the institutionalization of far-right
movements in local politics and secured their influence in the social and cultural life of the city. According to A.A., an old activist specializing in documentation, the presence of far-right actors in the city administration first started
to be felt with the mayor Michela Sironi from *Forza Italia*, who is claimed to
have instituted extremist figures in important decision-making bodies of the
city with her appointment in 1994 (A.A., interview 5 August 2019). During her
term in office, it is argued that some of the most notorious names among the
Veronese far-right circles gained political positions, including figures that have
been accused of attacking leftist activists and of incitement of racial hatred.[17]
From urban security councilors confiscating covers of the homeless,[18] to local
administrators sponsoring concerts that bring nazirock bands from around
Europe to be hosted for the first time in Italy, such as the Swedish *Ultima Thule*
and the British 'white power' rock band *Condemned 84*,[19] the institutional right
has opened the gates for a variety of far-right figures and outlooks to enter
local institutions. On one occasion, the official email of Verona municipality
was used to send invites for a cultural event underlining that "black shirt is
welcome"[20] with reference to the traditional fascist outfit, which later inspired
the title of a book on neofascist actors (Berizzi, 2022). Later in 2020, the same
local politician who sent the email declared on his social media account that

---

17   From the archival dossier *Allarmi Sono Fascisti*, 25 November 2000, Verona. Available
     online at: https://movimentandociaverona.files.wordpress.com/2017/04/allarmi-son
     -fascisti.pdf.
18   From the archival dossier *Allarmi Sono Fascisti* compiled by Kollektivo Porkospino and
     Coordinamento Cesar K., 25 November 2000, Verona. Available online at: https://movime
     ntandociaverona.files.wordpress.com/2017/04/allarmi-son-fascisti.pdf.
19   From the archival dossier *Veronesi Tuti Mati*, by Kollettivo Porkospino and Coordinamento
     Cesar K., 17 March 2001, Verona. Available online at: https://movimentandociaverona.files
     .wordpress.com/2019/10/veronesi-tuti-mati.pdf-valido.pdf.
20   From the archival dossier *Verona Citta dell'Amore e dell'Odio*, available at: https://mov-
     imentandociaverona.files.wordpress.com/2019/04/verona-cittc3a0-dellamore-dello
     dio-2019.pdf.

the only Republic in Italy was the 'Social Republic'[21] with reference to the fascism of the RSI. This declaration demonstrates the continuing legacy of fascist 'nostalgia' (Boym, 2001) in the Veronese far-right circles, calling for historical revisionism and a 'guilt-free homecoming' (Valencia-Garcia, 2020; Boyn, 2001).

Following a short period of center-left rule in the city administration with the leadership of Paolo Zanotto, Lega Nord made a grand entrance to the political scene in Verona with the election of Flavio Tosi as the mayor, who today serves as a deputy in the Italian Parliament from Berlusconi's Forza Italia party. During the two terms of Tosi from 2007 until 2017, figures from far-right movements were further institutionalized in the city administration and in other local agencies that run the urban infrastructure in Verona. Before his appointment in office, Tosi already championed close ties with the far-right universe, attending their rallies as the representative of Lega, conveying support.[22] During this period, the alliance between populist right and far-right actors started to be solidified as leading actors from the Veronese far-right movement scene declared their candidacy from Lega Nord.[23] This trend continues today as figures active in various far-right movements are entering local politics through political support by and candidacy in institutional parties such as Fratelli d'Italia and Lega.

On 22 March 2000, as a city councilor, Tosi together with other councilors proposed a motion of segregation on public transportation that led to the city being nominated as 'the Alabama of Italy', which foresaw the separation of entrances on city buses for Veronesi and *extracomunitari* (non-European immigrants). As justified in the official proposal: "*Extracomunitari* use AMT city buses without acquiring a ticket. While Veronese citizens contribute regularly to the maintenance of AMT buses with their taxes, most foreigners (certainly those that are clandestine) do not even know what taxes are."[24] At the local congress of MS-FT in 2006, it is claimed that he made the following statement: "There are many things that unite us: the strong bond we have with our land, the defense of family, love for our culture and our traditions. We are

---

21   L'Arena,"Bufera su Mariotti 'Unica Repubblica è quella Sociale'" (02 June 2020), Verona. Available online at: https://www.larena.it/territori/citt%C3%A0/bufera-su-mariotti -unica-repubblica-e-quella-sociale-br-1.8107525?refresh_ce.

22   From the archival dossier *A Verona tutta l'erba e uno (s)fascio,* available at: https://movime ntandociaverona.files.wordpress.com/2018/03/dossier-verona-corretto.pdf.

23   Ibid.

24   Consiglio Comunale di Verona, Pervenuto 266, 09 September 1999, *Mozione Urgente,* Verona. Translated from the original Italian text.

united by clear ideas and values for which we are willing to pay in person."[25] Thus, a passionate identification with the territory one feels attached to, coupled with the traditions and values that have come to define the identity of this place and the people inhabiting it, are the leitmotifs of the alliance forged between far-right movements and the populist right, or in other words, a sovereignist identitarian outlook.

The glorification of an exclusionary territorial identity fortified by defensive localism (Lipsitz, 2011) comes with moral narratives exalting local cultures and the traditional family model. In fact, the ex-mayor Tosi is renowned for his strong adherence to the Christian family model, exemplified in this support of events organized by ultra-Catholic groups as the representative of Lega Nord, including Family Day rallies and counterdemonstrations against Gay Pride in Verona, thereby playing an active role in the so-called 'anti-gender' movement (Garbagnoli & Prearo, 2018; Trappolin, 2022). In a 2005 counter-rally, he was spotted wearing a T-shirt that read "We are for Romeo and Juliet"[26] in utilizing Veronese local symbols that came to define the identity of Verona as a message against same-sex relationships and LGBTQ+ visibility in cityspace.

Also known as 'the sheriff' of Verona with a promise to bring 'urban safety' and a clean 'urban décor', one of the key elements in Flavio Tosi's political career was his campaign against the Roma and Sinti camps of Verona. This stance dates back to the 1990s when the city was receiving an inflow of migrants fleeing armed conflict in the Balkans coming to take refuge in these nomad camps. In a motion presented in the city council on the 29th of September 1995 with Tosi as the primary signatory, it is claimed that the wave of migration from ex-Yugoslavian territories had led to the "increase of theft, robbery, and violent acts conducted by Slavic citizens, of which Roma and Sinti families are also known for."[27] Lega Nord initiated an adamant anti-Roma and anti-Sinti campaign in Verona with the leadership of Tosi in 2001 carrying the slogan "Sign if you want to kick the gypsies out of our home," for which five members of the party including himself were charged for racial hatred under the *Mancino law*.[28] Eventually, the Roma and Sinti populations living in Verona

---

25   From the archival dossier *Verona Citta dell'Amore e dell'Odio*, available at: https://movimentandociaverona.files.wordpress.com/2019/04/verona-cittc3ao-dellamore-dellodio-2019.pdf.

26   A photo of him in this rally is available at the official webpage of the ultra-Catholic group Christus Rex: https://www.agerecontra.it/2018/10/tosi-ricordi-quando-sfilavi-contro-sodoma-e-gomorra.

27   Consiglio Comunale di Verona, Ordine del Giorno 29 September 1995, Pervenuto no. 466.

28   For more information on the court case, see: http://temi.repubblica.it/metropoli-online/verona-sindaco-tosi-condannato-per-razzismo.

faced increasing backlash on a daily basis in the early 2000s, involving also a suspicious fire inside their camp at *Forte Azzano* in 2004, the cause being unknown.[29]

Notwithstanding his conviction, Tosi did not give up and after his election as the mayor cleared out *Boscomantico* Roma camp for being 'a breeding ground for delinquency', alongside an old kindergarten occupied by the antifascist local collective *La Chimica* which was known to help migrants in need (La Terza, 2009). As put by ex-members of La Chimica: "For his electoral campaign, clearing the Roma camp was the first priority, clearing out La Chimica was the second. He won the election in June, and in August, he cleared us out." (Interview with S.P. & F.P., 10 June 2019) Tosi also came to the fore in national politics as a staunch advocate of a security practice introduced by the Minister of Interior of the time, Roberto Maroni of Lega Nord, involving the collection of digital fingerprints in nomad camps all around Italy, including those of children. The practice was later condemned by the EU Court of Human Rights for violating fundamental rights (Tessadri, 2008). This political campaign against Roma and Sinti communities living in Verona perfectly illustrates the top-down boundary-drawing of the sovereignist identitarian outlook (Demirsu, 2023), as the nomad camps at the periphery were rendered racialized spaces of criminality, deemed 'out of place' in the white middle-class touristified façade of Verona (Merrill, 2014; Saitta, 2015; Sequera & Nofre, 2018). In fact, Tosi continued his 'guardianship' of the historical center as a national deputy, leading a protest in April 2023 against the opening of a new emergency reception center for migrants (*centro d'accoglienza straordinaria*, hereafter CAS) at the heart of the touristic zone.[30]

As mentioned previously, the alliance forged by Tosi between Lega and far-right actors also involved a common enemy, namely the 'antifascists' as the victors of a war in which the far-right felt victimized as the 'losers of war', without the right to write their own history or take pride in it. A notorious figure from the far-right movement, Andrea Miglioranzi, entered the city administration with Tosi's electoral list as a candidate from MS-FT, coming from the nazirock subculture of VFS. While Miglioranzi was the first ever person in Italy to be found guilty and arrested under the *Mancino law* for instigation of racial hatred, he was nominated by Flavio Tosi in a provocative move as the

---

29   From the archival dossier *Verona Citta dell'Amore e dell'Odio*, available at: https://movimentandociaverona.files.wordpress.com/2019/04/verona-cittc3a0-dellamore-dello dio-2019.pdf.

30   Information on the protest can be accessed at: https://www.veronasera.it/politica/cen tro-accoglienza-profughi-filippini-bertaia-tosi-traguardi-21-aprile-2023.html.

official representative of the Veronese Institute of the History of Resistance and the Modern Age that aims to preserve the collective memory of the local antifascist resistance during WWII. The justification presented for this decision was the conviction that the winners of war have misrepresented the history, which ought to be rewritten in a different light.[31] From a 'historical revisionist' (Valencia-Garcia, 2020) vantage point, it was argued that the celebration of the Liberation Day on the 25th of April should be undertaken with "equal dignity for the partisans as well as the soldiers of Salò." (Miglioranzi quoted in Tosatto, 2007) Following a nationwide uprising against his nomination, Miglioranzi was appointed instead as the president of AMIA, the agency in charge of urban sanitation services, waste management, and recycling in the city of Verona and its province. According to one of the interviewees, who is an independent researcher on far-right groups in Verona, the agency is today filled with employees that are neo-Nazi sympathizers covered with tattoos in the shape of a swastika, listening to nazirock inside the premises of the agency (interview with E.M., 17 July 2019).

Following two terms of Tosi's mayorship, the subsequent mayor Federico Sboarina arrived from AN background, coming to office in 2017 as the candidate of an alliance between Forza Italia, Lega Nord, Fratelli d'Italia, and his own list *Battiti Verona* backed by local formations such as *Verona Domani* (Verona Tomorrow), *Verona Piu Sicura* (A Safer Verona) and *Indipendenza Veneto* (Veneto Independence). Once again, owing to this alliance far-right elements have ensured the upper hand in authoring a number of controversial motions in the city council, including the motion declaring the city of Verona a 'pro-life' city in 2018 against the national law no. 194 on the right to abortion.[32] Sboarina's candidacy list also included figures with direct links to far-right social movements (Marconi & Testi, 2019), most notably including the new 'identitarian movements' (Handler, 2019; Zùquete, 2018; Šima, 2021) such as *Fortezza Europa* and *Nomos*, who dwell on the more subtle themes of territorial identity, local culture, and homeland. Just like his predecessor Tosi, Sboarina undertook the role of creating a sanitized feeling of urban space that harbored a homogenous Veronese identity (Massey, 1994; Mitchell, 2000) by carrying out top-down boundary-drawing practices such as intimidating raids

---

31   From the archival dossier *Verona Citta dell'Amore e dell'Odio*, available at: https://movimentandociaverona.files.wordpress.com/2019/04/verona-cittc3ao-dellamore-dellodio-2019.pdf.

32   For the official declaration of this motion, see: https://ufficiostampa.comune.verona.it/nqcontent.cfm?a_id=9561&id_com=23361.

in the multiethnic neighborhood of Veronetta, targeting specifically 'ethnic' stores alongside his security councilor from Fratelli d'Italia.[33]

With Sboarina's administration, Lorenzo Fontana, who at the time was the leader of the Lega Nord group at the European Parliament, was made deputy mayor of the city of Verona, attending events of the 'cultural' identitarian organization *Fortezza Europa* as keynote speaker.[34] In 2019, under Sboarina's mandate and the backing of Fontana, who had later become the Italian Minister of Family and Disability, sponsorship was granted from the municipality of Verona and the region of Veneto for the organization of the *World Congress of Families* (hereafter WCF), bringing together anti-gender groups from around the world. The *Gran Guardia* palace, one of the most important convention centers owned by the Municipality of Verona located in its main piazza, was provided free of charge for this occasion when Verona became the locus of the transnational populist right and ethnonationalist groups brought together by Christian moralism, marketed as the 'model city' in the defense of traditional values (Demirsu, 2022).

This legacy of the populist right and its alliance with far-right elements within the local administration have been recently challenged by the landslide victory of the left alliance in the 2022 local elections with the leadership of Damiano Tommasi, who was elected the new mayor. Coming from a religious background himself, with a career in football that started in the local Hellas team, the new mayor promised an open and inclusive city, bringing different progressive groups together in his electoral campaign. This also included important elements of the antibodies, which for the first time found themselves in alliance with the local administration.[35] Doubtlessly, such political victory was contested firstly by his rival, the previous mayor Sboarina, who 'warned' the city-zens of Verona that Tommasi risked turning the city into 'a transgender capital'.[36] His statement was supported by the bishop of Verona, Giuseppe Zenti, in what was seen as a violation of secularism and a religious

---

33 From the archival dossier *Verona Citta dell'Amore e dell'Odio*, available at: https://movimentandociaverona.files.wordpress.com/2019/04/verona-cittc3ao-dellamore-dellodio-2019.pdf.

34 L'Arena (28 November 2017), "Bufera sul convegno degli avvocati a 'Fortezza Europa,'" available at: https://www.larena.it/territori/citt%C3%A0/bufera-sul-convegno-degli-avvocati-a-fortezza-europa-1.6130421.

35 For a detailed account of this electoral campaign under the slogan *Rete!*, you can find the official program here: https://www.reteperdamianotommasi.org/_files/ugd/239207_85efccf69fd04870a14b4cba6a4efc52.pdf.

36 For more information, see: https://www.ilpost.it/2022/06/24/lanimata-campagna-elettorale-per-il-ballottaggio-a-verona.

intervention in local politics, who invited the electorate to vote for the candidate supporting the family envisioned by God and not for the one who supported gender ideology, abortion, and euthanasia.[37] Notwithstanding these attempts, the victory of the new progressive city administration managed to challenge deep-seated exclusionary policies in a short period of time.

4   A 'Holy Alliance': Catholic Fundamentalism (*Integralismo*) and the Far-Right

The patron saint of Verona is the African bishop San Zeno (also referred to as *Zeno il Moro*-Zeno the Moor), with the impressive Basilica di San Zeno built at the spot where he is believed to be buried (Delibori, 2009: 15–17). Since then, notable saints have left a tradition of hospitality and volunteerism in the city throughout its history, such as the missionary *San Daniele Comboni* giving life to the Institute of Comboniani that has created a dynamic African community in Verona, or *San Giovanni Calabria* known to have taken care of disadvantaged children in Verona with similar civil society organizations dedicated to him today (Chelidonio, 2009). Notwithstanding this social reality, the city nonetheless came to be associated with another form of Christianity that has morphed towards an extremist and fundamentalist direction.

In the post-war period, Verona, like most of the Veneto region, was characterized by the cultural homogeneity of traditionalist Catholicism and the political dominance of Christian Democrats (Franzina, 2010). It has been argued that the latter has always had a benevolent eye for right-wing politics in Verona, whether it was the institutional right or non-institutional movements (Bonatelli, 2007). While piousness was a general trait shared in this region characterized as 'white' referring to its adherence to the Christian Democrat party, such religiosity had also manifested in more radical variants upholding illiberal values that had found it easier to flourish in a socio-political space as the city of Verona. These fundamentalist groups espousing a social space that is inhabited by a population that is native, white, and Catholic, have not only targeted immigrants or sexual rights activists, but also other Christian organizations who operate in Verona and work with immigrant communities seen as the promoters of an unwanted multiculturalism (Del Medico, 2009: 81).

---

37   The open letter of Zenti is quoted in La Repubblica, "Ballottaggio Tommasi-Sboarina a Verona, lettera del vescovo Zenti: 'Non votate chi sostiene idee gender, ma la famiglia' (20 June 2022). Available at: https://www.repubblica.it/politica/2022/06/20/news/verona _ballottaggio_tommasi_sboarina_lettera_vescovo_zenti_no_voto_idee_gender-354725174.

This rich reserve of fundamentalist Catholic organizations in Verona has also been enjoying substantial funding and sponsorship from the city administration for their operations. One such local religious association is called *Comitato Principe Eugenio* (Committee of Prince Eugenius), known to organize seminars that reflect the so-called 'clash of civilizations' thesis between Europe and Islam, arguing for the 'inferiority' of different cultures that jeopardize the perceived higher values of the Roman Catholic Church.[38] This organization has distributed pamphlets that personally attack Carlo Melegari, a sociologist, philanthropist, and an ex-priest who founded the association *Cestim* (*Centro Studio Immigrazione,* Center of Immigration Studies) that has been working with migrants in Verona as early as the 1990s. The reason this association and its founder were being targeted was due to their perceived advocacy of 'a multireligious society' against the Christian civilization of Europe, promoting instead an 'Islamized' Italy.[39] Such Catholic organizations promoting multicultural values are considered to betray their own faith by their fundamentalist counterparts, held to "hate Verona of traditions ... they are the enemies of the Catholic tradition" (quoted in Romagnani, 2009: 41). Hence, the defense of a nativist white Christian identity is sought not only against immigrants and different cultures *per se*, but also locals who support social inclusion and pluralism (Prowe, 2004; Kreisi et al., 2008; Duyvendak et al., 2022). As such, Comitato Principe Eugenio portrays a sort of anti-modern rewriting of history (Boym, 2001) in which one can find traces of the sovereignist rhetoric upholding mutually exclusive territories (Basile & Mazzoleni, 2020), that is also characteristic of the 'cultural difference' thesis. Another religious group with a similar outlook is *Famiglia e Civiltà*, that also adheres to a form of anti-modernist nostalgia in Verona, which it seeks to protect against unwanted change. The group has been targeting LGBTQ+ activism in the city since the 1990s, whose leader has been condemned with an administrative sanction following his comments equating homosexuality with pedophilia.[40]

These religious groups, together with their allies in the populist and the far-right circles, seek to immortalize the past upon urban space as a way of defending an identity which they feel has been under threat, thereby maintaining old

---

38   From the archival dossier *Allarmi Sono Fascisti*, 25 November 2000, Verona. Available online at: https://movimentandociaverona.files.wordpress.com/2017/04/allarmi-son -fascisti.pdf.

39   Original pamphlet archived in the dossier *Allarmi Sono Fascisti*, 25 November 2000, Verona. Available online at: https://movimentandociaverona.files.wordpress.com/2017 /04/allarmi-son-fascisti.pdf.

40   *L'Arena* "Chi insulta i Gay Paga", 07 June 1999, Verona.

hierarchies. Such instances directly manifested upon the nodal points (Moore, 2007) of the city included protests against rock concerts in *Piazza San Zeno* and *Arena di Verona*, and on one occasion against a concert of the Neapolitan antifascist band *99 Posse*, denounced as 'satanic rock'.[41] Likewise, in opposition to the prospect of organizing a rock concert in the Roman Arena in 1994, the ultra-Catholic network *Gruppi di Famiglie Cattoliche* staged a protest with the slogan *Rock in the Arena? Seven Times No!* due to their conviction that arts and music were "governed by a hierarchical order" just like the "difference in societies who could never be equal in their cultural worth" (the original document found in Del Medico, 2004: 129). According to the pamphlet distributed by these groups in Piazza Brà, *Arena di Verona* is considered to be the epicenter of the classical tradition, and therefore, should not serve as a venue for 'neo-tribal music' that incites immorality and drugs (Ibid.).

These episodes lucidly illustrate how historical landmarks are safeguarded by traditionalist groups that espouse a white Catholic Veronese identity believed to represent a higher elite culture, against groups that herald social change and difference in urban spaces, found to jeopardize homogeneity of the city's heritage and its authentic identity. This form of territorialization as collective action is aimed to preserve the touristified inward-looking historical center conveying a timeless uniform identity, against elements deemed 'out of place'. In this picture, the perceived inferiority of foreign cultures as the perfect example of contemporary racism (Balibar, 1991; Lentin & Karayakali, 2016; Frisina, 2020), merges with a negation of the counterculture of the left (Prowe, 2004; Kriesi et al., 2008), perceived as a degeneration of the native identity.

An important locus of ultra-conservative mobilization premised on the espousal of Veronese territorial identity is the carnivalesque celebrations of *Pasque Veronesi*, which are modern reenactions of the local anti-Jacobin uprisings against the French invasion of the city. The collective memory of this historical revolt was reinvoked by local Catholic groups as an inextricable part of *Veronesità*. Here, taking pride in the local identity against foreign invasion is rewritten with heavy traditionalist and reactionary undertones as the quintessential 'invented tradition' (Hobsbawm, 1990). This event came to be exalted as the 'first authentic Italian insurgence' against the Jacobin laicity of the French, being referred to as *Vandea Italiana* in relation to the anti-revolutionary insurgence that had taken place in Vandea, France (Romagnani, 2009). Ironically, this analogy is also used in far-right mobilizations, such as the anti-abortion

41   From the archival dossier *Allarmi Sono Fascisti*, 25 November 2000, Verona. Available online at: https://movimentandociaverona.files.wordpress.com/2017/04/allarmi-son -fascisti.pdf.

FIGURE 12   Italy depicted as under attack by Islam
according to Comitato Principe Eugenio
ORIGINAL PAMPHLET FROM THE
ARCHIVAL DOSSIER VERONESI TUTI
MATI, 17 MARCH 2001

rally organized by Forza Nuova in collaboration with the ultra-Catholic group Christus Rex with the slogan *Verona Vandea Europea* in 2018.

Today, the celebrations are organized by *Comitato per la Celebrazione delle Pasque Veronesi* (Committee of the Celebration of Veronesi Easters), with participants dressed in the historical military uniform of the 18th century carrying the *Contarina* flag of the Republic of Venice signifying Veneto independence. Cannons are blown from the Lamberti Tower in *Piazza Erbe* and Catholic mass is held in Latin with ancient Roman rituals. This form of nativist glorification of the past (Boym, 2001; Duyvendak et al., 2022) is a performative writing of the identity of Verona as a social space and its inhabitants (Aru, 2015). Thus, a timeless singular territorial identity is reinforced in reverence to the Republic of Venice, considered the true ruler of the native land during that historical period, which is then projected upon the present. The committee is composed of members of *Liga Veneta*, important local entrepreneurs, professors at the University of Verona, as well as members of local ultra-Catholic groups such as *Comitato Principe Eugenio* and the pro-monarchist anti-modernist *Sacrum Imperium* (Romagnani, 2009: 27). The celebration of this event has seen the participation of notable figures from the Veronese far-right, such as VFS, as well as institutional figures from the city administration (Romagnani, 2009). In short, the committee and the range of events they organize function to

consolidate loyalty to a territorial identity nested in localized myths and symbolisms that bind together identitarian groups from different walks of life.

The committee od Pasque Veronesi organizes other events usually related
to the history of Catholicism, such as the battle of Lepanto and the commemoration of martyrs who have fallen to secure victory against the Turks, still
construed as 'the Other' in the common ultra-conservative imagery, as exemplified in Figure 12.[42] According to the archive kept by the progressive network
of associations, in 1999 the group went to 'resacralize' a public venue that was
granted to Muslim immigrants a week ago to celebrate the end of Ramadan,[43]
an overt act of territorialization of Veronese urban spaces codified as white
Christian space. This formulation of the identity of Verona is imbued in a white
European culture understood as a union between 'the throne and the alter',
giving way to religious sermons in Verona today where a knife is blessed for the
crusade against Islam (Antonini, 2018).

Since the last decade, the most active ultra-Catholic group in the urban
scenery taking part in social conflict with progressive groups has been *Christus
Rex-Traditio*. This group's website opens with a greeting note that reads "Stop
the Islamization of Europe", and works as an archive of the abovementioned
religious associations that were active in the 1990s and early 2000s.[44] Defined
as an independent 'traditionalist' and 'sovereignist' Catholic organization,[45]
its membership retains close ties to Forza Nuova through mutual membership, including controversial figures such as the Austrian presbyter Don
Floriano Abrahamowicz known to support anti-Semite theories negating
the Holocaust.[46] Their leader advocates abolishing the *Mancino law*, is ada-
mantly against immigration and the Black Lives Matter movement, whilst
openly demonstrating his political support for Matteo Salvini, reckoned a 'true
Catholic' (Fieldnotes of online ethnography). As explicated in their official

---

42   Comitato Pasque Veronesi, *Locandina commemorazione dei caduti nella battaglia navale di
     Lepanto*, October 2019, Verona. Available online at: http://www.traditio.it/PASQUE%20V
     ERONESI/2019/settembre/28/lepanto.pdf.

43   From the archival dossier *Allarmi Sono Fascisti*, 25 November 2000, Verona. Available
     online at: https://movimentandociaverona.files.wordpress.com/2017/04/allarmi-son
     -fascisti.pdf.

44   The official website of Christus Rex is available at: https://www.agerecontra.it/chi-siamo.

45   "Chi siamo?" From the official website of Christus Rex, available at: https://www.agerecon
     tra.it/chi-siamo.

46   La Repubblica, "Prete lefebvriano: 'Camere a gas per disinfettare', Ma la sua comu-
     nità: 'Posizione personale'" (29 January 2009). Available online at: https://www.repubbl
     ica.it/2009/01/sezioni/esteri/benedetto-xvi-29/prete-lefebvriano/prete-lefebvriano.html.

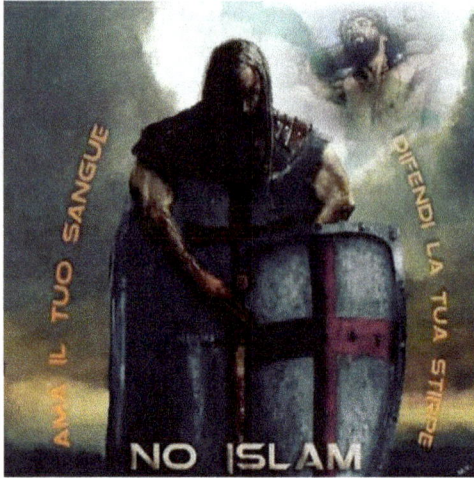

FIGURE 13   "Love your blood, defend your
              lineage: No Islam."
              FROM THE PUBLIC INSTAGRAM
              ACCOUNT OF A MEMBER OF
              CHRISTUS REX, 12 OCTOBER 2018

website, the association is not only against abortion and same-sex couples, but
also against 'exaggerated' rights for women and the co-education of sexes.[47]

In short, the sort of Catholicism dominant in Verona established solid
ties not only with the populist right but also far-right movements in exalting
a gated local identity defined by the negation of the 'other' in defense of a
white European ancestry, the native land, and the predictability of everyday
life provided by Christian morals against the backdrop of a globalizing world
constantly in flux. It is in these fertile grounds that a resilient bond is established between different institutional and non-institutional actors operating
in the landscape of Verona, who guard the borders of belonging inside a singular exclusionary identity where any foreign element is considered a "biological
and cultural degradation" (Del Medico, 2009: 71). As clearly illustrated by these
episodes, the making of a territorial identity manifests itself in urban topographies through the dual mechanism of top-down and bottom-up practices of
boundary-drawing.

---

47   From the official website of Christus Rex, available at: https://www.agerecontra.it/chi
      -siamo.

5   Hellas Fandom and the Stadium as a School of Hate

One of the most important dynamics in the everyday life of Verona is its local football team and the support it receives from its fan groups. As one of the two football teams to emerge from Verona, Hellas fans and their various associations throughout decades have come to be recognized among the most Nazi-fascist fandom in the Italian universe of hooliganism. Acquiring its name in 1903 from high school students attending *Liceo Ginnasio Statale Scipione Maffei* specializing in ancient Greek and Latin language, its stadium *Stadio Marcantonio Bentegodi* and the surrounding neighborhood became a school of far-right radicalization over the years. Also the most supported football team in the larger region of Veneto, the team is referred to as *gli Scaligeri* or *i Mastini*, with reference to the Scaliger dynasty taken as the golden era of the city, symbolized with the Scala emblem of a stair in the middle of two mastiff (*mastino*) dogs in their logo.

The historical fan group of Hellas ultras, *Brigate Gialloblù* has in the last four decades been the most consistent and long-lived youth movement in Verona (Dilemmi, 2009). The fandom is united in the expression of shared 'hatred', as they put it, towards groups or individuals qualified as 'others' who are deemed unfit for the Veronese identity or the urban decorum of this elegant touristic city. It is a school of hate where one socializes, providing an 'anything goes' kind of platform for neofascist and neo-Nazi expressions, who come together in the name of defending the identity of Verona. The anthem of the fan group is composed by the local neo-Nazi band *Sumbu Brothers*, entitled *Hellas Army*, a slogan taken up to brand the most radicalized branch within the *Brigate Gialloblù*. This ultras fraction is known to have a wide overlap with far-right movements in the city and frequently utilizes historical references to previous neo-Nazi organizations in the area, as exemplified by their posts on their Facebook page with the slogan *Got Mit Uns* accompanied by the Nazi eagle (see Figure 15), well-known themes in the city with reference to the criminal activities of Ludwig. The famous chant sung by the ultras during matches is adorned with overt neo-Nazi slogans: "We are a fantastic team, in the shape of a swastika. How beautiful it is that Rudolf Hess trains us?"[48] Visible from these symbolisms, the movement manifests a restorative nostalgia (Boym, 2001) towards fascism, culminating in scenes during the lockdown in 2020 where

---

48   The original chant in Italian: *Siamo una squadra fantastica ... fatta a forma di svastica ... che bello è ... allena Rudolf Hess.*

FIGURE 14   Image shared with the hashtag 'solo il
             nostro odio porta alla vittoria' (only our
             hate will lead us to victory). The banner
             reads 'noi odiamo voi' (we hate you).
             PHOTO FROM THE FACEBOOK PAGE *I*
             GUERRIERI DI VERONA, 30 MAY 2015

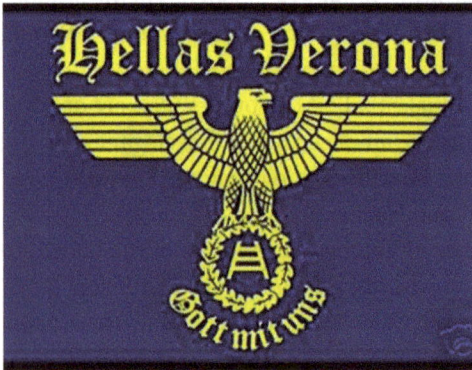

FIGURE 15   *Hellas Army* Facebook page – "Gott
             Mit Uns"
             FROM THE FACEBOOK PAGE OF AEK
             HELLAS ARMY, 13 OCTOBER 2012

the flag of the RSI was found hanging in front of the Bentegodi Stadium on the
25th of April Liberation Day in Italy.[49]

One particularly notable characteristic of Hellas ultras is the overtly racist content of their slogans inside the stadium. Traditionally, racism in the

---

49   For more information, see: https://daily.veronanetwork.it/news/la-mattina-del-25-apr
      ile-allo-stadio-e-comparsa-una-bandiera-della-rsi.

stadium, like much of the rest of the city, was channeled toward southern Italians, with particular antagonism towards Neapolitans due to rivalry in the stadium. Since the 1970s, slogans against the Napoli team included expressions such as *benvenuti in Italia* (welcome to Italy) with northern supremacy inherent in Padano nationalism (Pugliese, 2002). Similar themes as depicted on the banners that embellish the stadium included insults insinuating that Neapolitans are uncivil and dirty, such as *lavatevi* (wash yourselves) and *aqua e saon par el teron* (water and soap for the *terrone*/southerner) written in the local dialect. It is visible that the united feeling of hatred against difference is a form of community-building overcoming the sense of 'loss of identity' across different socioeconomic backgrounds.

Over time, the southerner was replaced by people of color as the main target of hate, culminating in the infamous case of hanging a black mannequin from the audience in 1996. These episodes have been accompanied by racist chants against players of color, as well as physical assaults against people of color near the stadium, in the main piazzas of the historical center, and in other middle-class areas.[50] On one occasion in 2019, a black Italian football player from the opposing team was subjected to monkey chants from the spectators, to which the latter responded by throwing the ball towards the chanting crowd. In the aftermath of this incident, the leader of the Hellas fan group (who happens to be also the leader of Forza Nuova Verona) claimed that the footballer "could never be truly Italian because he is black".[51] The city administration opted to back up its fan group, claiming the footballer 'defamed' the city of Verona by his reaction, even passing a motion entitled *Political Condemnation Against Those Who Defame the City of Verona*.[52] This incident has demonstrated how localist pride (Nevola, 2010; Paasi, 2011), understood through northern whiteness and imbued in a defense of the territorial identity, unites political actors in the city administration and the cultural movements of the far-right. The happy wedding between far-right groups, neo-Nazi social and cultural movements, and *curva* membership (a term used to refer to the ultras of a football team) gave

---

50   From the archival dossier *Verona Citta dell'Amore e dell'Odio*, available at: https://mov-imentandociaverona.files.wordpress.com/2019/04/verona-cittc3a0-dellamore-dello dio-2019.pdf.

51   For the original interview, see: https://corrieredelveneto.corriere.it/verona/sport/19_novembre_04/cori-bentegodi-capo-ultra-dell-hellas-verona-balotelli-mai-tutto-itali ano-c6c6419c-fee6-11e9-9bdb-6aaa04b7a1d7.shtml.

52   Official motion, *Mozione: Condanna Politica Per Chi Diffama la Città di Verona*, Pervenuto 1352, 04 November 2019, Presidenza del Consiglio, Comune di Verona.

way to a panoply of white supremacist rhetoric and racist symbolic violence against people of color in the stadium, including transnational symbolisms of the Ku Klux Klan and Celtic crosses, extending support for other European identitarian far-right groups such as the *Golden Dawn* in Greece, whose flag was hung in the stadium in 2013 accompanied by the slogan 'Free Greece'.[53]

As noted by Dilemmi (2009), beyond the artificial opposition and conflict construed in the stadium that pertains to the world of football, there is a visible bond between the ultras subculture and the exclusionary territorial identity anchored in social space that underwrites the collective identity shared with like-minded groups. The *Brigate Gialloblù*, for instance, consider themselves the defenders of a self-defined *Veronesità* on the national platform through their performances during matches (Dilemmi, 2009: 113). It is claimed that this territorial identity is first and foremost drawn from the historical center as the symbolic social space. The latter is to be protected from undesirable and non-aesthetic elements which do not fit the model of Veronese urbanite defined through white Christianity and urban elitism (Dilemmi, 2009). Thus, beyond symbolic violence and white supremacist slogans prevalent in the stadium, the historical center as an imagined pure space and the epicenter of Veronese identity has been the milieu of hooliganism in defense of the 'territory'.

Yet, one aspect overlooked by Dilemmi's (2009) analysis is the double function of the stadium, that is, temporarily eliminating class difference alongside forging a collective identity in a shared feeling of 'hate' towards difference. While the local elite is esteemed by Hellas fandom as the aspired profile of the urban protagonist, the group still considers itself as a working-class movement representing the authenticity of the native population, finding in itself a reflection of other working-class identitarian struggles in different contexts: "I am a team of the people. I am the gut and the belly of the city ... I am wine glasses [*goti* in dialect] and curses, *lesso* and *pearà* [local dishes]. I live in the streets, on the flags of houses in Borgo Roma. I am the dirty face of Piazza Toscana, the dignity of Borgo Venezia, the nobility of Liston right next to the Arena. I am not a tourist; I am not folklore. I am the pints of beer; I am the England of the working-class." (Brigate *Gialloblù*, Facebook post 28 March 2020). The stadium offers a space where class difference is replaced by a sense of unity through an 'authentic' territorial identity and the devotion to one's city that are the defining elements of this collective identity. Here, adhering to one's territorial identity can also be expressed in supporting other identitarian pursuits elsewhere,

---

53   From the archival dossier *Verona Citta dell'Amore e dell'Odio*, available at: https://mov-imentandociaverona.files.wordpress.com/2019/04/verona-cittc3a0-dellamore-dello dio-2019.pdf.

given the far-right and nativist tendencies well known among English hooligans (Morrow & Meadowcroft, 2019), where membership in the working-class is equated to 'authenticity'. The working-class fan, therefore, comes to share the same exclusive city-zenship with the better-off middle-class Veronesi in the stadium. As noted by a Hellas fan: "A community where everyone feels equal, there are all social classes imaginable. It's difficult to replicate this in any other context of aggregation. There isn't that type of classism that might exist among friends in the city square, at work, doing sports, in which you inevitably feel a sort of exclusion." (Interview with C.P., 8 July 2020). As such, supporting the city's leading team shifts the focus from social inequalities toward sociocultural issues (Prowe, 2004; Kriesi et al., 2008; Rydgen, 2018), where the perceived 'loss of identity' is addressed through clinging onto the immediate locality (Castells, 2010).

6   Identitarianism Is the New Black: The Identitarian Label and Territorial Belongings

In the last couple of years, most far-right actors, from the neofascist extreme right to Padania nativists, tend to gather under the umbrella of 'identitarianism' as their proclaimed political orientation. This also holds for local groups operating in Verona, offering interesting insights into the intersection of sovereignism and identitarianism with territorial claims to belonging that shape collective identity and collective action (Tarrow, 2011; Kriesi, 2011; Routledge, 2010). This study argues that a new generation of far-right movements, along with the evolution of existing ones, pioneers a rebranding of neofascist and white supremacist inclinations which are embellished with notions such as valorizing authentic identities tied to a homeland (Tudor, 2014; Zùquete, 2018; Šima, 2021), evoking sovereignty understood as mutually exclusive territories (Basile & Mazzoleni, 2020), coupled with nostalgia and reclaiming forgotten history (Hobsbawm, 1990; Boym, 200; Valencia-Garcia, 2020; Duyvendak et al., 2022). Such themes find strong resonance in fertile settings such as Verona and manage to channel collective action. Unlike openly supremacist or fascist ideals, benign-seeming ideals such as defending one's local culture or territorial identity escape legal persecution and are more 'sellable' in the political marketplace, especially for the younger generation in search of an identity to take pride in under conditions of multiple crises. This tendency is succinctly captured in the statement of a Veronese councilor, also a renowned representative of the identitarian wave, who underwent a legal investigation for making the Roman salute against a group of feminist protestors: "History has been written by winners and not the losers of the war. I think that there is also the other side of the medallion. Fascist? I prefer to define myself as an *identitarian*. Fascism, however, is an argument to be studied I believe, and not canceled like some are trying to do."[54]

Existing far-right groups in Verona are increasingly embracing the identitarian turn and framing their causes with a rhetoric of defending local tradition and culture from the threat of vanishing under unwanted multiculturalism and progressive values (Rydgren, 2018; Rucht, 2019; Basile et al., 2020). During the peak of the humanitarian crisis following the Arab Spring, Forza Nuova became the protagonist of the local mobilization *Verona ai Veronesi* (Verona to Veronesi), organizing rallies in the province of Verona with the support and participation of Lega Nord, VFS, and Christus Rex. This slogan is the quintessential exemplification of the sovereignist discourse that reigns identitarianism in Europe and elsewhere, where the conception of a native land and primordial entitlements to it is assumed by a local group appropriating the territorial identity to take back control (Tudor, 2014; Freeden, 2017; Zúquete, 2018; Basile & Mazzoleni, 2020). In 2015, *Verona ai Veronesi* organized a protest against the arrival of new refugees in *Costagrande* reception center located in the Lessinia mountain range, which they dubbed 'an invasion'. This reactionary protest was met with a counter-protest by the local network of progressive actors.[55] The initiative ultimately came under the radar of legal authorities and was investigated under the *Mancino law*. As the group was eventually absolved, it received solidarity from CasaPound Verona for having defended the Veronese identity against the 'shady business' of welcoming migrants (Facebook post of Il Mastino IV, 13 June 2021).

The identitarian turn criticizes the 'political correctness' of progressive politics, which are considered hypocritical at the expense of the genuineness of native identities and local traditions. As put by the leader of Forza Nuova Verona during a protest in 2017 against the mosque in Verona: "We have to take it to the streets ... to invert the course of our identitarian cancellation that is the offspring to 20 years of multicultural political correctness."[56] It is at this

---

54   Andrea Bacciga quoted in, Corriere del Veneto, 17 October 2017, available at: https://corrie redelveneto.corriere.it/verona/politica/17_ottobre_17/verona-consigliere-dona-libri-estr ema-destra-critica-m5s-049e496c-b32e-11e7-93e7-547794075405.shtml.

55   For more info: https://www.veronasera.it/cronaca/manifestazioni-lega-nord-forza-nuova -profughi-costagrande-no-sostegno-abitanti-avesa-21-luglio-2015.html.

56   Leader of Forza Nuova quoted in the local journal *Verona Sera* (7 June 2017), available at: http://www.veronasera.it/politica/striscione-forza-nuova-moschea-islam-terrore-7 -giugno-2017.html.

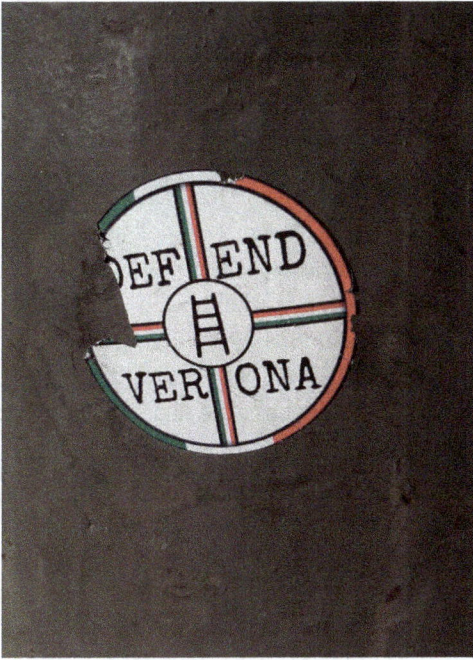

FIGURE 16   'Defend Verona' sticker with the
traditional scala symbol
PHOTOGRAPH: IPEK DEMIRSU

juncture that such groups propose conspiracy theories of ethnic replacement
in their homelands, a fear later voiced by the Italian Agriculture Minister in
2023, thereby calling for 'ethnic resistance': "The most racist project humanity
has ever seen ... A program of African and Asian immigration to Europe ... to
completely destroy hosting countries with the consequence of ethnic substitution." (Post on Facebook page of Verona ai Veronesi, 14 June 2019). A similar declaration underlining the intrinsic bond between a land and an identity
has been shared on the group's Facebook account following the groundbreaking participation of the progressive Damiano Tommasi at Verona Pride 2022,
claiming that the ideology of 'globalism' seeks to "cancel the first natural cell
of society, replacing it with a single individual without identity, without a land,
without a sex, and without identity."[57]

---

57   Public announcement of Forza Nuova Verona (Il Quadrato) on their Facebook account,
(16 July 2022). Available at: https://www.facebook.com/QuadratoVerona/posts/pfbid033
S1Qy4aepDnR3nkZ2spxtiqFJcJDS9GCcuKC7HBWq2GY9RTk7xqMNtvyLxbwZZVxl.

Another influential organization from Verona that represents the identitarian orientation with a national reach is *Comunità Solidarista Popoli Onlus*
(Solidarist Community Peoples NGO), which is in close collaboration with
CasaPound in Verona. *Popoli Onlus* was first founded in 2001 as a cultural
association and a meeting place for ex-far-right militants from the 1980s from
various backgrounds ranging from *Fronte della Gioventù* to *Terza Posizione*, to
adapt to the zeitgeist of the early 2000s under the motto of defending every
population's traditional identity in their own native land. As put by one of
their members: "Popoli Onlus is a sui generis organization because it is constituted by all ex-militants of the radical right in the '80s, with the primary aim of
helping peoples whose identities are oppressed, who is oppressed in their own
lands. Today, we meet for a common objective that has little to do with current
politics ... our idea to help and to support the identity and the tradition of people in their own territories." (Interview with C.P., 8 July 2020). Echoing the principles of sovereignist identitarianism, namely the defense of local identities
and traditions in a homeland perceived to have primordial ties to a given population (Tudor, 2014; Zúquete, 2018; Handler, 2019; Murdoch & Murhall, 2019;
Šima, 2021), Popoli Onlus is a particularly interesting organization as it operates outside Italy carrying such identitarian ideals in other parts of the world.

With its leaders concomitantly members of CasaPound,[58] the organization
presents itself as a humanitarian voluntary organization that provides aid in
areas devastated by war, epidemics, natural disasters, or poverty, prioritizing
those groups that are forced to fight for their independence, their traditional
values, and their own identity.[59] In line with their anti-globalization stance
against international organizations, the association's introductory statement
explicitly underlines that they do not follow a 'politically correct' agenda nor
do they have 'international patrons', but instead, through their own means
they support the 'fight for identity' of various populations, most notably the
community Karen in Burma and Palestinians. Such a battle for the natural feeling of pride for one's roots, it is claimed, is criminalized in Italy and equated
to a form of 'vulgar racism'.[60] According to an active member, the organization
provides medical aid, builds schools, and helps with the education program
in areas where it operates (Interview with C.P., 8 July 2020), yet some have

58   For more information, see: https://www.affaritaliani.it/politica/casapound-popoli-birma
     nia-solid-onlus-nerozzi-palladino-maggi-mya-karen-511330.html.
59   From the official website of Popoli Onlus: https://www.comunitapopoli.org.
60   From the About Us section of the official website of Popoli Onlus, available at: https:
     //www.comunitapopoli.org/chi-siamo.

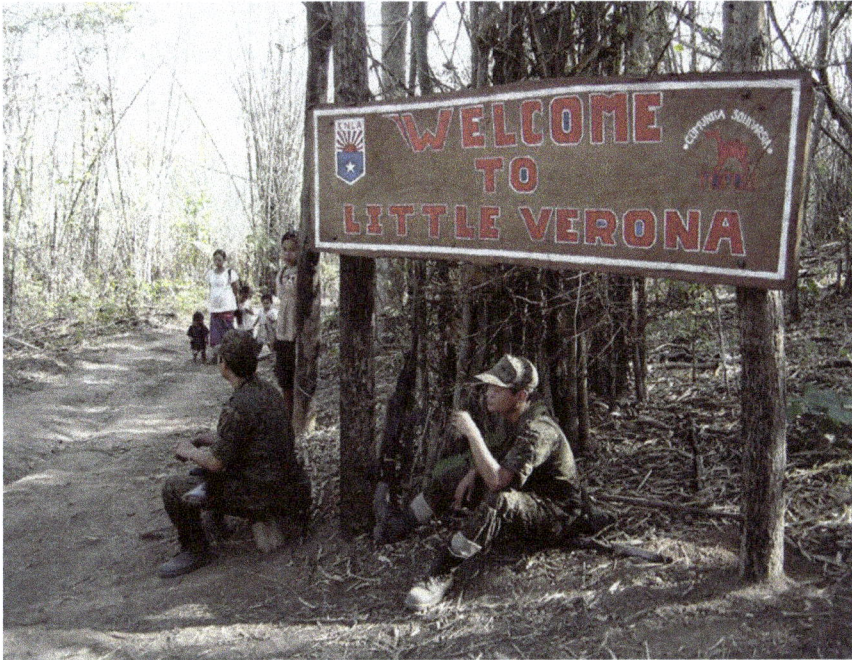

FIGURE 17   Exporting the ideal of territorial identity in places beyond, Popoli Onlus creates
'little Verona' in Myanmar
PHOTO FROM THE OFFICIAL WEBSITE OF POPOLI ONLUS

argued that humanitarian aid works as a façade to cover illegal operations such
as arms trafficking[61] with the founder of the organization along with other 6
Veronesi being arrested in 2002 for a coup attempt in Comoro islands (Del
Medico, 2004: 147).[62]

An excellent exemplar of new-age identitarian movements is the Veronese
organization *Fortezza Europa* (Fortress Europe) established by ex-members of
Forza Nuova and Fiamma Tricolore, located near *Basilica di San Zeno* in the
historical center. The four main ideals promulgated by this local movement are
namely *identity* to be defended from 'migratory chaos' and 'globalist thought',
family understood as genes, lineage, clan, *economic independence* (as they put
it, 'energetic auto-sufficiency'), and *aristocracy*, represented in the symbol of
the group with four arrows (Fieldnotes of online ethnography). The leader of

---

61   For more information, see: https://espresso.repubblica.it/palazzo/2012/11/05/news
/casapound-guerra-in-birmania-1.48032.
62   For more information on the arrest, see: https://www.repubblica.it/online/cronaca/com
ore/comore/comore.html.

the movement, who is also the lead singer of the nazirock band *Hobbit*, rooted in the Hobbit Camps tradition of MSI, explains their outlook: "Instead of fascists, we prefer being defined as identitarian. We don't live with our heads facing behind us; we believe in our ideals and fight for them, first of all against immigration and illegality. They say we named our movement after the Third Reich of Hitler, but we are not interested in the past. The fundamental threat for us Europeans is the migratory flood, that form of immigration where someone is trying to realize an ethnic substitution of European peoples, shaped over thousands of years starting from the solid pillars of the Greco-Roman civilization. And more immigration means more crime. For this reason, there are those who resort to do-it-yourself kind of justice."[63] Here once again, we see how the US-based Great Replacement theory articulated by transnational far-right actors in different contexts, and recently by ministers in the new Italian government, find expression in urban life.

Fortezza Europa finds resonance mostly among young Veronesi and runs the clothing brand *Movimento Verona* located in the same office, whose products are also sold by Forza Nuova's business office, *The Firm*. Apart from the local Scaliger symbolism, the products also include writings that that make reference to white supremacy, sovereignism, and a common European heritage understood in primordial terms through slogans such as *White Boys Verona, Supremacy, The Glorious Battle of Lepanto, Pro Border & Pro Nation,* and *European Brotherhood*. The clothing line is also carried by city councilors who frequent this organization, wearing European Brotherhood T-shirts embellished with Celtic crosses. As a result, this local identitarian movement, whilst upholding the native Veronese territorial identity that espouses exclusive city-zenship, underlines its part in the wider white Christian European heritage (Caiani, 2018). 'Fortress Europe' is to be protected against invasion of non-belonging (mostly non-white) subjects defined through ethno-national and religious characteristics, conveying a strong sovereignist sentiment (Basile & Mazzoleni, 2020), expressed through the perceived need to secure borders and impose social order in one's homeland. Moreover, this outlook is reflected upon everyday life as individuals partake in city life dressed in these outfits carrying sovereignist identitarian symbols and slogans as identifiers that visibly mark the borders of belonging (Lofland, 1973; Della Porta & Diani, 2006: 109). The inscription of exclusive city-zenship was exemplified in a backlash at a local high school in Verona, where young members of Fortezza Europa staged a protest with the slogans 'Pro Borders, Pro Nations, Just Order and Sovereignty'

---

63   Leader of Fortezza Europa quoted in *Corriere di Verona* (29 November 2017), available at: https://www.pressreader.com/italy/corriere-di-verona/20171129/281582355947895.

FIGURE 18   Protestors from Fortezza Europa outside a local high school with the slogan 'Pro
             borders, pro nations, just order, and sovereignty'
             PHOTO FROM THE FACEBOOK PAGE OF FORTEZZA EUROPA, 17 MAY 2018

against an initiative of the high school to raise awareness about the process of migration advocating the title 'No Borders, No Nations, Just People' (Facebook page of Fortezza Europa, 17 May 2018).

Collective action, understood as a defense of territorial identity ingrained in tradition and local values, is posed not only against ethnic or religious minorities, but also against sexual minorities. The anti-LGBTQ+ position of identitarian groups gave way to political contestation when an openly LGBTQ+ activist declared his candidacy in 2019 to represent the historical mascot that is an important part of the Veronese carnival traditions. The local carnival celebrations in Verona involve elections every year to choose who will represent the historical figure of *Papà del Gnoco* (father of gnoco), who is believed to have offered the Italian dish gnocchi to the city-dwellers during a time of famine. The candidacy of a gay LGBTQ+ activist disturbed local far-right groups, who, besides threatening the candidate,[64] organized an event with the participation

---

64   For more information, see https://www.veronasera.it/attualita/bacanal-del-gnoco-polemi
      che-elezioni-papa-carnevale-30-gennaio-2019.html.

of the mayor of Verona to remind the tradition of *Bacanal* (the carnival of Verona) as an indispensable tradition signifying the authentic native Veronese identity, whose construction negates sexual orientations deviating from heteronormativity:

> This year, the continuous and progressive move away from traditional principles meant that a further distortion could be created, allowing such policy to creep into the Veronese Carnival. The announcement of the candidacy for Papà del Gnoco 2019 of a character who presented himself to the press as a 'gay activist from Verona' leaves no room for misunderstandings about the candidate's willingness to exploit the carnival for the promotion of phantom LGBTQ+ rights. Our hope is that the mask will be definitively removed from the hands of those who would like to speculate on it for political and individual purposes in order to be restored to the genuine, popular, and traditional values that inspire it.
>
> Facebook page of Fortezza Europa, 31 December 2018

Identitarian groups that work as 'cultural associations' not only function to rebrand controversial extremist arguments into softer themes such as local identity, local traditions, and customs, but they also provide a platform for the multitude of far-right actors operating in the same area to establish direct ties with one another over a shared sovereignist identitarian outlook. *Nomos-Terra e Identità* (Nomos-Land and Identity) is one such 'cultural' association that promotes the local culture of Verona, with a president who was running in the local elections with Forza Nuova in 2008 and other members who are concomitantly part of Fortezza Europa. Their motto 'land and identity' succinctly demonstrates the centrality of the conception of 'place' for the collective identity of the movement. This identitarian group has been co-organizing events with other far-right groups, such as concerts with the nazirock bands *Hobbit* and *Topi Neri*,[65] as well as anti-migration events, including the 2019 conference 'The Lies About Migration' (*Le Bugie sull'Immigrazione*), in collaboration with CasaPound and the participation of the city's mayor (Facebook page of Nomos-Terra e Identità, 4 October 2019).

Online ethnography has further revealed that these identitarian groups upholding territorial identities on the local level, adhere to a global nativist agenda and follow themes disseminated by a 'transnational far-right network'

---

65   For more information on this event, see https://www.ilfattoquotidiano.it/2019/01/16/ver ona-lestrema-destra-organizza-un-concerto-in-memoria-di-jan-palach-provincia-e-com une-danno-il-patrocinio/4901994.

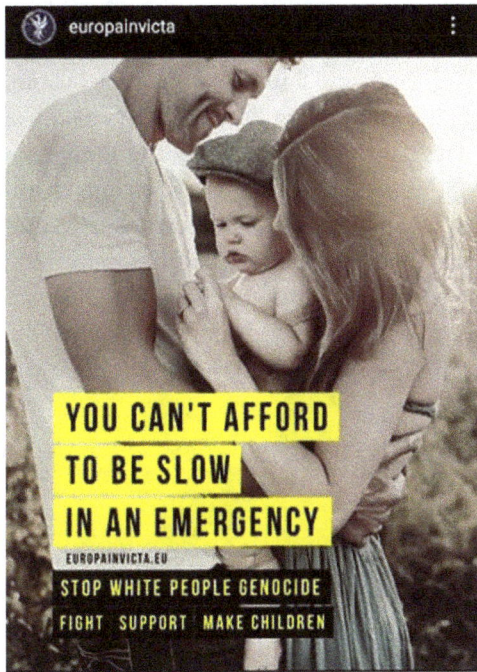

FIGURE 19 "You can't afford to be slow in an emergency. Stop white people genocide. Fight, support, make children"
FROM THE INSTAGRAM ACCOUNT *EUROPA INVICTA*, 18 DECEMBER 2019

(Caiani, 2018). It was observed that many young members of the abovementioned groups follow international social media accounts and share their posts promoting white supremacy with catchy frames and engaging imagery appealing to the younger generation. An interesting example is presented by the Instagram account *Europa Invicta*, praising European whiteness as a virtue to be defended against a so-called 'white people genocide' brought about by diversity and multiculturalism. The account shares images that aestheticize whiteness with Instagram-style visuality, using slogans to plead for all-white spaces ("An all-white space has a purity that is refreshing and serene", 26 June 2020), for the continuation of the 'white race' through reproduction against a perceived 'genocide' ("In the absence of borders, victims abound. Stop white people genocide. Fight, support, make children", 5 March 2020), for the centrality of the heterosexual family in maintaining the white identity biologically ("Clan, family, ancestors", 17 February 2020, "Pass on your genes", 5 January 2020; "Family is happiness", 10 January 2020), and for a defense of Europe identity that is first and foremost possible in protecting the homeland from unwanted arrivals ("In the absence of borders, victims abound", 5 March 2020; "Secure your homeland", 13 July 2020; "Honor and fatherland", "Europe belongs to Europeans", 30 November 2019; "M.E.G.A.: Make Europe Great Again", 14 February 2020; "Make Europeans Dangerous Again", 1 April 2020; "Europeans are the true nobility of the world", 26 April 2020) (Fieldnotes from online ethnography). In short, these local actors defending mutually exclusive territories as a birthright, with a predominant fear over being replaced by non-white immigrant populations, borrow from as well as contribute to transnational far-right frames on the significance of 'native identity' and 'native land', which in turn, shape collective action.

CHAPTER 5

The Antibodies of Hate in Verona: Spreading Expansive Place-Based Identity in an Outward-Looking Space

> Everywhere where there is interaction between a place, a time and an expenditure of energy, there is rhythm.
>
> LEFEBVRE, 2004: 15

∵

Situated in this social setting, so far depicted as the laboratory of intolerance where a holy alliance between far-right movements, ultra-conservative groups, and ethnonationalist politics have historically prospered, exists another Verona that not only seeks to resist the former, but instead pursues the realization of alternative spaces promoting prolific interconnections. Co-created by old and new Veronesi, whose shared feeling of 'not-belonging' is transformed into an *expansive place-based identity* located in an *outward-looking social space*, the existence of this assemblage of social movement actors (McFarlane, 2009) challenges identitarian closure from below. These actors operating in the mundane everyday (Holston, 2009) with their respective organizations share a collective identity and a common vision (Melucci, 1980; Johnston et al., 1994; Kriesi, 2011; Tarrow, 2011) in sustaining mutual trust constructed through a shared history and collective memory (Tarrow, 2011). In this way, they collaborate in the city of Verona not only on local issues but also in supporting transnational claims of justice, thereby demonstrating "how extra-local responsibilities to others become embedded in the day-to-day activities of place-based or territorial struggles." (Cumbers & Routledge, 2013: 218). Their everyday acts of city-zenship (Işın, 2009) as a form of collective action, and counter-claims of identity in the urban life of Verona resonate beyond the given locality (Işın, 2008).

During fieldwork, this assemblage of actors offering an alternative to exclusionary territoriality was referred to by a historical activist as the 'antibodies of hate', which I have opted to employ in defining their collective identity. The antibodies are composed of a closely-knit network of grassroots organizations from different walks of life and different issue-areas, which are remarkably positioned in the same neighborhood, namely the neighborhood of *Veronetta*

FIGURE 20   The transformation of the writing
                     'Verona Hates' to 'Verona Loves' by the
                     local antifascist graffiti artist Cibo
                     PHOTOGRAPH: CIBO. POSTED ON THE
                     ARTIST'S INSTAGRAM PAGE, 29 JUNE
                     2019.

adjacent to and partly overlapping with the historical center. It must be noted that the antibodies are not a form of 'neighborhood activism' (Martin, 2003), in the sense of uniting around a neighborhood-oriented agenda, but instead a constellation of various social actors who have chosen to operate in this partic-ular neighborhood. Moving from this *outward-looking space* which they helped create, the antibodies articulate a different representation of the city and a concomitantly different way of being 'Veronese' that is exercised in the every-day life of Veronetta, an alternative mode of membership to a community that is based on an *inclusive pluralist understanding of city-zenship* (*cittadinanza*), co-created by migrants, non-migrants, and other minority groups that radiates to the rest of the city.

These actors, previously dispersed in various neighborhoods, including the historical center, have over time chosen to settle in Veronetta. This was firstly due to the relatively low rents and the centrality, but also due to the legacy of leftist movements in this neighborhood, and most importantly, the onset of an indifferent tolerance set down by different migrant communities since the 1990s. Today, this informal network has come to be an indispensable feature of the identity of the neighborhood, seeking to sustain existing social bonds and to cultivate intercultural ties. This alternative representation of the city and the accompanying form of place-based identity do not only manifest through rallies and protests but more so through activist citizenship in urban life (Işın, 2008) involving the everyday art of co-inhabiting the city, through cultural events, book presentations, art exhibits, food exchanges, neighborly dinners, comedy shows, dance nights, football matches, farmer's markets and even wine tasting. As such, this assemblage of translocal actors negotiates for a dynamic and non-fixed spatial identity that is enriched and reinvigorated with new members, construed in a bottom-up process from the cosmos of Veronetta that has historically nourished different demographic groups, where face-to-face cross-cultural encounters can flourish in physical space (Boym, 2001: 76).

In addition to the influence of a cognitively drawn space that extends beyond the physical borders of the neighborhood itself, the 'collective iden-tity' (Melucci, 1980; Johnston et al., 1994) of the antibodies is defined by an allegiance to the local history of resistance since WWII presented in Chapter 3, extending to this day in the shared memory of everyday conflicts in cityspace with far-right actors. Hence, with a collective identity molded through a spatio-temporal axis as shown in Figure 21, the movement takes pride in belonging to a Verona that won a gold medal for its resistance to Nazi-fascist forces, today shouldering much of the opposition outside institutional politics against the two-way processes of boundary-drawing undertaken by sovereignist identitar-ian actors. As a matter of fact, their protracted struggles in the everyday have paved the way for the victory of a progressive local administration following the 2022 local elections through their alliance with political actors (as has been the case for far-right actors in past decades), thereby gaining the opportunity to carry their values in the city council.

The unifying values (Kriesi, 2011) that guide the movement uniting different groups are the indivisible and united struggles of *anti-fascism*, *anti-racism*, and *anti-sexism* in the urban spaces of Verona, as the motor of collective action. These three guiding principles are the glue of collective action and channel the movement's direction, uniting with global justice claims. Moreover, the antibodies prioritize *grassroots horizontal organization*, a non-hierarchical democratic intergroup relationship among different local actors that make up the movement, leaving out actors which are deemed too hierarchical in their approaches to collective action.

As such, the antibodies of Verona as a translocal assemblage of place-based social movement actors advocate global justice themes by translating them into their own social space. In fact, lived experiences in shared urban spaces have played an indispensable role in forging the bond that we observe today among the antibodies. They aim to redefine belonging, departing from the neighbor-hood of Veronetta which they have transformed into an outward-looking space,

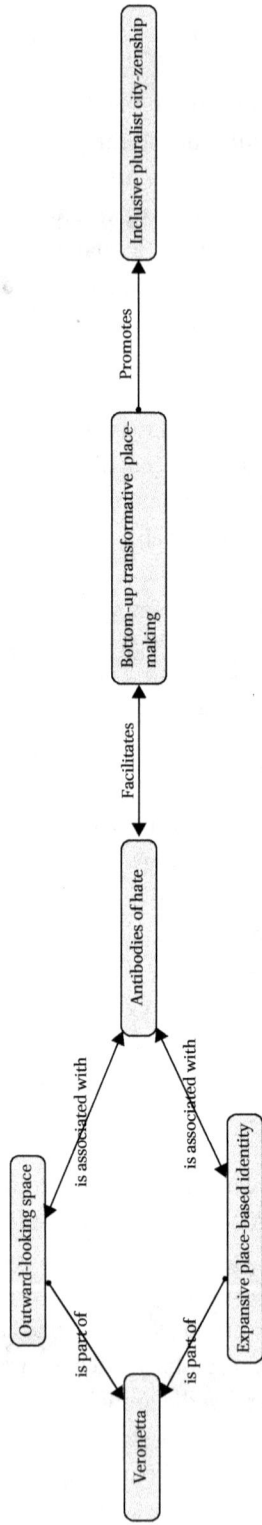

FIGURE 21   The socio-spatial analysis of the antibodies of hate in Verona

TABLE 2 A socio-spatial analysis of progressive actors in Verona

	Identity of place	Place-based identity	Collective identity	Collective action	Veronese city-zenship
	Veronetta as an outward-looking space	*Expansive place-based identity*	*Antibodies of hate*	*Bottom-up transformative place-making*	*Inclusive pluralist membership*
Assemblage of progressive actors	Juxtaposition of migrants, students, old residents, and civil society actors that make up the antibodies. Inclusiveness within diversity, intercultural values, and openness. Home to progressive actors with diverse backgrounds. Exemplify an alternative modus-vivendi radiating outwards. Resisting both to gentrification and reterritorialization attempts.	Progressive belonging to place, based on inclusion.	Anti-fascism Anti-racism Anti-sexism The collective memory of local antifascist resistance as a source of pride. A history of sharing spaces and engaging in solidarity across issues. Horizontal, grassroots organization that is democratic and non-hierarchical. Embracing global justice claims.	Bottom-up community building. Activist citizenship Everyday social ties Deterritorialization, opening up democratic spaces. Alternative representation of Verona that works to: (1) offer a different belonging to city-zens within, and (2) connect with similar causes of social justice in different settings.	City-zenship not fixed but evolving with new members, defined through shared values. The neighborhood of Veronetta as an experimental laboratory for exercising a different form of city-zenship that is offered to the rest of the city.

whilst upholding the collective memory of resistance in this challenging setting, connecting with places beyond in their grassroots united struggle guided by shared values. It is argued that today, the movement with its constitutive elements and the social space of the neighborhood have intertwined to such a degree that they have become one, with the collective identity being defined in and through the identity of Veronetta and the expansive place-based identity of its social fabric. Thus, the chapter will offer an analysis of this place-based collective identity, forged by time, space, interconnections, and a shared outlook, promoting an inclusive pluralist city-zenship model in Verona.

1   The Roots: A Historical Background of Secular Dissidence

The movement scene in Verona during the transformative years from the 1960s until the 1980s did not only include a rich panoply of actors from the extreme right, but also actors of the left with variegated ideological positions ranging from spontaneous movements inside squat houses to political parties. In addition to the incremental tension of the 'years of lead' (*anni di piombo*) that gave rise to a proliferation of political expressions, these formative years in the region of Veneto, including the city of Verona, involved an economic boom in which a traditionally agrarian society transformed into an industrial society with all the sweeping social and cultural changes that ensued. Notwithstanding the fact that Veronese politics witnessed the dominance of the centrist Christian Democracy, secular leftist groups managed to leave their imprint in local politics, especially in the form of 'counterculture' (Melucci, 1984; Della Porta & Diani, 2006) in the movement scene. Some of the leading activists of this period led an intellectual outlook that has been carried on by the movements active today in the Veronese socio-political scenery. Nevertheless, very little has been written about the social movements of the left in Verona during this period, as one respondent has put it, "[u]nfortunately, the militants of the time handed down almost nothing. Those that were radical or extraparliamentarian took a step back and assumed moderated positions if not a completely hostile stance to their revolutionary past." (Fieldnotes, 20 April 2021).

That being said, it is still worth mentioning those initiatives pertaining to this era that have undoubtedly paved the way not only for a local movement to flourish, but also conferred a space to such movement as its embodiment. In addition to the political parties of the period, including *Partito Comunista Italiano* (Italian Communist Party) and its youth branch *Federazione Giovanile Comunista Italiana* (Federation of Young Italian Communists) that were located in close proximity to the far-right *Fronte della Gioventù* in the historical center, there were also grassroots initiatives of social collectives led by progressive intellectuals, the social experiment of community schools, and squat houses hosting 'non-belonging' subjects (interview with P.N., 5 February 2021). Among these groups were *Circolo Operaio della Zai* (Worker's Club of the Industrial Zone), *Autonomia Operaia* (Worker's Autonomy) with their office in *via Cantarane* of Veronetta, followed by *Avanguardia Operaia* (Worker's Vanguard) focusing on the issue of housing in the 1970s and the systematic expulsion of the working-class from parts of the historical center to renew crumbling old houses, especially in the neighborhood of Veronetta, leading to the occupation of *Case Mazzi* in 1975 with around 170 families (Conti, 2017).

Among the nodal points of this leftist dissent were also *Centro Peruzzi* (Peruzzi Center) and later *Centro di Informazione* (Information Center) of Walter Peruzzi located in *via Santa Chiara* of Veronetta, the northern part close to Adige, which sought to create a secular dissident opinion in Verona. These social centers which had strong ties with trade unions managed to collect books and journals belonging to a line of counterculture very difficult to find for a period of ten years.[1] They gave form to a local 'restless intelligentsia' and their alternative culture in Verona, including intellectuals, artists, as well as students and workers who were following their works and ideological outlook (Canteri, 1991). This experience also opened room to the experiment of 'community schools' for adults in Verona between 1964 and 1974, where activists and teachers part of the new left would offer voluntary education to more than 800 workers and farmers from 16 to 45 years of age who lacked a secondary school diploma. Born from a group of Catholic student-workers movement in Milano, this cultural experiment found religious as well as secular manifestations in Verona, leading to 29 schools in the center as well as the province of the city (Lona & Olivieri, 2012).

Nonetheless, the dynamism of the left in those years came to a sudden halt with the kidnapping of a high-ranking American general called James Lee Dozier by the local branch of *Brigate Rosse* in 1981, who was working at the NATO base where the university campus stands today in Veronetta. The subsequent militarization of the city following this event, with widespread arrests of leftist militants, constant surveillance, and controls in every corner, managed to silence the panoply of left movements in the 1980s, thereby freeing the social space for neofascist and neo-Nazi groups to take advantage of extant discontent, as we saw in the previous chapter. According to a prominent

---

1   For more information on Walter Peruzzi, see: https://www.larena.it/argomenti/cultura/wal ter-peruzzi-il-sindacalista-che-cre%C3%B2-le-scuole-popolari-1.3084364?refresh_ce.

activist: "There was an exodus of alternative Veronesi after Dozier. One part went to South America, one part to India, and a small part remained here." (Interview with P.N., 5 February 2021). As a result, following the dynamism of the 1960s and the 1970s, the movement scene of the left experienced a large gap in the 1980s. This only changed with new social and cultural initiatives in the mid-1990s, acquiring new life especially with the first waves of immigration arriving in Verona. Another major influence that devastated the alternative subculture scene and the continuity of progressive movements was the impact of heroin dependency that took over the whole Italian peninsula, having an even heavier hold on Verona as a city located at important crossroads, leading to the city being referred to as the 'Bangkok' of Italy. Drug dealers and heroin addicts became part of daily life with a high visibility in the heart of the historical center from *Piazza Erbe* to *Piazza dei Signori*: "When I was little, towards the end of the '70s, the historical center was full of heroin addicts, which lasted until the end of the '80s. Later, they were evicted from the center, but until then you would see these guys, their faces totally wasted, asking for 100 lire. It was one of the first memories I had as a 5-year-old." (Interview with E.T., 19 April 2019). The grip of addiction also took over political movements that were operating in the same part of the city during this period: "In that period there was this great mess between heroin addicts, anarchists, then the fascists also arrived … it was a huge mess." (Interview with P.N., 5 Feb. 2021).

That being said, one figure that sought to carry on the legacy of activism of the past to the present was the late Giorgio Bertani, referred to as 'the rebel publisher', whose death during my fieldwork in 2019 shook the movement deeply. Bertani belongs to the tradition of radical left of the 1960s, and obtained national fame when he was part of a group of four socialists from Verona and four anarchists from Milano who kidnapped the Spanish vice-consulate on the 8th of September 1962 to request the liberation of anti-Franco dissidents condemned to death. For years, struggling in the frontlines of leftist movements in the difficult setting of Verona, Bertani's legacy in the city was predominantly his intellectual work as an independent publisher, among the first in Italy to publish books of Dario Fo, Felix Guattari, Gilles Deleuze, and Jacques Derrida, who at the time did not enjoy their current fame. He also collaborated and published books on feminism together with the feminist circle of Verona called *Diotima*, involving academics at the university who have had a substantial impact on the wave of difference feminism worldwide. Old and new movements of the left in Verona have studied his books and shaped their political outlook with the counterculture that he offered in a city that was governed by reactionary forms of belonging. Part of his collection of books and journals was passed on to associations of the antibodies with whom he stood alongside and shared neighborly relations in his dear neighborhood of Veronetta (Tibaldi, 2020). His outlook on activism is perfectly summed up in his following statement: "In Verona, and in the world, against the inhuman wind that blows, we will know how to respond with intelligence, culture, and a creative and joyous rebellion." (Giorgio Bertani quoted in Tibaldi, 2020). Against this historical backdrop, the following section will offer an analysis of the indispensable components that make up the movement of antibodies, their united fight, their shared memory, and their collective identity tied to the space from which it was born and continues to flourish.

2   The Constitutive Elements of the Antibodies of Hate

2.1   *La* Sobilla *and the Heritage of Collective Memory*
Following a long period of 'depoliticization' of the left in Verona for much of the 1980s and the early 1990s, the new generation was left without a point of reference or a guide to carry out their activism: "We were born in an impoverished environment, without any local points of reference. We had to invent ourselves." (Interview with M.L. during fieldwork, 18 August 2021). As such, one of the first constituents of the antibodies of hate born out of the punk and metal subculture in Verona came into existence as an anarchist cultural center in 1991 named *Centro Culturale di Documentazione Anarchica Pecora Nera* (Black Sheep Anarchist Cultural Center of Documentation). The legacy of this group continued in different spaces of Veronetta inside different associations through the library of *Biblioteca Giovanni Domaschi*, named after the Veronese antifascist anarchist in the local resistance against the RSI and Nazi occupation between 1943 and 1945. Giovanni Domaschi was the son of a farmer from Poiano, living on the verge of famine in his childhood, who started working at the age of ten in the industrial area near Porta Vescovo train station. He was an anarchist and an anti-militarist who opposed World War I, ultimately founding *Gruppo Operaio Anarchico* (Anarchist Workers' Group) in 1920 in the neighborhood of Veronetta, considered one of the first antifascist establishments in the city (Domaschi, 2007). Such reverence for the personality of Domaschi has thus come to characterize the particular strand within the larger movement.

This tribute highlights the centrality of Veronese local resistance as a building block of the 'alternative' place-based identity proposed by this network of actors, a collective memory that defines collective action (Melucci, 1980; Johnston et al., 1994; Della Porta & Diani, 2006). Pecora Nera was the first counterspace in the Veronese terrain to harbor non-belonging subjects (Bacchetta et al., 2019) and to fight against exclusionary practices in the city, employing insurgent urban citizenship (Holston & Appadurai, 1996) in negotiating the frontiers of belonging. Not only serving as an extensive archive of the history of local resistance and dissident groups with counterdiscourses (Fraser, 1990), this space was a school of activism that produced its own subjects. As put by a local activist from another collective: "This was a school to us when we were teenagers. This is the nest from which we originate" (Interview with S.P., 10 June 2019). This non-conformist way of being Veronese was thus anchored not only in a common past, but also in everyday experiences in lived spaces.

Notwithstanding the lack of experience at the time of its young founders, they worked to give life to this space first and foremost through the realization of an underground cultural center: "We were organizing meetings, events, presentations, and concerts in the space we had underground, which served to finance ourselves as well as other initiatives which we felt close to, such as the construction workers in Sardinia who were on strike." (Interview with M.L., 15 July 2019). The collective did not only focus on issues present in Verona, but sought to create an outward-looking space by offering solidarity to causes in other parts of Italy and beyond from the onset, echoing Massey's (2004) 'responsibility of distant others'. Hence, the banner hanging in the middle of their office read, "Our country is the whole world, our law is freedom." (From the photo archive of CCDA Pecora Nera). One of its primary focuses was anti-militarism in support of political conscientious objectors, since the military tribunal undertaking these trials was located in Verona: "Their difficulty was to make their gesture of protest be heard. If you fail to give visibility to your protest, its reach diminishes. So, we tried to be the megaphone for guys who decided to take this radical action." (Ibid.) Thus, this 'counterspace' (Mitchell, 2000) in a highly militarized city sought to realize a center that accommodated non-conforming subjects and helped amplify their voices beyond the locality.

Pecora Nera was located in the abandoned rooms under the roof referred to as 'pensilina' where once stood the bus stop in Piazza Isolo of Veronetta, and drew other antagonistic subjects to its orbit who came to occupy neighboring empty rooms. This improvised collective socio-spatial reality formed the first precursors of the movement network, perfectly situated side by side in their little but influential space, with a red flag waving on top to mark it as a leftist island: "There was this rooftop, and underneath it, rooms that were relatively large. Some had underground spaces too. On one side, there was Pecora Nera which was about to run its course and coming to the end of its days, on the other side the rebel publisher Giorgio Bertani, and next to them we occupied another room as Kollettivo Porkospino and we also hosted migrants who slept under the rooftop." (Interview with A.A., 5 August 2019). An experienced local activist reminisces about this period when the movement was positioned literally 'under the same roof', in a part of Veronetta close to everyday hang-out hubs of the movement, where antibodies continue to socialize today: "This was at the heart of Veronetta, we had on our side *Osteria ai Preti* [local tavern], another important point of reference with a history of its own. There were all the formations located one next to another under a shelter in Piazza Isolo." (Interview with S.P., 10 June 2019). The movement started to reach out to homeless migrants and help them find shelter within the *pensilina* experience, which involved at the time migrants arriving primarily from Eastern Europe and the Balkans. During this period, the city administration under Sironi was undertaking a top-down maintenance of 'urban décor', rendering cityspace sanitized and aesthetic (Mitchell, 2000), free of 'non-decorative' elements (Mazzei, 2018), with the service of the local cleaning agency already occupied by notorious figures from the far-right: "They would pass at 5 am in the morning, they took away the cardboards they slept on, and water down the whole place so that they could not place them back on the floor." (Interview with A.A., 5 August 2019).

As an antagonistic space filled with non-belonging subjects, Pecora Nera was eventually evacuated by the city administration: "This was an important moment in our struggle. For the first time we put our bodies against an abuse because they wanted to demolish it." (Interview with S.P., 10 June 2019).

FIGURE 22   Image of 'pensilina', the old bus stop
PHOTOGRAPH: ARCHIVE OF CCDA PECORA NERA

Accommodating 'unwanted' subjects of the city (Wacquant, 2016), Pecora Nera caught the attention of the city councilor Romano Bertozzo from Lega Nord in 1997, who proposed to revalorize San Pietro Castel by "rehabilitating marginal realities of the city" including "the Roma community, Albanians, seasonal migrants, gays, and *members of Pecora Nera.*" (L'Arena, Cronaca 20 July 1997, *emphasis added*) As such, social groups who were deemed 'out of place' (Merrill, 2014; Saitta, 2015) in the 1990s included sexual minorities, migrants coming to work from the south as well as those coming from Eastern Europe, and finally, radical left groups who were denied the tolerance extended to far-right movements commanding the city.

As Pecora Nera was emptied out, it left a large space which was later taken on by a growing number of homeless migrants as a shelter, coming from different countries of origin. Unfortunately, the *pensilina* experience came to a bitter end when a Polish migrant named Cesar Karabowski lost his life due to a fire that took place in the underground room of Pecora Nera at night, where he was taking refuge: "It shook us all obviously. There were some of us who were with him during the same day. We went to his funeral; it was an emotionally heavy episode." (Interview with A.A., 5 August 2019) The event marked a turning point for the shared memory of the movement, leading up to the realization of the first anti-racist umbrella network *Coordinamento Cesar K.* in September 2000, with myriad local actors cooperating to fight racism and to address the needs of newcomers in the city. Concurrently, following the demolition of the *pensilina* experience, Pecora Nera had largely dissolved, leaving but two volunteers who took on the responsibility of maintaining the anarchist library with a great number of books. Since such conservation required a large space, they took refuge for ten years in the old office of *Circolo Pink* in *via Scrimiari,* the leading LGBTQ+ association of Verona, which in the early 2000s became a new sanctuary for 'non-belonging' subjects (Bacchetta et al., 2019). As put by the dissident librarians: "After 5–6 years of changing places, we land inside Circolo Pink which was a period of political learning for all of us and of cross-pollination for many groups." (Interview with M.L., 15 July 2019).

Following these two milestone experiences of space-sharing with other actors, the group of *Biblioteca Domaschi* took on their own path and inaugurated *La Sobilla* in a rented space on the 15th of November 2014 at the eastmost border of Veronetta next to the city walls that function as physical borders of the neighborhood. La Sobilla was established strictly as a cultural association and a container of various groups and ex-activists who are no longer affiliated with any collective, offering a new home to *Biblioteca Domaschi.* Still functioning today, the activities of this group involve book presentations and public debates, photography and art exhibitions, talks with journal editors, and movie nights. The group is interested in connecting with others who work on the global themes of migration, feminism/LGBTQ+ activism, and a critical reflection on anti-capitalism, aiming to stimulate a counterculture in the city. Contrary to the politically charged activism of the Pecora Nera period, the priority today lies in remaining a strictly cultural association, whilst being able to host diverse political outlooks (Ibid.). As noted by one of its younger members: "It is like an island in the context of Verona, where political and social themes that regard this territory are discussed weekly, also in a radical manner, but never in a sectarian or identitarian manner." (Interview with O.P., 8 June, 2019).

Functioning primarily as a 'subaltern counterpublic' (Fraser, 1990), La Sobilla also became the birthplace of *Non Una di Meno Verona* (Not One Woman Less, hereafter NUDM) in 2017, the local branch of a transnational feminist movement which has in recent years became an active element re-invigorating the movement. La Sobilla has also been collaborating regularly with other groups, such as the activists of the Sports Camp *Gigi Piccoli* (ex-members of *La Chimica*), with whom they have had the experience of sharing physical space both in *pensilina* and Circolo Pink's old office in via Scrimiari. Another such cultural association that prioritizes the issue of social inclusion is *Veronetta 129*, which co-hosts certain events together with La Sobilla: "The big collaborations are narrowed down to associations close to us, close in identity and close geographically. Firstly, we collaborate with Gigi Piccoli since La Sobilla 'goes to the field' [*va in campo*] during the summer, and they come to us during the winter as they do not have an indoor space. Another one is Veronetta 129 with whom we share the synergy of organizing the Middle East Cinema festival *Mediorizzonti*." (Interview with M.L., 15 July 2019). From this testimony, one can observe the importance attributed to physical proximity in the movement space of Veronetta among different actors that shape their collective identity, as well as the shared outlook premised on a united struggle.

Among the leading events that La Sobilla organizes today are *Brutti Caratteri* which is a book exhibition of independent publishers and radical writers, and the famous *l'Asta* (The Auction) that is an auction sale of 'unpresentables' full of humorous ironies. This latter is a collaboration with the Sports Camp *Gigi Piccoli,* an event that works to strengthen social ties, bring together dissenting voices, and reinforce socialization among the antibodies and their followers through the lightness of humor. First starting in the 1990s with Pecora Nera, it has become a trademark 'ritual' (Della Porta & Diani, 2006) defining the collective identity of the movement, filled with inside jokes about ultra-Catholic groups, the far-right and their symbolisms, presented as artifacts to be auctioned: "It's a particular auction where you hear very funny proposals.

FIGURE 23   A book presentation at La Sobilla
PHOTOGRAPH: IPEK DEMIRSU

It's a moment that many look forward to. It seems like pure entertainment, but instead, it's a bridge between individuals who have a sense of irony. It helps us to live together in this setting." (Interview with A.V., 23 April 2019).

2.2   The Evolution of a Social Center 'Alla Veronese': La Chimica Before and After

As noted by a prominent activist, the experience of a real social center with the meaning attributed to the term in the Italian context came about with the realization of *La Chimica* (interview with M.L., 15 July 2019). Yet, before going there, its inception must also be analyzed starting with the first experimentation of squatting in the *San Pancrazio* area. This project started off with an initial group in San Pancrazio by occupying houses that used to belong to the bishop of Verona, one of which was inhabited by three anarchist conscientious objectors to military service, together with members of what was going to be *La Chimica* in the years to come. In 1997, the next move was to squat an old Austrian fort in the province of *Santa Lucia*, called *Forte 115*, where migrants were also taking refuge: "Since our initial squatting experiences, we always had a contact with migrants." (Interview with A.A., 5 August 2019). The occupation of Forte 115 was interrupted by officials several times as the activists went on to reoccupy the same space: "We re-entered on 25th of April [Italian Liberation Day] and organized a 3-day festival with punk groups coming even from abroad, from Germany and other countries." (Ibid.) As such, from its onset the group was establishing ties with both newcomers in their city as well as reaching beyond borders to connect with like-minded social actors sharing similar global claims to justice on a transnational scale, thereby building 'networks of solidarity' (Leitner et al., 2008).

Following these formative experiences of activism, this initial group created *Kollettivo Porkospino* (Collective Porcupine) and took part in the *pensilina* experience with the space they occupied next to Pecora Nera, named *l'Isola* (Island). The collective had a punk porcupine mascot to convey the outlook of the group designed by a cartoonist: "It seems like a little animal, but it's capable of pulling out its spikes and stinging, and this was the concept of 'Porkospino'. We had this porcupine with the guitar, dressed like a punk with All Star shoes. He was a good fella; he did many good things." (Ibid.) The porcupine represented the collective identity of the group, characterized by the style of outfit and music taste that define membership and reinforce solidarity within the movement (Della Porta & Diani, 2006), which despite being small and innocuous, was able to 'sting' in a city governed by a nativist localism. Formed by a mixture of younger generation of activists, who came from the aforementioned experience of squatting, alongside an older generation from the 1970s and the 1980s, the birth of *Porkospino* carried the hope of bringing the Italian 'social center' experience in the mid-sized city of Verona, compared to the likes of *Leoncavallo* in the metropolitan city of Milan: "In that period the concept of 'social center' was considered a panacea of all ills. There was a great attention placed to establishing a real social center also here in Verona." (Interview with A.A., 5 August 2019).

Hence, the initiative of Kollettivo Porkospino which was born out of a need and desire to realize outward-looking spaces joined the assembly of actors in the *pensilina* of Piazza Isolo, the part of Veronetta closest to the touristic center and thus under a constant diffident gaze. During this period, the piazza was depicted as a 'no-go zone' (Wacquant, 2016) par excellence by the local journal *L'Arena*, mostly due to homeless migrants who took refuge around the *pensilina*. Following the traumatizing death of Cesar Karabowski at the old office of Pecora Nera, the activists of Kollettivo Porkospino sought to rechannel their collective action, which was made possible with the discovery of a new space they could transform, thereby giving life to *La Chimica* as the social center that brought national and international attention to Verona.

FIGURE 24   The portrayal of Piazza Isolo as
             abandoned by 'Veronesi' due
             to the undesirable presence of
             'extracomunitari' disturbing the locals
             and the urban décor (*L'Arena*, 10
             September 1999, original article).

Coming from the rooted tradition of social centers in Italy, defined by self-management (*autogestione*) and self-financing (*autofinanziamento*) on squatted edifices as venues of alternative social, cultural, political exchanges where the Italian no-global network found expression (Becucci, 2003; Mudu, 2004), *La Chimica* came to life with the occupation of a massive abandoned chemical factory. Located along the Adige River to the northwest of the city center, the factory used to belong to an American company called The Quaker: "It was an extremely rich social center, full of initiatives and activities. It not only had a recognition at the level of Verona, but at least at a national level if not international." (Interview with S.P. & F.P., 10 June 2019). As the mandate of Mayor Sironi came to an end, for the first time the center-left came to power with the leadership of the new mayor Paolo Zanotto in 2001, and the activists thought this was the right moment to take action: "It was a magical period for Verona, we had a moment of lucidity and we realized, it was now or never." (Ibid.) Despite the dominance of the social centers linked to the *Disobbedienti del Nord-Est* (Disobedients of North-East) no-global movement in the Veneto region (Becucci, 2003), *La Chimica* insisted on remaining an independent local reality which led to the schism establishing Café Metropolis later on (explained under Paratodos).

The group completely renovated this abandoned place, which included cleaning the asbestos that was falling off from its ceiling. Similar to their previous experiences of squatting, they shared this space with migrants from

Tunisia and Morocco who were already living inside when the latter arrived, continuing their activities in co-existence. In no time, this old chemical factory turned into an outflow of alternative youth culture, full of social, cultural, and political activities that stimulated new ideas and new outlooks in a city that chose to cling strongly onto a romanticized past and unchanging traditions. One of the most important activities undertaken in this period was the organization of the enogastronomic festival *Terra e Libertà/Critical Wine* (Land and Liberty/Critical Wine), counterposed to the most important commercial wine festival in Italy taking place in Verona every year, named *Vinitaly*.

Starting off with the efforts of the internationally famed wine critic and anarchist Luigi Veronelli, who was searching for a space where they could host a wine festival on organic wine with small local producers as opposed to the big producers participating in *Vinitaly*. La Chimica pitched in and offered their space. Thus, the group undertook the organization of the first national Critical Wine in Verona in April 2003, at the same time as Vinitaly that was taking place in another part of the city. The event revolved around ecological themes of production and consumption, slow food, reflections on the use of land, and 'going back' to the land as radical politics, alongside other political issues such as opposing war, supporting migrants, and negating local identitarian belongings.[2] The attention placed on ecological themes was undergirded with other transversal themes of belonging, of one's attachment to the land, and a bottom-up reformulation of citizenship. A way of reclaiming the land that did not rely on localism or a short-sighted nostalgia was being developed in these events full of gusto, one that invoked an environmental sensibility in valorizing the local against particularistic localisms: "The myth of the origins, the attachment to the roots ... already produced their monsters of whining nostalgia and of nationalistic hate. The planetary sensibility loves the particulars but negates every particularism ... values the local because it can smell the odor of decay in every localism."[3]

The first event enjoyed a landslide success with over 3000 visitors, owing to a great number of national and international producers who sent their products for tasting: "It was something massive! There were even Japanese producers who were sending their products to us thanks to the invitations of Veronelli, who was a giant in this field. They wouldn't go to Vinitaly, they would

2 *Wine News Italy*, "TERRA E LIBERTA'/CRITICAL WINE" N. 4, 08 March 2006, Verona (author's translation). Available at: https://winenews.it/it/terra-e-liberta-critical-wine-n-4-a-verona-dal-7-al_292445.

3 "Che cos'è Terra e Libertà/Critical wine" (author's translation): http://www.lariocriticalwine.org/index.php?option=com_content&view=article&id=6&Itemid=15#6.

come to us!" (Interview with S.P. & F.P., 10 June 2019). After the first organiza-tion of Critical Wine in *La Chimica,* the event was hosted in different settings, including *Mag 47* of Brescia, *Forte Prenestino* of Rome, *Bulk* and *Leoncavallo* of Milan, *Ex-collocamento* of Torino, and many more.[4] The great success of Critical Wine in the mid-sized city of Verona, identified as the fortress of the far-right, had two outcomes: firstly, it meant defining oneself through the land but not possessive of it; and secondly, it challenged one of the most import-ant events of mass tourism in Verona and the monopoly of international big producers. This second impact meant Verona was not only to be known as the face of *Vinitaly* and its marketing of the city, but also the birthplace of Critical Wine by offering an alternative appreciation of enogastronomy that is trans-local in its approach, yet politically oriented and environmentally responsible. In short, the event offered a different representation of the city and reinter-preted the identity of Verona (Martin, 2003; Banini & Ilovan, 2021; Schwarz & Streule, 2022).

Unfortunately, the success of *La Chimica* social center did not last long, as the occupied ex-factory started to catch the attention of the city administra-tion and was eventually evicted, as a counterspace so evidently 'out of place' (Merrill, 2014) in the larger Veronese setting. The next phase for this group was in the neighborhood of *Borgo Venezia,* also known for the high number of migrant families, located to the east of Veronetta. Here, the group first occu-pied an old school in *via Del Capitel,* and later an abandoned prefabricated kindergarten in *Piazza Zagata* where they continued to undertake their activ-ities including Critical Wine as well as *Brutti Caratteri* in collaboration with Biblioteca Domaschi. This new location continued to radiate new ideas and alternative outlooks to the rest of the city and hosted influential figures such as Antonio Negri who came to give talks. With the arrival of Flavio Tosi as the mayor of Verona, this space was also evicted as was promised in his electoral campaign: "They demolished it to the ground as it was prefabricated. When Tosi arrived, he came with the bulldozers, and they waited inside with eggs to throw at them. Since then, a social center in the full meaning of the term doesn't exist in Verona." (Interview with E.T., 19 April 2019). Notwithstanding the eviction, the activists continued to organize weekly farmers' markets with local producers working on ecological production, slow food, and organic farming in the same piazza without the permission of the city admin-istration: "It was a way to say, we are still here. We will continue to do our

---

4 For more information on Critical Wine, see: http://www.arivista.org/riviste/Arivista/308 /18.htm.

thing even if we don't have the space anymore." (Interview with S.P. & F.P., 10 June 2019).

From 2007 until 2011, the group 'took refuge' in the large office of Circolo Pink in *via Scrimiari* of Veronetta, alongside Biblioteca Domaschi, and joined this stimulating experience of collaboration and physical co-existence, which shaped the outlook of the movement and consolidated their horizontal union in the shared principles of antifascism, anti-racism, and anti-sexism. Since 2012, the final destination of La Chimica has been a sports camp right outside the city walls marking the borders of Veronetta. After repetitive experiences of being criminalized and evicted by the city administration, on top of the long series of physical assaults they were subjected to by far-right groups, including, in one episode, an arson attempt at their center, the group started to be much more wary and lowkey in their new home. Hence, the *Sports Camp Gigi Piccoli* was born out of the same group that took on the management of this non-profit small sports camp with a football field and continued with their weekly farmers' market, operating under the name *Gruppo di Acquisto Sociale Piccoli* (Group of Social Purchasing Piccoli, hereafter GasP!). The new space also changed the name attributed to the same group of activists, which were since then referred to as La Chimica, thereafter being referred to as 'Gigi Piccoli' by other associations, with the spatiality of the sports camp coming to define the identity of the group.

More recently, the new space with the same group started to be involved in another reality that they had noticed in their vicinity, namely the operations of an emergency reception center located near the sports camp with an inpour of asylum seekers and refugees following the humanitarian crisis of 2015. They had noticed that a number of individuals who arrived in Lampedusa were sent off directly to this CAS in Verona near their sports camp: "We learned that there was this CAS with around 100 people, who had arrived in Lampedusa or Siracusa, immediately put in buses and sent to various reception centers in Italy. So, what do we do for these guys? The only thing we could do was this sports camp, if they wanted, they could come here to play football. We opened the doors. It also worked as a uniting factor for them to organize and discuss their situation and needs." (Interview with S.P. & F.P., 10 June 2019).

The sports camp, despite being located outside the city walls marking Veronetta, is indicated in the cognitive map of the respondents as part of the neighborhood due to the social activities and relations it authors, as an outward-looking space promoting greater sociability and intercultural exchange. The activists of Gigi Piccoli express how the arrival of these new-comers gave new meaning to collective action, since they had remained very few in number over the years. This new presence gave them a motive to carry

FIGURE 25   First GasP! market in Gigi Piccoli after the lockdown in 2020
              PHOTOGRAPH: IPEK DEMIRSU

on and keep the sports camp open. As a social space pioneering everyday acts of conviviality and community building (Bacchetta et al., 2019; Neal et al., 2019; Demirsu, 2023a), Gigi Piccoli was described by M.R., a refugee living in Verona for the sustained contact among migrants and non-migrants, sparking a feeling of homeliness and emotional attachment:

> When I first arrived three years ago, I only knew this place. We played [football] and music, because here they have lots of gatherings. We cook African food as well as Italian food. I also like playing with the kids that are around. They help me learn the language. You know, kids talk to you even when you don't want to listen [laughter]. And you need to respond. I like this.
>
> Interview with M.R., 13 May 2019

Today, Gigi Piccoli stands as a core element of the antibodies, continuing the legacy of La Chimica in conveying global themes of justice, cultivating interconnections, and offering new dynamism to the network that operates in

FIGURE 26   Gigi Piccoli, Spring of 2019
PHOTOGRAPH BY S.P. FOR PHOTO-ELICITATION

the radius of Veronetta who defy singular territorial identities (Massey, 1994; Banini, 2011). In addition to providing an open venue for their farmers' market and a football court bringing migrants and non-migrants to engage in sports, this space also provides 'a garden' to the larger movement network, who can organize their summer events here, including weddings of same-sex couples, thereby becoming a significant 'nodal point' (Moore, 2007) for the movement in a short period of time. For newcomers, taking part in the sociocultural life that the network of associations can mean forging new friendships and becoming part of community relations (Nicholls, 2008), as well as providing the counterspace for their own political mobilization. Such blossoming of new connections inevitably transforms the lived space, and as a consequence, shapes the outlook of those co-inhabiting it (Massey, 1994; Aru, 2015).

This process does not involve a simplistic and unidirectional 'integration' project, but a sociocultural cross-pollination that gives way to a new reality that is co-written by migrant and non-migrant individuals alike (Demirsu, 2023a). Hence, these local initiatives help foster alternative ways of being 'Veronesi' based on fluid and porous identities that impact the character of the neighborhood radiating outwards to the rest of the city in cultivating an inclusive pluralist city-zenship (Massey, 1994; Nicholls, 2008; Banini, 2017). This grassroots creation of a 'humane public sphere' (Boym, 2001) is clearly captured in the narration of the same rapport with kids from the point of view of a local Veronese activist:

> When they come here and see our friends with little kids, they don't wanna leave. There is a willingness and need to spend time with little ones because, most probably, they come from a world where they were surrounded by children. They miss this here in Verona. This is human-ity. The kids here live in a provincial area of Verona, where normally at school their classmates would yell 'he is black!' when they see an African. But this boy will never do so. It's surely an education for them as well.
>
> Interview with S.P., 10 June 2019

2.3   *Circolo Pink and the Protracted Struggle for City-zenship of Sexual Minorities*

Circolo Pink is a local association working on the rights of LGBTQ+ individuals in a city notoriously negating the recognition of sexual minorities. The group dates back to *ArciGay Verona*, which was founded in the first half of the 1980s as the local branch of the national *Assocazione LGBT* Italiana* (Italian LGBT* Association). The 1980s and 1990s in Verona were marked by a very belliger-ent outlook against sexual minorities by the alliance of ultra-Catholic groups, the populist right, and far-right movements, including threats and physical violence alongside consecutive motions passed in the city administration refusing to provide equal treatment of sexual minorities.[5] Congruently, every-day urban life was also overwhelmed by 'heteronormative scripts of appropri-ateness' (Brown & Browne, 2016) in bottom-up acts of boundary-drawing. As noted by a leading activist, in Verona, the boundaries of belonging were drawn first and foremost to keep sexual minorities 'outside' as unwanted subjects, preceding sovereignist ethnonational sentiments of anti-immigration: "At the time, although there already was the issue of immigration, it was not as instrumentalized. During that period, there was a lot of homophobia here in Verona; for instance, when there was Gay Pride, I remember there were so many insults by the people passing by ... Unfortunately, it's a provincial city that reacts in this way." (Interview with A.A., 5 August 2019). Not only in the everyday life of the city, but also within the city administration, what is referred to as 'anti-gender' political rhetoric (Garbagnoli & Prearo, 2018; Trappolin, 2022), became commonplace, reaching the extent of a councilor

---

5   For more information, see: https://www.malorarivista.it/2020/07/16/una-storia-di-mozi oni-omofobe.

from Lega Nord suggesting on one occasion the castration of gay men on 22nd of June 1995.[6] Pursuing their existence in this hostile setting and being refused equal city-zenship, the first move to respond to the unheard needs of sexual minorities came from Arcigay Verona in the form of a support hotline *Telefono Amico Gay e Lesbico* to help individuals that faced problems due to their sexual identity. In the context of the 1980s with the AIDS crisis, the group also worked on the frontlines in a campaign providing information and helping the prevention of HIV, with the possibility of having an anonymous HIV test at the office of Arcigay Verona.

In 1995, Verona became the first and only European city to pass a motion (no. 336)[7] negating the *A3-0028/94 European Parliament resolution*, which recommended member states to implement equal rights for individuals of different sexual orientations and the abolishment of legal provisions that criminalize or discriminate against homosexual or lesbian individuals.[8] The EU resolution foreseeing equal treatment was rejected by a majority in the Verona city council on the grounds that it could invoke "negative effects on the psychological development of young members of society, and the corrosive impact of 'promiscuity' that can be present in homosexual or heterosexual families, and could lead to the demise of one of the fundamental tenets of the family order, namely the stable union between a man and a woman."[9] In response, Arcigay Verona launched the Committee *Alziamo La Testa* (Let's Lift Our Heads) in 'acting out' (Işın, 2009) their negated citizenship: "The 1995 motion changed the lives of many individuals, including ours, because it made us very visible all of a sudden and made us take careful decisions on the local and the national level." (Interview with C.Z., 10 February 2021). The first move was to block the traffic in front of the municipality building in order to generate a public debate on the decision and to raise awareness in public opinion. Subsequently, on 30 September 1995, a large rally with over 5000 participants was organized, hosting other national LGBTQ+ movements in Verona.

The Municipality had institutionalized a favorable position toward 'profamily' groups composed of ultra-Catholic associations the same year that the

---

6   For more information, see: http://www.deportati.it/aned/le-sezioni/verona/verona-in-consiglio-comunale-saluto-romano.

7   Original document of the motion can be found at: http://www.circolopink.it/wp-content/uploads/2015/01/Mozione-336.pdf.

8   European Parliament (1994) Report of the Committee on Civil Liberties and Internal Affairs on equal rights for homosexuals and lesbians in the EC, A3-0028/94 (26 January 1994), [Accessed on 23 September 2020] Available at: http://aei.pitt.edu/49350/1/A10612.pdf.

9   Consiglio Comunale di Verona (1995) Mozione no. 336, Unità Affari Consiglio (14 July 1995), Verona. Translated from the original Italian text.

Il Consiglio Comunale di Verona dibatte un documento di Elmo Padovani, che valorizza la famiglia come unione naturale fra uomo e donna e la maternità. Le sinistre, le associazioni gay e i laicisti, contrari, dichiarano guerra ai cattolici e alla maggioranza dei veronesi.

CI SONO DUE VERONE: QUALE DELLE DUE È LA VOSTRA?

C'è la Verona dei pederasti che, applaudendo ai cosiddetti "matrimoni" omosessuali e alle adozioni di bimbi da parte dei pedofili, vuole legalizzare il vizio e preparare l'immoralità per le generazioni future. Per questa Verona del vizio sono schierate, ovviamente, tutte le sinistre, certi catto-progressisti, i laicisti e, stando alla stampa, perfino due consiglieri di Forza Italia e uno della Lega Nord, nonché i mezzi di controllo sociale (giornali, TV ecc.) infeudati ai progressisti.

C'è poi la Verona tradizionale e civile, che si riconosce nel matrimonio mono-gamico e nella famiglia come unione naturale fra un uomo e una donna e che vuole per sé e per i propri figli una società moralmente più sana. Per questa Verona sono: la Lega Nord, Alleanza Nazionale, il Centro Cristiano Democratico, la stragrande maggioranza dei consiglieri di Forza Italia, il Patto Segni e buona parte del Partito Popolare (se saprà superare le ambiguità del suo capogruppo.)

I VERONESI DICONO SÌ AL DOCUMENTO PADOVANI

Perchè non riconosce come vero matrimonio il concubinato omosessuale e rigetta l'immorale risoluzione del Parlamento Europeo (condannata anche da Giovanni Paolo II) che vorrebbe legalizzarlo.

Perchè valorizza l'istituto del matrimonio, la salute e il ruolo materno della donna, nonché il suo diritto inalienabile di potersi dedicare pienamente alla famiglia e ai figli.

Perchè favorisce il ritorno a quei principi morali diffusi, naturali e cristiani, che, soli, possono arrestare il degrado della famiglia e della società, condannando l'aborto e il divorzio (suscitando invece riserve l'educazione sessuale nelle scuole e alcune tracce di egualitarismo familiare che si ritrovano nel documento).

Perchè sostiene, anche economicamente, i coniugi che si trovano in ristrettezze o in difficoltà.

L'empia parodia della Crocifissione, durante una sfilata gay a San Francisco (USA). Sono queste le "conquiste civili" che ci preparano i progressisti?

Stampato in proprio - FAMIGLIA E CIVILTÀ - *Associazione per la difesa della famiglia e della Civiltà Cristiana* - Casella Postale MBE n. 148 - Via C. Cattaneo, 24/C - 37121 VERONA - Tel. 045/6095306 - Verona, 1° giugno 1995

FIGURE 27   The original pamphlet (1995) by the ultra-Catholic group Famiglia e Civiltà, claiming there are two different cities of Verona: Verona of 'pederasts' who believe in same-sex marriage and the traditional and civil Verona.
PHOTOGRAPH: CIRCOLO PINK ARCHIVE, VERONA

notorious motion was passed, in tandem with two other motions (motions no. 383 and no.393 defining family solely as a union between a man and a woman) to instill the traditional Catholic conception of family as the only viable model. Such an overt stance filled the LGBTQ+ activists with a burning sensation of injustice:

> At that point, our struggle was born to put the term 'family' into discussion. It's not 'family' but 'families'. We departed from this conception and initiated a legal battle with ultra-Catholic groups and city councilors that were involved. These battles had one goal, and that goal was to get justice, to become a legal subject as homosexuals, so that one could not attack a person because they are gay, because that gay person was now part of a legal subjectivity. This would mean that they could not claim that homosexual people cannot have equal rights as them.
>
> Interview with C.Z., 10 February 2021

Seeing that their mobilization was not powerful enough on the local level to push the city administration to change their stance, the group first reached out to national authorities in Rome and then the supranational body of the European Parliament to make their voices heard. Only 27 years later, with the arrival of a progressive alliance in the local administration following the 2022 elections that the abovementioned motions were revoked,[10] owing to the collaboration of the new progressive mandate with LGBTQ+ activists in what constituted a historical victory for the antibodies. This was in stark contrast to the previous center-left administration under Paolo Zanotto, who refrained from any type of involvement with LGBTQ+ associations.

After *Alziamo La Testa*, LGBTQ+ activists continued their struggle for recognition by the local authorities under a new slogan, *Cittadinanza Va Scritta* (Citizenship Is To Be Written), organizing a rally with the attendance of other "democratic and antifascist groups" nationwide.[11] By then, Circolo Pink was already established as an independent association and moved to the neighborhood of Veronetta in 1996. Due to internal schisms within Arcigay Verona, Circolo Pink set off a new movement, one that was much more politically engaged, more inclusive of other minority groups and their causes, as well as more openly confrontational with the municipality. As a matter of fact, among

---

10   The official decision can be found at the Municipality of Verona website: https://ufficiostampa.comune.verona.it/nqcontent.cfm?a_id=9561&id_com=29840.

11   Circolo Pink, "Un Percorso di Cittadinanza," (8 February 1994–8 February 2002), 2002 Verona. From the private archive of Circolo Pink.

the main tenets of the group, held to equal importance as LGBTQ+ rights, were antifascism and anti-racism in confronting far-right groups and their more radical neofascist variants in Verona cityspace. This outlook, which shares the indivisible principles of the antibodies that they have helped establish, has eventually differentiated Circolo Pink from Arcigay Verona.

One of the first moves of Circolo Pink as a new association in the Veronese political landscape was to mobilize for the recognition of the deportation of gay, lesbian, and transexuals to concentration camps during WWII: "Previously, official ceremonies of 25th of April would focus exclusively on the death of 6 million Jews. As Pink, we went to talk with the officials for the recognition of our subjectivity, because clearly, if you are not being referred to as a subject, you do not exist." (Interview with C.Z., 10 February 2021). In 2001, Circolo Pink was granted representation at the 25th of April Liberation Day ceremonies, alongside more traditional associations functioning on a national level, such as ANED (*L'Associazione Nazionale Ex Deportati nei Campi Nazisti*, National Association of ex-Deportees in Nazi Camps) and ANPI (*L'Associazione Nazionale Partigiani d'Italia*, National Association of Partisans of Italy). This victory established a major milestone in their 'Course to Citizenship' (*Un Percorso di Cittadinanza*),[12] bringing due recognition as a legal subject instead of private individuals, and dignity to the sexual minorities who had lost their lives in concentration camps. The indivisibility of antifascism and anti-racism alongside their LGBTQ+ mobilization today takes the form of becoming a civil party alongside ANED to the court case investigating the celebration of the football team Hellas in 2017, during which the leader of the football fan group is recorded praising Adolf Hitler and thanking him for making the celebration possible.[13]

In the early 2000s, Circolo Pink moved its office to *via Scrimiari* in Veronetta, turning it into the second most decisive period for the collective identity of the antibodies after the *penisilina* experience, becoming a school of mobilization and co-existence on every possible level. Other central elements of the antibodies took refuge inside the Circolo Pink office in *via Scrimiari* and shared this physical space for individual and collective projects, thereby leaving an imprint on the collective memory and shaping the direction of collective action. In the absence of a space to host a large number of books, Biblioteca Domaschi harbored here for eight years, and so did La Chimica for four years following their eviction. The assemblage continued to enlarge with the arrival

---

12   Circolo Pink, "Un Percorso di Cittadinanza," (8 February 1994–8 February 2002), 2002 Verona. From the private archive of Circolo Pink.

13   For more information, see: https://www.veronasera.it/cronaca/processo-castellini-cori -balotelli-hitler-27-gennaio-2021.html.

FIGURE 28   Circolo Pink office in *via Scrimiari*, depicting different movement
dynamics in the same social space
PHOTOGRAPH BY M.G. FOR PHOTO-ELICITATION

of a younger generation of activists inside the same office, including the student groups *Studiare con Lentezza* (Studying Slowly) and *I Giovani Indignati* (The Indignant Youth). The office became a movement locus par excellence with its new members and a grassroots legal assistance office for migrants run by volunteers of *Coordinamento Cesar K.*, becoming what they referred to as "a space where Veronese antifascism met each other and constructed many things together." (Interview with C.Z., 10 February 2021). Inside the *via Scrimiari* office was born also the subdivision SAT-Pink (*Servizio Accoglienza Trans/Transgender*, Reception Center for Trans/Transgender), helping transgender people have access to health professionals accompanying them for their transition, as well as providing a platform to discuss their decision and to voice questions.[14] This service was the first of its kind in the region of Veneto, still continuing to function on its own.

As such, the office in *via Scrimiari* worked as a 'counterspace' or a 'counterpublic' (Fraser, 1990; Mitchell, 2000) where identities that did not belong to

---

14   For more information, see: https://www.satpink.it/about-us.

the dominant territorial identity met to construct an alternative belonging in Verona, one that is actively involved in authoring an inclusive outward-looking identity. The social ties that were cemented in this shared time and space still impact the dynamics of reciprocity and collaboration today among the anti-bodies: "In the old office we became a catalyzing center for other groups; many were staying in our office. Biblioteca Domaschi had moved its office inside ours, the student groups were also meeting at our office, the legal assistance office for migrants was born here in an LGBT office ... because they all knew that although we were an LGBT association, every subject had a right to cit-izenship." (Interview with C.Z., 10 February 2021). While bringing together under the same roof different groups that constituted much of the antibodies movement in Verona, Pink also hosted a variety of community-building events among groups from different walks of life, thereby offering an alternative cul-tural reference point (Johnston et al., 1994). For almost 15 years, this space came to be known not only locally but also nationally for the rich collaborative initiatives as a vibrant ground brewing 'a culture of resistance' ingrained in this place (Nicholls et al. 2013). The harmonious co-existence is captured lucidly in Figure 28, taken by M.G.:

> This photo shows two souls of the old Pink office. Because on the left, we see a girl who is busy preparing something. So, there's mobilization in the sense of self-management [*autogestione*], where everyone contributes in the way they can. Maybe she is washing dishes, or she brought food to cook. To the right, there's another girl, maybe a trans we don't know, who is putting on make-up. Hence, there's the part related to fun; Pink is not only about politics but also entertainment. These are the two souls of the same place.
>
> Interview with M.G., 25 April 2019

Towards the end of its lifetime, this office also served as a refuge for the Roma and Sinti population for several months, who were evicted from their nomad camp by the city administration. However, this meant that all events had to be suspended, and some members of the LGBTQ+ community who did not agree with this prolonged stay decided to leave Pink, leading to another inter-nal schism. In the end, the principle was to provide an open space for those subjects who felt excluded and unwanted in the Veronese landscape: "This was another group for whom Pink found a space. It was a great moment of sharing because Roma people at the time (not anymore because now the immigrants came in their place), were considered the last step on the social ladder. So, they were [considered] all thieves, all scoundrels, all robbers, while we initiated a relationship with this community. I was the babysitter of their children; we would go to the park together." (Interview with C.Z., 10 February 2021). As such, Circolo Pink from the onset espoused the indivisible united struggle that works as the glue within the movement, undertaking everyday acts of citizenship in urban space (Işın, 2009).

Eventually, Circolo Pink moved to their current office in *Via Cantarane*, close to *Porta Vescovo*, where they still continue their operations, sharing their space with NUDM in the last couple of years. Here, a new subgroup was founded in 2017 in response to the humanitarian crisis and the subsequent new waves of asylum seekers in Italy, called *Pink Refugees*: "With the birth of Pink Refugees, the LGBTQ+ migrant group, Pink found new life thanks to this new subjectivity. Also because, in my opinion, its political action as an LGBTQ+ group was over for a while. But in defense of the rights of migrant individuals, it found new vigor." (Interview with C.Z., 10 February 2021). Initially, migrants with different sexual orientations were very cautious about their visibility and involvement in the mobilization of Pink as they worried about possible repercussions from their local communities. However, with time and help from the activists, these individuals started to feel more secure and became more active even in public rallies.

During Verona Pride of 2019, they led the cortege in the frontline, transforming Verona Pride into the first Pride rally in Italy to be led by a refugee group: "We tried not only to represent gays, lesbians, and trans people, but we also invited the LGBTQ+ migrant community. In fact, that year an article came out saying that it was the first ever Pride in Italy to have migrants in the frontline." (Interview with S.C., 9 February 2021). During the rally, the leader of Circolo Pink introduced the group to the crowd, saying they were the 'hope for this country', the ones that were going to bring change. One of the migrants took the microphone to thank Pink for the encouragement to speak up about his homosexuality. He said he was very happy to be here as a gay man because he could finally have the rights that were negated to him in his country (Fieldnotes, 18 May 2019 Verona). That year, Pink Refugees took the initiative and went to other Prides around Italy with their own banners and T-shirts to represent asylum seekers and refugees with different sexual orientations, "because they felt themselves part of a movement." (Interview with C.Z. 10 February 2021). Pink Refugees has thus demonstrated how membership rights can be negotiated through insurgent urban citizenship in active participation (Holston & Appadurai, 1996): contributing, on the one hand, to the expansive place-based identity adopted by the antibodies of Verona and their alternative construction of city-zenship, and on the other hand, to larger citizenship struggles of sexual minorities and migrant groups in Italy.

FIGURE 29   Verona Pride, 18 May 2019
                PHOTOGRAPH: IPEK DEMIRSU

2.4   Paratodos: *Workshop of the Multitude in the Movement Scene of Verona*

Paratodos is a self-managed workshop that encompasses several different dynamics in one large space that looks like an old warehouse located on the outskirts of *Veronetta*, beyond the city walls in the bordering neighborhood of Borgo Venezia. Despite its location, this movement scene is also considered by many of the respondents as part of the 'extended Veronetta' (*Veronetta allargata*) due to the sociability, intercultural exchanges, and counterdiscourses it authors (Fraser, 1990), which are considered to be the characteristics of this neighborhood (Banini, 2017). It aims to provide assistance to individuals living in vulnerability and asylum seekers, in addition to organizing vibrant cultural events, and participating in political mobilizations.

The group that constitutes Paratodos dates back to *Café Metropolis* which used to be in *via Nicola Mazza* of Veronetta, first established as a schism from *La Chimica* by those who decided to leave this movement in the early 2000s and start a new political course that involved younger activists. Undoubtedly more than a simple *café,* this initiative following the political theory of Antonio

Negri was hosting political and cultural events in Veronetta. The group was part of the tradition of *Disobbedienti del Nord-Est* in Veneto, and had close ties with initiatives from Padova, such as the social center of *Pedro* and *Radio Sherwood*. Such involvement was considered by some elements of the antibodies as an 'external intervention to the local movement of Verona', preferring instead to remain an independent place-based grassroots movement (Fieldwork notes, 6 June 2019). As Café Metropolis, this group had thus continued in its own path, separate from the core actors of the antibodies, up until they started to work with migrants. Their initiatives offering bottom-up support to generate social inclusion intensify their collaboration with the rest of the assemblage. These included Italian courses for foreigners by volunteers (which continues in Paratodos), helping with migrant kids' schoolwork, and a pizza-making course that helps the participants find jobs in Italian society. Café Metropolis was eventually scattered, partly due to the local administration's interventions, and partly due to the young members going off to study in other cities.

Together with the local grassroots trade union ADL Cobas (*Associazione Diritti Lavoratori Comitato di Base*, Association for the Rights of Workers Grassroots Committee), old members of Metropolis Café decided to move into a new space that gave life to Paratodos: "It's new but it's old, in the sense that as a political reality it existed for a while, but just like *Sobilla* they decided to change their office, and in doing so, turned into something else. It merged with ADL COBAS, a grassroots trade union very active in Veneto, and therefore trans-formed." (Interview with O.P., 8 June 2019). Owing to the vast space available, *Paratodos* became the 'indoors' venue for the movement, just as Gigi Piccoli functions as the outdoor space, parallel to the intensifying collaboration with other groups such as La Sobilla, Circolo Pink, InfoSpazio and the transnational feminist group NUDM, becoming particularly involved and connected with the rest of the antibodies during the period of my fieldwork.

With new members coming from different backgrounds joining the new Paratodos, their focus continued to be placed on migration, not only regarding Verona but Europe in general, following the humanitarian crisis of 2015: "In 2015, the migration movement towards the Balkan route started to become more pronounced, so we united with many other groups around Italy in a cam-paign with the primary objective of helping the migrants complete their jour-ney. We organized buses on the basis of the different needs of different areas, and we accompanied them in their walk, providing them with the necessities that we could offer, such as tents, generators, boots, power banks ... anything that was necessary to keep on going." (Interview with B.P., 1 February 2021). This intense experience across borders in collaboration with both national and international groups had influenced the kind of work the volunteers wanted

FIGURE 30   Palestra Popolare Jacovacci inside Paratodos
PHOTOGRAPH BY M.R. FOR PHOTO-ELICITATION

to pursue once they returned to their hometown in Verona, who turned their attention to the newly arriving asylum seekers and refugees in this city. With some initial events addressing problems encountered in African countries, a group of Senegalese and Gambian newcomers started to visit Paratodos on a regular basis, which offered them a space where they could freely hang out outside the CAS. From casual conversations, the volunteers understood that they could use a gym to work out and let some steam off. So, the group collected a number of recovered gym equipment and created a free access gym corner, which eventually evolved into *Palestra Popolare Jacovacci* (Community Gym Jacovacci). The gym was named after the black Italian boxer Leone Jacovacci, whose career ended following the racial laws under fascism. Its activities involve boxing classes and training classes twice a week alongside free access to the gym equipment.

The growing exchange with newcomers informed Paratodos of the shortcomings in the CAS reception system, be it the legal process of obtaining refugee status or the daily needs of individuals in this prolonged limbo: "Thanks to this interaction, we started to enter the world of refugees, the world of reception centers and migration that was not only limited to the Balkan route but also other routes. But above all, we started to understand the conditions that people who undertook migration to arrive in Italy, in particular here in Verona." (Ibid.) Other actors from the antibodies were invited to join in this new dialogue established with asylum seekers and refugees, who have come to constitute a new political agency in the city, negotiating their 'membership rights' (Holston & Appadurai, 1996) and bringing 'new sites of struggle' (Işın, 2008) for the local network to take part in, in their united fight. The possibilities of interconnection offered by Paratodos, creating new relations and new city-zens of Verona, have been pointed out by one of the refugees who frequent this space:

> We have events here. They know how things work and through these meetings, they explain them to us. Meetings to explain to those newly arrived how the government has changed the laws and how there are no more humanitarian permits. They also gave us this gym if you want to do physical activity, you don't have to pay. I like coming here, everyone presents themselves. I like it because the people are very friendly. They teach Africans how to make pizza. A friend of mine attended their course, then we had dinner together and he made us pizza. Later, he even found a job doing pizza. The refugees like them and they like the refugees.
>
> Interview with M.R., 13 May 2019

Since 2015, Paratodos has also hosted the community theatre *Teatro Popolare Verona* (Verona Community Theatre) that had constituted much of the cultural events, helping fund the expenses of maintaining this space. First coming into being by a group of young artists who wanted to perform theatrical acts inside the vast space available at Paratodos, Teatro Popolare became a success in organizing performances that were politically underpinned, drawing a sizeable audience from 'the other Verona' with a different outlook, thereby introducing discussion on critical themes. The group aims to make theatre accessible to people from different walks of life, stimulating the 'counterculture' flourishing in Veronetta: "Before, we knew nothing about theatre. I didn't even go to the theatre. But thanks to the experience of these people, interesting themes and contents were brought up." (Interview with B.P., 1 February 2021).

Following the pandemic, organizing and hosting events for a large audience became impossible; therefore, the group channeled their attention to the needs that this emergency had generated. They started to mobilize for the basic necessities of individuals and families who have lost their jobs after months of lockdown or have endured a reduction in their income, therefore, falling short of affording primary needs. This involved recovering edible unsold food from local markets, and organizing a weekly 'free market' called *sos Spesa*. In a short amount of time, they enlarged their circle and made deals with supermarkets, farmers, and other local producers. Hence, the project achieved both the ecological purpose of revalorizing edible food destined to be trashed, and most importantly, provided a weekly grocery to approximately 50 families in need (Ibid.).

2.5   *Non Una di Meno Verona: Introducing Transfeminism in the City*

NUDM is a transnational grassroots feminist organization established in Argentina as *Ni Una di Menos* in 2015, with the aim of representing women in the 99% and ending gender-based violence. The group focuses on issues such as the right to abortion, the gender pay gap, feminicide, colonialism, transgender activism, and the rights of sexual workers, whilst building alliances with the environmental movement, labor movement, as well as indigenous and migrant movements. The new wave of feminism that the organization upholds takes intersectionality as a principle and seeks to reinterpret human rights from a feminist perspective. To draw attention to the devalued female labor in the market and the non-waged invisible labor such as caregiving, domestic, and reproductive work, one of the group's primary sites of mobilization has been the global feminist strike on the 8th of March International Women's Day.[15] In a short period of time, the movement spread across Latin America, reaching all the way to Europe and giving life to NUDM in Italy, constituted by local associations and initiatives around the country with the objective of pushing for structural, social, and political change. First established in 2016 in Rome, other cities including Verona followed suit, and subsequently the movement came to be materialized in Italy as an umbrella movement hosting a great variety of activists operating in different settings.

Within the transnational dynamics of this new wave of feminism, the activists that today constitute the Verona branch come from a long tradition of homegrown feminism in Verona, which already enjoyed an international reputation since the 1980s as a significant voice shaping 'difference feminism': "There is a new transfeminism in Verona, but this movement recalls a story of the feminist Verona to which also the university has contributed." (Interview with B.U., 16 April 2019). This tradition dates back to the feminist philosophical group of *Diotima* that was established inside the University

---

15   For more information, see https://www.vice.com/amp/en/article/3kpk53/-womens-str ike-organizer-cecilia-palmeiro-feminism-for-the-99-percent.

of Verona in 1983, following the theory of Luce Irigaray and the experiences of the Women's Bookshop of Milano (*Libreria delle Donne di Milano*).[16] This theoretical tradition also gave way to feminist spaces and initiatives during these years, including *Circolo della Rosa* founded in 1992 with the objective of creating a feminine space of culture, literature, art, and cultural exchange, as well as *Il Filo di Arianna* (Arianna's Thread) that aimed to offer "a space where women can carry out their studies and research ... talk about their gains and experiences, and offer new ways of studying."[17] As a result, feminist activists operating in Verona in the past and today were influenced by Veronese feminist philosophers, whose works have been translated into different languages around the world.

In this sense, the feminist movement in Verona, despite the conservativism and the Christian model of family that came to represent the city, had strong intellectual roots and an existing network from the onset. This historical initiative struggled to create 'subaltern publics' (Fraser, 1990) for women in cityspace, whilst contributing to the intellectual growth of feminism on a global scale. From an intergenerational perspective, old and new experiences in the Veronese territory touched one another and culminated in collaborations such as *Tre Generazioni* (Three Generations), which as the name suggests, brought together three generations of feminists based in Verona from 20 years of age until 75 years of age. One activist testifies her experience coming from this background and later going on to establish NUDM Verona with a new outlook:

> The movement is the offspring of the '70s. That is the reason one of our slogans is: 'We are the daughters of the witches you could not burn'. We definitely have a bridge with our grandmothers and mothers of the '70s, because we find ourselves still having to struggle for the rights they have fought for us. Yet, at the same time this is a new feminism, one that is much larger, a feminism that has transformed itself to transfeminism that wants to be intersectional and inclusive.
>
> Interview with F.M., 12 February 2021

As a result, coming from a long line of homegrown feminism, blended with women's struggles in different settings, *NUDM Verona* was born in 2017 inside the cultural collective *La Sobilla* where they undertook the initial phases of their activism. Today, the group works around interconnected themes,

---

16   Official website of Diotima, available at: http://www.diotimafilosofe.it/presentazione.
17   Official website of Il Filo di Arianna, available at: http://www.filodiariannaverona.it /l%e2%80%99associazione.

involving the right to have safe options for abortion, equal pay and equal treatment at the workplace, politics of desire, the rights of LGBTQ+ individuals as well as migrant women, sexual education, consent, and domestic violence. With respect to the last two, the group launched a legal desk (*Sportello Legale Contro Violenza e Discriminazione*) at the beginning of the COVID-19 pandemic, extending solidarity to individuals who have suffered violence or discrimination, including legal assistance with the voluntary help of professionals.

The group openly shares the three unifying principles that characterize the 'collective identity' of the antibodies (Johnston et al., 1994; Kriesi, 2011), namely, the indivisible united struggle of antifascism, anti-racism, and anti-sexism. Since its establishment, NUDM Verona has been active, coming under the limelight in the local setting of Verona and reaching beyond. This has been due to two reasons: (1) their frontline confrontation against far-right elements and regressive decisions passed inside the city council, and (2) their success in connecting local struggles with similar national and transnational struggles. From the outset, the group had a vast field to work on given the adamant anti-gender stance on the part of the city administration, backed up by ultra-Catholic and far-right movements seeking to reinstall 'traditional family values'. Urban public spaces in Verona have long been demarcated by these heteronormative scripts (Hubbard, 2000; Brown & Browne, 2016), assigning appropriateness not only with respect to race, class, and religion, but also sexuality (Hubbard, 2000). The innovative, intersectional, inclusive, and translocal approach of NUDM Verona produced a form of mobilization in urban life that was playful and constructive in challenging the taken-for-grantedness of the 'ideal protagonist' of city life, leading a creative bottom-up transformation in the city (Carmo, 2012).

The group entered what was going to be a prolonged conflict with identitarian figures (Handler, 2019; Zùquete, 2018) and their ultra-conservative backings, turning into a pronounced socio-political cleavage (Johnston et al., 1994) that accentuated competing representations of the city and competing identities (Dillard, 2013; Nicholls, 2013). The first episode took place inside the city council on the 26th of July 2018 during the discussion of a proposed anti-abortion motion, entitled "Initiative for the prevention of abortion and support for motherhood on the 40th anniversary of Law 194/1978,"[18] to which NUDM activists presented themselves dressed as the Handmaids (*ancelle*) from the

---

18   *Comune di Verona*, "Iniziative per la prevenzione dell'aborto e il sostegno alla maternità nel 40° anniversario della Legge 194/1978", Mozione 434 NV, 1 October 2018, Verona. Original copy of the motion is available online at: https://www.comune.verona.it/media /_ComVR/Cdr/SegreteriaConsiglio/Allegati/mozioni/2017-2022/434_moz.pdf.

TV series Handmaid's Tale in a flash mob protest. The conflict escalated into a scandal when an identitarian city councilor from the political group *Battiti per Verona* rose from the benches to give the protestors the fascist Roman salute inside the city council,[19] which he later claimed was just a greeting with the right hand.[20] On the 6th of October 2018, a revised motion proposed by the councilor Alberto Zelger from Lega was passed with 21 votes in favor and 6 against, declaring the city '*Verona città in favore della vita*' (Verona the city in favor of life), conferring public funding to anti-abortion groups. The motion worked as a precedent for other cities around Italy, presenting Verona as a model city in the pro-life movement,[21] which was justified on sovereignist identitarian grounds of promoting Italian birthrates against the threat of Muslims taking over the country (Demirsu, 2022; Demirsu 2023).[22] Hence, the leitmotif of the motion reflected the transnational Great Replacement theory, imbued in an outlook viewing Italian women as the reproducers of the white Christian nation (Yuval-Davis, 1999), in response to a demographic anxiety (Gökarıksel et al., 2019) of being replaced by Muslim immigrants (Balibar, 1991; Goldberg, 2006). This stance is part of a larger far-right theme resonating in different settings, exemplified by the slogan 'procreation, not immigration' pioneered at the Budapest international demography summit.[23]

Following the motion being passed, NUDM Verona launched a nationwide rally, drawing activists not only from the local network, but also from other branches of NUDM Italy, as well as various national social centers. Under the motto 'State of Permanent Agitation' (*Stato di Agitazione Permanente*), the group sought to reclaim the right to safe abortion guaranteed by law no. 194 that has become *de facto* void in its application due to the growing number of doctors refusing to implement it. The rally helped consolidate the collective identity espoused by the movement of antibodies, which was, as theorized by Melucci (1980), summoned when challenged and united in collective action: "Thanks to Zelger we went out to the streets to protest together, immigrants, gays, women in solidarity." (Fieldnotes, 13 October 2018) The consolidation of the movement ties was not only done so with respect to the panoply

---

19   For this incident he is undergoing a legal process, see: https://www.repubblica.it/polit
     ica/2018/07/27/news/saluto_romano_destra_verona_consiglio_comunale-202795134.

20   For more information on the event, see: http://www.veronasera.it/politica/saluto-rom
     ano-aborto-consigliere-bacciga-consiglio-comunale-proteste-27-luglio-2018-.html.

21   See: https://www.valigiablu.it/mozioni-attacco-aborto.

22   Interview with Zelger: https://video.repubblica.it/politica/verona-il-leghista-della-mozi
     one-anti-aborto-senza-bimbi-italiani-saremo-invasi-dagli-islamici/316126/316755.

23   More information on the summit can be found at: https://www.theguardian.com/world
     /2019/sep/06/viktor-orban-trumpets-far-right-procreation-anti-immigration-policy.

of participants and the counterdiscourses being utilized, but also spatially as urban space became a factor in defining the movement. Passing from Piazza Brà and arriving at Piazza Santa Toscana in Veronetta, the group announced that the cortege had arrived 'home' at the 'neighborhood of solidarity', thereby underlining the outward-looking spatial identity of the neighborhood as well as the expansive place-based identity it authors: "With the spirit of Veronetta, let's sing to say no to all barriers." (Ibid.) During this event, in the displays of solidarity from the windows and balconies of residents as well as by shopkeepers, the neighborhood transformed into the rally itself, becoming one with the antibodies. While it has been previously argued that a protest can come to constitute a 'sense of place' (Della Porta et al., 2013), it was the identity of the neighborhood that turned into collective action (Fieldnotes, 13 October 2018).

Doubtlessly, the biggest accomplishment of NUDM Verona, which brought international attention to this mid-sized Italian city, was the organization of *Verona Città Transfeminista* (Verona Transfeminist City) that took place simultaneously with the World Congress of Families held in Verona in March 2019, aiming to contest the latter and offer a competing event to represent the city. The WCF is an organization renowned for bringing together Christian

FIGURE 31   NUDM Verona rally in the neighborhood of Veronetta in 2018
PHOTOGRAPH: IPEK DEMIRSU

fundamentalists, far-right groups, and the populist right from different countries around the world to redeem the values of the traditional family as the foundation of society, to oppose the practice of abortion as well as same-sex relationships outside heteronormative scripts. The event was sponsored by the municipality of Verona, the Region of Veneto, and the Ministry of Family and Disability led by the Veronese minister from Lega, Lorenzo Fontana. As a result, it was not only offered public venues for the conference, but also the historical center for the 'pro-family' rally that took place at the end of the event. On the other hand, NUDM Verona whilst being denied access to the city center, the venues and the funding, still managed to organize a 4-day event centered around the neighborhood of Veronetta with the help of antibodies and their transnational connections. The aim was to reclaim the city and its identity as a 'Transfeminist City', challenging from below its international branding as 'The City of the Traditional Family'. In this example once again, the deep cleavage that was present between the two opposing movements accentuated the demand for mobilization around competing identities (Johnston et al., 1994).

The term 'transfeminism' chosen to represent Verona, as elaborated by a historical feminist trans activist, signifies the liberation of all subjects with the whole variety of sexual orientations welcomed by NUDM, and does not refer to trans activism exclusively. It is claimed that this slogan was articulated to confront the 'fascist face' of Verona, as a way of giving a new face to the city, a new image that was inclusive and in becoming (Fieldnotes, 28 March 2019). The alternative event by NUDM Verona resulted in a massive mobilization drawing national and transnational activists, scholars, and politicians around the world from Latin America, including the founder of the movement in Argentina, to Eastern Europe and the Middle East. Given the absence of the type of public venues and resources that the organization of WCF had enjoyed, the event by NUDM found home in the spaces managed by the antibodies in Veronetta, such as La Sobilla, Paratodos, ANPI, Circolo Pink, as well as movement hubs present in the neighborhood including the bookstore Libre! and local bars. It involved discussions by international academics, book presentations, films, art exhibits, theatrical performances, and other cultural events around the theme of sexual rights and sexual liberation. The 4-day event reached its zenith with a massive rally of *Verona Città Transfeminista* marshaling an estimated 300,000 participants from around the world, considered the biggest rally in the modern history of the city, turning into a 'profestival' par excellence (Carmo, 2012). The organization was finalized with a transnational assembly of different NUDM branches from various countries and feminist organizations from various settings, in order to share local problems endured in different contexts and to collectively mediate transnational responses. As such, the objective of this translocal/transfeminist/intersectional mobilization was to "face a global reactionary agenda that wants to subordinate women's bodies, as well as all non-white and non-heterosexual bodies." (Facebook page of NUDM Verona, 29 March 2019).

The great success of this intense organization with the leadership of NUDM Verona, consolidated the former's position within the antibodies in introducing new strategies of mobilization, new ways of offering tangible alternatives beyond mere confrontation, an intersectional and inclusive agenda that unites different causes into one indivisible struggle, and thus new ways of forming links that resonate across borders uniting with global themes of justice. It was a quintessential undertaking of 'activist citizenship' (Işın, 2008) where counterclaims to identity were made in the local echoing to the transnational, one that opened room to non-white and non-heterosexual identities, where new scales of the struggle were collectively built. Most importantly, the organization by NUDM Verona aimed at the reappropriation of the identity of Verona as an object of collective action, successfully rebranding it as a 'transfeminist city' against a sovereignist identitarian marketing of the city: "The city-zenship [*cittadinanza*] in Verona takes action and responds well when NUDM Verona

FIGURE 32   Verona Città Transfeminista, 30 March 2019
              PHOTOGRAPH: IPEK DEMIRSU

organizes or proposes something new, and this for us is a signal that there is a real need to discuss such arguments, especially in a city of the right, of the fascists we can even say, to overcome certain rhetoric, mentality, and culture." (Interview with F.M., 12 February 2021).

2.6   *Veronetta 129: Making Cultures Cross Paths in Verona*

Another relatively recent formation that entered the movement scene in Verona has been the cultural association *Veronetta 129*, which works exclusively on the themes of social inclusion of newcomers, on intercultural exchange between old and new Veronesi, and finally on breaking deep-seated stereotypes. The founders of the association have a background of teaching Italian to foreign speakers at the association of Cestim, which was among the first grassroots initiatives in Italy during the 1990s established to address the inclusion of migrants. Coming from this background, yet finding a more progressive direction of their own, Veronetta 129 was established first in 2012 with the impetus of the Arab Spring that marked this period. In their events they seek to undertake an 'everyday activist citizenship' (Işın, 2008; Işın, 2009) as a motto of existence, without which they would have succumbed to the defensive localism that reigns much of the city: "When the rest of life is not going well, at least there is the association ... in the sense that even if we get infuriated about what is going on around us, being active is a psychological support to keep on going. If you are not active, you have given up." (Interview with A.V., 15 February 2019).

Functioning both as an Italian language course for foreigners and a cultural association, Veronetta 129 has been actively involved in fighting racism, primarily in the neighborhood they are located in, in their own creative quotidian ways. Two of the cornerstone projects they have been organizing are the project *Indovina Chi Viene a Cena* and the film festival *Mediorrizzonti*. The former is a nationwide grassroots initiative undertaken in 90 different municipalities around Italy, which involves migrants hosting non-migrant guests at their own homes, cooking their traditional dishes from their country of origin, thereby inverting the dichotomy of host/guest: "They host at their own homes to show that there are houses, there are habits, and there are people who live a settled life here, who speak Italian well and have interesting things to tell, and you become a guest in their home, not on the other way around. The perspective and the roles change." (Interview with A.V., 15 February 2019). Both events, at their core are a criticism of the *'accoglienza'* (hospitality) approach that promotes integration from the vantage point of the local community 'hosting' newcomers in 'their' hometown: "All our projects are on the contrary. We share lived spaces as equals, so it's better to get to know one another to understand how we can enrich each other's lives." (Ibid.). As social dinners proved to be impossible to organize during the pandemic, the group continued their activity online through cooking classes presented by migrants who would give instructions to cook a traditional dish together with other participants, thereby continuing the intercultural exchange in the absence of face-to-face proximity.

The second activity undertaken by the group is an annual film festival about Middle Eastern countries, called *Mediorrizzonti*, that seeks to break deep-seated convictions and to provide different lenses from which to observe these societies: "If you hear about the country only when there are political events involved, you don't understand it well. So, I thought about a way to introduce these countries to the Italian public, to organize events where we could project a film and focus on certain themes ... because maybe in the movie there is a new argument which allows the viewer to acquire a greater understanding of that context." (Interview with I.V., 7 April 2019). The films chosen to present the society in question are low-budget, preferably by female directors, and tend to provide an out-of-the-ordinary insight into Middle Eastern society, depicting the protagonism of local actors in these settings.

In both projects, Veronetta 129 collaborates the most with La Sobilla, as the two share members and the perspectives of undertaking cultural events as a form of urban activism. Veronetta 129 also cooperates with other missionary or religious groups on an ad hoc basis on the themes of social inclusion and anti-racism. An interesting example of this collaboration was *Volti da Ascoltare* (Faces to Listen to), organized together with the missionary organization *Combonifem* and the local artist Marco Danelion, which took place at the garden of the institute hosting Combonian nuns. The event was about matching refugees from Africa and Latin America hosted by the Combonians with Italian participants, and involved a three-day workshop on using clay to create a bust sculpture of their partner while getting to know them personally during the whole process. Just like *Indovina Chi Viene a Cena*, the objective here was to promote intercultural exchange through elongated social contact between old and new Veronesi from different walks of life who inhabit shared urban spaces. As such, rather than a unidirectional integration process, Veronetta 129 has been championing a bottom-up two-way integration reflecting the outward-looking identity of the social space they take part in, thereby promoting an inclusive pluralist city-zenship model in Verona.

The central theme of anti-racism also comes to the fore in the activities of this organization, engaging in practices of transformative placemaking (Bacchetta et al., 2019) to redefine belonging in and through cityspace. One exemplary neighborhood initiative was organized in collaboration with another local association D-HUB, whereby all residents of Veronetta were invited to partake in collectively painting anti-racist banners that were to be

FIGURE 33   *Siamo Tutti Esposti* in the garden of Ex-Nani
PHOTOGRAPH: IPEK DEMIRSU

hung on the balconies and windows of residents. Two schools in the neighbor-hood participated in the project by encouraging their students to come up with catchy anti-racist slogans. According to one of the organizers, their aim was to reclaim Veronetta as an 'anti-racist space', also in response to the new offices of far-right neofascist organizations (Fieldnotes, 16 March 2019), by embellishing the physical materiality with banners carrying the values that define the iden-tity of this place (Aru, 2015; Banini, 2017), animated in the place-based identity of its residents (Lynch, 1981; Massey, 2005).

2.7   AfroVeronesi: *Challenging Latent Claims of Whiteness in Belonging*

I discovered the formation of *AfroVeronesi* by the end of my fieldwork. Although I did not get the chance to participate actively in their events, it was immediately clear to me that their outlook and efforts in a context like Verona made a remarkable difference in rewriting pregiven scripts of belonging. The initial ideas of this crucial addition to the antibodies were incepted in 2019 among three young women, all children of migrants born and/or raised in Verona, with a shared vision of identity and citizenship that defied the norm.

As put by a member of the group, their objective was to "deconstruct precon-
ceptions and prejudices towards black people, demonstrating to Veronesi as
well as Italians that 'second generation' exists, and that they are not invisible
actors but instead active members of society." (Interview with H.A., 18 April
2023). The motivation of H.A. for taking part in this formation was an unpleasant experience encountered during the application for Italian citizenship at
the age of 18, despite being born and raised in Italy, where she was questioned
regarding her 'Italianness' throughout the formal process. She stated that such
experience left a bitter doubt about her identity and made her a first-hand witness to institutional racism (Ibid.). Similar shared experiences are expressed
in the events and social media content of AfroVeronesi: "One of the biggest
discriminations for us 'second generation' youth is being born and/or raised in
a state that does not recognize us as 'Italian' from a cultural and a judicial point
of view." (Facebook post of AfroVeronesi, 1 March 2021).

A first meeting took place in early 2020 to talk about racism, identity, and
citizenship: moving from personal experiences of individuals in Verona,
arriving at national as well as transnational themes of belonging that the so-
called 'second generation' youth confront in their everyday lives. These individuals, usually confounded with newly arriving migrants and refugees, find
themselves in a limbo of (mis)recognition, consequently seeking to render
their experiences visible. In order to do so, AfroVeronesi utilize social media
platforms to reach a wider audience, cultural events such as music and film
festivals, and lastly, political mobilization to promote social inclusion and
dismantle racist stereotypes. The term 'second-generation' itself, used to connote children of first-generation migrants, is considered an oxymoron since
most of these individuals have no experience of migration *per se*: "I did not
go through a migratory process. So, I see [the term] second-generation as a
contradiction. Yes, we are the second generation in relation to our parents. But
we were born and raised in the host country." (Ibid.). As such, they strive to
be role models for the younger generation from mixed backgrounds, exemplifying the possibilities of multiple belongings binding Veronesità, Italiannes,
and African heritage. The association challenges exclusionary definitions of a
territorial identity in Verona, instead asserting that "whoever holds Verona in
their heart, not only those born but also raised in this city, therefore who had
experiences here, should be considered Veronese with no concern over their
physical traits." (Interview with H.A., 18 April 2023).

The informal group officially became an association in September 2020
and started to collaborate with local schools on intercultural communication, social inclusion, and diversity. In a short period of time, they became
an integral part of the extant movement scene, establishing ties with other

FIGURE 34   'Different from whom?': Demonstration of AfroVeronesi in Piazza Brà for
international Zero Discrimination Day
PHOTO FROM THE FACEBOOK PAGE OF AFROVERONESI, 1 MARCH 2021

social collectives that have been active in Verona including NUDM, Pink Refugees, and Paratodos. While operating locally, the association also cooperates with national networks fighting against racism, such as *Razismo Brutta Storia* (Racism Bad [His]tory) and *Italiani Senza Cittadinanza* (Italians without Citizenship). Today, the group is composed of approximately 30 young Veronesi from 25 to 30 years of age with a background in an African country. They define their identity as a source of 'added richness' for the city of Verona and for Italian society at large, and their role as a 'bridge' between the Italian and African cultures (Ibid.). Although they do not have a permanent office space, they often utilize the spaces offered by Museo Africano (The African Museum) managed by Comboni missionaries for their events, located in the northern part of Veronetta, also referred to as San Giovanni in Valle. Notwithstanding this organic link, the group remains autonomous and adheres to progressive sexual politics that is often not in accord with other religious groups.

   In short, the aims of the association are in line with the united struggle the antibodies uphold, primarily with respect to the anti-racism cause, fight against discrimination based on skin color, sexual orientation, gender identity, socioeconomic status, and disability (Facebook post of AfroVeronesi, 1 March 2021). The struggles of children of migrants in Italy for the acquisition of citizenship status and the fundamental rights that the title carries (Hawthorne, 2022) reverberate in the city as claims to city-zenship for the equal recognition of belonging. The efforts of AfroVeronesi have epitomized such translocal linkages that the African diaspora in Europe has been pioneering. The group is also active on transnational issues such as the Black Lives Matter movement, which started in the US following the shooting of George Floyd in 2020, rapidly spreading in other contexts, including Italy. In Verona, this group took the initiative to join this global protest representing their own locality by voicing the systematic and everyday forms of racism endured in Italy, especially following the murder of Willy Monteiro Duarte less than four months after Floyd's death.

3 Collective Identity and Collective Action in Urban Space: Core Values, Issue-Based Formations, and Tactical Alliances of the Antibodies

The 'antibodies of hate' have, over the years, formed a number of formalized issue-specific networks and ad hoc alliances with other local actors that operate in Verona. The concretized formations have historically taken place in relation to the aforementioned three fundamental principles that unite these actors, namely antifascism, anti-racism, and anti-sexism. It is worth reiterating that the conceptualization of an *indivisible united struggle* is the social glue that keeps these closely-knit actors together whose understanding of collective action is based on the conception of a common fight in defense of all three values contemporaneously, seeking to create open and democratic spaces within Verona where these values can blossom and flourish in everyday exchanges. These three principles came to constitute one united vision over time, transforming the hostile setting prevalent in the city. They were solidified with the collective memory of the recent struggles going back to the Veronese antifascist resistance during WWII, whose memory is invoked on every occasion. Moreover, an idea of democracy understood as bottom-up activism through grassroots initiatives against rigid institutional traits and hierarchic forms of organization has shaped the direction of their activism: "[A]n idea of grassroots movement departing from the people, this is the common trait." (Interview with B.M., 8 October 2021). Hence, their approach to collective action evolved over time in tandem with the *expansive place-based identity* associated with the urban space of Veronetta, merging the movement itself with a social space. A collective identity that is by and large written in and through situated spatial experiences, a shared history, and shared values is perfectly summed up in a speech given by a prominent activist during a demonstration against far-right groups in Piazza Isolo of Veronetta:

> In a city that became the symbol of the far-right all over Italy, we need to remember that it was once the cornerstone of Italian resistance against Nazi forces. We want to stress today how important it is in a square that is historically dear to us, where we have struggled against racism and fascism in this city, to talk about a Verona that knows how to raise its voice, that knows how to create not the laboratory of the far-right but also another type of laboratory ... A laboratory of relations, the great capacity to produce hospitality, the great capacity to produce projects. We are the ones who know how to bring together different worlds with bridges. We are forging relations. But most importantly, they are the past, and we are the future because we are already in all the real relations of this neighborhood and of this city.
>
> Fieldnotes, 24 November 2019

Notwithstanding the fact that these actors have continued their activities within their own organizations and collaborated with other components of the network on various occasions, the collective action has, in certain instances, given way to parallel forms of more formal collaborations that encompass actors also outside of the antibodies. The first instance was the realization of *Il Coordinamento Cesar K.* (Cesar K. Coordination) following the traumatic event that left its impact on the collective memory of the antibodies. This semi-formal alliance, with its primary focus on racism, was founded in September 2000 after the poignant death of the homeless Polish migrant Cesar Karabowski taking refuge in the evicted office of Pecora Nera in Piazza Isolo. A personal acquaintance to some of the activists operating under the same roof of the *pensilina*, this incident shook many deeply, who have united to fight all forms of racism in Verona. Dedicated to the memory of Cesar, the initiative was named after him in an attempt to bring together city-zens willing to transform the environment of hostility towards difference. As indicated by the founding statement of the group, the objective was to "give voice to those who cannot accept anymore the environment of intolerance that dominates Verona ... the politics of exclusion and the deprivation of fundamental rights from those considered 'different' ... with the consequence of reducing spaces of democracy for all."[24] In this quest for creating open, inclusive, and breathable spaces

---

24   Chi è Cesar K. (Who is Cesar K.?): http://www.ecn.org/reds/estremadestra/destraoo1ces arK.html.

for all the inhabitants of the city, the Coordination addressed local issues such as the 'reparative prayer' by the organization *Famiglia e Civiltà* with the attendance of Lega Nord ahead of the upcoming Gay Pride,[25] microaggressions of far-right groups condoned by the city administration, the racial profiling of non-European inhabitants as 'criminals' by members of Lega Nord, whilst also extending a sense of responsibility for distant others (Massey, 2004) in blocking trains that were carrying arms for the war in Iraq from Italy (interview with B.M., 8 October 2021).

The initiative was a juxtaposition of elements that were part of the core group of the antibodies alongside other actors that belong to a different social reality, including religious missionary groups such as *Beati I Costruttori di Pace*, as well as the local office of the national association of atheists and agnostics UAAR (*Unione Atei Agnostici Razionalisti*), both LGBTQ+ groups of Circolo Pink and Arcigay Verona, the anarchist library Biblioteca Giovanni Domaschi, Kollettivo Porkospino, as well as institutional leftist groups including the communist party *Partito Rifondazione Comunista*. This unlikely alliance bringing institutional and grassroots actors together was united to promote a collective identity whose action frame was based on a sense of belonging to 'the other Verona', one that is inclusive, open, and welcoming of difference; therefore, an *expansive place-based identity* tied to one's city (Melucci, 1980; Massey, 1994). As put by one of the old members: "Verona has been a laboratory of far-right for many years. Then, there is a diversified galaxy in this city composed of voluntary workers, Catholic associations, organizations of the left, anarchist groups, student groups, and whatnot. Twenty years ago, *Coordinamento Cesar K.* was born out of these elements and put together various social actors to contrast far-right and their supporters in the city administration." (Interview with C.Z., 10 February 2021).

For some of these groups that today constitute the antibodies, Cesar K. was also a formative experience in which different struggles met and joined forces, thereby solidifying the indivisible tripartite values we observe today: "It was the first attempt to coordinate a list of groups that we were in contact with for a while. It was also where we got to know the whole world of LGBTQ+ activism and a new friendship began there." (Interview with S.P., 10 June 2019). Moreover, the bottom-up model of social inclusion also gave way to a grassroots 'migration office' to help with bureaucratic hurdles and other everyday issues of newcomers, in which city-zenship is reconstrued and membership

25   Chi è Cesar K. (Who is Cesar K.?): http://www.ecn.org/reds/estremadestra/destraoo11ces arK.html.

rights re-negotiated. The work undertaken in this office by local volunteers posed a counterclaim to identity in the everyday life of the city against nativist territorial belongings.

The momentum that was set off by *Coordinamento Cesar K.* was later taken on by a looser network named *Assemblea 17 Dicembre* (Assembly of 17 December), which is still active. This informal initiative operating in Verona was formed following the revolts of asylum seekers staying at the reception center of *Ostello della Gioventù* in via Santa Chiara of Veronetta, who decided to organize a demonstration occupying the street in front of the city's police headquarters by blocking it with large dumpsters. As the demonstrations took place in December 2017 to protest the adverse living conditions they were experiencing, the informal network was mobilized in solidarity, and named their initiative after this date. The migrant group that organized the revolts underwent a backlash by the officials, being separated and sent off to remote parts of the Verona province, some to the secluded Lessinia mountain range, others to south of Verona at the borders with Mantua. To provide solidarity to this group of newcomers, the older and the younger generation of social actors formed *Assemblea 17 Dicembre*: "From there, the old group with Pink, Sobilla, and all the others that we were always in contact with, including younger activists ... We start again to meet with the motivation of constructing a network that would support the cause of the migrants." (Interview with S.P., 10 June 2019) From the same group of asylum seekers that the network was in contact with was born Pink Refugees the same year with the initiative of a Muslim gay immigrant from an African country, who succeeded in mobilizing local activists to address the particular issues faced by LGBTQ+ migrants.

This network is also active online under the name *Veronesi aperti al mondo-Verona città aperta* (Veronesi open to the world-Verona open city) to share important news and events with a wider audience, to mobilize on issues regarding migration, to help newcomers in the city, and to signal cases of racism or racist assaults. On their Facebook group, the concept of a 'united struggle' based on the tripartite principles is accentuated with a self-description that states: "We are a network of antifascists, antiracists, and antisexists of Verona."[26] On the digital plane, the group explains its objectives as addressing the shortcomings of the official reception system and mitigating the wave of fear and rage in the territory without falling into the rhetoric of 'sending them back', instead organizing locally to create plausible solutions for incoming

---

26   Facebook Group of Assemblea 17 Dicembre functioning as Veronesi aperti al mondo-Verona città aperta, available at: https://www.facebook.com/Assemblea17dicembre.

asylum seekers and refugees to take part in city life as new members of the local community.[27] In 2018, they occupied a square in front of the city's Prefecture, turning it into a 'beach' since the officials went on a vacation and left seven refugees without a decision on their permit. Activists of *Assemblea 17 Dicembre* helped these newcomers not only by protest, but also by guiding them in making legal applications and in re-obtaining their right to safe accommodation.

The antibodies of hate have also formed collective initiatives around the identity of place that they have been fostering and seeking so meticulously to maintain, based on the movement space that the neighborhood of Veronetta offers. Such mobilization around an outward-looking spatial identity not only resists exclusionary territorialism, but also constructs tangible alternatives to nurture a different form of belonging co-written by new and old members. The cosmos of Veronetta and the values that underwrite this 'conceptual space' (Miller, 2013) are celebrated, produced, and reproduced in the everyday life of its inhabitants. One such initiative arrived with the dynamism of the Arab Spring when in 2014, a group of actors and everyday hubs collaborated to organize under the name *PrimaVera Veronetta* (Veronetta Spring) to organize a festival to celebrate the spatial 'counterculture' (Melucci, 1984; Fraser, 1990; Della Porta & Diani, 2006) that "animates the neighborhood."[28]

The network of antibodies organized a similar mobilization invoking the identity of Veronetta in response to the opening of a new office of Forza Nuova at the heart of the neighborhood, with the intention of a so-called 'ethnic resistance'. On the same day of the inauguration of this new office called *Casa dei Patrioti* (House of Patriots), CasaPound's national leader declared that he would give a talk in this organization's office in the same neighborhood in a parallel street which had arrived two years ago in 2017. This suddenly heightened presence of competition among far-right groups in the oasis of Veronetta that the antibodies worked so vigilantly to realize, gave way to a collective response. Therefore, in an assembly to mobilize this new initiative called *Veronetta Vive* (see Figure 35 below), a leading feminist activist made the following remarks:

> The fact that a fascist group declares Veronetta as the frontlines of a so-called 'ethnic resistance' is very troubling. Maybe Forza Nuova is a radical group, but *their intentions of wanting to exclude people, wanting to get*

---

27   Facebook Group of Assemblea 17 Dicembre functioning as Veronesi aperti al mondo-Verona città aperta, available at: https://www.facebook.com/Assemblea17dicembre.
28   Facebook group of PrimaVera Veronetta: https://www.facebook.com/PrimaVera-VERONE TTA-447694348632925.

rid of people are shared in other parts of the country by other individuals in vague and elusive ways. Because Veronetta is a multiethnic neighborhood, it has been equated with urban decay, whereas, in fact, it is the most beautiful neighborhood of Verona. It is maybe the only neighborhood where you can have the feeling of living in a city that is free, welcoming, and culturally stimulating. It is a neighborhood that dreams of a different future. *They do not belong here. They are not part of our history together. They are not what we want to become.*

Fieldnotes, 10 December 2019, emphasis added

As conveyed vividly in these remarks, the antibodies define their sense of belonging on the axis of time and space (Melucci, 1980), a collective history ingrained in the memory of struggles fought together in everyday transformative placemaking (Bacchetta et al., 2019), and the subsequent social space which gives body to the collective identity created through such bottom-up community building efforts. The ensuing mobilization involved underlining the rich social life together with the intercultural fabric of the neighborhood, as various associations and public spaces opened their doors to host events, thereby turning the everyday life of the neighborhood into political mobilization. As the existing social ties and conviviality were emphasized in this attempt to invoke the identity of Veronetta itself as a counterspace that rejects hate-based belongings, the mobilization was finalized with a flash mob by NUDM in Piazza Santa Toscana.

> It's a mobilization in the strictly political sense, but also a movement of city-zenship [*cittadinanza*] that always exists, not only today. Today, we want to make ourselves more visible. But in Veronetta, there is always this movement; if we think about all the realities that constitute it, the associations, more or less politically involved to engage residents, also foreign residents, places to meet all city-zens without any differentiation. These moments of encounter, of exchange, of relation, and of support are small yet concrete things in life. And I think that also this is a way of doing politics.

Interview with E.N. during fieldwork, 10 December 2019

A more encompassing and more structured initiative was taken in September 2019, to organize a three-day festival in another district of the city which could accommodate a large number of participants in an open space. This initiative, called *Festival delle Città InVisibili* (Festival of Invisible Cities), inspired by the book of Italo Calvino, was organized by the antibodies, including Paratodos,

FIGURE 35   Logo of Veronetta Vive
FROM THE FACEBOOK PAGE OF VERONESI APERTI AL MONDO – VERONA
CITTÀ APERTA, 15 DECEMBER 2018

GasP! farmers from Gigi Piccoli, NUDM Verona, Assemblea 17 Dicembre, Circolo Pink and Pink Refugees, alongside other actors such as environmental and anti-speciesist groups, the university student group *La Sirena* promoting LGBTQ+ rights, associations working on arts and crafts such as *Le Fate* and *DHUB*, missionary organizations *Nigrizia* and *ComboniFem* working with migrant communities from Africa and different African cultures. The aim of this initiative was to organize a festival that could introduce the 'other Verona' to the rest of the city for individuals who might be experiencing the same kind of 'non-belonging' (Bacchetta et al., 2019) and to those who are in search of alternative spaces and alternative forms of belonging. As put by the organizers:

> The idea originates from the willingness to offer a space in which different actors of the struggle in Verona and its province can collaborate, come together, and discuss among themselves as well as with the 'outside'. Verona comes to be portrayed in national and international newspapers as the laboratory of the far-right. We want to demonstrate the presence of other initiatives that courageously resist these groups, but above all, we intend to launch a collective political project that can give a new face to

FIGURE 36   Mobilization of Veronetta Vive, with the banner that reads 'Veronetta resists/
exists'
PHOTOGRAPH: IPEK DEMIRSU

the city and create new connections with outer reality. In this way, Verona can escape from this shadow upon itself in the common imaginary.[29]

This symbolic reclaiming of the city is done by reappropriating the image of the city, the representation of 'identity of place' (Aru, 2015; Banini, 2017), which is ultimately linked to the identity of its inhabitants (Lynch, 1981).

As illustrated by these collaborations, the antibodies of hate who are wedded in an indivisible united struggle form ad hoc alliances with other actors who are not intrinsic to the movement, which is solidified through shared values, a horizontal organizational style, a collective history, a movement space, and a place-based identity. These collaborations usually take place with the parallel reality of the Catholic left, including religious associations and missionary groups, but also moderate or institutional secular associations. For

29   Post from the Facebook Page of *Le Citta InVisibili,* 2 September 2019: https://www.faceb
ook.com/FestivalVerona.

instance, under the umbrella organization *Nella Mia Citta Nessuno è Straniero* (In My City No One is a Foreigner), a large array of groups from different backgrounds, including certain components of the antibodies, unite sporadically to confront racism in Verona. Nevertheless, many of these groups either do not share the three core principles and the organizational style that the antibodies uphold, or they are not as actively involved in the collective construction of an alternative spatial identity in the movement/countermovement contestations. As a result, they remain a parallel reality. One substantial fault line is sexual rights, particularly the issue of abortion and same-sex marriages, as the antibodies are critical of leftist Catholic figures and institutions in Verona for their extension of support to anti-abortion and so-called 'anti-gender' groups: "[T]he moment in which you accept that a fundamentalist Catholic group, the no-gender groups come to your place to have a conference, this is a form of support." (Interview with C.Z., 10 February 2021).

Another fault line is the organizational style of the antibodies, which is horizontal and non-institutional. A significant organization that deserves a mention here with a deep-rooted relationship to the antibodies is the Verona branch of *Associazione Nazionale dei Partigiani Italiani* (National Associations of Italian Partisans), located in Veronetta, next to the renovated campus at Santa Marta sharing its office with the Veronese Institute for the History of Resistance and the Modern Age. These twin organizations carry an undeniable symbolic importance, representing the collective history that the antibodies take pride in and resort to in distinguishing their collective identity for a sense of alternative belonging to the city. As such, they are revered for embodying the legacy of antifascism in Verona and for keeping this memory alive. Also, the Verona branch of the national student association *L'associazione Unione degli Universitari* (UDU Verona) is closely linked to ANPI Verona and can be considered an organic part of the latter. During national festivals celebrating Italy's liberation from Nazi-fascism, the antibodies gather in the office of ANPI Verona to celebrate this historical milestone as a central pillar uniting their place-based movement with similar antifascist movements around Europe and beyond. When neofascist groups such as CasaPound engage in verbal or physical violence against members of ANPI or their office, the antibodies quickly mobilize and extend their support.

That being said, ANPI is neither completely intrinsic nor extrinsic to the movement, but rather connected with a loose bond. This is due to differences in outlook as ANPI is considered too 'institutional' on the national level, enjoying a formal relationship with public authorities based on memorialization, in contrast to the antibodies constituted mainly by grassroots independent actors that constitute a movement dynamic: "ANPI is an association that works on ceremonies, such as 25th of April ... It is interested in promoting events that are directed towards the past, only to the historical perspective of the resistance. So, when you propose to them to be involved in things that are more active, at times they participate, but in general they don't. They have a different imprint than us, much more institutional, much more respectful of institutional practices ... institutions understood as authority, of hierarchies, etc." (Interview with O.P., 8 June 2019).

That being said, it is through such organic as well as instrumental alliances among the core elements of the antibodies, as well as the movement's collaboration with the larger left-wing environment in Verona made up of actors who are not necessarily an intrinsic part of the movement, that the local elections were won in 2022 with the progressive leadership of Damiano Tommasi. With the exception of the administration of Paolo Zanotto, who was notably known to avoid taking a stance on sexual politics and sexual rights, this groundbreaking victory of progressive actors after decades of far-right politics was enabled by the collaboration of institutional and non-institutional actors to challenge exclusionary territorialism that has come to characterize the city. As a result, the active involvement of the antibodies in this political campaign, with their experience of protracted struggles, paved the way for their shared values and collective vision to finally enter local administration, reversing some of the most problematic motions passed in the history of the city.[30]

4   The Neighborhood as Movement Space and Everyday Hubs of Counterculture

As demonstrated by the evolution of individual groups, by a shared history of the movement, and by the moments of collaboration with other actors in the sociopolitical scene, the antibodies as a movement are composed of diverse civil society organizations in Verona, who unite around a collective identity and a common vision that draw their lifeblood from the cosmos of Veronetta, which they helped create. Since the early 2000s, much of their activities and socialization have taken place in this 'lived space' (Aru, 2015), which has over time acquired meaning and emotional attachment of countless city-zens who do not feel an attachment to the inward-looking territorial identity prevalent in the historical center, radiating a different spatial belonging instead.

---

30   Official Press Release of the Municipality of Verona abolishing the 1995 anti-LGBTQ+ motion: https://ufficiostampa.comune.verona.it/nqcontent.cfm?a_id=9561andid_com= 29840.

As demonstrated by a number of constitutive elements of the movement, the urban topography does not strictly correspond to the cognitive map defined through the type of social relations characterizing it. This phenomenon was epitomized by the spaces of Sports Camp Gigi Piccoli and Paratodos that fall outside the city walls demarcating the physical borders of Veronetta despite being indicated by the respondents as part of an 'extended Veronetta' (*Veronetta allargata*). Therefore, this section seeks to draw a cognitive map uniting material places with the identity of place by tracing important nodal points where the social fabric of Veronetta is cultivated from below.

As put by Routledge (2013), collective action uses and benefits from social ties and cultural codes, which are spatially defined, and in this sense, the proximity of shared urban spaces is a valuable starting point. This study goes a step further in arguing that the collective action of the antibodies channeled towards an inclusive pluralist city-zenship is cultivated in the outward-looking space of Veronetta and ingrained in the expansive place-based belonging it nourishes, which in turn materializes their collective identity. Hence, collective action is not merely constituted by protests, demonstrations, and rallies, but also through the everyday art of living together in a progressive space that cherishes plurality and intercultural contact. It is in this context of what I call *neighborhood as movement* that certain nodal points (Moore, 2007) or social movement scenes (Melucci, 1984; Della Porta & Diani, 2006) in the everyday life of the neighborhood come to the fore, where a counterculture is articulated and where the socialization of these actors take place, consolidating traditional forms of political mobilization.

In these everyday hubs of counterculture, the social, cultural, and artistic life associated with the expansive place-based identity that underwrites the movement manifests itself through 'carrying out rituals and other cultural performances that gather people together at certain places, or ... more mundane activities in which people, mostly unconsciously, become identified with localities via the action of memory, emotion, imagination and sociality.' (Byrne & Goodall, 2013: 65). Although they are not spaces that directly produce activism, they nonetheless sustain alternative belongings and an inclusive pluralist city-zenship model through everyday transformative placemaking practices (Bacchetta et al., 2019), with an open outlook reaching to places beyond.

4.1   *Giardino Ex-Nani: From 'Casa del Fascio' to Social Street*

Giardino Ex-Nani is one of the few green areas in Veronetta, operating as a public garden, located at the heart of the neighborhood in *via XX Settembre*. The garden used to belong to the impressive Renaissance style 16th century *Palazzo Bocca Trezza*, whose final task was to function as an art school more than a

FIGURE 37   Community event at Giardino Ex-Nani
PHOTOGRAPH: IPEK DEMIRSU

decade ago. Notwithstanding the renovations it underwent throughout its history, today, the building is not in a condition to open its doors and is undergoing another round of reconstruction. Its garden, however, is open to the public with two other smaller structures on both ends: a two-floor building that is managed by the association *DHUB* funded by the municipality of Verona, and a larger building that is currently closed. This older building carries an ironic story about the transformation of urban space, and a concomitant transformation of the identity of place.

During the fascist period, this second building was known as *casa del fascio* (house of 'fascio', named after the fascist symbol), referring to the local branch of fascists with the Roman eagle on top (Fieldnotes, 10 March 2019). Apparently, the garden and the surrounding buildings were mainly used by the Fascist Party during the 1920s and 1930s, where a leading Veronese figure, Piero Cosmin, reactivated the Federation of the Fascist Party on the 13th of September 1943. Cosmin had also declared himself as the prefect of Verona during the RSI mandate and condemned to death members of the fascist party that voted for '*ordine del giorno Grandi*' (Rossi et al., 2019). In the middle of the garden, one finds a fountain with an inscription around it that reads '*Il Comitato Madonna Verona ai Fasci di Combattimento XII*' (The Committee of Madonna Verona to the Fascists of the 12th Combat), referring to the 12th year of the fascist regime, namely the year of 1934. Still carrying visible marks of the fascist imprint in urban materiality, in 1980s the building with the Roman eagle sign was transformed into *casa del popolo* (house of the people) and was turned into a bar run by local communists who would organize dance nights, make movie projections, and celebrate the leftist *Festa dell'Unità* of *Partito Communista Italiano* (Italian Communist Party, PCI), named after the party's newspaper *l'Unità* founded by Antonio Gramsci.

Although this auxiliary building is not functional today, the smaller building that it faces at the entrance of the garden is a significant everyday hub fostering sociality and hosting various city-zen initiatives. The management of the garden and this smaller building has been granted by the municipality to the association *D-Hub* that brings together three themes: recycling and reuse, craftivism, and solidarity with women living in vulnerability. Born in 2013, this voluntary association has a separate workshop where recycled fabric is put to use in order to create new products for an 'ethical fashion'. The workshop works primarily with women who underwent hardship to provide them with tailoring skills. Since 2015, the association took over the managing of the garden ex-Nani and started to organize social events with the objective of community building in the neighborhood. With the launch of the informal online initiative *Social Street Via XX Settembre*, community lunches and dinners started to be held regularly in this small building, aiming to foster solid social ties among various inhabitants of Veronetta who can share their knowledge, interests, and needs, eventually building lasting relationships. The project was part of an international initiative that first originated in Bologna in 2013, which aimed to carry neighborhood ties both online through social media and offline through face-to-face relationships: "Right after I moved to Veronetta, I met Mirriam who told me about this curious reality of Social Street. Actually, I knew about this initiative from other cities, such as Bologna. But living this experience was much more exciting than hearing about it! Through Social Street, I feel more at home. I got to meet lovely people and experienced lots of conviviality. It's a different way of living the neighborhood." (Interview with F.S., 24 May 2019).

From the experience of Social Street that takes place at Ex-Nani, two other community initiatives were born, namely *Re-Cup* and *Ri-Ciak*. The first is a project similar to *SOS Spesa* by Paratodos, yet one that predates the pandemic, where volunteers recover unsold edible produce and distribute it to individuals who lack the means to do regular grocery shopping. The second is an initiative by residents of Veronetta to revalorize an old non-functioning movie

FIGURE 38   A Social Street weekly dinner
PHOTOGRAPH BY F.S. FOR PHOTO-ELICITATION

theatre to use it as a 'neighborhood cinema' that can show films reflecting the multiculturalism of the urban area. Unfortunately, the garden has been under construction since 2021 under revalorization efforts by the city administration, with casa del fascio being transformed into a private establishment, and the prospects of the rest of the garden as a hub of sociality are dubious at best (Interview with A.V. during fieldwork, 25 May 2022).

This lived space that underwent a sweeping transformation through history, has harbored a prolific sense of activist citizenship located in everyday urban life (Işın, 2009). Especially for newcomers, taking part in this sociocultural life that *Ex-Nani* offers meant forging new friendships and becoming part of the relational space. Such blossoming of new connections inevitably defines the neighborhood itself, and consequently, shapes the outlook of those co-inhabiting it (Massey, 1994; Aru, 2015). The account of a South Asian gradu-ate student testifies how migrants experience integration as co-creators of the identity of place: "Before participating in the activities of this local associa-tion, I didn't have many friends. After being introduced to this association, if I have some problems, I can talk to many, many people now. I feel happy to be attending Social Street and Re-Cup; otherwise, I wouldn't go." (Interview with N.S., 7 June 2019).

4.2   *The Red Triangle:* Osteria ai Preti, Circolo Arci Cañara, *and* Malacarne Barassociazione

Among the everyday hubs of the movement, three historically significant café-pub type businesses referred to as 'bar' in the Italian context, come to the fore in shaping the identity of Veronetta over different periods of the movement since the 1980s. Witnessing the embodiment of 'the other Verona' that has been dissenting to the prevalent singular timeless identity, these three localities have come to be defined from the outside as *triangolo rosso* (red triangle), closely monitored by the city administration for their non-conformist outlook, and experiencing episodes of violence inflicted by far-right groups. They are part of the movement not in the sense of mobilization *per se*, but in the counterculture they have cultivated throughout the years, operating as 'movement areas' (Melucci, 1984; Della Porta & Diani, 2006). In these hubs, everyday socialization consolidates interpersonal bonds of the antibodies and their sympathizers, thereby reproducing the expansive place-based identity in every encounter:

> Instead of being movement places, these are places to get together for people who take part in the movement. Usually, we come here to hold meetings. If you don't have an office, you can meet others in these bar-osteria type localities. They have been targeted by fascists. They went to these places and beat people up. They have named it the 'red triangle'. It started out like this, with physical aggression, not verbal, which were not isolated episodes.
>
> Interview with I.S., 7 June 2019

The oldest of these milieus is *Osteria ai Preti*, operating as a bar and a cultural association that also hosts various events such as concerts, art exhibits, theatrical shows, and book presentations. It is also historically one of the favorite hangout places of Veronesi, who experience a strong 'not-belonging' to the upper-middle class white Christian profile that dominates the touristic center. Osteria ai Preti has been a locus of everyday politics and has been providing its space for the movement also during demonstrations and rallies, as the 'home base' to come back to after mobilization. It is the place of birth for groups such as *Kollektivo Porkospino*, who would get together here to discuss their projects over a Veneto-style *aperitivo* drink. An activist from a younger generation defines the sense of place-based belonging that he receives from this space: "*Ai*

FIGURE 39   Osteria ai Preti
PHOTOGRAPH BY O.P. FOR PHOTO-ELICITATION

Preti represents the community, the collectivity of Veronetta in the way that one lives here, which is much less conformist to any given canon. This is the image of the Veronetta that I feel at home, because I have the bars I can go to where I feel good. I find people similar to me. I don't have to worry about how I dress or what I say. Maybe if I go to the other side [of Adige] I can come across a fascist." (Interview with O.P., 8 June 2019).

Malacarne Barassociazione is another nodal point of the triangle, coming into existence in 1999, founded inside an old butcher of the neighborhood by the son of an ex-partisan who fought in the resistance,[31] as a bar and a cultural association with a little area also for concerts and other cultural events. It is also considered a hangout place that upholds the core values of the antibodies and reflects the identity of Veronetta: "Of course, they are get-together places. You go there to have fun. Yet, they are also present for political mobilization, especially Malacarne. They frequently organize events, a bit of literature, meetings,

---

31   For more information on Malacarne, see https://architettiverona.it/diverse-architett ure/dai-sogni-alla-memoria-malacarne-e-nosetta.

FIGURE 40   Malacarne Barassociazione
            PHOTOGRAPH BY A.R. FOR PHOTO-ELICITATION

debates, and different arguments. They are also active from the point of view of antifascism and anti-racism." (Interview with A. R., 1 June 2019).

The last and the newest nodal point of the red triangle is *Circolo ARCI Cañara* (*Cañara Associazione di Promozione Sociale*, Cañara Association for Social Promotion), which was founded in 2012 as part of the rooted ARCI (*associazione ricreativa e culturale italiana,* recreative and cultural Italian association) tradition in Italian civil society, cultivating bottom-up initiatives with a progressive outlook in different settings and different issue-areas. Located in *via Interrato Aqua Morta* in the vicinity of Osteria ai Preti and Malacarne, Cañara has become part of the counterculture that emanates from this urban scenery, defined by a more eclectic, imaginative, and non-conformist outlook. Once again, this space hosts cultural events that bring together activists and other citizens who are drawn to the alternative form of belonging, including concerts, exhibitions, comedy shows, and literary get-togethers.[32]

---

32   For more information, see: https://www.arci.verona.it/circoli-arci/elenco-circoli/5-arci
      -canara.html.

4.3 Archival Space of the Collective Struggle: Info-Spazio 161 and the Legacy of Giorgio Bertani

This space is a novelty in the cosmos of Veronetta, coming into existence in 2019 to offer an archive that focuses on the more recent collective memory of the antibodies, rather than the historical episode of the antifascist resistance in WWII. The small office dedicated to the documentation of social conflict in the city of Verona covers particularly the period from the 1980s until today, with rich material sources of official documents such as motions and proposals in the city council, press releases, news articles, brochures, and flyers of far-right, the ultra-Catholic, and Venetist social actors, as well as those produced by the antibodies themselves. Hence, the space is dedicated to documentation as a form of activism to preserve the 'collective memory' (Melucci, 1980) of dissident voices in the Veronese landscape, including a number of 'dossiers' that chronologically narrate episodes of racism, xenophobia, far-right violence, sexism, and homophobia called 'chronology of hate', with references to primary sources.

One of the people involved in maintaining this space is a long-term activist from what once was Kollettivo Porkospino, considered to be the middle generation in the movement, undertaking much of the online work of documenting, archiving, and organizing the chronology of the collective struggle since the early 1990s, alongside a younger generation of activists called *Suburban*, operating with the slogan 'urban resistance'.[33] One part of this archival space is dedicated to the legacy of the 'rebel publisher' from Verona, Giorgio Bertani, who was part of the *pensilina* experience in the early 2000s. The section dedicated to him pays respect to this important cultural and political figure who was considered a bridge between the movements of the past and movements of the present, and hosts a part of his personal archive consisting of a collection of journals, books, and other publications, considered as an intellectual heritage of the movement.

4.4 Antifascist Bookstore: Libre!

One final hub in Veronetta worthy of mention is the cooperative bookstore *Libre!*, where readers can become partners through a symbolic contribution. Libre! is defined as an 'extremely inclusive' social reality that negates bordering tendencies present in an exclusionary territorial identity. It is the continuation of the legacy of the local bookstore *Rinascimento*, which used to be located in

---

33   For more information, see https://infospazio161.noblogs.org/centro-di-documentazi one-giorgio-bertani.

FIGURE 41   Bookstore *Libre!*
              PHOTOGRAPH BY E.S. FOR PHOTO-ELICITATION

the historical center near Porta Borsari as a locus of the Veronese left culture
with organic links to the Italian Communist Party. Born from this background
as a 'cultural emporium' in Veronetta, Libre! immediately established working
relations with other associations and social collectives in Veronetta, having in
common "an identity of shared visions, meetings, and exchanges." (Interview
with L. L., 22 October 2021).

    The bookstore seeks to avoid big commercial publishers, and works instead
with independent publishing houses and editors. The space is divided into
two parts: the anterior area is dedicated to the bookstore itself, and the pos-
terior area is a room where social and cultural activities take place, such as
yoga classes, art workshops, weekly farmer's market, and collaborations with
the University of Verona, in particular the *PoliTeSse* research group (*Politiche e
Teorie della Sessualità*) from the Department of Humanities, working on politics and theories of sexuality. The ties with a number of professors from the
university who belong to this counterculture are also evident from a large part
of the bookshelves dedicated to their publications and research areas, usually
around the themes of antifascism, anti-racism, and anti-sexism/homophobia.

As the owners come from the legacy of antifascist resistance in Verona, they also collaborate frequently with ANPI Verona and ANED, thereby playing a significant role in the city in maintaining this collective history. The bookstore is thus considered part of the movement manifested in urban space, giving form to a collective identity in the lived experience of the neighborhood:

> It's a particular bookstore that supports small independent publishers. It's one of those places that creates opportunities to meet people beyond the events that they offer, such as book presentations and whatnot. They also have events where you eat and drink. It's a cooperative; whoever can become a partner by paying 100 euros. This fusion is very interesting. In this sense, it has brought a positive change in Veronetta.
>
> Interview with E.C., 13 May 2019

Movement-Countermovement Dynamics in and through the City: Practices of Territorialization and Competing Inscriptions of Belonging

> The city is wilder than you think
> And kinder than you think.
> It is a valley and you are a horse in it.
> It is a house and you are a child in it.
> Safe and warm here in the fire of each other.
>
> ROBERT MONTGOMERY

∴

The previous chapters have investigated the socio-spatial evolution of two distinct sets of competing social actors operating in the same cityspace, their historically unfolding alliances, and their mobilization for contending constructions of city-zenship. In this sense, these chapters explored the relationship between place-based identities and collective action in everyday life, demonstrating how a group's association with the social space can act as a strong basis for their collective identity as well as a strong motor for mobilization that resonates beyond a given locality. Hence, we have seen in the micropolitics of the everyday, the possibility of developing two opposing forms of place-based identities in the same mid-sized Italian city and their side-by-side dialectical evolution in relation to one another. Having unpacked from a comparative angle the historical course of antagonistic social actors in Verona, their collective identities and values, this chapter will go on to shed light on the manifestation of movement-countermovement dynamics in the microcosmos of the city. Therefore, the section will provide insights into the forms of everyday collective action that reflect upon the lived spaces of Verona in acts of territorialization, reterritorialization, and deterritorialization (Soja, 1971; Brighenti, 2010, 2010a, 2014; Klauser, 2012; Halvorsen, 2015), especially with respect to the boundary-drawing practices between the historical center and the neighborhood of Veronetta. It will go on to sketch the activism of competing actors in the context of gentrification and conclude with an analysis of contending

© IPEK DEMIRSU, 2024 | DOI:10.1163/9789004692909_008

representations of Verona, whereby alternative imaginings of the city turn into a medium of connecting with similar actors and similar struggles in distant places. Hence, this section investigates how situated collective action mobilized through spatial identities finds expression upon the urban morphology in everyday acts of territorialization and symbolic representation, with repercussions for the experience of city-zenship. In this sense, the cognitive map of the city of Verona is divided into two territories constantly in the making, with diverse identities themselves, fuzzy borders, and ongoing struggles of representation, namely the outward-looking movement space of Veronetta and the inward-looking white sanitized space of the historical center.

1   One City, Two Territories, and Two Identities of Place: Veronetta and the Historical Center

As previously underlined on several occasions, the neighborhood of Veronetta offers an alternative conception of city-zenship with its celebration of diversity owing to the antibodies of hate that have chosen to settle here over time alongside the extant migrant communities that had laid the groundwork for the blossoming of mutual tolerance. It is not merely a 'movement area' or a 'social movement scene' accommodating social actors (Melucci, 1984; Della Porta & Diani, 2006; Nicholls, 2008), but instead I argue that the neighborhood is an inseparable part of the movement itself with its distinctive identity of place, its alternative form of expansive place-based belonging linking to places beyond, and its authentic counterspaces creating counterdiscourses in rewriting the relationship between the Veronese landscape and the self (Mitchell, 2000; Fraser, 1990). Hence, Veronetta as a social space fuels the collective identity of the antibodies, and offers a real-life experiment for the possibility of an inclusive pluralist city-zenship that the movement seeks to promote in Verona:

> In my opinion, it offers more opportunity or willingness for an alternative identity; that's what many people come to look for in Veronetta, because it has an alternative identity. So, those who desire an identity different with respect to the rest of the city come here, not only to reside but also to take part in everyday life ... It's an enclave where things go a bit differently than the rest of the city. The sociality that highlights multiculturalism ... It is a neighborhood more salient in terms of identity. If the same association in a different neighborhood assumes a slightly different identity, it is because the context gives such identity, the social reality gives identity to the place, but also the place gives identity to what happens there.
>
> Interview with E.N., 9 April 2019

TABLE 3   Movement/countermovement dynamics in and through urban space

	Historical center	Veronetta	Representation of Verona
Sovereignist Identitarianism	Territorialization and boundary-drawing practices (aggression, naming, stickers) in line with top-down attempts to keep 'urban décor' in this touristscape free of unwanted subjects.	Revanchist reterritorialization against the outward-looking identity under the so-called '*ethnic resistance*' (phantom presence, night patrols, naming, textual graffiti, and stickers).	The branding of Verona Vandea marketed to the outside world. Verona as the model city of sovereignist identitarian expressions on the transnational level.
	Ensuring *exclusive city-zenship* in the everyday (white, middle-class, Christian traditionalism, territorial culture).	Targeting antifascist activists, their associations, and hangout places. In line with the process of gentrification in replacing migrants, marginalized groups, and counterspaces of the antibodies.	Presenting Verona as a model city for other national & international identitarian actors.
Antibodies of Hate	Claims-making towards administrative authorities through protests, sit-ins, and rallies. Deterritorialization attempts to open up space for a multiplicity of subjects in the touristic center.	Everyday rituals of transformative placemaking (community building, visualizing the identity of Veronetta upon urban space, 'correcting' textual graffiti, deterritorialization, stickers).	Representing the 'other Verona' in connecting with global justice claims and extralocal actors. Verona as an open city where inclusive pluralist city-zenship is possible.

TABLE 3   Movement/countermovement dynamics in and through urban space (*cont.*)

	Historical center	Veronetta	Representation of Verona
	Exporting *inclusive pluralist city-zenship* by challenging the borders of the exclusionary territorial identity dominant in the inward-looking space.	Resisting the erosion of the identity of Veronetta generated by revanchist reterritorialization and gentrification. Cultivating spaces of intercultural exchange outside the logic of profit.	Verona as the model transfeminist city in the global struggle for sexual rights.

Today, we are talking from the inside because we live in this neighborhood every day. We are part of the residents, the associations, the life, and the culture of this neighborhood. We are the people who come from all around the world, from other Italian cities to study here ... A complexity, a multiplicity that doesn't talk about integration, but talks about interaction, cooperation, relations, and mutualism. We are those who are inside Veronetta, and we will hear the voices of those who live in Veronetta. Today, the outsiders, the clandestine and the irregulars in this neighborhood are the fascists.

> Speech delivered during a protest against the new office of
> Forza Nuova in Veronetta, fieldnotes 22 December 2018

Today, this informal network has come to be an indispensable feature of the outward-looking identity of the neighborhood, seeking to sustain existing social bonds and cultivate further inclusiveness and exchange among the various realities that constitute it. In promoting practices of community-making embedded in a pluralist environment (Nicholls, 2008; Bacchetta et al., 2019), these local groups bring together inhabitants of various backgrounds, generations, and gender identities in ritualized face-to-face exchanges that permit the proliferation of an expansive place-based belonging: "I believe that Veronetta is a beautiful neighborhood that ought to be sustained, because it was created over the years. It's something that created itself." (Interview with

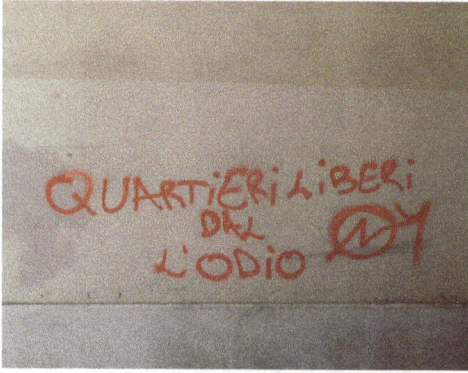

FIGURE 42   'Neighborhoods free of hate' writing on
             a wall in Veronetta
             PHOTOGRAPH: IPEK DEMIRSU

P.N., 5 Feb. 2021). This little material, cognitive, and lived 'enclave' is situated as opposed to the rest of the city taken as the playground of the multiplicity of far-right actors supported by the city administration: "Let's say that Verona is a city where the right, from the moderate right to far-right, finds a fertile ground. In this respect, the whole city is like this." (Interview with B.P., 1 February 2021). As a result, the city is understood as being divided into two spatial identities defined by two different sets of belonging:

> Verona is a difficult city when it comes to personal relations, so we tend to create our own bubble in terms of friends and those who share our world-view. Veronetta gives form to this conception of sociality. It's not perfect, but nothing is. And surely more than the rest of the city, Veronetta gives me a reason to want to continue living here and be involved in things that are not going well. Maybe living in another neighborhood would have been much more complicated because other neighborhoods mirror the true reality of Verona.
>
> Interview with A.V. 15 Feb. 2019

> Verona is a bit particular as a city. At times, it demonstrates incredible signs of closure, and on the other hand, it has initiatives and groups that are on the contrary.
>
> Interview with I.V., 7 April 2019

Within this divide regarding spatial identities, the historical center employs a special place not only as the touristified facade of the city (Sequera & Nofre,

FIGURE 43   Racist writing at the bus stop in front of Arena
di Verona in the historical center that reads
'Negroes in Africa'
PHOTOGRAPH: IPEK DEMIRSU

2018), but also one that embodies the Veronese territorial identity for the far-right universe, which is promoted as a 'model city' for transnational identitarian actors. The historical center is a space that encapsulates heritage, history, local myths, and traditions sparking a sense of pride. It is a heavily touristified area (Sequera & Nofre, 2018), 'guarded' by far-right groups from unbelonging subjects in order to defend this showcase of territorial identity presented to the outside world, visibly marked by a heteronormative order (Hubbard, 2000; Brown & Browne, 2016). In short, it is the seamless white sanitized touristic space harboring defensive localisms (Massey, 1994; Lipsitz, 2011), embellished with hegemonic narratives of a glorious past conducive for restorative nostalgia (Zukin, 1998; Mitchell, 2000; Boym, 2001; Moore, 2007).

Those that are financially well-off are from the historical center and are positioned towards the right. There are also people who do not have such privileges and want to be part of it. So, the historical center is a globe in itself of right-wingers.

Interview with N.C., 11 February 2021

In the last two or three years, a new form of racism has been spreading that targets differences identified in how one dresses, the accent, or opinions being expressed, which is then provoked and assaulted. There is no organization with a program or a structure to ... pursue targeted violence. Instead, all is born out gradually, especially during the weekends and always in the historical center, a symbol of the identity that is to be protected from contamination, with a desire for violence nurtured by an aversion towards difference.

Ex-chief Prosecutor of Verona Guido Papalia, quoted in LA TERZA, 2009: 153

As a result of a sense of entitlement to local privileges and the 'everyday chauvinisms' that they incur (Saitta, 2021), the center came to be identified with what has been referred to as *'destra imborghesita del centro storico'* (Siviero, 2018); in other words, right-wing elements that came to be identified as the bourgeois of the historical center: "If you cross the bridge and go to Piazza Erbe, there it's the far-right zone, the middle-class right, those that to go have *aperitivo* and stay there all night." (Interview with F.M., 12 Feb 2021). It is, therefore, no coincidence that the wide array of far-right and populist right movements identify with the city center and seek to defend it from unwanted intrusion. In a similar vein, the process of rendering the city of Verona as a global tourist hub is considered a development that indulges localist pride, as put by a member of CasaPound: "Verona managed to position itself incredibly on a global level as a reference point for touristic attraction, as a point of interest for international visitors. Today, a series of valorizations of the city are wonderful and unique. For the love that I have for my city, I see it as a positive development." (interview with C.P., 8 July 2020).

In sum, the historical center with its rich historical monuments and architecture, is appropriated for the marketing of heritage and for building an exclusionary territoriality, where belonging is defined through this white and sanitized space in the negation of non-belonging elements such as migrants, different sexual and political orientations. As one responder has summarized it succinctly, "[i]f you're different, remain in your own diversity and don't come spoiling my local." (Interview with D.P., 4 February 2021). Such an outlook epitomizes sovereignist identitarian tendencies prevalent on the national level in various contexts, reifying national borders and homogeneity within. On the other hand, the neighborhood of Veronetta, adjacent to the touristic area and part of the historical center itself, has come to be identified with a contending expansive place-based identity, upholding a different set of values on conviviality and social ties, where the alternative construction of city-zenship reflects wider struggles of citizenship rights in Italy and beyond. The fuzzy borders of these two 'territories' are rewritten in everyday encounters, as contending actors seek to mark urban space with their version of spatial belonging that is part of larger identity struggles across borders.

2   Acts of Territorialization between Adjacent Social Spaces of Verona

2.1   *Guarding the Borders of the Historical Center*
As the symbolic fortress and the touristic showcase of the nostalgic territorial identity for far-right and identitarian groups in Verona, the historical center has been defended and 'guarded' against non-belonging elements. The practices of territorialization undertaken by these groups have involved both what Wahlström has differentiated as 'control of territorial borders' as well as 'control within a territory' (2010). The controlling of borders involves militants of far-right movements and local hooligans guarding the material borders of the historical center, monitoring entrances, and keeping out unwanted elements. The latter is an attempt to maintain a sanitized white space on the part of the city administration with institutionalized far-right elements at various bodies of urban security and urban hygiene, who seek to eliminate traces of poverty, marginalization, and urban decay from within the touristic center (Saitta, 2015; Mazzei, 2018). As a result, this inward-looking space, carefully maintained as if it were frozen in space and time (Zukin, 1998), harbors hegemonic narratives of a glorious past that nurtures identitarian claims. As is the case in other hostile settings around the world, those actors who increasingly appropriate sovereignist rhetoric claiming an exclusive entitlement to a 'homeland' (Freeden, 2017; Basile & Mazzoleni, 2020; Basile et al., 2020) engage in acts of territorialization in their locality to 'defend' and 'protect' this space symbolizing a nativist belonging.

The historical center and Veronetta are not only separated by the natural border (Lefebvre, 1991 [1974]) of the river Adige with the bridges that offer passage between the two, but are also separated by cognitive boundaries that are re-negotiated by everyday acts of boundary-drawing and erasing. One of the most aggressive forms of boundary-drawing to protect the touristscape

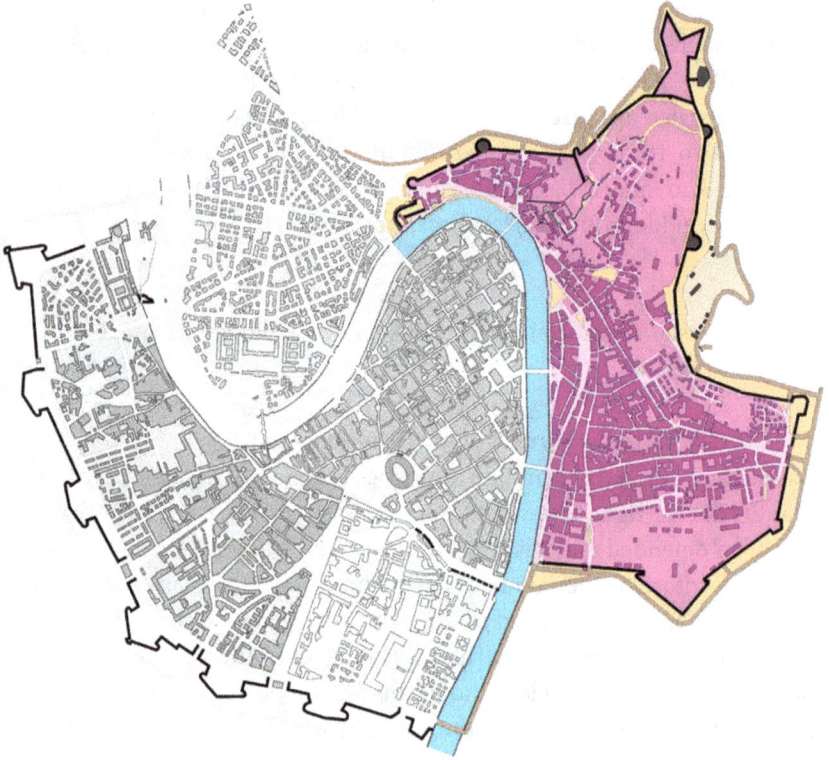

FIGURE 44   Map depicting the border between the historical center and Veronetta
ILLUSTRATION: AMT3: TRASPORTI, TURISMO, TERRITORIO. AVAILABLE AT:
HTTPS://WWW.AMT3.IT/EN/PERMESSI/VERONETTA

as a perceived source of territorial identity taken up by far-right groups since the 1990s is everyday micro-violence around the borders between these two spaces. These episodes densify around the *Ponte dei Navi* bridge connecting the most racialized street in Veronetta *via XX Settembre* to *Porta Leoni* as the Roman southern gate of the center, today leading to the main piazzas. As a result, entrances to the historical center from Veronetta have been guarded by far-right militants from various backgrounds, resulting in some of the most brutal episodes of everyday violence in Verona. Such practices have been evidently absent at the borders with other adjacent neighborhoods such as Borgo Roma, Borgo Milano, or Borgo Trento. The boundary-drawing sought by the systematic threatening and aggression undertaken by far-right actors against non-belonging subjects arriving from Veronetta is lucidly explicated by a historical LGBTQ+ activist:

> In the city center, the 'lounge' of the affluent was Piazza Erbe, where certain people would act as the owners. For us, it was almost dangerous crossing the bridge and going to the other side because it was controlled by the far-right, by people who knew that we were coming from Veronetta ... I remember the years when we had our office in *via Scrimiari*. We would go out in groups. We couldn't go out alone. Neither us nor other Veronese [activist] groups. Veronesi themselves could not cross the bridge from Veronetta to the center. Verona is a small city where everyone is recognized; the far-right most probably knows where we live.
>
> Interview with C.Z., 10 Feb 2021

This testimony clearly demonstrates Bauman's (1995) definition of a no-go zone, which for some means 'no go in', whereas for marginalized others, it means 'no go out' as confinement (Bauman, 1995: 10). As a matter of fact, on 5th of May 2001, leading to an elevated chapter of tension between LGBTQ+ associations and far-right actors, two prominent LGBTQ+ activists from Verona were violently assaulted at the entrance of the historical center near Porta Leoni, one being beaten in the face with a belt by local members of Forza Nuova who were condemned by the tribunal in Verona.[1] The underlying cause for the tension was the fact that LGBTQ+ activists were planning to organize a demonstration in *Piazza Brà*, one of the most important piazzas of the city accommodating the world-famous Roman Arena. As a social space demarcated by heteronormative scripts of appropriateness (Brown & Browne, 2016) in a city boasting a return to traditional values, these actors sought to defend what they perceived as their own territory from elements 'out of place' (Merrill, 2014).

Everyday acts of territorialization through violence against non-belonging subjects reached a zenith with the murder of Nicolo Tommasoli, exactly at the cognitive borders between the historical center and Veronetta at *Corticella Leoni* on the night of 30th of April 2008, who was singled out by his 'alternative' outfit representing the difference of a non-conforming lifestyle (Melucci, 1980; Johnston et al., 1994). These episodes exemplify the ways in which extremist elements have taken on the self-proclaimed role of guarding the boundaries of the historical center, to be protected as the sanctuary of a native Veronese

---

1 From the archival dossier *A Verona tutta l'erba e uno (s)fascio,* available at: https://movime ntandociaverona.files.wordpress.com/2018/03/dossier-verona-corretto.pdf.

tradition and identity (Brighenti, 2010; Brighenti, 2014; Halvorsen, 2015). Yet, everyday violence endured by the antibodies has worked to reinforce a sense of collective identity, and to consolidate solidarity among different groups that constitute the movement: "This has posed for many years a strong threat for us. There have been dozens of aggressions, but this has re-awakened a movement. That is, all the disgrace that took place (also the death of Nicola Tommasoli), cemented a Veronese movement that throughout the years learned to speak for itself, because it's not always easy to speak inside a movement that has very different positions and very different methodologies." (Interview with C.Z., 10 February 2021).

The use of violence in territorializing the historical center did not only take place at the overlap of the cognitive and material borders, but also inside the main squares in bottom-up forms of 'controlling the territory' (Wahlström, 2010), where non-belonging subjects are threatened and forcefully 'canceled' from the urban scenery. One particular example on point is the aggression of a same-sex couple in Piazza Brà, who were targeted and attacked for having demonstrated affection in public, thereby defying the heteronormative order (Hubbard, 2000; Brown & Browne, 2016).[2] Another such incident came to the fore when two antifascist activists from the younger generation started working at a restaurant in the heart of Piazza Erbe, who came to be continuously pursued and threatened by members of CasaPound due to their political orientation (Fieldnotes, 1 July 2019). With respect to the systematic threats endured by these two activists and those who came to their support, antibodies made the following post on social media: "After ten years after the death of Nicola Tommasoli, nothing seems to have changed in Verona. No one with opinions that do not conform to those held by neofascist groups can feel at ease in the streets of the city. Not even at one's workplace. Security, a precious theme for the right, far-right or not, seems to be a privilege of the few and for the few." (Facebook post by Veronesi aperti al mondo-Verona città aperta, 18 July 2019).

2.2   *Deterritorializing Practices in the Historical Center*
It is argued that landscapes that are sites of dominant identity constructs can concomitantly function as sites of resistance (Winchester et al., 2003). It is those everyday practices of resistance (Semi et al., 2009) that can deterritorialize public spaces by negating pre-defined ownership or exclusionary forms of territorial belongings. These practices open up such privileged sites

---

2   For more information on aggression towards gay couple in the city center, see: https://corrie redelveneto.corriere.it/verona/cronaca/18_agosto_14/verona-coppia-gay-aggredita-un-gru ppo-ragazzini-piazza-bra-39b9d0e2-9f93-11e8-b2ca-5158fc8ef2ca.shtml.

to a multiplicity of subjects by disturbing the boundaries that were previously placed. Such deterritorialization efforts (Brighenti, 2014; Halvorsen, 2015) can work to expose hierarchies and inequalities inscribed in a given space, imposing limited access to marginalized groups (Holston & Appadurai, 1996). The historical center is not only a touristified space embodying local heritage that calls for singular identities, but also an administrative space of power where the principal bodies of the municipality and other local authorities are situated. As such, it is the space where the antibodies go to address their claims-making in most of the protest events, depending on the necessary authorization, which is frequently denied, according to the activists (Fieldnotes, 24 November 2019, 18 July 2020).

Notwithstanding sporadic protest events or rallies in the various piazzas of the historical center, the public space that the antibodies have been systematically trying to 'liberate' in ritualized practices of deterritorialization has been *Piazza dei Signori* (also referred to as *Piazza Dante*). I prefer to use the term 'deterritorialize' instead of 'reterritorialize' due to the fact that these groups, in their daily endeavors, have not sought to claim exclusive possession of this urban space, instead, aiming to render it accessible to a variety of protagonists outside the logic of profit. As such, deterritorialization here is an attempt to introduce inclusive pluralist city-zenship in an inward-looking space, challenging the cognitive boundaries that are set by exclusive territorial city-zenship. Thus, deterritorialization efforts are treated as everyday acts of city-zenship (Işın, 2009) in contested urban spaces. The square comes to be referred to as *Piazza Dante* after the famous Italian poet, writer, and philosopher Dante Alighieri, also known as the father of the Italian language, whose statue is placed in the middle of the square. The square is located right next to Piazza Erbe in a central touristic area, whilst accommodating the administrative building of the Prefecture of Verona. As a matter of fact, before the total 'conquest' of the historical center by identitarian actors alongside the process of its touristification, this square was considered a 'movement area' (Melucci, 1984; Della Porta & Diani, 2006) in the 1970s where local groups from the radical left would meet, which explains the choice of the antibodies to operate in this part of the touristic center (Interview with P. N., 5 Feb. 2021).

Following the complete territorialization of the historical center by far-right figures as the Veronese progressive movements and leftist politics were pushed out towards Veronetta, one of the first significant episodes of 'deterritorialization' took place on the 25th of April 2006 in Piazza Dante. A group of ultra-Catholics, Padania nativists, and Venetists collaborating under the *Committee of Pasque Veronesi* organized the celebration of San Marco Day on the same day as the celebration of the Italian Liberation Day from Nazi-fascism, in an attempt to rewrite the local history to emphasize Verona's allegiance to the Republic of Venice as opposed to post-war antifascist Italy. Such restorative nostalgia involving an anti-modern rewriting of history with local myths and symbols (Boym, 2001) was cogently exemplified by the 18th century traditional outfits of the participants who were preparing to hold a mass in Latin at the square. To protest the event and deterritorialize this piazza from a historical revisionist rewriting (Valencia-Garcia, 2020), activists from the LGBTQ+ association Circolo Pink and the social collective La Chimica dismantled the stage that was prepared for the organizers, and occupied the square to prevent the event from taking place: "That day, around 30 activists from Circolo Pink and La Chimica liberated Piazza Dante from Catholic fundamentalists and fascists, resisting as much as possible to the evacuation by the police forces. It was related to one of the first attempts to change the meaning of the Italian Liberation Day by the circle of nostalgic separatists and fundamentalists who have tried to turn it into San Marco Day." (Facebook post by *Centro Documentazione Bertani*, 25 April 2021) They were eventually taken to the police station and identified, yet released in the afternoon, continuing with another event to commemorate victims of Nazi-fascism for the occasion of Liberation Day in the other principal square of the center, Piazza Brà.

Piazza Dante came to the fore once again in 2008, when various student groups, from secondary school to university level, with the lead of the youth collective *Studiare con Lentezza* (Studying Slowly), decided to employ a ritualized presence in Piazza Dante during the summer period every until 2015. The aim was to challenge the representation and the maintenance of the historical center as the epitome of urban décor: "We had this idea because the question of spaces is a question that was there for ages. Verona is, so to speak, a symbol of the question of space, of décor, of a city that has to be clean, where you should not see things or people that contrast the character of the city." (Interview with F.M., 12 Feb 2021). With the leadership of the younger generation, the antibodies went on to 'frequent' Piazza Dante as 'non-belonging subjects', which would involve spontaneous acts of making music, singing, dancing, and having collective debates in the square. Despite the fact that the group consisted of residents, because they were found to be spoiling the sanitized and timeless touristic setting marketed to the outside world, they were regularly evicted by the local police and taken to the police station: "There were guys playing bongo drums, so the police would always intervene ... Spontaneously staying in the center became a political claims-making." (Interview with, C.Z. 10 Feb 2021)

Later in 2018, an informal network called *Assemblea 17 Dicembre* (Assembly of 17 December) constituted by the antibodies working on the issue of immigration occupied *Piazza dei Signori* in front of the city's Prefecture, turning

FIGURE 45   Piazza dei Signori (Square of the Lords) turned into 'Spiaggia dei Signori' (Beach
of the Lords) in solidarity with refugees left without a decision on their permit
FROM THE FACEBOOK PAGE VERONESI APERTI AL MONDO —VERONA CITTÀ
APERTA, 6 AUGUST 2018

it into a 'beach' since the officials went on a vacation and left seven refugees
without a decision on their permit. In temporarily transforming this space
that represents 'authority' into a place of 'solidarity' with a sense of humor, the
volunteers of *Assemblea 17 Dicembre* renamed the piazza *Spiaggia dei Signori*
(Beach of the Lords). In this example, protest itself comes to construe a sense
of place in the acts of occupying, reappropriating, and attributing new meaning to a space (Della Porta et al., 2013), which tends to be embedded in the local
whilst producing global frames, in this case, solidarity with asylum seekers and
refugees.

2.3   *Revanchist Reterritorialization and 'Ethnic Resistance' in Veronetta*
The growing visibility of an outward-looking multicultural urban space in the
close vicinity of the white sanitized homogenous space of the historical center led to an attempt at reterritorialization in Veronetta (Soja, 1971; Brighenti,
2010; Brighenti, 2014), as the neighborhood entered the orbit of far-right and
identitarian movements. Such a mission was undertaken by two prominent
far-right groups, namely *CasaPound* and *Forza Nuova*, with the slogan of 'ethnic resistance' to reinstate a white Veronese identity once again in one of the
most historic neighborhoods of the city that was now considered a racialized
space. This strategy in the locality clearly conveys the demographic anxiety
underpinning the Great Replacement theory, which is voiced at the national

FIGURE 46   'Ethnic resistance' by Forza
             Nuova Verona
             FROM THE TWITTER ACCOUNT
             OF FORZA NUOVA VERONA, 24
             NOVEMBER 2018

level by government officials as well as by other far-right counterparts on the transnational level.[3] While the so-called migrant 'invasion' is pointed out as the primary culprit, allegedly 'threatening' non-migrants living in the area, the actual target has been the network of progressive associations that work to realize a plural and open space in Veronetta. These intentions were already being signaled before the official entrance of far-right groups in the neighborhood, in the form of violent raids accompanied by fascist chanting that took place on repeated occasions in some of the hangout places of leftist activists that are considered to constitute 'the red triangle' explicated in Chapter 5.[4]

First in 2017, when *CasaPound* opened a new office near the university campus, another notorious far-right group, *Forza Nuova*, followed suit a year later to inaugurate their new office in this multicultural neighborhood, causing feelings of unrest and insecurity on the part of the inhabitants. Naming their new office as *Casa dei Patrioti* (The House of Patriots), Forza Nuova announced the objectives of their 'outpost' in the neighborhood:

> Because there is and there should always be someone willing to demonstrate the shield and the blade to those who seize our Land and our

3   For a discussion on Italian Agriculture Minister's statement and the use of the 'ethnic replacement' theory by international far-right figures, see: https://www.bbc.com/news/world-eur ope-65324319.
4   For more information on these raids, see: https://www.larena.it/territori/citt%C3%A0o/botte -e-razzismoalla-festa-di-laurea-vanno-condannati-1.6019569.

Identity. This is the reason for the birth of The House of Patriots Verona in the neighborhood of Veronetta, where the only struggle without borders is the struggle against ethnic replacement. The House of Patriots might be the last Veronese identitarian reference point in a neighborhood considered 'lost' by experienced politicians and by the most hopeful identitarian consciences. The House of Patriots will be ... the New Order *to discover an anti-system and politically incorrect culture in a degraded and multi-ghettoized neighborhood in which the myth of the 'melting pot' has already failed.*

Facebook page of Forza Nuova Verona, 16 December 2018, *emphasis added*

This declaration demonstrates the spatial struggle to reclaim white spaces that are considered to be threatened by non-white immigrants (Tudor, 2014; Murdoch & Murhall, 2019), while framing such cause in a sovereignist rhetoric of taking back control in one's territory and defending one's identity (Freeden, 2017; Basile et al., 2020) against a perceived failure of multiculturalism (Prowe, 2004; Kriesi et al., 2008; Zùquete, 2018; Šima, 2021). Moreover, the term 'resistance', usually associated with left-wing, progressive movements, is appropriated to invoke a sense of righteousness and just cause, portraying the autochthon 'white' population as the victims in an existential struggle.

The same day of the opening of *Casa dei Patrioti*, CasaPound organized a celebration for the first anniversary of their own office in Veronetta named *'il Mastino'* after the Scaliger ruler, with the participation of their national leader Gianluca Iannone, who claimed: "Looking back in this past year, we have realized that we are the only ones who undertake the defense of Veronetta and that il Mastino is the only Veronese bulwark where the love for the nation is kept."[5] What is particularly striking in this declaration is the connection being made between reterritorialization efforts in urban space and a sense of loyalty to the nation, as ethnonationalist motives underwrite everyday boundary-drawing practices in other hostile settings. These two groups, who not only compete with progressive movements but also among themselves, have carried such rivalry in Veronetta, thereby raising concerns over an 'escalation of fascist violence' in the neighborhood: "Veronetta should not become a field of competition between different Veronese fascisms." (Facebook post by member of *Assemblea Veronetta Vive*, 21 December 2018).

---

5 Iannone quoted in Corriere di Verona (23 December 2018), available at: https://www.veronas era.it/attualita/forza-nuova-casapound-antifascisti-veronetta-22-dicembre-2018.html.

These new offices have rarely functioned and remain closed most of the days (in fact, *Casa dei Patrioti* was closed permanently after a year), and therefore fail to constitute a part in the everyday life of the neighborhood. That being said, they still serve a significant symbolic function of a revanchist reterritorialization, to reclaim this space through textual graffiti and stickers, coupled with episodes of violence towards migrants and antifascist activists during night patrols, thereby causing a sense of insecurity on the part of the residents. For instance, just a couple of days after the inauguration of the Forza Nuova office, a Romanian migrant woman walking in Veronetta while talking on the phone in her native language was insulted with racist slurs and then physically attacked.[6] Around the same period, writings threatening the LGBTQ+ association Circolo Pink appeared on the walls in Veronetta, an association that was previously targeted by Forza Nuova as 'non-belonging' subjects in the conceptualization of the ideal heteronormative protagonist of city life.

Migrant and non-migrant respondents alike have chosen to bring this issue up as a negative development, conceived as a provocation of existing actors. This position is conveyed in the testimony of A.R. from Eastern Europe, who first arrived in Verona as a student 15 years ago, later on settling here:

> It's a place of discomfort, a negative change from a political perspective to have two representations of extreme right in the neighborhood. Unfortunately, they are gaining more support in Verona and in the north in general. Pointing out migration, always putting the blame on who is different ... Obviously, the fact that they opened here in a multiethnic neighborhood is a provocation, because they could've chosen any other neighborhood. Instead, they chose here to provoke, to create moments of conflict, of uneasiness.
>
> Interview with A.R., 1 June 2019

Cross-cutting these acts of everyday reterritorialization by far-right groups, involving a phantom presence in the neighborhood and violent threats, lies the sovereignist idea of 'taking back control in our own territory' (Basile & Mazzoleni, 2020): "These new presences settled to bring their outlook inside a neighborhood taken to be 'different' ... It's not only a question of ethnic resistance, but also one of creating outposts here to say 'it's not your home anymore, antifascists', assuming antifascism to be an insult. Inside this boiler of right-wing

---

6 For more information on the episode, see: https://corrieredelveneto.corriere.it/verona/polit ica/18_dicembre_26/straniera-insultata-strada-verona-ipotesi-razzismo-482b8d8c-0901-11e9 -b824-08206b89cf3f.shtml.

FIGURE 47   Writing insulting Circolo Pink appear
             four days after the inauguration of Casa
             dei Patrioti
             PHOTO FROM THE FACEBOOK
             PAGE OF CIRCOLO PINK, 26
             DECEMBER 2018

sovereignism, the first things to enter are politics of gender and immigration."
(Interview with E.N., 9 April 2019). In short, sovereignist ideals translate as acts
of territorialization and reterritorialization of urban space (Brighenti, 2010;
Brighenti, 2014) in the form of aggressive revanchism of defending old privileges, traditional values, and nativist identities (Smith, 1996).

2.4 Everyday Rituals of Placemaking as Resistance to Reterritorialization

The set of social relations, the forms of belonging, and the everyday rituals of
a place play a significant role not only in shaping the identity of individuals
who occupy such space, but also in the identity of the space itself. As argued
from the outset, the neighborhood of Veronetta has a different identity of
place in relation to the rest of the city, accompanied by a different understanding of spatial belonging that is both upheld and promoted by individuals who

frequent it. Faced with the series of revanchist reterritorialization attempts to instill an exclusively white Christian belonging predominating the rest of the city, the antibodies valorize the identity of Veronetta in their daily exchanges as an outward-looking pluralist space, cultivating their expansive spatial belonging. The neighborhood owes its distinct identity to everyday rituals of 'transformative placemaking' (Bacchetta et al., 2019), in the daily community-building efforts and practices of conviviality (Neal et al., 2019) sustained by the antibodies, through which an alternative form of city-zenship is made possible (Işın, 2009). By evoking the defining characteristics of Veronetta and the alternative forms of belonging it generates as a form of everyday collective action, the antibodies resist reterritorialization attempts, refusing representations that depict the neighborhood as a 'no-go zone' of micro-criminality associated with marginalization.

Three examples come to the fore following the opening of the new offices of far-right groups in Verona, namely the ad hoc initiatives *Senza Memoria Non C'è Futuro* (Without Memory There's No Future) and *Veronetta Vive* (Veronetta Lives), together with the collective art project *Siamo Tutti Esposti* (We Are All Exposed). The first initiative of visually accentuating the antifascist and anti-racist identity of Veronetta was in response to the new office of CasaPound at the end of 2017, for the occasion of the Holocaust Memorial Day. A group of collectives and associations from the antibodies, with the lead of *Assemblea 17 Dicembre*, placed photographs depicting the horrors of the Holocaust in various urban spaces of Veronetta and distributed vouchers in order to spatially criticize fascist ideologies and their modern vestiges (Facebook post of Veronesi aperti al mondo-Verona città aperta, 27 January 2018). This strategy of visualizing the consequences of Nazi-fascism was a spontaneous act of transformative placemaking, whereby the materiality of Veronetta was rewritten with an antifascist outlook that is evoked to guide the future. This included hanging a big banner that read 'Without memory, there is no future' in front of the new office of CasaPound in Veronetta, signed by *Assemblea 17 Dicembre*.

The second initiative called *Veronetta Vive*, in response to the new office of Forza Nuova one year later, was a collaborative event organized by different associations, collectives, bookstores, and cafés in the neighborhood to highlight once again the inclusive and pluralist understanding of city-zenship born out of this area. These actors concurred that the best way to resist identitarian closure was to demonstrate how they co-inhabit the everyday in Veronetta:

> Veronetta is the place that we inhabit, work, and spend our time in, expressing our passions and interests. Where our steps and our lives cross each other, intermingling with other lives and other worlds. It is a place

FIGURE 48   A photograph of Holocaust victims, hung on a Veronetta street sign dedicated to a
historical neofascist figure in Verona.
PHOTO FROM THE FACEBOOK PAGE OF VERONESI APERTI AL MONDO –
VERONA CITTÀ APERTA, 27 JANUARY 2018

where we can delude ourselves to live in a welcoming city that is culturally stimulating. In the streets of this neighborhood, we feel at home ... *In
Veronetta, there is no room for those who disregard its profound essence, its
open and cosmopolitan spirit, its indescribable gaze looking beyond its borders.* There is no room for those who consider it as land to be conquered,
for those who seek to 'clean' it. Because what we have here is precious
and should be defended. That is why we want Veronetta to respond to the
obtuse closure of racism and intolerance by opening up its spaces, filling
up its streets and squares with life.

> Facebook post by member of *Assemblea Veronetta Vive*,
> 21 December 2018, *emphasis added*

With this collectively set up objective, various actors and movement spaces
collaborated to demonstrate the identity of Veronetta underwritten by social
inclusion, pluralism, and cosmopolitanism, but most importantly as a space
that is part of the collective identity of the antibodies: namely an antifascist,
anti-racist, and anti-sexist space at its core. The initiative was concluded
by a flash mob in Piazza Santa Toscana organized by NUDM Verona, whose

FIGURE 49   Antifascist witch spell by NUDM Verona in Piazza Santa Toscana of Veronetta
PHOTOGRAPH: IPEK DEMIRSU

members dressed as witches putting an antifascist spell: "Under our eyes, you will always be. Ours is a greatly immense network, you see. Let every fascist tremble. Let them shiver. The revolution is feminist. Let every male chauvinist tremble, let them shiver. Veronetta is antifascist!" (Fieldnotes, 22 December 2018).

The last undertaking of transformative placemaking against reterritorialization attempts of far-right groups was the project of *Siamo Tutti Esposti* (We Are All Exposed), aiming to visibly portray the anti-racist identity of the neighborhood. Organized by the cultural associations *Veronetta 129* and *D-HUB*, this event invited all residents of Veronetta to meet at the community garden of Ex-Nani to collectively paint banners carrying anti-racist slogans. These banners were later chosen by volunteers residing in Veronetta and hung from their windows or balconies to 'expose' the anti-racist spirit that governs everyday life in the neighborhood, rendering the expansive place-based identity radiating from Veronetta materially tangible in its streets, houses, stores, and offices.

FIGURE 50   A banner that reads "Our homeland is the entire world" hanging from a balcony in
               Veronetta
               PHOTO FROM THE FACEBOOK PAGE OF *VERONETTA 129*, 17 MARCH 2019

2.5   *Naming as Territorialization*

Toponymic maps of a city tell a lot about the identity of place (Banini, 2017) and its representation (Martin, 2003; Banini & Ilovan, 2021; Schwarz & Streule, 2022), in which naming a space assigns a certain type of belonging (Berg & Kearns, 1996; McKittrick, 2007). The practice of naming can assume sexual, racial, or colonial entitlements, and therefore, "naming place is also an act of naming the self and self-histories" (McKittrick, 2007: xxii). As a result, toponymic decisions can also be read as acts of territorialization, where a particular set of belonging is inscribed into urban space. The case of Verona highlights how the simple act of naming a place can become a matter of political controversy, whether they are attempts made by city councilors with far-right affiliations on an institutional scale, or ad hoc practices of renaming places by social movements in the everyday city life.

A striking example of this practice happened in 2008 when one of the main streets of Veronetta along the Adige River was dedicated to *Nicola Pasetto*, a notorious historical far-right figure from Verona, with the initiative of councilors from *Alleanza Nazionale*. From a young age, Pasetto was involved in and became the leader of the Verona branch of *Fronte della Gioventù*, the youth movement of the post-fascist political party *Movimento Sociale Italiano* (MSI) (Milesi et al., 2005). He was among the leaders of Hellas ultras and was eventually elected to Verona city council from MSI in 1980. A year later, on the 4th of April 1981, he was found guilty of violently attacking leftist activists that were hanging posters against death penalty, which MSI at the time was trying to bring back.[7]

The street named after Pasetto is not only a central road dividing Veronetta from the historical center, but also an area with historical significance to the antifascist resistance in Verona during WWII, where partisans were executed by fascist forces. This is demonstrated by the fact that it intersects another major street dedicated to those who fought in the local resistance, named *Viale dei Partigiani*. The latter has been subjected to further reterritorialization attempts by Forza Nuova, who decided to mark over this street sign with their stickers: "Here we have a negative superimposition, a cancellation of memory. During WWII, the police headquarters was near here, where the university building stands today next to the river. So, they used to execute partisans, and would leave the dead bodies next to this wall. What remains today is this street's name as a place of commemoration. On top, we see the stickers of Forza Nuova. It's like spitting on the tombs of the partisans when neofascists

---

7   For more information, see: https://veronacittaaperta.blogspot.com/2009/01/nicola-pase tto-deputato-picchiatore.html.

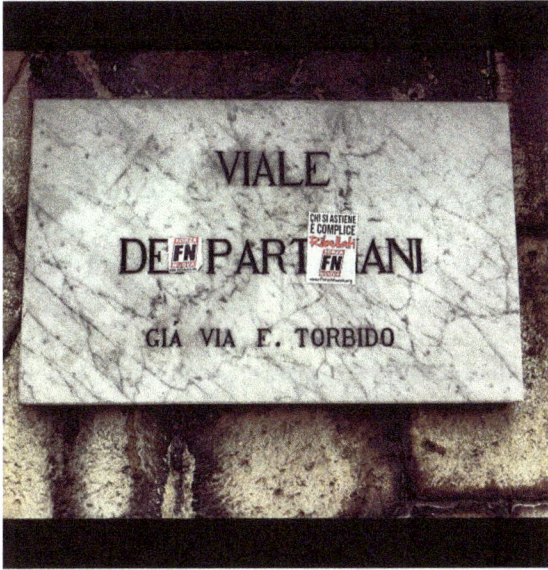

FIGURE 51   Via dei Partigiani dedicated to the memory of the
partisans who were executed during the Italian
Social Republic, with stickers of Forza Nuova
covering some of the text
PHOTOGRAPH BY M.G. FOR PHOTO-ELICITATION

put their own stickers on top." (Interview with M.G., 25 April 2019) Both of
these roads mark the physical borders of Veronetta, with their toponomastics
conveying the contending political belongings through urban space.

In 2018, a committee inside the city council formed by far-right politicians from *Fratelli d'Italia* and their identitarian allies active in the Veronese
movement scene presented a joint proposal to name a street or a square after
Giorgio Almirante,[8] the historical leader of MSI. Almirante is a political figure
who served in the National Republican Guard during the Republic of Salò and
was a staunch adherent of the Manifesto of Race under fascist rule. While this
proposal was accepted with a majority of the votes awaiting implementation,
another proposal was presented in the city council to name a street or a public park after the historical fascist intellectual Julius Evola, and later for Ezra

---

8 Original motion presented to the City Council of Verona, 15 June 2018, Pervenuto 406,
   Mozione per intitolare una strada o una piazza a Giorgio Almirante. Presidenza del Consiglio.
   Available at: https://www.comune.verona.it/media/_ComVR/Cdr/SegreteriaConsiglio/Alleg
   ati/mozioni/2017-2022/406_moz.pdf.

Pound.[9] The antibodies have protested these attempts to nostalgically enti-
tle urban spaces after local, national, or international forerunners of fascism,
which inevitably leave an impact on the identity of place and the place-based
identity of those who inhabit thereof. In 2020, old and new elements of the
antibodies mobilizing under the informal Facebook group *Veronesi aperti al
mondo-Verona città aperta* (Veronesi open to the world, Verona open city),
organized a public gathering to prevent the association of Veronese urban
spaces with fascism, instead reminding the identity of Verona as a city that
deserved a gold medal for its resistance to Nazi-fascism in Italy (Facebook post
of Veronesi Aperti al mond – Verona città aperta, 24 January 2020).

Another form of territorialization through urban toponomastics in selec-
tively rewriting collective memory of place is the far-right attempts to officially
cancel commemorative landmarks dedicated to the antifascist resistance. One
such example of historical revisionism (Boym, 2001; Valencia-Garcia, 2020) is
the motion presented by a city councilor in 2019 demanding the verification of
the historical episode coming to be known as the battle in defense of *Palazzo
delle Poste* by local antifascist forces against the German troops.[10] As explicated in detail in Chapter 3, this historical event, constituting a cornerstone
in the legacy of antifascist resistance in Verona, had earned the city a golden
medal, which the antibodies take pride in and construct their collective identity. It is commemorated yearly by the city council, whose memory is inscribed
in this 'nodal point' (Moore, 2007) by a plaque honoring those who fought
to defend the building. Moreover, the piazza next to the building is named
after the intellectual father of the local antifascist resistance, Piazza Francesco
Viviani. Having a large space dedicated to the legacy of the antifascist resistance at the heart of the historical center did not sit well with far-right actors.
In an attempt to cancel the antifascist memory upon cityspace, the councilor
claimed in the proposed motion that there was no historical document verifying the episode. His plea was backed up by the Verona branch of CasaPound,
who organized a protest in front of the commemorative plaque,[11] whilst claiming on social media: "Yet another historical nonsense aimed at fueling the

9   Original proposal by city councilor Andrea Bacciga (3September 2019), *Richiesta di inti-
     tolazione di un giardino/parco o una via a Ezra Pound*, Alla Commissione Toponamastica,
     All'Assessore Danielo Polato della Commissione.
10   Originial motion presented at the City Council of Verona, entitled *Convocazione della
     Commissione Toponomastica per verificare l'esistenza comprovata da documentazione stor-
     ica della battaglia in difesa della Palazzo delle Poste*. (Prevenuto 1321, 6 September 2019).
11   For more information on the protest, see: https://www.veronanews.net/i-veronesi-non-si
     -prendono-in-giro-nessun-documento-sulla-battaglia-delle-poste-lazione-di-casapound.

myth of resistance which otherwise would have very little to rely on." (From the Instagram account *il Mastino IV*, 9 September 2021).

Alongside institutional decisions inside the city council to (re)name urban spaces with the fascist legacy in the making of a perfect touristic destination for nostalgic identitarian actors elsewhere are also *everyday ad hoc practices of naming* undertaken by social movement actors. An example of this practice was spotted during my fieldwork in Veronetta in the street *via Museo* near the Natural History Museum of Verona (see Figure 52 below). This street was renamed *via Alessandro Pavolini* in an impromptu fashion through a sticker by the youth branch of CasaPound, *Blocco Studentesco*, communicated by their lightning symbol. Pavolini was a prominent figure during fascism, participating in the March to Rome in 1922 and later becoming the secretary of the Republican Fascist Party founded in 1943. This act upon cityspace, therefore, symbolizes the continuing allegiance of the far-right universe to the Republic of Salò, which played an indispensable role in shaping the identity of the city today. These actors seek to inscribe a nostalgia of the fascist past (Boym, 2001) imbued in historical revisionism (Valencia-Garcia, 2020) against the outward-looking expansive identity that Veronetta has come to be known for.

FIGURE 52   Via Museo in Veronetta, ad hoc renamed after Alessandro Pavolini by *Blocco Studentesco*
PHOTOGRAPH: IPEK DEMIRSU

2.6   Urbs Picta: *Rewriting Belonging on Urban Space through Street Art*
Despite the fact that many social movements utilize the communicative space of social media and other digital platforms (Postill & Pink, 2012; Caiani, Della Porta & Wagemann, 2012; Mosca, 2014; Johan, 2018), the street remains a 'privileged site' (Pavoni et al., 2021) of political expression through the visibility of everyday realities (Brighenti, 2010a). Street art has been a lasting medium of micropolitics in urban space, involving not only the graffiti subculture, but also posters, stickers, collages, and other drawings, particularly prominent in areas with competing social movements and contending identities (Tarrow, 2011; Pavoni et al., 2021). The city offers a conducive setting for these forms of mediated interactions, which can evolve into prolonged dialogues, owing to the visible surfaces 'written over' by actors that seek public attention (Brighenti, 2010b). Some of these textual and visual messages on urban space are everyday visible attempts of boundary-drawing, in which walls become 'territorial devices' for marking a certain type of belonging (Ibid.).

2.6.1   Political Graffiti
In the city of Verona, while the historical center has been meticulously kept 'clean' with respect to any form of graffiti, Veronettta as a neighborhood has become the frontline in the so-called 'graffiti wars' between contending actors. These visible everyday practices of territorialization are mostly observable at the borders separating the two neighborhoods, where the 'natural boundary' of the Adige River overlaps with the 'conceptual boundaries' made visible through various forms of street art (Lefebvre, 1991 [1974]). In addition to these, the southern border of Veronetta, which used to be the military barracks of Passaqua where the university campus stands today, and the easternmost borders of Veronetta opening to the neighborhood of *Borgo Venezia*, all physically marked by city walls, are the areas with the greatest concentration of conflictual territorialization practices mediated through textual graffiti. An example was provided by one of the respondents on the southern border of the neighborhood in the university zone, who presented this photo as 'urban dialogue' conveyed on walls, preferring 'corrections' rather than cancellations that would constitute censorship in the name of urban decor:

> Two weeks ago, when I passed here, it was written 'Veronetta Zona Nera' [Veronetta Black Zone], so fascist zone, a zone to delimit. Also, the font of the letters they use is very particular; it's fascist writing. Instead, a couple of days ago I was passing by, and they had put white hearts instead of the word 'black'. So, someone went to neutralize what was written before. It's

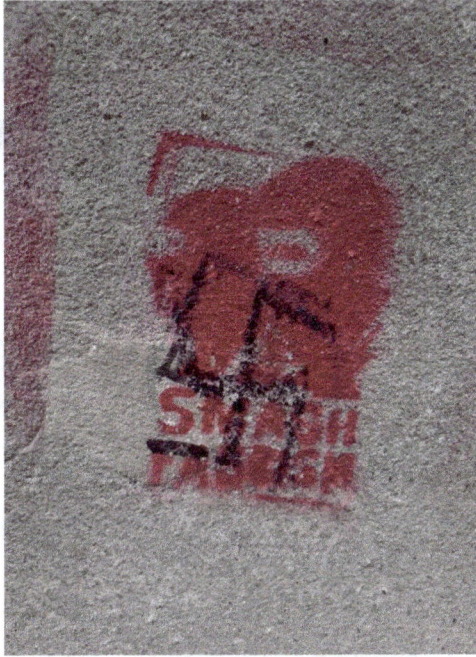

FIGURE 53   Two contending graffiti on a wall right
before Ponte dei Navi: an antifascist
sign reading 'Smash fascism' and a
Swastika symbol on top
PHOTOGRAPH: IPEK DEMIRSU

right in front of the university in *via San Francesco*. They wanted to send
a threatening message, saying don't pass from here, this is a black zone,
it's 'ours'.

Interview with I.S., 7 June 2019

A similar example of a high concentration of contending territorializations
along the borders of Veronetta is found around an underpass inside the city
walls encircling Veronetta, opening to the adjacent neighborhood of Borgo
Venezia. This example was presented by another respondent as the most contested area of 'graffiti wars' in Verona: "This is where the battle is concentrated
for those who feel they need to write something ... there is a conflict between
nationalists and antifascists. This arch is important for this reason: it is where
the graffiti battle is concentrated. They even climb up; they do acrobatics to

FIGURE 54   The writing declaring Veronetta 'black zone' corrected with white hearts, which
             now reads Veronetta zone of hearts
             PHOTOGRAPH BY I.S. FOR PHOTO-ELICITATION

write things. It is the crossroads of opposing antagonisms." (Interview with
M.S., 8 June 2019).

The social conflict that is expressed on the walls of Veronetta is also carried
out on online platforms, as participating groups in this form of territorialization either declare authorship on social media, or comment on the works of
the opposing party. As such, movement-countermovement dynamics manifest
themselves on the *online-offline continuum* through material spaces as well as
digital ones (Hine, 2000; Airoldi, 2018; Pavoni, 2021). The following Facebook
post on urban graffiti in Veronetta exemplifies this inter-spatial dimension of
mobilization:

> This morning, we met to discuss the writings and symbols that have
> appeared in some of the principal streets of Veronetta. We are talking
> about Celtic crosses and the *scala* sign in the classic Veronese neofas-
> cist style. There are so many things that can be written and painted on
> the walls of our streets to render them richer and more colorful than
> before. It's an idea that we understand in practice, but we are very distant

from the content that these symbols and writings convey. We are tired of repeating, still in 2019, the political analysis of this city ... almost always related to the reactionary and sovereignist world.

Facebook page of the local antifascist youth group *Suburban*, 23 September 2019

These visible practices of territorialization through political graffiti tend to be used by far-right movements and their new-age identitarian variants to specifically target and provoke antagonistic groups on themes that involve sexual orientation, sexual rights, immigration, political correctness, climate change, and the historical rereading of WWII. While these actors tend to utilize a sovereignist, defensive, and nostalgic language upon urban space, the network of progressive groups resort to humor and sarcasm in response as a method of deterritorializing an urban space where racist, sexist, or fascist messages have been left. These visible interactions on material space render the walls of the city, especially those of Veronetta, readable texts epitomizing the social tensions going on in the city, often with national and transnational themes that transcend the particular locality. As such, the city walls conferring public visibility exhibit claims and counterclaims to identity, and therefore to city-zenship, in everyday urban life (Işın, 2008; Işın, 2009). In other words, these practices of territorialization (Brighenti, 2010; Brighenti, 2014) demonstrate how movements act from space, on space, in space, and create new space (Routledge, 2010), whilst unveiling movement-countermovement contestation in the microcosmos of the city (Meyer & Staggenborg, 1996). Moreover, such 'publicity' of visible urban surfaces keeps the opposing groups alive and renders their arguments available to the rest of the city (Dillard, 2013).

One example of this practice was a writing left by the local branch of CasaPound, with the group referring to themselves as the 'Mastino Gang' (using the initials M.G.), that read: "You are on Facebook whining, we are on Tinder with the [female] comrades," implying that while male antifascist activists were busy doing activism on social media, far-right militants were busy hooking up with leftist girls on the dating application Tinder. This message, among other important discursive cues it conveyed, once again demonstrates cogently the online-offline continuity (Hine, 2000; Airoldi, 2018; Caiani, 2019; Pavoni et al., 2021) of collective action and how digital practices impact material urban spaces in acts of territorialization (Brighenti, 2010a; Brighenti, 2010b). The response given by the antibodies was painting over the writing with the drawing of vaginas to convey female empowerment. This episode was accompanied by an online declaration on Facebook by Circolo Pink with a post entitled 'From the social to the walls, but the violence is always the same', who continued to point out not only the sexist language used by the far-right militants, but

il_mastino_verona

Liked by ████████ and **others**

il_mastino_verona Questo è BODY SHAMING.
#antifamariangelafantozzi #IlMastino #Verona
#veronetta #viamazza #fantozzi #fantozzicontrotutti
#antifa

FIGURE 55   The Verona branch of CasaPound (Il Mastino) mocking the graffiti
                    writing "You are beautiful like antifascism" by claiming that the
                    statement constitutes 'body shaming'
                    FROM THE INSTAGRAM ACCOUNT OF IL MASTINO, 12 APRIL 2020

FIGURE 56   A neofascist writing on a wall in Veronetta that reads, "You are beautiful like the
            march to Rome". The writing is humorously corrected to read instead as "You are
            beautiful like a super-aromatized rotting apple"
            PHOTOGRAPH BY A.V. FOR PHOTO-ELICITATION

also the repressed frustration due to their pages being banned on social media platforms for hate speech (Circolo Pink Facebook Page, 11 September 2019). A feminist activist commented on the episode later, underlining the importance of the social conflict taking place on the walls of Veronetta: "Veronetta is a contested territory but on the walls. On the walls there is a battle of writings. Once they directly targeted us, they wrote slogans aimed at us near the university campus. What did we do? We went to correct these writings. It's a conflict over the walls of Verona, of slogans, on the Internet and physically, always with Veronetta as the context." (Interview with F.M., 12 February 2021).

Another salient and lingering theme is the end of WWII as far-right actors seek to revindicate this historical episode which they believe has made them the 'losers' of war, thereby silencing them in the Italian political scene (Milesi et al., 2005: 68). Notwithstanding the fact that these new generation of far-right actors who refrain from identifying themselves with fascism and prefer 'identitarian' as their political orientation, they nonetheless advocate a 're-reading' of the WWII and the history of fascism under a more dignifying

light for the 'losers' of history.[12] In northeast Italy, such historical revindica-
tion (Valencia-Garcia, 2020) and a search for 'guilt-free homecoming' (Boym,
2001) by far-right groups finds expression around the controversial issue of
Foibe massacres, which involved the killings of Italians in northwest Croatia
by Yugoslavian partisans towards the end of WWII. This historical episode with
particular repercussions in the regions of northeast Italy is appropriated by
far-right groups in invoking a sense of victimhood on the part of the ex-fascists
and their current heirs, while depicting groups with socialist and communist
political orientation as perpetrators of violence and traitors. Every February,
around the time of the commemoration of Foibe killings, local far-right groups
mobilize against antifascist organizations. This tension is exacerbated by the
physical proximity of the office of CasaPound in Veronetta located in *via Nicola
Mazza*, and the Verona branch of ANPI, representing the antifascist partisan

FIGURE 57   Writing left by CasaPound at the entrance of ANPI office that reads,
"ANPI: Defends followers of Tito? Negationism and Money"
PHOTO FROM THE FACEBOOK PAGE OF MOVIMENTANDOCI VERONA, 12
FEBRUARY 2020

12   Interview with Andrea Bacciga, city councilor and member of local identitarian groups in
Verona, Corriere del Veneto, 17 Ocboter 2017, available at: https://corrieredelveneto.corri
ere.it/verona/politica/17_ottobre_17/verona-consigliere-dona-libri-estrema-destra-crit
ica-m5s-049e496c-b32e-11e7-93e7-547794075405.shtml.

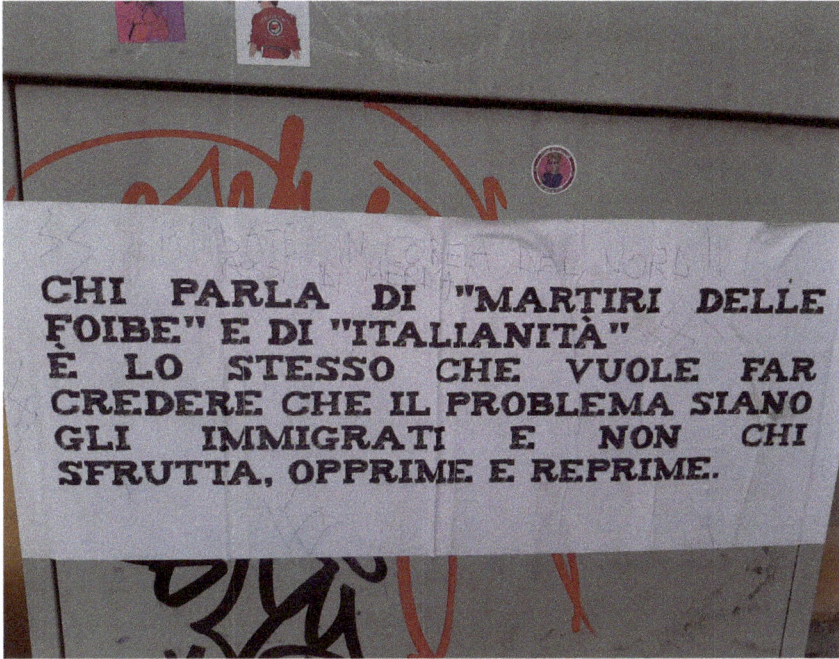

FIGURE 58   An anonymous writing near Porta Vescovo of Veronetta that reads: "Those who talk about the 'martyrs of Foibe' and 'Italianness' are the same as those who want us to believe that the problem is the immigrants and not those who exploit, oppress, and repress"
PHOTOGRAPH: IPEK DEMIRSU

resistance located in the adjacent *via Cantarane*. As a result, the attempt to reappropriate history assumes a spatial dimension reflecting upon cityspace, where street art renders visible an ongoing ideological argumentation open to reflections by other city-zens as the 'audience'.

Lastly, acts of territorialization among contending movement actors also convey opposing positions on global issues and interpret transnational themes from local lenses. On many of these issues, far-right groups tend to employ a skeptical and suspicious stance, at times favoring conspiracy theories about the 'new world order' and the role of liberal institutions supported by progressive actors. The latter are seen as the culprits of a perceived downfall of authentic cultures and traditions, whose seemingly 'benevolent' motives are believed to be veiling a hidden agenda (Rydgren, 2018; Rucht, 2019). Contention can range from the war in Syria to global warming, in which the material surfaces of Veronetta give way to a 'dialogue' between antagonistic positions. One example is a writing found on a garbage can that reads 'Defend Rojava' in support of

FIGURE 59   Writing making a call to defend Rojava is corrected to read 'Defend
             Assad' with the addition of the Wolfsangel sign
             PHOTO FROM THE FACEBOOK PAGE OF THE ANTIFASCIST LOCAL
             YOUTH ASSOCIATION *SUBURBAN*, 29 OCTOBER 2019

the Kurdish population in Syria, which is corrected over to read 'Defend Assad'
with the neo-Nazi *Wolfsangel* sign next to it.

2.6.2   Political Stickers
Walking from *via XX Settembre* at the heart of Veronetta, one crosses over the
Adige through *Ponte dei Navi* to arrive first at the old Roman gates, passing

FIGURE 60   A pole intensely marked with political stickers at the entrance of via
Capello, the street leading to Piazza Erbe. The stickers belong to far-
right and local identitarian groups such as Fortezza Europa, Blocco
Studentesco, and CasaPound.
PHOTOGRAPH: IPEK DEMIRSU

the House of Juliet as the most lucid example of Disneyification of Verona
(Zukin, 1998), and finally arriving to *Piazza Erbe* as one of the most important
nodal points marking territorial belonging through its architecture and history.
Throughout this walk, an observant eye would notice myriad forms of political

FIGURE 61   'Be Lions' sticker by Lotta Studentesca, the youth branch of Forza Nuova,
             between Piazza Erbe and Piazza Brà.
             PHOTOGRAPH: IPEK DEMIRSU

stickers on urban materialities such as walls, streetlights, traffic signs, and other
visible surfaces: from inside Veronetta, more intensely marked by the network
of progressive movements advocating open spaces and inclusive identities,
towards the bridge and all the way until the main piazzas, where traces of far-
right and identitarian actors promoting a singular exclusive city-zenship identity become salient. Unlike urban graffiti that is considered against the urban

FIGURE 62   The pole of a traffic sign near Osteria ai Preti of the 'red triangle' in
             Veronetta. Stickers belonging to various antifascist and feminist groups
             convey messages against white pride and against male violence, as well
             as demarcating the area as an antifascist zone.
             PHOTOGRAPH: IPEK DEMIRSU

décor in the marketing of heritage, these stickers manage to infiltrate without
much notice into the most touristic parts of the historical center.

Other sites of territorial marking through political stickers include 'nodal
points' (Moore, 2007) in the cognitive map carrying high symbolic value for

FIGURE 63   An art installation entitled 'Hangover' made by a local association
             involving a mannequin vomiting stickers of neofascist and far-rights
             groups that were collected from the walls of Veronetta in 2019.
             PHOTOGRAPH: IPEK DEMIRSU

the contending social actors, where competing forms of spatial belongings are
intensely felt, such as hangout places associated with various movements. These
stickers can simply communicate the existence of a group with their symbols,
convey a message to the public in general, or a message directed to an antagonistic group in particular, which in turn is interpreted by the respondents as

a form of "dialogue between invisible entities." (Interview with M.G., 25 April 2019). Both groups also practice systematic cleaning of stickers left by a competing group, or placing stickers right on top to highlight 'reterritorialization' of the same space by an opposing presence. For instance, for the celebration of Liberation Day on the 25th of April, an art project called 'Hangover' realized by the antibodies collecting far-right stickers in Veronetta, was put on display as an angry mannequin vomiting hateful stickers. On the other hand, the strategy of reclaiming urban space was witnessed during participant observation in *Verona Pride* (18 May 2019) and *Lotto Marzo* march of NUDM Verona (8 March 2019), where the antibodies, who have low visibility and minor presence in the historical center, gain a chance to rip off identitarian stickers with heteronormative and anti-immigration messages, or to place their own stickers over theirs usually with antifascist, anti-racist, and anti-sexist messages.

3   Gentrification, the Far-Right, and Future Projections

Previously noted as the 'no-go zone' (Wacquant, 2016) par excellence in the cognitive map of Verona, the neighborhood of Veronetta has transformed into an outward-looking space to construct a bottom-up form of expansive place-based belonging. As discussed in detail previously, this was made possible by the juxtaposition of an existing environment of tolerance set down by various migrant communities since the 1980s, and the arrival of the antibodies of hate who, over time, came to be embodied by this social space that they helped create. Notwithstanding its transformation over time, the neighborhood could not easily escape earlier stigmatizations it was subjected to, including the label of 'the Bronx of Verona':

> Veronetta was known as the Bronx of Verona. It was a difficult neighborhood, very difficult. Now, it's a completely different reality. That's how I see Veronetta. It's a lovely neighborhood. I never felt insecure walking around here. They have been instrumentalizing it for years and years, claiming that it's impossible to walk around Veronetta.
> Interview with F.S., 27 May 2019

While the neighborhood continues to be referred to as 'the ghetto', and characterized by urban decay alongside criminality by far-right and populist right actors, Veronetta has been undergoing a thorough gentrification process with the penetration of commercial interests, engendering the replacement of working-class and immigrant families with the middle-class (Semi, 2015; Polat,

2020). In fact, administratively being part of the historical center, the municipality has been sponsoring a project to market the section of Veronetta next to the river where it accommodates some important touristic sites as the 'East Side' of Verona, shifting away from the analogy with the Bronx.[13] It has been argued by a number of the respondents that the depiction of Veronetta as a racialized space associated with micro-criminality, which is undertaken not only by local newspapers and the populist right, but also the so-called 'ethnic resistance' of far-right groups, has been working to justify the expulsion of certain categories of people alongside the penetration of business interest into the neighborhood. Thus, one notes the curious convergence of interests between investors and far-right groups for pushing out unbelonging non-decorative elements (Mazzei, 2018), to recreate a white, middle-class, and profitable space close to the city center (Smith, 1996), where gentrification comes to constitute the reproduction of ethnic boundaries in urban space (Polat, 2020): "For such groups, it's already something positive. They are glad because different cultures are automatically being cleaned out, the *extracommunitari* [non-Europeans] are slowly going away." (Interview with R.B. & T.B., 2 October 2021).

As such, regardless of any intentionally plotted plan, there is a mutually reinforcing mechanism in place between the process of gentrification and the revanchist reterritorialization efforts on the part of far-right groups.

> There are many excuses for which the two groups have decided to settle in this part of the city: to take over this territory, to give it back to Italians, to overcome urban decay. The local leader of Forza Nuova said that Veronetta was chosen because there is a high presence of migrants with respect to other parts of Verona, and therefore, according to his logic, there is also more criminality. It must be said that other neighborhoods of Verona have a higher percentage of the migrant population. But Forza Nuova, just like CasaPound, likes to lie just to ride on this mediatic denigration against Veronetta for years with the aim of hastening the process of gentrification; that is, the expulsion of the poor groups of the population from the neighborhood, happening right under our noses. The not-so-indifferent presence of a migrant population makes it easier to cry for the offended homeland.
>
> Facebook post of Potere al Popolo for the occasion
> *Veronetta Vive*, 22 December 2018

---

13   For more information on the project, see: https://www.veronasera.it/attualita/funicol are-percorsi-scoprire-verona-east-side-12-aprile-2019.html.

One does not know whether it is a strategy devised on the table, but the two things go in tandem: it seems that the fight against urban decay could not otherwise but push away those people that are in difficulty, the poor … and restructuring for the new rich or the so-called hipster that come from outside … From this point of view, it is the usual gentrification as we know it, the neighborhood ending up losing its genuineness, its somewhat uniqueness in Verona. Whether it is something studied, I have thought about it. I thought about whether or not the presence of *Casa dei Patrioti* [Forza Nuova] was functional in some way to create tension.

Interview with M.L., 15 July 2019

The gentrification process is interlinked with *touristification* and *studentification* processes (Sequera & Nofre, 2018; Sequera & Nofre, 2019), involving the expulsion of old tenets either to divide apartments and rent rooms to university students, or the mushrooming of bed and breakfasts (hereafter, B&Bs) that accommodate tourists who do not spend time in Veronetta except to sleep. Alongside these processes, we see the traditional manifestations of

FIGURE 64   Writing in Veronetta against the process of gentrification, signed with an antifascist sign
PHOTOGRAPH: IPEK DEMIRSU

gentrification, such as the restoration of ancient palazzi to render them luxury apartments, the requalification of the Austrian military barracks Passalacqua and Santa Marta, and the proliferation of new trendy hangout places near the university campus. These intermittent dynamics that constitute the multivariate reality of the gentrification, touristification, and studentification processes must be handled individually.

To begin with, similar to any other neighborhood in different parts of the world, the process of gentrification, while bringing new energy, new investments, and new attention to a given urban area, concomitantly signifies the replacement of old residents with a more desired profile usually exemplified by the middle-class, white, and heteronormative protagonist (Smith, 1996; Semi, 2015). Such transformation corrodes the identity of place, as it washes over the social relations that constituted it in the first place (Zukin, 2015; Polat, 2020). In the case of Veronetta, the presence of the university campus coupled with the proximity of the main tourist attraction sites were the two chief motors that ignited the replacement of the old inhabitants, as landlords preferred to transform their apartments either into B&Bs or into student accommodations in order to maximize profit: "Take into account that if a neighborhood is not doing well, the houses cost less and it attracts investors, especially if there is the university. One can say, 'I'll buy an apartment, I will redo and rent it.' So slowly Veronetta is being renovated, re-organized, which means that the housing prices go up, and so those that are poor, Italian or non-Italian, move to other areas." (Interview with I.V., 7 April 2019) As such, in what was once known as the 'working-class neighborhood', a place where the elderly can afford houses and newly arriving migrants can come to settle and start their businesses, the soaring prices started to push out even those born and raised in Veronetta: "I love Veronetta. I was born and raised there. But I had to move to *San Pancrazio*, because I cannot afford a house in Veronetta any longer, despite the fact that it is the place I spend most of my time." (Interview with E.C., 11 April 2019). The replacement of the old residents also signifies the changing identity of place, as Veronetta loses its pluralist and open spirit that has been offering an alternative belonging to marginalized groups, instead being pulled into the 'Disneyification' of the historical center (Zukin, 1998):

> I see a lot of B&Bs, and I also see the opening of new art galleries, all the new realities that, if you don't observe meticulously, can even be positive developments since they bring new jobs. But on the other hand, they represent the requalification of a working-class quarter into something else, much more alluring, and much more expensive for those who can afford

it. It's positive because the neighborhood is requalified, and becomes relived. It's negative because the prices are going up, and people start to move away. For instance, I notice the sudden emergence of garages with elevators where large SUVs enter and exit. It almost seems external to the neighborhood; they seem like external people, but instead, they are the new residents that came to live in the restructured buildings ... I know a lot of people who always lived in Veronetta until a couple of years ago, and they had to move to Borgo Venezia because they are slowly pushed away. *This is a great risk of transforming Veronetta into an appendix of the historical center.*

> Interview with M.L., 15 July 2019, *emphasis added*

Aside from the restructuring of single buildings or apartments, the neighborhood has experienced a large-scale gentrification project on the vast area occupied by the two historical military barracks left to the neighborhood during the Austrian rule, namely Passalacqua and Santa Marta, which together also constitute the largest green area inside the city. While the former was utilized during the post-WWII as an American military base for the South Europe Task Force (SETAF) until well into the 1980s, the latter was by and large abandoned. With an extensive requalification project in the early 2000s, this large area part of Veronetta was first destined to be the new NATO military base: "We were alarmed by the news that there would be a big NATO base, one that is operative. At the time, they were bombarding ex-Yugoslavia from the bases in Italy. So, having here in the middle of the city an operative military base for many different reasons was unacceptable." (Interview with B.M., 8 October 2021).

Such a decision taken by the Minister of Defense was confronted by an intervention of an ad hoc formation within the antibodies who decided to act not only for the neighborhood of Veronetta, but also out of a sense of responsibility for distant others (Massey, 2004), thereby culminating in the Committee Passalacqua and Santa Marta for Verona (*Comitato Passalacqua e Santa Marta per Verona*). The Committee, which was hosted by the old office of Circolo Pink in *via Scrimiari*, used several grassroots tactics to prevent this large area amounting to more than 160,000 meters square from transforming into yet another military presence in a neighborhood that was by then experimenting with its newly blossoming expansive belonging as an outward-looking space. The grassroots Committee worked to revalorize this area as a green space offering recreative services and sports camps, a space for "everyone who wishes to finally live in a pacific, creative way as a community inside this interethnic and

multicultural neighborhood ... free of prejudice and violence".[14] Their repertoire of action included collecting of 5000 thousand signatures for the area to
be requalified as a civilian area, distributing informative flyers (see Figure 65
below), sit-ins in front of the municipality building, and mobilizing around the
compelling slogan 'Military tanks or baby strollers?'. Such endeavor managed
to successfully carry the issue to the Italian parliament in Rome, eventually
resulting in the area being conceded to the city of Verona for a civilian requalification project.[15]

The subsequent requalification project divided the vast area into three
sub-categories: the main building of Santa Marta bakery was to be renovated
and integrated into the university campus, while the remaining areas would
be opened up to new affordable housing and a new public park.[16] Instead,
the housing project that was eventually undertaken has come to offer highly
expensive luxury housing heavily criticized by the residents of Veronetta as
well as members of the antibodies, who consider it as the embodiment of market interests ruling over the needs of the existing inhabitants. Hence, the end
decision is perceived to transform the neighborhood into a 'real estate speculation site' with the aim of realizing a luxury area out of urban decay: "Before it
was a military zone and this committee struggled to transform it into a public
space, green, etc., but part of the project was absorbed by speculation. This, for
me, leads to the birth of a neighborhood within a neighborhood." (Interview
with M.L., 15 July 2019) Strikingly, this entrepreneurial undertaking that came
to constitute the most extensive gentrification mechanism in the neighborhood is found to be in tandem with the penetration of far-right groups, as both
dynamics seek to "negate and eliminate everything that Veronetta represents."
(Fieldwork notes during *Assemblea Veronetta Vive*, 10 December 2019)

Parallel to the process of gentrification that has been going on for a longer
period of time, more recently, the process of touristification has been spilling
over to Veronetta from the historical center. While the increasing tourist presence is not necessarily considered a negative development, contributing to the
economic and cultural life of the neighborhood, however, the mushrooming
of B&Bs in Veronetta is a matter of concern for the residents since the neighborhood is turning into a dormitory of transient visitors: "Veronetta will soon

---

14   Text from the original flyer of Committee Passalacqua and Santa Marta for Verona (3
     December 1999), provided by the respondents.
15   For more information on the Committee, please see: https://altreconomia.it/ecco-per
     che-il-paese-va-allasta-immobiliare-italia-ae-26-2.
16   Comune di Verona, *Riqualificazione del complesso ex caserme S.Marta e Passalacqua.*
     Accessed on 24 September 2021, available at: https://www.comune.verona.it/nqcont
     ent.cfm?a_id=18300&tt=verona_agid.

Preferite i carri armati o le Carrozzine ?

Se permetteremo che la NATO occupi le caserme Passalacqua e S. Marta, invece degli spazi verdi e delle strutture per il quartiere e per l'Università, avremo divise militari, armi, filo spinato. Ai carri armati preferiamo le carrozzine. Facciamoglielo vedere!

Venerdì 3 dicembre 1999

Sit-in in Piazza Brà, h.17
davanti al Comune

CONTRO LA CESSIONE DELLE CASERME ALLA NATO.
PER IL LORO UTILIZZO PUBBLICO E CIVILE, A BENEFICIO
DEI CITTADINI DEL QUARTIERE E DELLA CITTA'

Comitato "S. Marta e Passalacqua per Verona"

FIGURE 65   Flyer by the Committee Passalacqua and Santa Marta for Verona, with the slogan 'Military tanks or baby strollers?'
ORIGINAL DOCUMENT PROVIDED BY A LOCAL ACTIVIST

turn into a big B&B. They say it's a tourism of a passage. That is, they sleep here in Veronetta, but they go to the center to spend the day. So, it's not perceived as a place where a tourist goes to visit." (Interview with A.V., 15 February 2019). Among the new realities that are entering the neighborhood with the effect of student life and the increasing salience of tourism, residents express mixed feelings about different types of businesses that are becoming ever more visible:

> It's another thing if one opens a new restaurant or a new art gallery; I'm fine with those. But a restaurant and a hostel are two different things, because the former is a service that I also have access to. It's a variety that renders the neighborhood more livable. A hostel or a B&B signifies one resident less. If the tenets change over time, one day, there is a group of American students, and the next year there is a Sri Lankan family, it is fine with me. It means they can get to know you as a neighbor. They can greet you, they go to the same shops that you go to, and they have something in common with you. Instead, if only tourists start to arrive, it erodes this social fabric. I have nothing against tourists, I work with them, I recommend Veronetta to them. But there has to be a limit. You cannot transform the whole neighborhood into a B&B.
>
> Interview with M.G., 6 April 2019

Hence, the residents do not necessarily regard new locales, art galleries, and bookstores in the neighborhood as an *a priori* negative development since they render the neighborhood a more vibrant social space and contribute to its outward-looking spirit. Undoubtedly, the presence of the university is another significant factor in this direction, with the proliferation of 'trendy' stores, cafés, restaurants, and cultural centers that serve the interests of university students. That being said, a complete takeover of tourism interests in Veronetta to the point in which it loses its own identity and intercultural community ties, undergoing Disneyification as part of the historical center, is a matter of concern: "Veronetta in a couple of years will not be the same neighborhood. Esthetically speaking, it's a beautiful neighborhood. Doubtlessly, it will maintain something of itself. It will become more 'hipster', the part of Verona that is 'radical chic', but not anymore working-class. It won't be any longer a bit disorganized but free as it is now." (Interview with, A.V., 23 April 2019) Hence, the residents and members of associations that are part of the antibodies express a shared concern over the looming intensive touristification of Veronetta with the penetration of business interests in this alternative social space. Such a process is found to jeopardize the outward-looking identity of place and the expansive place-based belonging that radiate to the rest of the city, offering a 'home' to marginalized and non-belonging groups with its open spaces. As a result, Veronetta risks becoming just another 'boutique' neighborhood (Zukin, 2015).

Topographically speaking, the multivariate transformation the neighborhood is undergoing is more salient near the river Adige bordering the historical center, concomitantly where the university is located. On the other hand, the process is still less visible in the eastern part,[17] close to Porta Vescovo that borders the neighborhood of Borgo Venezia, which lacks the cultural and movement dynamics predominant in Veronatta despite also being a working-class multicultural neighborhood itself. Moreover, while Veronetta administratively and historically is part of the historical center, Borgo Venezia is positioned in the eastern periphery of Verona. Remarkably, the same east-west divide within Veronetta goes for the presence of antagonistic social actors as well, with the far-right presence felt the most around the university area and the western border near the historical center, whilst the core elements of the antibodies have their offices and collectives on the easternmost border near Porta Vescovo where the outward-looking identity of Veronetta and the expansive belonging it cultivates are still relatively intact:

> This is home to me. This is the place where I can recognize Veronetta, because lots of migrants pass by. There is the office of my political group, in front there is the Pakistani that I go to eat. There is ANPI. It's a safe zone and it's still not gentrified. There are still a number of the so-called 'ethnic stores': there is the Muslim here, there is the Sri Lankan, the Arab barber that cuts my hair. If this is the east, going west toward the university, there are different types of locales and a different profile of people who hang out.
>
> Interview with O.P., 8 June 2019

Yet, this topographic distribution of movement actors has not always been the case, as explained in detail in Chapter 5. The actors that constitute the antibodies of hate, whose collective identity has merged with the identity of space in Veronetta since the 1990s, were first active in Piazza Isolo found on the western end of the neighborhood. Along with the inhabitants of the neighborhood, the gentrification process pushed them away from their first shared home under the 'pensilina', which was one of the first areas to be gentrified in the neighborhood, ultimately turning into a big underground parking lot that serves the historical center: "In my opinion it [the eviction of pensilina] was on purpose, to prevent the solidification of ties between the movement and the neighborhood,

---

17   With the exception of a small fraction of new apartments as part of the requalification of Passalacqua and Santa Marta, on the southernmost borders of the neighborhood.

which was against their worldview. Better to eliminate it before it goes out of hand." (Interview with B.M., 8 October 2021). Thus, the elements of the movement have been moving towards the eastern borders, either towards the city walls marking Veronetta and beyond: "This change is a geographic change, in the sense that also the groups, I am referring particularly to Pecora Nera but also Circolo Pink, are constantly being pushed towards the periphery of the neighborhood and probably they will be expelled finding themselves outside of the city walls." (Interview with M.L., 15 July 2019). Consequently, the identity of place marked by sociality and movement relations is carried outside the architectural and administrative borders of Veronetta into the beginning of Borgo Venezia that is perceived in the cognitive map of city-zens as part of an 'extended Veronetta'.

Against this background, various elements within the antibodies are wary of a possible link between the so-called 'ethnic resistance' undertaken by far-right groups on the one hand, and the process of gentrification on the other hand that is eroding the pluralist identity of Veronetta nourishing differences. These dual mechanisms in tandem generate a force that pushes out not only the working-class and ethnic minorities, but also antagonistic actors that challenge populist policies, thereby treated as 'unwanted others'. During their short presence, far-right actors have proven that a primary target has been the antibodies who are associated with the neighborhood, and who cultivate an alternative form of place-based belonging that defies the territorial belonging upheld by the former. Therefore, it has been voiced on several occasions that whether or not intentionally planned, the presence of the far-right encourages the gentrification process and vice-e-versa, accentuating the mutually reinforcing mechanisms between the revanchist reterritorialization attempts of these actors and the process of gentrification of Veronetta that also eliminates traces of everyday grassroots dissent.

> What scares me is that it might be a maneuver not only by this administration, but also by its predecessors, to turn Veronetta into something else because it intimidates them. You seek to send away old inhabitants and make new people arrive, gentrification. The fact that Forza Nuova and CasaPound arrived here, they said it clearly, it is the frontlines in the 'ethnic conflict'. Veronetta is also one of the neighborhoods that vote the most for the left, together with Borgo Venezia. So, what I'm trying to say is, it's a tough nut for the rest of Verona. It's not that everyone is a communist, but there's definitely more tolerance.
>
> Interview with historical activist A.A., 5 August 2019

The phenomenon of gentrification has increased housing prices. Then, the new offices of two groups arrive who want a piece of Veronetta for themselves in these spaces. They could've opened near the stadium. They could've opened it in San Zeno, instead, they chose here. It seems to me that there is an objective to turn it into something else, with respect to what it has been and what it still is. So, in my opinion, there could be a link. There is this legend of urban decay in Veronetta. I never experienced it until CasaPound and Forza Nuova settled in this neighborhood. The only time I found myself in difficulty was when a member of a far-right student group was following me on his bicycle when I was returning home from the university. That's the only tension that there is, not the urban decay that they are trying to link to the question of migrants. Those who are willing to defend the requalification of Veronetta are the ones who made me feel insecure.

> Interview with sexual rights activists and
> university students F.S. & N.S., 10 July 2019

The two far-right groups present in Veronetta are seeking to reinstate the native Veronese identity in a historical neighborhood of Verona, which they consider to be defaced by the existence of different ethnic groups equated with criminality and urban decay on the one hand, and progressive leftist groups seen as their 'enablers' on the other hand. What is most striking is that identitarian groups who claim to represent 'the real people' do not enunciate or directly criticize the phenomenon of gentrification. Their loud silence speaks volumes, especially for a movement such as CasaPound built upon the theme of 'public housing' also articulated in the guiding doctrine of the group, the Manifesto of Verona (Cammelli, 2018). Whilst remaining silent on the replacement of lower-income residents from the neighborhood, these groups nonetheless express their objective of 'freeing' the neighborhood from certain ethnicities and political collectives, which they believe caused its degeneration:

> We didn't choose Veronetta by chance. It's a highly symbolic gesture for us. It's not a provocative choice from the point of view of political antagonism or anything of the sort. We want to dismantle the fact that any neighborhood of Verona would belong to any group in particular, or even worse, any particular ethnicity. We will demonstrate how Veronetta, by night, has become a place of drug dealing, and by day, a place of chaos, of dirtiness, due to the fact that there is overpopulation that is not

FIGURE 66
A T-shirt with the slogan 'Veronetta
Offender' next to a tattoo with the
Scaligeri symbol representing the
territorial identity of Verona
PHOTO FROM THE FACEBOOK PAGE
OF IL MASTINO IV, 23 JUNE 2021

controlled. We are not trying to accuse any single race; we are not racist.
We do not claim that a single race is the cause of disorder. Instead, certain
ethnicities are left absolutely free to act and to break the law, which is
demonstrated by the local news every day.

> Interview with Pietro Amadeo from Forza Nuova
> in Verona Daily, 22 December 2018.[18]

Here, identitarian themes are quite visible in the aspired 'reconquest' of
Veronetta, one that seeks to distance itself from the stigmatizing label of 'racism', instead arguing for public order and control in one's own native territory.
Despite the fact that these groups do not directly express their views on the
ongoing process of gentrification, their outlook of revalorizing the neighborhood for Veronesi city-zens and restoring territorial belongings resonate with
the projects of rendering Veronetta more 'presentable', the 'East Coast' instead
of the 'Bronx', a continuation of the historical center once again harboring the
true *Veronesità*. This outlook was also visible during the campaign against the
anti-COVID lockdowns in the past two years, in a call to relive the city again
by the local CasaPound branch Il Mastino: "Go and live your city. It's a call
we are making to all young Veronesi: live the squares, the streets, and go back
to living life in these symbolic places of our city-zen identity [*identità citta-
dina*]. Every millimeter of this city is 'your zone' … the so-called 'antifa zone'
does not exist in Verona. Verona is your city, and no neighborhood will ever
be a filthy banlieue." (Facebook post by Il Mastino Verona IV, 11 June 2021).

---

18   The interview can be accessed at: https://fb.watch/8qFYg5W-zD.

As a result, whilst remaining silent on the replacement of low-income groups, the far-right's reterritorialization of Veronetta with the slogan of 'ethnic resistance' is premised on future aspirations that are in line with the unfolding of the gentrification process, rendering it as an 'appendix' of the historical center touristscape, presenting itself as a white, clean, and orderly space harboring a homogenous territorial identity.

4   Struggle over the Representation of the City: Verona, the City of ...

Against the backdrop of everyday struggles in lived spaces and material realities of Verona, antagonistic actors also compete over the representation of the city (Martin, 2003; Banini & Ilovan, 2021; Schwarz & Streule, 2022) to be presented both to an internal and an external audience, in an attempt to rearticulate the identity of Verona that encapsulates their vision of city-zenship. The latter serves not only in delineating the boundaries of belonging to the city for those who inhabit it, but also 'marketing' such identity constructs to the outside world, which is a way of connecting and networking with like-minded transnational actors. Amounting to a semantic appropriation of a territory through its preferential depiction, competition over the representation of a city impacts the form of social relations that are acceptable within it (Banini & Ilovan, 2021). Contending 'place-frames' (Martin, 2003) guide collective action, in our case, those of two opposing movements operating in the same city, not merely with respect to urban politics but also in mobilizing the locality to connect with wider struggles of identity.

On the one hand, sovereignist identitarian actors articulate the representation of Verona as a model city in the defense of a territorial identity and the traditional values that are tied to this imagined homeland against the perceived corrosive effects of the type of modernity brought about by globalization. On the other hand, the antibodies strive to offer a different representation of the city of Verona, originating from the good practices that they have established in the neighborhood of Veronetta, as a city with a great history of antifascism, as an open city to those who seek a home, and a transfeminist city that actively engages in larger discussions pertaining to sexual rights. As such, these actors compete in representing the city of Verona to a wider audience at home and elsewhere, and thereby connect with actors advocating similar progressive values in places beyond.

4.1   *Verona Vandea of Europe*

A passionate identification with the territory one occupies, coupled with a nostalgic rereading of modern history, and a rediscovery of traditional values that have come to define belonging to this place, have been a leitmotif for the alliance of sovereignist identitarian groups from ultra-Catholics to Veneto nativists that command everyday life in the city. Given such a sociopolitical setting heavily imbued in a defensive localism (Lipsitz, 2011), these actors posit Verona as a city at the frontlines of a battle to defend local identities of the white Christian civilization, which is conceived to be jeopardized by a dubious multiculturalist project pioneered by international actors and their local allies. Nonetheless, taking pride in the local heritage of the immediate community in Verona and a claim to defend the territorial identity can manifest themselves in hues of white supremacy (Murdoch & Murhall, 2019) on the one hand, and sociocultural authoritarianism on the other hand (Mudde, 2000; Rydgren, 2018; Caiani, 2019). Such a self-proclaimed representation of the city is marketed not only in rewriting belonging for city-zens, but also for an external audience, starting from the Italian society and going beyond, drawing to its orbit European and American counterparts that are part of an identitarian transnational network.

To begin with, the city has come to the forefront on a national level as the model city that pioneered in implementing some of the most controversial policies, such as collecting digital fingerprints of children of Rom and Sinti origin introduced by the Minister of Interior of the time, Roberto Maroni of Lega Nord (Tessadri, 2008), as one of the first Italian cities to pass a motion banning kebab stores in the historical center,[19] and as the only European city to revoke a European Parliamentary resolution on the equal treatment of individuals with different sexual orientation.[20] The maintenance of a safe and sanitized space and a singular identity (Lipsitz, 2011; Saitta, 2015; Mazzei, 2018) found resonance in other parts of the country, even in the most progressive cities such as Bologna, where the mayor of Verona was invited to give 'lessons' on the Verona model and how to deal with 'unruly' multiethnic neighborhoods such as Bolognina.[21] In the meanwhile, the city had also become a favorite

---

19   For more information, see: https://www.ladige.it/cronaca/2016/02/22/verona-il-sind aco-stop-ai-kebab-in-centro-storico-1.2686441.

20   European Parliament (1994) Report of the Committee on Civil Liberties and Internal Affairs on equal rights for homosexuals and lesbians in the EC, A3-0028/94 (26 January 1994), accessed on 23 September 2020, available at: http://aei.pitt.edu/49350/1/A10 612.pdf.

21   Details of the visit can be found at: https://www.bolognatoday.it/cronaca/flavio-tosi-vis ita-bolognina.html.

FIGURE 67   Celebration of Pasque Veronesi in 2014 with traditional 18th-century
             costumes and the Contarina flag in Piazza Brà
             PHOTO FROM THE VENETIST WEBSITE VEJA.IT, 12 MAY 2014

meeting spot for neofascist and nativist subcultures around Europe, hosting events such as nazirock festivals bringing nazirock bands from around Europe, some hosted for the first time in Italy, such as the Swedish Ultima Thule and the British 'white power' rock band Condemned 84.[22]

An important locus of identitarian mobilization premised on the espousal of the Veronese territorial identity is the carnivalesque commemoration of *Pasque Veronesi* (Veronese Easters), which is a modern reenactment of anti-Jacobin revolts during the French occupation of the city under Napoleon's rule in 1879. As explained in detail in Chapter 3 and Chapter 4, this episode came to be exalted as *Vandea Italiana* in relation to the anti-revolutionary insurgence that had taken place in Vandea, France (Romagnani, 2009). The marketing of the heritage of *Pasque Veronesi* to identitarian counterparts elsewhere manifests itself in the slogan *Verona Vandea Europea* utilized by the alliance of extreme right actors and traditionalist ultra-Catholic groups in drawing European counterparts to the image of an anti-modernist Verona (Demirsu, 2023). In fact, the slogan was famously utilized for an anti-abortion event, with the participation of noted identitarian actors from different cities in Italy and

---

22   From the archival dossier *Veronesi Tuti Mati*, by Kollettivo Porkospino and Coordinamento
      Cesar K., 17 March 2001, Verona. Available online at: https://movimentandociaverona.files
      .wordpress.com/2019/10/veronesi-tuti-mati.pdf-valido.pdf.

other European countries, including a city councilor from Trieste, the mayor of Ásotthalom in Hungary known for his extreme right position and his infamous 'migrant hunter' police force at the border of Serbia, a representative from the Polish National Radical Camp known for its ultranationalist and even neo-Nazi tendencies, and another representative from People's Party Our Slovakia who had been involved in creating an anti-Rom militia unit. These actors operating in different settings come together in their joint struggle to defend their homelands, their local traditions, and their native population seek to create 'fortresses' around Europe and elsewhere, where exclusionary territorial identities can prevent non-white, non-heterosexual, and non-decorative elements inside white pristine spaces. The heritage of *Pasque Veronesi* as an anti-Jacobin local uprising against foreign invasion offers a perfect historical rewriting in the representation of Verona to the outside world (Banini & Ilovan, 2021; Schwarz & Streule, 2022), as the new 'Vandea' of Europe upholding anti-modernist nostalgia (Boym, 2001), of going back to a primordial identity tied to the territory and its memory with nativist entitlements (Mudde, 2000; Zùquete, 2018; Duyvendak et al., 2022). This leitmotif is clearly conveyed in the speech given by the national leader of Forza Nuova during the event: "For Forza Nuova, Verona represents itself as *Europe's Vandea*, and is a candidate for the near future to be an authentically revolutionary laboratory in the fight against the enemies of the People of Europe, liberticidal laws against the family, and against life."[23]

The theme of 'gender ideology' as framed by these reactionary groups (Garbagnoli & Prearo, 2018; Trappolin, 2022) is frequently reappropriated by the sovereignist identitarian alliance in promoting the city as the last bastion of the heteronormative Christian family values that the 'continuation' of the white European lineage relies on. The motion passed in 2018, declaring the city as '*Verona città in favore della vita*' (Verona the city in favor of life), thereby conferring public funding to anti-abortion groups, is one cogent example. The motion worked as a precedent as representatives in other cities around Italy, such as Ferrara, Rome, and Milano, who copied the exact text of the Veronese motion and tried to push forward similar decisions to limit access to abortion, turning Verona as a 'model city' in the pro-life movement.[24] What was even more striking was the justification of the motion also on 'nativist' grounds (Mudde, 2007; Duyvendak et al., 2022), put succinctly by the promoter of the

---

23   Roberto Fiore cited in the local newspaper *L'Arena*, 22 November 2018 (emphasis added). Available at: https://www.larena.it/territori/citt%c3%a0o/forza-nuova-e-aborto-prote sta-degli-attivisti-contro-il-convegno-1.6928732.

24   For more information, see: https://www.internazionale.it/reportage/annalisa-camilli/2018 /11/23/verona-estrema-destra-aborto-europa.

motion, Alberto Zelger: "We need to help women have kids. Otherwise we will be invaded by Muslims who will impose on us the Islamic law once they gain the majority."[25] The narrative of pro-life is thus imbued in fear of 'losing control' in one's own territory and a territorial identity primordially defined (Tudor, 2014; Zùquete, 2018; Murdoch & Murhall, 2019), thereby reflecting the Great Replacement theory that has been traveling across borders embodied in the slogan 'procreation, not immigration' in Hungary to chants in Charlottesville, US asserting 'you will not replace us'.[26]

Against this backdrop, the city proved to be not only a particular case in the Italian peninsula, but a strategic showcase for transnational identitarian movements when it was chosen to host the WCF with the official sponsorship of the municipality of Verona and the regional administration of Veneto. This annually held international conference is organized by a US-based coalition of conservative actors operating globally, known for bringing together Christian fundamentalist and far-right groups around the world under a 'pro-family' banner, promoting the traditional Christian family model against women's rights and LGBTQ+ rights. As a matter of fact, the title of the conference hosted in Verona was 'The Wind of Change: Europe and the Global Pro-family Movement'. In 2017, the event was held in Budapest, Hungary hosted by President Orban, and in 2018 in Chisinau, Moldovia hosted by President Igor Dodon, who also attended as a keynote speaker of the event the following year in Verona. The choice of Verona in 2019 was no coincidence, and neither were the previous choices of venue for the event, all 'model' cities functioning as strategic nodes in the rise of the populist right and far-right movements (Demirsu, 2022; Demirsu, 2023), whose alliance is premised on sociocultural authoritarianism (Mudde, 2000; Rydgren, 2018; Caiani, 2019): "The fact that having the WCF here was absolutely not by chance, it could not have happened in another city. I mean, the first choice could not have been other than Verona." (Interview with E.N., 9 April 2019)

Among the participants of the conference were national and international anti-gender associations from US, Europe, and Africa; populist politicians from Eastern Europe, such as Katalin Novak from Hungary; leading religious figures, such as the Russian Archpriest Dimitri Smirnov; far-right groups, such as CasaPound and Forza Nuova; and some members of European nobility. There

---

25   Interview with Alberto Zelger: https://video.repubblica.it/politica/verona-il-leghista
      -della-mozione-anti-aborto-senza-bimbi-italiani-saremo-invasi-dagli-islamici/316
      126/316755.

26   A more detailed account of the Great Replacement theory can be found in: https://time
      .com/5748503/trump-abortion-immigration-replacement-theory.

were also representatives of the then Italian government of the time, including the Interior Minister of the time, Matteo Salvini from Lega, and the Minister of Families and Disability, Lorenzo Fontana, who himself is from Verona and used to be vice mayor of the city under the previous administration, known for his ardent support of Russian President Putin's anti-LGBTQ+ laws. This transnational network of identitarian groups from different walks of life, seeking to 'take back control' in their own localities and to reinstall an imagined 'natural order' protected by tradition, have united in this event under the banner "God, Homeland, Family" (*Dio, Patria, Famiglia*), a slogan once articulated during fascist rule in Italy. The natural heteronormative family, understood as the building block of a 'healthy' European society, was praised during the panels of the event, which witnessed controversial moments, which involved proposed methods to cure homosexuality and the distribution of plastic souvenir fetuses to endorse the anti-abortion stance (Fieldnotes, 31 March 2019). The conference resulted in a joint 'Verona Declaration' communicated at the closing ceremony, which lucidly illustrates the choice of Verona as the event venue and its successful marketing to the outside world as the city of Christian family values: "Verona, a noble city of art, of culture, and of ancient civilization, which for centuries has been called the 'City of Love' proclaimed itself in October 2018 to be the 'City for Life'; today it has also become the 'City for the Family'."[27]

4.2   *Verona, the Transfeminist Open City*

The antibodies of hate do not succumb to the labeling of Verona as a model city for the alliance of sovereignist identitarianisms, undertaking the effort to deconstruct such representation. Instead, this assemblage of situated actors seeks to present 'the other face of Verona' for those city-zens who are in search of a non-exclusionary place-based belonging, and to the outside world as an exemplar a grassroots movement intrinsic to the city thriving even under the most hostile conditions. The outward-looking spatial identity espoused by these actors does not negate the local Veronese culture, yet seeks to reappropriate it, rewrite it, and take it as a starting point to offer an alternative representation of the city of Verona for its own inhabitants and for places beyond. Resisting the monopolization of the local identity and the appropriation of the city's image by far-right actors, the antibodies have been seeking to depict the city of Verona as an 'open' city, where different subjects can strive as part of an inclusive pluralist belonging. This motto is succinctly captured

---

27   The original text of the Declaration can be found at: https://profam.org/verona-declarat ion-adopted-at-wcf-xiii-on-31-march-2019.

FIGURE 68   March for the Family in the historical center on the last day of WCF
                        in Verona
                        PHOTOGRAPH: IPEK DEMIRSU

by the rebranding of the city as the 'Transfeminist City' on the 30th of March 2019: "This movement has united all diversity ... it is the pulsating heart of what Verona can also become. In our recent rallies, we have demonstrated that the cultural and political constructions of the people who take part in the movement provide light upon a city that has been obfuscated by a pseudo-political culture that rendered Verona a black stain in the eyes of the entire world." (Interview with D.P., 4 February 2021). The primary aim of the antibodies is to render visible the expansive place-based identity they have realized in Veronetta to the rest of the city, ultimately extending across borders to touch distant localities that similarly struggle with nativist closure: *"We cannot stop at Veronett. Otherwise, we will merely be an oasis in the desert.* If we only talk to ourselves, we become self-referential, sterile. We depart here, but we do not stop here, reaching the whole galaxy without limits." (Interview with L.L., 22 October 2021, *emphasis added*).

The antibodies have been redefining the identity of Verona through their online and offline mobilization, accentuating the characteristics of the city that is welcoming to newcomers and inclusive of diversity. One example of online representation is the relabeling efforts such as the Facebook group 'Veronesi open to the world, Verona open city' (*Veronesi aperti al mondo, Verona città aperta*), where the antibodies communicate important news and new initiatives with a larger local following. Moreover, the alternative spirit of Verona is highlighted in grassroots initiatives and demonstrations that resonate in other settings to connect with or offer solidarity to distant actors and causes. Historically, a significant turning point was the 1995 decision that rendered Verona the only city to refute the EU resolution on the equal treatment of sexual minorities when the antibodies, with the lead of Arcigay at the time, managed to raise their voice and carry their cause not only on the national scale through two significant demonstrations, *Alziamo La Testa* and *Cittadinanza Va Scritta*, but went further to reach the supranational level of presenting their case at the European Parliament. This tendency was later exemplified by the great success of the Critical Wine initiative by the social collective La Chimica, carrying the name of Verona on a global level as an example of ecological agriculture promoting small producers without favoring any sort of localist loyalties.

A more recent example can be found in the rally called *PassaPorti: Marcia Contro Ogni Forma di Razzismo, Per una Citta Aperta e Solidale* ('PassaPorti': March Against Every Form of Racism, for an Open and United City) that took place in Piazza Brà in 2019, with the participation of numerous organizations including Pink Refugees, leftist trade unions, migrant communities and religious representatives from the Muslim and Jewish community of Verona. The event uniting with the global anti-racist movement for the occasion of the International Day for the Elimination of Racial Discrimination, aimed to bring out the anti-racist face of Verona as a city that could benefit from the richness of its migrants' cultures, and criticized the hierarchy ingrained in the concept of citizenship, where some passports are allowed entry in many parts of the world whilst others are denied mobility beyond the national borders (Fieldnotes, 23 March 2019). A similar example was presented by the Black Lives Matter demonstration organized by AfroVeronesi in this mid-sized Italian city.

Hence, the antibodies of hate have not only sought to realize a 'happy oasis' in the neighborhood of Veronetta, but have also been seeking to export the bottom-up transformative placemaking efforts they have accomplished to the rest of the city, connecting with global social justice claims. By reappropriating and playing with the local traditions and symbols that have been reified by identitarian groups, the antibodies deconstruct these symbolisms to reconstruct them in a way that represents a pluralist antifascist, anti-racist, and anti-sexist *Veronesità*. One animated platform for this occasion is Verona Pride, which has been utilizing historical symbolisms of the city, and transforming them into symbols of an expansive place-based belonging. These examples include the *scala* coat of arms that represents the Scaliger golden age, the Contarina flag that has come to represent *Venetismo*, or Juliet as the touristic face of Verona, which are transformed with the colors of the rainbow in advocating the rights of sexual minorities and people of color. In so doing, the antibodies turn local symbolism into signifiers of translocal claims to justice, reflecting their place-based collective identity. LGBTQ+ activists have also attempted to reclaim local Veronese traditions, such as the candidacy of a gay activist to represent the mascot of the carnival in Verona, *Papa del Gnoco* (the Father of Gnoco), which is a ritual monopolized by identitarian actors as part of the Veronese territorial identity (Fieldnotes, 1 March 2019). A previous example in 2007 saw the candidacy of a historical trans activist as the mayor of Verona with her own electoral list of councilors, promising to address issues of social class, racism, and sexual rights in one of the most hostile settings in Italy: "The decision of my candidacy as a trans woman to the position of the mayor is surely particular, but also necessary in a city like ours. This list is important not only for those who live in Verona, but for all Italy, and for the whole movement of LGBTQ+."[28]

Carrying their local struggles embellished with local symbols and culture that are 'liberated' from the monopoly of sovereignist identitarian groups, the antibodies have managed to put 'the other Verona' in the spotlight on a national, supranational, and transnational level, with their experience resonating in other contexts and in uniting with similar causes. Parallel to the theoretical insights that movement/countermovement dynamics provide visibility to both sides, keeping opposing movements alive (Meyer & Staggenborg, 1996; Dillard, 2013; Nicholls et al., 2013), the antibodies have successfully mobilized on various occasions to reverse the marketing of the city of Verona as the model city of traditional white Christian values. This is done by offering a contrasting image of Verona in a representation that accentuates the antifascist, anti-racist, and anti-sexist united struggle. In 2018, NUDM activists

---

28   Laurella Arietti's candidacy letter published by *Italia Laica*, available at: http://www.ital ialaica.it/forum/27002.

FIGURE 69   Verona Pride 2021 logo
             FROM THE FACEBOOK PAGE OF
             VERONA PRIDE, 14 MAY 2021

adopted the international symbol of the 'handmaid' from the television series The Handmaid's Tale in protest of the 'pro-life' motion and were subsequently greeted by a far-right councilor with the Roman salute. The antibodies capitalized on this opportunity to redeem the image of Verona as a city where the issue of women's rights is inseparable from the antifascist struggle and vice-e-versa: "A resistance started to take place emanating from Verona with the Handmaids." (Interview with E.N., 9 April 2019). As a result of this episode, they positioned the city on the frontlines of both the pro-choice movement and the antifascist movement.

The escalation of the conflict between feminist and LGBTQ+ activists, supported by the rest of the antibodies, on the one hand, institutional and non-institutional identitarian figures, on the other hand, reached a crescendo when the municipality announced Verona would be hosting the 2019 WCF summit. Notwithstanding the profile of prominent international politicians and religious figures from different countries at the summit, the concomitant organization of NUDM Verona entitled *Verona Città Transfemminista* overshadowed the former with the participation of its own transnational network alongside the antibodies and their followers. Reaching an unprecedented arrival of approximately 300,000 participants in this mid-sized Italian city, Verona came to symbolize the fight against the rise of a populist and far-right alliance in support of sexual rights and liberties as well as the rights of other minority

FIGURE 70   The political campaign of the trans activist Laurella Arietti for the mayorship of
Verona in 2007
PHOTO FROM THE FACEBOOK PAGE OF CIRCOLO PINK, 9 DECEMBER 2020

groups: "Everyone now is talking about the oceanic demonstration of NUDM. Before, when I used to say I was Veronese, they would look at me with compassion, saying 'Oh, the city of fascists'. Now, when I say I'm Veronese they tell me, 'You guys managed to organize that incredible demonstration. I was also there!'" (Interview with B.M., 8 October 2021). Hence, the three-day event marketing Verona as a 'transfeminist city', organized by a small group of local activists with scarce resources, that has managed to gather participants from around the world, including Latin America and the Middle East, attests to the power of their situated collective identity moving from the locality to connect with similar citizenship struggles in distant places.

NOI MAREA

VOI VANDEA

FIGURE 71   Two simultaneous organizations by competing groups
PHOTO FROM THE FACEBOOK PAGE OF NUDM, 31 MARCH 2019

On the whole, the antibodies of hate demonstrate the possibility of existing, resisting, and flourishing in an improbable territory, whilst offering another image of the city that allows room for an inclusive pluralist city-zenship: "The greatest success of this movement has been resisting to what has been going on in this city. It could have given up, but it didn't. This, in my opinion, is our greatest success, to never have given up to the strong aggression of the far-right." (Interview with C.Z., 10 February 2021). The representation of the city is not limited to the semantic field, but can also shape the everyday exchanges in shared urban spaces, thereby transforming the relation they might form with the place they live in. Moreover, alternative imaginings of the city can also serve as a medium to connect with similar causes in different places, in which collective mobilization gives voice to such representations on a transnational scale. Thus, the imagining of the 'other Verona' that is nourished by global claims to social justice departs from the outward-looking identity of space that is flourishing in Veronetta, but expands to the rest of the city and places beyond, touching other local efforts in countering exclusionary territorial belongings, wherever they may be.

The long course of activist city-zenship, the history of solidarity, community-building, experimentation, and bottom-up transformative placemaking efforts have nurtured values of openness and plurality that the antibodies have been authoring, allowing for prospects of expanding the boundaries of belonging. The fact that the antibodies have not only survived for so long, solidifying their ties among different constitutive elements and with city-zens of the city, but have also proven to the outside world that a successful grassroots movement is possible even in the most unlikely hostile setting lacking the necessary resources, is an invaluable example for similar struggles in the rise of sovereignist identitarianism around the globe:

> Verona is famous everywhere for the discriminatory policies of the right, but it's also becoming famous for the grassroots resistance with very few resources, which renders it so powerful. Not being a Milano, not being a Bologna, not being a big center where you have all the opportunities, a heterogeneity of people and resources, it nonetheless demonstrates how a small provincial city with numerically few people that organize can still extend to many. Also, not getting discouraged in smaller places, being able to mobilize and organize concretely even with few people in a hostile environment creates a chain effect through networking with other small groups. Being small does not equate to not having enough resources to be able to engage with others, even those who have not been active before.
>
> Interview with, E.N. 9 April 2019

Conclusion: (Re)spatializing Collective Action between Identity of Place and Place-Based Identities

In the nexus of social movements, urban life, and a sense of place, this book has been an effort to offer a diachronic socio-spatial analysis of antagonistic actors that operate in Verona following the insights of the extended case method (Gluckman, 1961; Burawoy et al., 1991; Burawoy, 2009), extending over a three-year fieldwork conducted in urban and digital spaces of various urban areas in connecting different theoretical traditions. By tracing the evolution and the everyday struggles of actors competing over the boundaries of belonging, the study aimed at restructuring our theorizing of collective identity and collective action in demonstrating the heuristic potential of social space, and subsequently that of everyday urban life in the field of social movements. The utilization of the dual concepts of *identity of place* and *place-based identities* for studying movement/countermovement dynamics in the microcosmos of an Italian city renowned for its hostile social setting has allowed us to examine the manifestations of wider global trends of identity politics in everyday urban encounters. The first concept has been employed to convey those material and cognitive characteristics that make a space turn into place, while the second concept comes to signify a common vision and a shared set of values derived from inhabiting the same place. The study took off with the exploration of a tempting curiosity on the particular environment of Verona as the stronghold of sovereignist identitarianisms on the one hand, and the relentless transformative placemaking struggles of progressive groups extraordinarily positioned in one single neighborhood, which animates their collective identity, on the other hand. Notwithstanding the limitations imposed by my positionality in the field, substantially restricting access to participant observation and semi-structured interviews with far-right actors, the study has nevertheless accomplished to obtain invaluable insights allowing for a sound comparative analysis of antagonistic movements in cityspace owing to the triangulation of a rich set of empirical data.

With the rise of populist politics worldwide, sustained by groups from the extreme right end of the political spectrum, the book has shed light on a new identitarian rebranding and a sovereignist outlook uniting these actors with nativist claims to territoriality. At this conjuncture, the city of Verona comes to the fore as a model forecasting these global trends in the Italian peninsula, culminating in what some experts have defined as a 'Veronification' of Italian politics to point out the rise of the far-right (De Medico quoted in Torrisi, 2019, Bernini, 2022). Hence, with a curious hunch to understand what kind of social dynamics in the urban life of Verona made it possible for the success of far-right actors, leading to a remarkable tolerance in everyday life to exclusionary practices of boundary-drawing, I have undertaken this multi-method investigation in Verona to unpack an alliance extending from the local movement scene to the city administration, and reaching transnational counterparts. As a result, the analysis has shown that an oath to take back control in the 'native' territory by promoting an exclusionary form of city-zenship is imbued in the perception of a primordial tie between an 'authentic' identity and the land. In this respect, the study has revealed the two-way process of boundary-drawing as a result of the institutionalization of far-right elements inside the city administration: (1) a top-down institutional mechanism of 'guarding urban décor and heritage' through exclusionary administrative policies (Mitchell, 2000; Saitta, 2015; Mazzei, 2018), coupled with (2) a bottom-up mechanism of micro-level acts of 'territorialization' to reclaim ownership of social space (Brighenti, 2010; Brighenti, 2014; Halvorsen, 2015) and 'everyday chauvinisms' in the city premised on an existential aversion towards otherness (Saitta, 2021).

Such nativist closure reflecting the rise of far-right and populist right discourses upon urban realities is not particular to Verona, as observed by scholars working in various settings such as Athens in Greece (Papatzani, 2021), Messina in Sicily (Saitta, 2022), Timişoara in Romania (Creţan & O'brien, 2019), and even Toronto in Canada (Silver et al., 2020). Through a detailed investigation of intertwined socio-spatial mechanisms in Verona, this book has offered a systematic analysis of the evolution and operations of such actors within and beyond cityspace, by employing novel theoretical lenses that can easily be adopted in different contexts. The book juxtaposes the concepts of 'sovereignism' (Freeden, 2017; Basile & Mazzoleni, 2020; Basile et al., 2020), commonly used in Italian language and politics despite being relatively unexplored by international scholars, alongside the growing trend of 'identitarianism' (Tudor, 2014; Zùquete, 2018; Handler, 2019; Murdoch & Murhall, 2019; Šima, 2021) as a search to recuperate loss of identity by restoring a golden age. In so doing, it uncovers several dynamics at play on multiple layers: (1) the union of populist right, far-right, and ultra-conservative groups from the institutional to non-institutional actors around a shared understanding of 'sovereignist identitarianism', which foresees (2) mutually exclusive territories of peoples, where objects to be defended are the homeland and the white native identity tied to the construction of this social space, (3) and therefore, the mobilizing strength of an exclusionary place-based identity in the contemporary politics of uncertainty, with the instinct of clinging even stronger to the immediate locality

(Castells, 2010), (4) resulting in two-way mechanism of boundary-drawing in advocating exclusive city-zenship. The notion of an *exclusionary territorial identity* works as a glue bringing various actors under the same cause, converging into a shared collective identity in defense of the local, which is a concept that finds resonance in other settings, connecting with actors elsewhere defending the same cause. This phenomenon was exemplified by the realization of 'little Verona' in Myanmar by a Veronese identitarian group supporting territorial identity claims of foreign actors. In the case of Verona, such place-based identity translates into ethnonationalist characteristics of being white, Christian, and mittel-European (as opposed to South European) in relation to the geographical construct of Padania, manifested through the local dialect, local traditions, and local heritage, as a territorial way of belonging that has for generations been tied to this land.

As invoked by the question of micro-macro entanglements in the extended case method, it is shown that while every locality has a distinct identity of place that shapes the form of attachment to it and the type of social relations it fosters, the sovereignist motto of taking back control of a homeland and reinstating an authentic identity translates smoothly in myriad diverse contexts and on different scales by groups who feel threatened by the workings of globalization. From conceptualizations of national sovereignty trickling down to everyday bordering practices in cityspace, the sovereignist logic targets particularly unwanted multiculturalism and its effects on daily lives. These themes that emerge from Verona are even more meaningful when analyzed in the light of anachronistic ethnonationalist citizenship policies at the national level, unresponsive to the claims made by children of migrants for equal rights (for a detailed discussion, see Hawthorne, 2022), parallel to supremacist worries of being ethnically replaced by non-white migrants and their offspring. On a transnational level, the case of Verona lucidly demonstrates how boundary-drawing and border-keeping practices today in Fortress Europe against incoming waves of migration are reflected in urban life. The aforementioned concerns over 'ethnic replacement' expressed personally by the Italian Agriculture Minister in 2023 are, in fact, part of a larger 'Great Replacement' theory articulated by notorious far-right figures in the western world, from New Zealand to Norway,[1] translating into urban life as 'ethnic resistance' in multicultural neighborhoods. In urban spaces, these acts of revanchist reterritorialization at times operate in tandem with gentrification efforts in pushing out non-decorative elements.

---

1   For more information, see: https://www.bbc.com/news/world-europe-65324319.

The historical center of Verona, admired as the romantic setting of Shakespeare's play Romeo and Juliet, is the suitable social space in the marketing of a 'model city' that incarnates identitarian values, local traditions, and myths, in other words, the *Veronesità* that these actors so ardently seek to protect and promote. The historical center inscribed with scripts of belonging and non-belonging, with its heritage invoking pride for an anti-modern nostalgia (Boym, 2001), is endorsed as an exemplary place for the transnational network of far-right and conservative actors. Therefore, the historical center as a space of touristification (Sequera & Nofre, 2018) in the last couple of decades concurrently signifies the cleansing of marginal elements in the name of urban décor for the marketing of an exclusionary territorial identity as 'heritage' (Massey, 1994; Mitchel, 2000; Moore, 2007). The *inward-looking identity of the historical center* that the alliance of sovereignist actors draws on for their collective identity, and which they seek to 'guard' through everyday territorialization efforts, thereby pulls to its orbit 'identitarian tourists' yielding a similar orientation, as lucidly illustrated in the case of the Verona Vandea in 2018 and the WCF in 2019.

Nonetheless, this has been merely part of the story and a partial depiction of the social conflict that manifests itself in this mid-sized Italian city. The investigation of social movement actors in Verona led to the discovery of the cosmos of Veronetta and its *antibodies of hate* that exemplify the possibilities of cultivating inclusive and pluralist social ties even in the most improbable hostile setting. Once one crosses over one of the bridges connecting the historical center to the eastern bank of River Adige, the wanderer gets the feeling of entering a completely different social space with its own identity, as put succinctly by one respondent, "almost like a world of its own" (Interview with N.C., 11 February 2021). The conceptual strength of social space once again displays its utility through the duality of the identity of place and place-based identities, with Veronetta radiating an *outward-looking identity* in contrast to the rest of the city and fostering an *expansive place-based identity* to subjects who share a non-fixed and open form of belonging to cityspace, owing to the everyday efforts of an assemblage of actors fighting intolerance who operate alongside migrant communities in the neighborhood. Hence, in understanding the relationship of the antibodies to the neighborhood of Veronetta, from which they operate and connect with places beyond, the research has applied the socio-spatial categories for a rereading of their collective identity and collective action. This complex assemblage composed of grassroots actors and horizontal initiatives seeks to open up democratic spaces through transformative placemaking practices (Bacchetta et al., 2019) and deterritorialization efforts, thereby offering an alternative form of place-based belonging emanating primarily from Veronetta.

The push factors of touristification and far-right territorialization in the historical center, besides the pull factors of an indifferent tolerance initially set by migrant communities, low housing prices, and a history of counterculture, concurrently have led these groups from different walks of life to resettle in Veronetta since the beginning of the 1990s. From a spatio-temporal axis, the antibodies have crossed paths from the early *pensilina* experience, which came to an end with the earliest gentrification projects, subsequently taking refuge in the Circolo Pink office in *via Scrimiari*. Such space-sharing experiences have been indispensable in forging their collective identity and the form of collective action they have been undertaking in the wider area of Verona. Thus, the investigation of this assemblage has elucidated once again the reciprocal constitution of social space and social actors: there would be no antibodies without the neighborhood of Veronetta, and no Veronetta understood as a conceptual space surpassing its material borders without the antibodies. This observation can be extended to other urban contexts cultivating pluralist belongings in different settings, where the social space itself becomes an author of mobilization harboring wider struggles of identity, and where a cosmopolitan place-based identity becomes entrenched in the collective identity of a movement.

In their democratic and horizontal organizational structure constituted by independent associations, centers, collectives, and transnational movements operating at the local, those values that unite the antibodies are defined through a situated collective memory premised on the indivisible struggles of antifascism, anti-racism, and anti-sexism, values that connect the antibodies with similar causes in distant settings. What allows these otherwise autonomous actors to collaborate in the everyday is firstly taking pride in the collective memory of the Veronese antifascist resistance reflected in contemporary struggles, secondly, the shared spaces and experiences that have solidified their bond, and lastly, the experimental laboratory of an outward-looking neighborhood they have helped create promoting their vision of an *inclusive pluralist city-zenship* as opposed to the predominant exclusive city-zenship model. Therefore, against the dual mechanism of top-down policies pioneered by the city administration and the bottom-up boundary-drawing practices by far-right movements in the city, the antibodies have found strength and perseverance in uniting around a common cause that is locally defined, yet one that opens up to places beyond and connects with progressive counterparts elsewhere and their struggles. Once again, the place-based repertoire of action undertaken by this assemblage involves everyday practices of activist citizenship, transformative placemaking, collective deterritorialization efforts, and an alternative representation of the city on the semantic plane. It is by large part thanks to such protracted struggle and decades of resistance that the 2022 local elections saw the victory of a progressive political alliance in the city administration for the first time in decades, led by the newly elected mayor Damiano Tommasi, which not only ensued in the abolishment of anti-LGBTQ+ motions from the 1990s along with the extraordinary participation of the mayor in Verona Pride 2022, but also enabled the very first Afrodescendant councilor Veronica Atitsogbe to enter the city council, who happens to be a founding member of *AfroVeronesi*.

The form of city-zenship that the antibodies have been struggling for, expanding the boundaries of place-based belonging, carries the life force of grassroots movements striving in hostile settings elsewhere who confront nativist closure on different levels. These involve local anti-racist, antifascist, and anti-sexist struggles in various European cities that have come to be marked by reactionary backlash, such as Dresden, Chemnitz, Budapest, or Trieste. Moreover, the themes presented here regarding city-zenship in urban space reflect wider struggles for the recognition of citizenship rights on the national level. This can be traced in the political claims of children of migrants who struggle for an alternative conceptualization of belonging not only in cityspace but also with respect to underlying assumptions of whiteness in the current Italian citizenship laws (Hawthrone, 2022). Another manifestation can be found in the claims for equal citizenship rights by LGBTQ+ actors, such as the rejected *Zan Bill* that sought to extend the Mancino Law to include violence against sexual minorities and people with disability as a hate crime. These citizenship struggles for the recognition of equal rights are undoubtedly present in other national contexts beyond Italy, with migrant movements, LGBTQ+ and feminist movements, anti-racist and antifascist movements making their voices heard around the globe, extending from the intimacy of everyday life to transnational platforms.

The antibodies of hate in Verona and elsewhere offer a sense of belonging to subjects that have long suffered non-belonging, including political dissenters, sexual minorities, migrant communities, people of color, or simply individuals with different experiences and different outlooks upon the world. Whilst stimulating a competing image of the city and an alternative city-zenship within, micro-macro entanglements reveal how the antibodies employ global causes of social justice in their own locality on the one hand, and unite their own local struggles with other transnational actors working on similar issues on the other hand. In the case of Verona, these translocal linkages have been exemplified by the experiences of *Critical Wine* as a local manifestation of a transnational ecological movement, *Verona Città Transfemminista* as a transnational uprising against the international anti-gender network, and the local mobilization uniting with the global *Black Lives Matter* movement pioneered by AfroVeronesi. In a mid-sized city with scarce resources known for its socio-political hostility and intolerance, managing not only sheer survival in a liberated little urban neighborhood, but constructing an alternative social reality that overflows to the rest of the city, connecting with distant places is what makes the case of the antibodies so appealing as an example for other contexts where hostile localism reigns. Table 4 below summarizes the findings of the comparative analysis of these two antagonistic movements through a socio-spatial examination of collective identity and collective action.

These significant insights from the extended case of Verona contribute to the avenue of research at the intersection of urban studies and social movements in three ways. Firstly, owing to its methodological approach, the study shows the continuities of online and offline spaces of collective action on the one hand, and captures the spatial manifestation of social movements visually by utilizing visual methods of inquiry on the other hand. Secondly, it provides a novel perspective into the relational spatiality of movement-countermovement dynamics in the struggle to define belonging by applying a 'bird's eye view' (Nicholls et al., 2013) to social conflict among antagonistic social actors, both situated in the same city while being part of competing global trends on identity struggles. As put by Massey, the aim has been "[e]xposing the maps of power, through which identities are constructed" (Massey, 1999: 11), which moves beyond macro-explanations of opportunity structures and micro-explanations of individual membership to complement these approaches in introducing: a. a comparative diachronic analysis of the evolution of antagonistic actors in relation to one another and b. a synchronic everyday analysis of their interaction in urban space. The final and most important contribution has been the implementation of the social space approach borrowed from critical geography, as it is defined through 'identity of place' and 'place-based identity'. In so doing, the research has aimed to restructure the existing theoretical insights on collective identity and collective action by demonstrating the heuristic strength of spatial concepts in an analysis of mobilization among antagonistic movements with repercussions within and beyond (Burawoy et al., 1991).

While social movements scholarship has been giving due attention to the role of spatiality through the vast urban social movements literature (Castells, 1983; Dikeç, 2002; Martin & Miller, 2003; Pickvance, 2003; Harvey, 2012; Mayer, 2009; Dochartaigh & Bosi 2010; Soja, 2010; Nel·lo, 2016; Domaradzka, 2018), the concept of 'space' has hitherto been employed in its physical existence as a container that accommodates material resources, social actors, and social relations. This is visible in the groundbreaking works of Routledge (2010, 2013)

TABLE 4 A comparative socio-spatial analysis of antagonistic actors in Verona

	Identity of Place	Place-based identity	Collective identity	Collective action	Veronese city-zenship
Alliance of far-right, right-wing populist, and ultra-conservative actors	*Inward-looking space of the historical center* Symbolic space embodying local history, myths, and symbols. Fixed timeless homogenous identity. Sanitized white touristscape, marketing of heritage. 'Model city' for the transnational identitarian network.	*Exclusionary territorial identity* Nativist belonging to place, based on exclusion.	*Sovereignist identitarianism* Nativist feeling of ownership over homeland, mutually exclusive territories. Identity understood as primordial ties to territory. Historical revisionism. 'Anti-gender' approach to sexual rights, promoting traditional family. Anti-globalization and anti-immigration.	*Two-way Boundary-drawing* Institutionalization of extremist elements in the city administration, exclusionary policies rendering the city a 'model' on a transnational level (*top-down boundary-drawing*). Everyday guarding of cognitive borders, ethnic resistance, and other acts of territorialization upon urban space (*bottom-up boundary-drawing*).	*Exclusive membership* Whiteness of mittel-Europa as against Southern European identity, middle-class aspirations, idealizing local symbols and myths, use of local dialect in symbolizing privilege in one's homeland, heteronormative traditional Christian moral values, shared territorial culture and outlook.

TABLE 4   A comparative socio-spatial analysis of antagonistic actors in Verona (*cont.*)

	Identity of Place	Place-based identity	Collective identity	Collective action	Veronese city-zenship
Assemblage of progressive actors	*Veronetta as an outward-looking space* Juxtaposition of migrants, students, old residents, and the civil society actors that make up the antibodies. Inclusiveness within diversity, intercultural values, and openness. Home to progressive actors with diverse backgrounds. Exemplify an alternative modus-vivendi radiating outwards. Resisting both gentrification and reterritorialization attempts.	*Expansive place-based identity* Progressive belonging to place, based on inclusion.	*Antibodies of hate* Antifascism Anti-racism Anti-sexism The collective memory of local antifascist resistance as a source of pride. A history of sharing spaces and engaging in solidarity across issues. Horizontal, grassroots organization that is democratic and non-hierarchical. Embracing global justice claims.	*Bottom-up transformative place-making* Bottom-up community building. Activist citizenship. Everyday social ties. Deterritorialization, opening up democratic spaces. Alternative representation of Verona that works to (1) offer a different belonging to city-zens within, and (2) connect with similar causes of social justice in different settings.	*Inclusive pluralist membership* City-zenship not fixed but evolving with new members, defined through shared values. The neighborhood of Veronetta as an experimental laboratory for exercising a different form of city-zenship that is offered to the rest of the city

who has skillfully elaborated how movements act from the material conditions of space, on space (appropriating), in space (protests), and make space (Routledge, 2013:1). Likewise, significant progress has been made thanks to the stimulating works of Nicholls on the link between city life and mobilization around a tolerant or exclusionary identity (Nicholls, 2008; Nicholls et al., 2013), and the canonical work by Melucci (1984) (which is also borrowed by Della Porta and Diani [2006]) in underlining how certain neighborhoods become 'movement areas' or 'social movement scenes' that offer not only a space to organize collective action but also everyday cultural activities that foster the movement identity involved with this space. The work of Miller (2013) must also be reminded here, pointing out how social movements operate on different spaces, namely material space, conceptual space, and lived space. Doubtlessly, this research has benefited from this line of scholarship at the intersection of space, identity, and mobilization. There are also other valuable contributions to the field in demonstrating the spatiality of nationalisms in different contexts, operating primarily through the exclusion of difference and the selective writing of local histories (Soja, 1971; Herb & Kaplan, 1999; Mitchell, 2000; Moore, 2007; Siatta, 2015; Cretan & O'brien, 2019; Silver et al., 2020; Papatzani, 2021; Saitta, 2021; Gawlewicz & Yiftachel, 2022). Lastly, while the link between place-based identities and collective action has been accentuated in a number of recent studies (Sbicca & Perdue, 2013; Bruttomesso, 2018; Yuen, 2018), this was done so in relation to ad hoc events such as protests and temporary occupations, thereby, overlooking the indispensable connection between the collective identity of social movement actors and the identity of place which they take part in and identify with on an everyday basis, shaping their objectives and vision.

Once we move beyond seeing space merely as a surface and start conceptualizing it as an agent in its own right constituted through social interconnections, we can talk about the identity of a given place and the type of place-based identities it fosters, which have the potential to become a fundamental part of the collective identity of movement. The representation of a city, its characteristics, and its ideal protagonist turn into collective action itself, whereby different imaginations of the same space can blossom into different and competing constructions of city-zenship. The 'extension of theory' (Burawoy, 2009) foreseen by the extended case method, therefore, is realized with a detailed account of social space and its impact on collective action among opposing actors.

In this sense, with a conceptualization of space as the product of social relations harboring multiplicity and therefore never a fixed static entity (Massey, 2005), we can observe the fluidity between the local/global divide

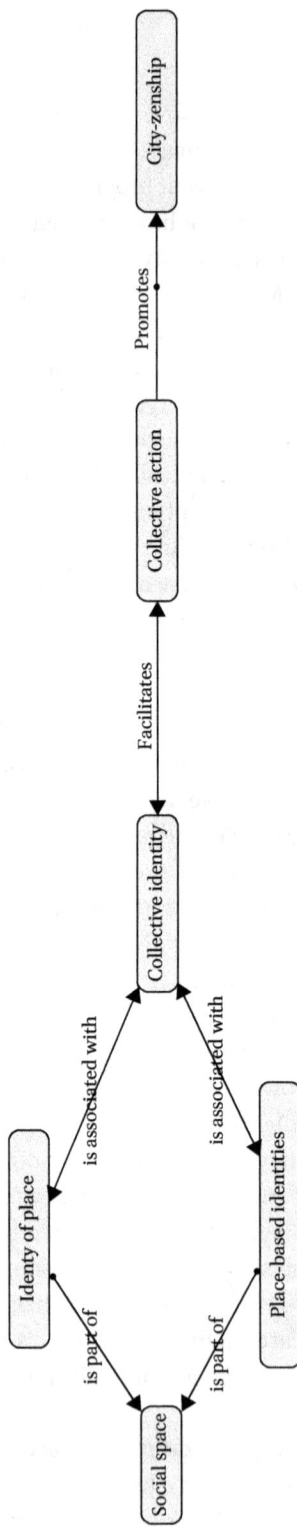

FIGURE 72   Revisiting the relationship between space, identity, and collective action

on the one hand, digital space and urban materialities on the other hand, in which defending the local 'authenticity' or transforming it from below both turns into global objectives of mobilization. In so doing, we can reflect upon the continuities between citizenship struggles in national and transnational settings and city-zenship struggles in urban space. The contesting aspirations that travel across borders demonstrate the two distinct effects of territorial boundaries on human existence: "[T]hose which the residents wish to defend and remain within; and those which the residents wish to remove or cross." (Kearns, 1995: 167) From the extended case of Verona, this study has sought to show the link between the construction of the identity of Verona as an inward-looking timeless homogenous space guarding what *was*, performed through a territorial identity adhered to by far-right and identitarian movements in the everyday. Thus, Verona Vandea is the Verona of the historical center, encapsulating its extraordinary history, its traditional values rooted in Christianity, its order and security as a touristic space, its richness and middle-class values, and above all, its whiteness. The image of a different Verona, one in which an inclusive pluralist understanding of city-zenship can flourish, radiates instead from the neighborhood of Veronetta, a laboratory of community-building with a history of its own identified through the complex set of social relations it authors. This outward-looking space created with the juxtaposition of the university, the migrant communities, and the assemblage of antibodies animates the collective action of this grassroots movement, who connect with like-minded actors in places beyond. The expansive place-based identity that overflows from Veronetta draws to its orbit subjects looking for an alternative sense of belonging.

From place-based identities to collective identity translating into collective action, our socio-spatial experiences in a given place shape our vision of the world, whether we want to accept and defend what is passed down to us or to resist and transform it. While global themes are deciphered according to the locality, local struggles, in turn, find resonance elsewhere by connecting with similar causes in diverse contexts. It is in this nexus that depending on how one sees the world and the society they live in, a sense of place can work either as an anchor for reactionary impulses towards social change or act as the motor for transforming social relations and rewriting belonging. We are situated social beings shaped by our experience in the space-time axis, notwithstanding the age of mobility (Urry, 2010) and uprootedness that characterize much of modern society. Our corporeal existence (*dasein*) is essential in locating our perspectives on social injustice and the solutions we come up with for a better society, whether such ideals are expressed on urban walls or Instagram photos. The way forward for future research is to further explore the significance of social space for mobilizations across diverse contexts, focusing particularly on everyday social processes in material and non-material urban realities. As illustrated by the present work, this is possible by systematically implementing the socio-spatial categories of identity of place and place-based identity to investigate social movements struggling on the opposite ends of identity politics.

Bibliography

Adinolfi, G. & Fiore, R. (2015) *Noi Terza Posizione*, Roma: Settimo Sigillo-Europa Libreria Editrice.

Agnew, J. & Brusa, C. (1999) "New Rules for National Identity? The Northern League and Political Identity in Contemporary Northern Italy," in *National Identities*, vol. 1, no. 2, pp. 117–133.

Airoldi, M. (2018) "Ethnography and the Digital Fields of Social Media," in *International Journal of Social Research Methodology*, vol. 21, no. 6, 661–673.

Akkerman, T., de Lange, S. L., & Rooduijn, M. (2016) *Radical Right-Wing Political Parties in Western Europe: Into the Mainstream?*, London: Routledge.

Allen, A.M. (1910) *A History of Verona*, London: Methuen & Co. Ltd.

Amorese, A. (2013) *Fronte della gioventù. La destra che sognava la rivoluzione: La storia mai raccontata*, Firenze: Ecclettica Edizioni.

Andretta, M., Piazza, G. & Subirats, A. (2015) "Urban Dynamics and Social Movements," in (eds.) Donatella Della Porta and Mario Diani, *The Oxford Handbook of Social Movements*, Oxford: Oxford University Press.

Anthias, F. & Yuval-Davis, N. (1992) *Racialized boundaries: Race, nation, gender, colour and class and the anti-racist struggle*, New York: Routledge.

Antonini, C. (2018) "Il laboratorio dell'intolleranza," in *LEFT* (21 Seprember 2018) [Accessed on 6 November 2019] Available at: https://left.it/left-n-38-21-settem bre-2018/.

Aronowitz, S. (1992) *The Politics of Identity: Class, Culture, Social Movements*, London: Routledge.

Aru, S. (2015) "Identità, spazi e luoghi," in A. Alaimo, S. Aru, G. Donadelli, F. Nebbia (eds.) *Geografie di Oggi: Metodi e strategie tra ricerca e didattica*, Milano: FrancoAngeli.

Atkinson, P. & Hammersley, M. (2007) *Ethnography: Principles in practice*, London: Routledge.

Avanza, M. (2018) "Plea for an Emic Approach Towards 'Ugly Movements': Lessons from the Divisions within the Italian Pro-Life Movement," in *Politics and Governance*, vol. 6 no. 3, pp. 112–125.

Ayoub, P.M., Wallace, S.J., & Zepede-Millan, C., (2014) "Triangulation in Social Movement Research," in Donatella Della Porta (ed.) *Methodological Practices in Social Movement Research*, Oxford: Oxford University Press.

Bacchetta, P., El-Tayeb, F., & Haritaworn, J. (2019) "Queers of Colour and (De)Colonial Spaces in Europe," in (eds.) Paola Bacchetta, Sunaina Maira & Howard Winant, *Global Raciality: Empire, PostColoniality, DeColoniality*, New York: Routledge.

Baldini, G., Bressanelli, E. & Gianfreda, S. (2020) "Taking back control? Brexit, sovereignism and populism in Westminster (2015–17)," in *European Politics and Society*, vol. 21 no. 2, pp. 219–234.

Balibar, E. (1991) "Is There a 'Neo-Racism'?" in *Race, Nation, and Class: Ambiguous. Identities*, (eds.) Etienne Balibar and Immanuel Wallerstein. London: Verso.

Balsiger, P. & Lambelet, A. (2014) "Participant Observation," in Donatella Della Porta (ed.) *Methodological Practices in Social Movement Research*, Oxford: Oxford University Press.

Banini, T. (2011) "Introduzione alle identità territoriali," in Tiziana Banini (Ed.) *Mosaici identitari. Dagli italiani a Vancouver alla kerppa islandese*, Roma: Nuova Cultura.

Banini, T. (2017) "Proposing a Theoretical Framework for Local Territorial Identities: Concepts, Questions, and Pitfalls," in *Territorial Identity and Development*, vol. 2 no. 2, pp. 16–23.

Banini, T. & Pollice, F. (2015) "Territorial Identity as a Strategic Resource for the Development of Rural Areas," in *Semestrale di Studi e Ricerche di Geografia*, vol. 27 no. 1, pp. 7–16.

Banini, T. & Ilovan, O. (2021) "Introduction: Dealing with Territorial/Place Identity Representations," in Tiziana Banini and Osana-Ramona Ilovan (eds.), *Representing Place and Territorial Identities in Europe*, Berlin: Springer.

Barak, N. (2020) "City-zenship and National Citizenship: Complementary and Competing but Not Emancipated from Each Other," in Rainer Bauböck and Liav Orgad (eds.) *Cities vs States: Should Urban Citizenship be Emancipated from Nationality?* (EUI Working Papers), Florence: Robert Schuman Centre for Advanced Studies.

Barbosa, R. & Casarões, G. (2023) "Statecraft under God: Radical Right Populism Meets Christian Nationalism in Bolsonaro's Brazil," in *Millenium: Journal of International Studies*, vol. 50 no. 3, pp. 669–699.

Basile, L. & Mazzoleni, O. (2020) "Sovereignist Wine in Populist Bottles? An Introduction," in *European Politics and Society*, vol. 21 no. 2, pp. 151–162.

Basile, L., Borri, R. & Verzichelli, L. (2020) "'For Whom the Sovereignist Bell Tolls?' Individual Determinants of Support for Sovereignism in Ten European Countries," in *European Politics and Society*, vol. 21 no. 2, pp. 235–257.

Bauböck, R. (2003) "Reinventing Urban Citizenship," in *Citizenship Studies*, vol. 7 no. 2, pp. 139–160.

Bauman, Z. (1995) "Making and Unmaking of Strangers," in *Thesis Eleven*, no. 43, pp. 1–16.

Becucci, S. (2003) "Pratiche di sovversione sociale: il movimento dei dissobedienti," in *Quaderni di Sociologia*, vol. 33, pp. 5–20.

Becker, H.S. (1996) "The Epistemology of Qualitative Research," in (eds.) R. Jessor, A. Colby, and R. Shweder (1996), *Ethnography and Human Development: Context and Meaning in Social Inquiry*, Chicago: University of Chicago Press.

Bejarano, C.A., Juárez, L. L., Mijangos García, M.A., & Goldstein, D.M. (2019) *Decolonizing Ethnography: Undocumented Immigrants and New Directions in Social Science*, Durham: Duke University Press.

Benford, R. D. & Snow, D. A. (2000) "Framing Processes and Social Movements: An Overview and Assessment," in *Annual Review of Sociology*, vol. 26, p. 611–639.

Berg, L. D. & Kearns, R.A. (1996) "Naming as Norming: Gender, and the Identity Politics of Naming Places in Aotearoa/New Zealand," *Environment and Planning D: Society and Space*, vol. 14, pp. 99–122.

Bergen, N. & Labonte, R. (2019) "'Everything is Perfect and We Have No Problems': Detecting and Limiting Social Desirability Bias in Qualitative Research," in *Qualitative Health Research*, vol. 30 no. 5, pp. 783–792.

Berger, P.L. & Luckmann, T. (1966) *The Social Construction of Reality: A Treatise in the Sociology of Knowledge*, New York: Penguin Books.

Bernard, H.R. (2006) *Research Methods in Anthropology: Qualitative and Quantitative Approaches*, Lanham: Rowman & Littlefield Publishers.

Bernini, L. (2022) "Tre generazioni e tanti brividi," in *Jacobin Italia* (20 October 2022), [accessed on 21 November 2022], available at: https://jacobinitalia.it/tre-generazi oni-e-tanti-brividi.

Berizzi, P. (2022) *È gradita la camicia nera: Verona la città laboratorio dell'estrema destra tra l'Italia e l'Europa*, Milano: Rizzoli.

Biguzzi, S., Domenichini, O., Bonente, R., & Crepaldi, R. (2015) *Verona tra guerra e Resistenza 1943–1945*, Verona: Istituto Veronese per la storia della resistenza e dell'età contemporanea, [accessed on 21 September 2020], available at: http://www.ivrr.it /didattica/verona-tra-guerra-e-resistenza-1943-1945.

Boellstorff, T., Nardi B., Pearce, C. & Taylor, T.L. (2012) *Ethnography and Virtual Worlds: A Handbook*, Princeton: Princeton University Press.

Bonatelli, P. (2007) "Le radici dei fascisti 'resistenti'," in *Il Manifesto* (22 July 2007), [accessed on 24 September 2020], available at: https://archiviopubblico.ilmanife sto.it/Articolo/2003113395.

Bosi, L. & Reiter, H. (2014) "Historical Methodologies: Archival Research and Oral History in Social Movement Research," in Donatella Della Porta (ed.) *Methodological Practices in Social Movement Research*, Oxford: Oxford University Press.

Boym, S. (2001) *The Future of Nostalgia*, New York: Basic Books.

Bozzetto, L.V. (1996) *Verona e Vienna. Gli arsenali dell'imperatore. Architettura militare e città nell'Ottocento*, Verona: Cierre Edizioni.

Brighenti, A.M. (2010) "On Territoriology: Towards a General Science of Territory," in *Theory, Culture & Society*, vol. 27 no. 52, pp. 52–72.

Brighenti, A.M. (2010a) *Visibility in Social Theory and Social Research*, New York: Palgrave Macmillan.

Brighenti, A.M. (2010b) "At the Wall: Graffiti Writers, Urban Territoriality, and the Public Domain," in *Space and Culture*, vol. 13 no. 3, pp. 315–332.

Brighenti, A.M. (2014) "Mobilizing Territories, Territorializing Mobilities," in *Sociologica*, vol. 1 pp. 1–25.

Brinkmann, S. (2017) "The Interview," in N.K. Denzin & Y.S. Lincoln (eds.) *Collecting and Interpreting Qualitative Materials*, London: SAGE Publications.

Brown, G. & Browne, K. (2016) *The Routledge Research Companion to Geographies of Sex and Sexualities*, Oxon: Routledge.

Bruttomesso, E. (2018) "Making Sense of the Square: Facing the Touristification of Public Space through Playful Protest in Barcelona," in *Tourist Studies*, vol. 18 no. 4, pp. 467–485.

Byrne, D. & Goodall, H. (2013) 'Placemaking and Transnationalism: Recent Migrants and a National Park in Sydney, Australia,' in *PARKS*, vol.19 no.1, pp. 63–1.

Burawoy, M., Burton, A., Ferguson, A.A., Fox, K.J., (1991) *Ethnography Unbound: Power and Resistance in the Modern Metropolis*, Berkeley: University of California Press.

Burawoy, M. (2009) *The Extended Case Method: Four Countries, Four Decades, Four Great Transformations, one Theoretical Tradition*, Berkeley: University of California Press.

Caiani, M., Della Porta, D. & Wagemann, C. (2012) *Mobilizing on the Extreme Right: Germany, Italy, and the United States*, Oxford: Oxford University Press.

Caiani, M. & Kröll, P. (2014) "The transnationalization of the Extreme Right and the Use of the Internet," in *International Journal of Comparative and Applied Criminal Justice*, vol. 39 no. 4, pp. 331–351.

Caiani, M. & Della Porta, D. (2018), "The Radical Right as Social Movement Organizations," in Jen Rydgren (ed.) *The Oxford Handbook of the Radical Right*, New York: Oxford University Press.

Caiani, M. (2018), "Radical Right Cross-National Links and International Cooperation," in Rydgren, J. (ed.), *The Oxford Handbook of the Radical Right*. Oxford: Oxford University Press.

Caiani, M. (2019) "The Rise and Endurance of Radical Right Movements," in *Current Sociology*, vol. 67 no. 6, pp. 918–935.

Calogero, P. (2017) "Magistratura, servizi segreti e terrorismi di destra e sinistra. La responsabilità dello Stato," in Carlo Fumian and Angelo Ventrone (eds.) *Il Terrorismo di Destra e di Sinistra in Italia e in Europa*, Padova: Padova University Press.

Cammelli, M.G. (2015) *Fascisti del Terzo Millennio*, Verona: Ombre Corte.

Cammelli, M.G. (2018) "The Legacy of Fascism in the Present: 'Third Millennium Fascists' in Italy," in *Journal of Modern Italian Studies*, vol. 23 no. 2, pp. 199–14.

Canteri, R. (1991) *Gli anni caldi 1966–1975*, Verona: Arte Grafica.

Carmo, A. (2012) "Reclaim the Streets, the Protestival and the Creative Transformation of the City," in *Finisterra*, vol. XLVII no. 94, pp. 103–118.

Castells, M. (1983) *The City and Grassroots: A Cross-cultural Theory of Urban Social Movements*, Berkeley: University of California Press.

Castells, M. (2010) *The Power of Identity*, West Sussex UK: Blackwell Publishing.

Cazzullo, A. (2012) "I mille volti di Verona: dalla destra alla Lega," in *Corriere della Sera* (19 March 2012), [accessed on 9 May 2019] available at: https://www.corriere.it/crona che/12_marzo_19/verona-citta-amata-all-estero-ha-da-sempre-il-complesso-di-non -contare-abbastanza-aldo-cazzullo_4e8e80aa-718f-11e1-b597-5e4ce0cb380b.shtml.

Cevese, R. (2005) "Market, bazar, phone center: pratiche commerciali e percezione dello spazio a Veronetta," in *DiPAV-QUADERNI. Quadrimestrale di psicologia ed antropologia culturale*, vol. 14 no. 3, pp. 71–92.

Chalfen, R. (2011) "Looking Two Ways: Mapping the Social Scientific Study of Visual Culture," in Eric Margolis & Luc Pauwels (eds.) *The SAGE Handbook of Visual Research Methods*, London: SAGE Publications.

Chalfen, R. (2011a) "Differentiating Practices of Participatory Visual Media Production," in Eric Margolis & Luc Pauwels (eds.) *The SAGE Handbook of Visual Research Methods*, London: SAGE Publications.

Chelidonio, G. (2009) "Le Radici Tradizionali e Cultura della 'Veronesita,'" in (ed.) Maurizio Delibori, *Quale Veronesità: Identità e radici culturali ed umane veronesi in un mondo globalizzato*, Verona: Editrice Grafiche P2.

Conti, I. (2017) *Carlo Furlan: Una vita per l'ambiente e per la sua città*, Verona: Cierre Grafica.

Creţan, R. & O'Brien, T. (2019) "'Get out of Traian Square!': Roma Stigmatization as a Mobilizing Tool for the Far Right in Timişoara, Romania," in *International Journal of Urban and Regional Research*, vol. 43 no. 5, pp. 833–847.

Cumbers, A. & Routledge, P. (2013) "Place, Space and Solidarity in Global Justice Networks," in David Featherstone & Joe Painter (eds.), *Spatial Politics: Essays for Doreen Massey*, Oxford: John Wiley & Sons.

D'Agostino, P. (2002) "Craniums, Criminals, and the 'Cursed Race': Italian Anthropology in American Racial Thought, 1861–1924," in *Comparative Studies in Society and History*, vol. 44, no. 2, pp. 319–342.

De Certeau, M. (1984) *The Practice of the Everyday*. Berkeley: University of California Press.

De-Shalit, A. (2020) "Thinking Like a City, Thinking Like a State," in Rainer Bauböck and Liav Orgad (eds.) *Cities vs States: Should Urban Citizenship be Emancipated from Nationality?* (EUI Working Papers), Florence: Robert Schuman Centre for Advanced Studies.

De Spiegeleire, S., Skinner, C. & Sweijs, T. (2017) *The Rise of Populist Sovereignism: What it is, where it comes from, and what it means for international security and defense*, The Hague: The Hague Centre for Strategic Studies.

De Vita, A. (2008) "Veronetta si-cura. Note di filosofia e metodologia della partecipazi-one," in *Culture della sostenibilita'*, anno II no. 3, pp. 127–138.

De Vita, A. & de Cordova, F. (2013) *Veronetta un territorio in relazione*, Research Report for Project FEI 2011 Action 8, Department of Human Sciences, Verona: University of Verona.

De Vita, A. & de Cordova, F. (2018) "Veronetta: un quartiere in movimento a partire dall'Università," in Paolo Di Nicola (ed.) *Veronetta, quartiere latino: Una ricerca tra Università e Città a Verona*, Milano: FrancoAngeli.

Del Medico, E. (2004) *All'estrema destra del padre: Tradizionalismo cattolico e destra radicale, Il paradigma veronese*, Ragusa: Edizioni La Fiaccola.

Del Medico, E. (2009) "Il mondo chiuso del fronte identitario," in *Venetica*, vol. 1 La Città in Fondo A Destra, Integralismo, fascismo e leghismo a Verona, pp. 67–94.

Della Porta, D. (2004) *Comitati di Cittadini e Democrazia Urbana*, Milano: Franco Angeli.

Della Porta, D. & Diani, M. (2006) *Social Movements: An Introduction*, New Jersey: Blackwell Publishing.

Della Porta, D., Fabbri, M. & Piazza, G. (2013) "Putting Protest in Place: Contested and Liberated Spaces in Three Campaigns," in Walter Nicholls, Byron Miller, and Justin Beaumont (eds.) *Spaces of Contention: Spatialities and Social Movements*, Oxon: Routledge Publishing.

Della Porta, D. & Mattoni, A. (2014) *Spreading Protest: Social Movements in Times of Crisis*, Colchester: ECPR Press.

Della Porta, D. (2014) "Social Movement Studies and Methodological Pluralism: An Introduction," in Donatella Della Porta (ed.) *Methodological Practices in Social Movement Research*, Oxford: Oxford University Press.

Della Porta, D. (2014a) "In-Depth Interviews," in Donatella Della Porta (ed.) *Methodological Practices in Social Movement Research*, Oxford: Oxford University Press.

Della Porta, D. & Diani, M. (2015) "Introduction: The Field of Social Movement Studies," in D. Della Porta and M. Diani (eds.) *Oxford Handbook of Social Movements*, Oxford: Oxford University Press.

Delibori, M. (2009) "I Veronesi e La Veronesità," in (ed.) Maurizio Delibori, *Quale Veronesità: Identità e radici culturali ed umane veronesi in un mondo globalizzato*, Verona: Editrice Grafiche P2.

Demirsu, I. (2017) *Counter-terrorism and the Prospects of Human Rights: Securitizing Difference and Dissent*, Cham: Palgrave Macmillan.

Demirsu, I. (2022) "The 'Anti-gender' City of Verona and Grassroots Spatial Resistance: An Interspatial Analysis of Contentious Politics," in *About Gender: International Journal of Gender Studies*, vol. 11 no. 22, pp. 754–797.

Demirsu, I. (2023) "Identitarian Movements in the Touristic City: The Marketing of Hate in Verona," in *International Journal of Urban and Regional Research*, vol. 47 no. 5, pp. 725–744.

Demirsu, I. (2023a) "Visualizing Conviviality in the Fortress of the Italian Far-Right: The Case of Veronetta," in *Ethnic and Racial Studies*, DOI: 10.1080/01419870.2023.2247469.

Denzin, N. & Lincoln, Y. (2017) "Introduction: The Discipline and Practice of Qualitative Research," in Normal K. Denzin & Yvonne S. Lincoln (eds.) *The SAGE Handbook of Qualitative Research*, London: SAGE Publications.

Desai, R. & Sanyal, R. (2011) *Urbanizing Citizenship: Contested Spaces in Indian Cities*, Thousand Oaks: Sage Publishing.

Di Nicola, P. (2018) "Università e territorio: luci ed ombre della presenza dell'Università a Veronetta," in Paolo Di Nicola (ed.) *Veronetta, quartiere latino: Una ricerca tra Università e Città a Verona*, Milano: FrancoAngeli.

Diani, M. (1992) "The Concept of Social Movement," in *The Sociological Review*, vol. 40 no. 1, pp. 1–25.

Diani, M., & McAdam, D. (2003). *Social movements and networks: Relational approaches to collective action*. Oxford: Oxford University Press.

Diani, M. (2015) *The Cement of Civil Society: Studying Networks in Localities*, New York: Cambridge University Press.

Diani, M., Ernstson, H., & Jasny, L. (2018) "'Right to the City' and the Structure of Civic Organizational Fields: Evidence from Cape Town," in *Voluntas*, vol. 29 no. 4, p. 637–652.

Dikeç, M. (2002) "Police, Politics, and the Right to the City," in *GeoJournal*, vol. 58 no. 2–3, 91–98.

Dikeç, M. (2017) *Urban Rage: The Revolt of the Excluded*, New Haven: Yale University Press.

Dilemmi, A. (2009) "'Heil Hellas!': tenere la destra in curva. Sociabilità e immaginario della destra radicale sugli spalti scaligeri," in *Venetica*, vol. 1 La Città in Fondo A Destra, Integralismo, fascismo e leghismo a Verona, pp. 95–134.

Dillard, M.K. (2013) "Movement/Countermovement Dynamics," in D.A. Snow, D. Della Porta, B. Klandermans, and D. McAdam (eds.) *The Wiley-Blackwell Encyclopedia of Social and Political Movements*, New Jersey: Blackwell Publishing.

Dochartaigh, N. & Bosi, L. (2010), "Territoriality and Mobilization: The Civil Rights Campaign in Northern Ireland," in *Mobilization: An International Quarterly*, vol. 15 no. 4, pp. 405–424.

Domaradzka, A. (2018) "Urban Social Movements and the Right to the City: An Introduction to the Special Issue on Urban Mobilization," in *Voluntas*, vol. 29, pp. 607–620.

Domaschi, G. (2007) *Le mie prigioni, le mie evasioni. Memorie di un anarchico veronese dal carcere e dal confino fascista*, (ed.) Andrea Dilemmi, Verona: Cierre Edizioni.

Duyvendak, J.W., Kesic, J., & Stacey, T. (2022) *The Return of the Native: Can Liberalism Safeguard Us Against Nativism?*, Oxford: Oxford University Press.

Eder, K. (2015) "Social Movements in Social Theory," in D. Della Porta and M. Diani (eds.) *Oxford Handbook of Social Movements*, Oxford: Oxford University Press.

Emerson, R.M., Fretz, R.I., & Shaw, L.L. (2011) *Writing Ethnographic Fieldnotes*, Chicago: Chicago University Press.

Evangelisti, V. (2009) "Ludwig, un caso chiuso?," in *Venetica*, vol. 1 La Citta' in Fondo A Destra, Integralismo, fascismo e leghismo a Verona, pp. 57–66.

Farina, A. (2020) "Porta Nuova Strage Evitata," in *La Cronaca di Verona* (28 February 2020). [Accessed on 20 March 2020] Available at: https://www.cronacadiverona.com/porta-nuova-strage-evitata.

Fasanella, G. & Zornetta, M. (2008) *Terrore a nordest*, Rizzoli: La Biblioteca Universale Rizzoli.

Featherstone, D. & Painter, J. (2013) "Introduction: 'There Is No Point of Departure': The Many Trajectories of Doreen Massey," in David Featherstone & Joe Painter (eds.), *Spatial Politics: Essays for Doreen Massey*, Oxford: John Wiley & Sons.

Ferrari, M.L. (2018) "Convergenze parallele: storie e percorsi del quartiere e dell'Università," in Paolo Di Nicola (ed.) *Veronetta, quartiere latino: Una ricerca tra Università e Città a Verona*, Milano: FrancoAngeli.

Fillieule, O. & Broqua, C. (2020) "Sexual and Reproductive Rights Movements and Counter Movements from an Interactionist Perspective," in *Social Movement Studies*, vol. 19 no. 1, pp. 1–20.

Fillieule, O. & Neveu, E. (2019) *Activists Forever? Long-term Impacts of Political Activism*, Cambridge: Cambridge University Press.

Flick, U. (2009) *An Introduction to Qualitative Research*, London: SAGE Publications.

Flick, U. (2017) "Triangulation," in N. K. Denzin & Y. S. Lincoln (eds.) *The SAGE Handbook of Qualitative Research*, London: SAGE Publications.

Fligstein, N., & McAdam, D. (2012). *A theory of fields*. New York: Oxford University Press.

Franzina, E. (2010) "I 'terzogeniti': fascisti e fascismi a Verona," in (ed.) Emilio Franzina *Dal fascismo alla fiamma: Fascisti a Verona dalle origini al MSI*, Verona: Cierre Edizioni.

Fraser, N. (1990) "Rethinking the Public Sphere: A Contribution to the Critique of Actually Existing Democracy," in *Social Text*, no. 25/26, pp. 56–80.

Freeden, M. (2017) "After the Brexit Referendum: Revisiting Populism as an Ideology," in *Journal of Political Ideologies*, no. 22, pp. 1–11.

Frisina, A. (2013) *Ricerca Visuale e Trasformazioni Socio-Culturali*, Torino: UTET Università.

Frisina, A. (2016) "Introduzione," in Annalisa Frisina (ed.) *Metodi visuali di ricerca sociale*, Bologna: il Mulino.

Frisina, A. (2020) *Razzismi contemporanei: Le prospettive della sociologia*, Roma: Carocci editori.

Galletta, A. (2013) *Mastering the Semi-Structured Interview and Beyond: From Research Design to Analysis and Publication*, New York: New York University Press.

Gamberoni, E. (2009) "La Veronesità a Confronto con Culture Diverse nel Turismo e Nell'Accoglienza," in (ed.) Maurizio Delibori, *Quale Veronesità: Identità e radici culturali ed umane veronesi in un mondo globalizzato*, Verona: Editrice Grafiche P2.

Gamberoni, E. & Savi, P. (2016) "Stranieri residenti e spazi urbani a Verona. Note di ricerca." In Luca Romagnoli (ed.) *Spunti di ricerca per un mondo che cambia. Studi in onore di Emanuele Paratore*, Roma: Edigeo.

Garbagnoli, S. & Prearo, M. (2018) *La crociata 'anti-gender': Dal Vaticano alla manif pour tuos*, Torino: Kaplan.

Gargiulo, E. & Piccoli, L. (2020) "Mean Cities: The Dark Side of Urban Citizenship," in Rainer Bauböck and Liav Orgad (eds.) *Cities vs States: Should Urban Citizenship be Emancipated from Nationality?* (EUI Working Papers), Florence: Robert Schuman Centre for Advanced Studies.

Gatson, S.N. (2012) "The Methods, Politics, and Ethics of Representation in Online Ethnography," in N.K. Denzin & Y.S. Lincoln (eds.) *Collecting and Interpreting Qualitative Materials*, London: SAGE Publications.

Gattinara, P.C. & Pirro, A. (2018) "The Far-Right as Social Movement," in *European Societies*, vol. 21 no. 9, pp. 447–462.

Gattinara, P.C. (2019) "Forza Nuova and the Security Walks: Squadrismo and Extreme Right Vigilantism in Italy," in Tore Bjørgo and Miroslav Mareš (eds.) *Vigilantism against Migrants and Minorities*, London: Routledge.

Gastaldo, M. (1987) *La città e lo psichiatra. La Verona di Vittorino Andreoli*, Verona: Il nuovo Veronese.

Gawlewicz, A. & Yiftachel, O. (2022) "'Throwntogetherness' in Hostile Environments: Migration and the Remaking of Urban Citizenship," in *City*, vol. 26 no. 2–3, pp. 346–358.

Geertz, C. (1973) *The Interpretation of Cultures*, New York: Basic Books Publishers.

Gezgin, E. (2023) "Between Privileges and Sacrifices: Heteronormativity and Turkish Nationalism in Urban Turkey," in *Journal of Homosexuality*, vol. 70 no. 10, pp. 2072–2095.

Girolami, M.P. (2000) *Verona: Art, History, Culture*. Verona: Edizioni KINA Italia/LEGO.

Glick-Schiller, N., Cağlar, A., & Guldbransen, T.C. (2006) "Beyond the Ethnic Lens: Locality, Globality, and Born-Again Incorporation," in *American Ethnologist* vol. 33 no. 4, pp. 612–633.

Glick-Schiller, N. & Cağlar, A. (2018) *Migrants and City-Making: Dispossession, Displacement, and Urban Regeneration*, Durhan: Duke University Press.

Goldberg, D.T. (2006) "Racial Europeanization." *Ethnic and Racial Studies*, vol. 29 no. 2, pp. 331–364.

Goodwin, J. & Jasper, J.M. (2003) *The Social Movements Reader: Cases and Concepts*, New Jersey: Blackwell Publishing.

Gökarıksel, B., Neubert, C. & Smith, S. (2019) "Demographic Fever Dreams: Fragile Masculinity and Population Politics in the Rise of the Global Right," in *Signs: Journal of Women in Culture and Society*, vol. 44 no. 3, pp. 561–587.

Greven, T. (2016) "The Rise of Right-Wing Populism in Europe and the United States: A Comparative Perspective," in *Friedrich Ebert Stiftung Perspectives* (Berlin, May 2016). [accessed on 14 March 2019], available at https://library.fes.de/pdf-files/id/12892.pdf.

Griffin, Roger (1996) "The 'Post-Fascism' of the Alleanza Nazionale: A Case Study in Ideological Morphology," in *Journal of Political Ideologies*, vol. 1 issue 2, pp. 123–145.

Grossberg, L. (2013) "Theorizing Context," in David Featherstone & Joe Painter (eds.), *Spatial Politics: Essays for Doreen Massey*, Oxford: John Wiley & Sons.

Gunning, J. & Baron, I. Z. (2014) *Why Occupy a Square? People, Protests, and Movements in the Egyptian Revolution*, Oxford: Oxford University Press.

Glaw, X, Inder, K., Kable, A., Hazelton, M. (2017) "Visual Methodologies in Qualitative Research: Autophotography and Photo Elicitation Applied to Mental Health Research," in *International Journal on Qualitative Methods*, vol. 16, pp. 1–8.

Gluckman, M. (1961) 'Ethnographic Data in British Social Anthropology', *Sociological Review*, vol. 9, pp. 5–17.

Hall, B. (2019) "Gendering Resistance to Right-Wing Populism: Black Protest and a New Wave of Feminist Activism in Poland?" in *American Behavioral Scientist*, vol. 63 no. 10, pp. 1497–1515.

Hall, S. (2021) *The Migrant's Paradox: Street Livelihoods and Marginal Citizenship in Britain*, Minneapolis: University of Minnesota Press.

Halvorsen, S. (2015) "Encountering Occupy London: boundary making and the territoriality of urban activism," in *Environment and Planning D: Society and Space*, vol. 33, pp. 314–330.

Handler, H. (2019) *European Identity and the Identitarians in Europe*, (Flash Paper No. 1/2019), Vienna: Policy Crossover Center.

Harald, B. & Jonathan, D. (2019) *Sanctuary Cities and Urban Struggles: Rescaling Migration, Citizenship, and Rights*, Manchester: Manchester University Press.

Harper, D. (2012) *Visual Sociology*, Oxon: Routledge.

Harvey, D. (2008). "The Right to the City," in *New Left Review*, vol. 53, pp. 23–40.

Harvey, D. (2012) *Rebel Cities: From the Right to the City to the Urban Revolution*, New York: Verso Books.

Hatuka, T. (2018) *The Design of Protest: Choreographing Political Demonstrations in Public Space*, Austin: University of Texas Press.

Hawthorne, C. (2022) *Contesting Race and Citizenship: Youth Politics in the Black Mediterranean*, Ithaca: Cornell University Press.

Heinisch, R., Werner, A. & Habersack, F. (2020) "Reclaiming National Sovereignty: The Case of the Conservatives and the Far Right in Austria," in *European Politics and Society*, vol. 21 no. 2, pp. 163–181.

Herb, G.H. & Kaplan, D.H. (1999) *Nested Identities: Nationalism, Territory, and Scale*, New York: Rowman & Littlefield Publishers.

Hine, C. (2000) *Virtual Ethnography*, London: SAGE Publications.

Hjorth, L. & Pink, S. (2014) "New Visualities and the Digital Wayfarer: Reconceptualizing Camera Phone Photography and Locative Media," in *Mobile Media & Communication*, vol. 2 no. 1, pp. 40–57.

Hobsbawm, E. (1990) "Introduction: Inventing Traditions," in Eric Hobsbawm & Terence Ranger (eds.) *The Invention of Tradition*, Oxford: Oxford University Press.

Hochschild, A. R. (2016) *Strangers in Their Own Land: Anger and Mourning on the American Right*, New York: The New Press.

Holston, J. & Appadurai, A. (1996) "Cities and Citizenship," in *Public Culture*, vol. 8, pp. 187–204.

Holston, J. (2009) "Insurgent Citizenship in the Era of Global Urban Peripheries," in *City & Society*, vol. 21 no.2, pp. 245–267.

Hubbard, P. (2000) "Desire/Disgust: Mapping the Moral Contours of Heterosexuality," in *Progress in Human Geography*, vol. 24 no. 3, pp. 191–217.

Hubbard, P. (2005) "Space/Place," in D. Sibley, P. Jackson, D. Atkinson, & N. Washbourne (eds.) *Cultural Geography: A Critical Dictionary of Key Concepts*, London: I. B. Tauris.

Işın, E.F. & Wood, P.K. (1999) *Citizenship and Identity*, Thousand Oaks: SAGE Publications.

Işın, E. F. (2008) "Theorizing Acts of Citizenship," in E.F. Işın and G. M. Nielsen (eds.) *Acts of Citizenship*, London: Zed Books.

Işın, E.F. (2009) "Citizenship in Flux: The Figure of the Activist Citizen," in *Subjectivity*, Issue 29, pp. 367–388.

Işın, E.F. (2013) "Introduction: Democracy, Citizenship and the City" in E.F. Işın (ed.) *Democracy, Citizenship and the Global City*, London: Routledge.

Jenkins, J.C. (1983) "Resource Mobilization Theory and The Study of Social Movements," in *Annual Review of Sociology*, vol. 9, pp. 527–553.

Johan, F. (2018) "Multi-sited Online Ethnography and Critical Discourse Studies: Exploring Disguised Propaganda on Social Media," in *7th Critical Approaches to Discourse Analysis across Disciplines Conference* (CADAAD), 4–6 July Aalborg, Denmark, available at: https://easychair.org/smart-program/CADAAD-2018/2018-07-05.html#talk:68217.

Johansen, S. & Le, T.N. (2014) "Youth Perspective on Multiculturalism Using Photovoice Methodology," in *Youth & Society*, vol. 46 no. 4, pp. 548–565.

Johnston, H., Larana, E. & Gusfield, J.R. (1994) "Identities, Grievances, and New Social Movements," in E. Larana, H. Johnston & J.R. Gusfield (eds.) *New Social Movements: From Ideology to Identity*, Philadelphia: Temple University Press.

Kaplan, D.H. (1994) "Two Nations in Search of a State: Canada's Ambivalent Spatial Identities," in *Annals of the Association of American Geographers*, vol. 84 no. 4, pp. 585–606.

Kearns, A. (1995) "Active Citizenship and Local Governance: Political and Geographical Dimensions," in *Political Geography*, vol. 14 no. 2, pp. 155–175.

Kearns, A. & Forrest, R. (2000) "Social Cohesion and Multilevel Urban Governance," in *Urban Studies*, vol. 37 no. 5–6, pp. 995–1017.

Klandermans, B. (2004) "The Demand and Supply of Participation: Social-Psychological Correlates of Participation in Social Movements," in David A. Snow, Sarah A. Suole, & Hanspeter Kriesi, *The Blackwell Companion to Social Movements*, Oxford: Blackwell Publishing.

Klandermans, B. & Mayer, N. (2006) *Extreme Right Activists in Europe: Through the Magnifying Glass*, London: Routledge.

Klauser, F.R. (2012) "Thinking through Territoriality: Introducing Claude Raffestin to Anglophone Sociospatial Theory," in *Environment and Planning D: Society and Space*, vol. 30, pp. 106–120.

Klein, O. & Muis, J. (2018) "Online Discontent: Comparing Western European Far-Right Groups on Facebook," in *European Societies*, vol. 21 no. 4, pp. 540–562.

Krase, J. (2009) "A Visual Approach to Multiculturalism," in Giuliana Prato (ed.) *Beyond Multiculturalism*, Farnham: Ashgate Publishing.

Kriesi, H., Grande, E., Lachat, R., Dolezal, M., Bornschier, S., Frey, T. (2008) *West European Politics in the Age of Globalization*, Cambridge: Cambridge University Press.

Kriesi, H. (2011) "Social Movements," in D. Caramani (ed.) *Comparative Politics*, Oxford: Oxford University Press.

La Terza, A. (2009) "Dietro la paura," in *Venetica*, vol. 1 La Città in Fondo A Destra, Integralismo, fascismo e leghismo a Verona, pp. 135–172.

Lamour, C. (2022) "A Radical-Right Populist Definition of Cross-National Regionalism in Europe: Shaping Power Geometries at the Regional Scale Beyond State Borders," in *International Journal of Urban and Regional Research*, vol. 46 no. 1, 8–25.

Lefebvre, H. (1991 [1974]) *The Production of Space*, Oxford UK: Blackwell Publishing.

Lefebvre, H. (2004) *Rhythmanalysis: Space, Time, and Everyday Life*, London: Continuum.

Leitner, H., Shepard, E. & Sziarto, K.M. (2008) "The Spatialities of Contentious Politics," in *Transactions of the Institute of British Geographers*, vol. 33, pp. 157–172.

Lentin, A. & Karakayali, J. (2016) "Bringing Race Back In: Racisms in 'Post-Racial' Times," in *Movements: Journal for Critical Migration and Border Regimes Studies*, vol. 2 no.1.

Lévy, P. (1997) *Collective Intelligence: Mankind's Emerging World in Cyberspace*, Cambridge, MA: Perseus Books.

Lipsitz, G. (2011) *How Racism Takes Place*, Philadelphia, Temple University.

Lofland, L.H. (1973) *A World of Strangers: Order and Action in Urban Public Space*, New York: Basic Books Inc. Publishers.

Lofland, L.H. (1998) *The Public Realm: Exploring the City's Quintessential Social Territory*, New York: Aldine de Gruyter.

Lofland, J., Snow, D.A., Anderson, L., Lofland, L.H. (2006) *Analyzing Social Settings: A Guide to Qualitative Observation and Analysis*, Belmont: Wadsworth/ Thomson Learning.

Lona, A. & Olivieri, N. (2012) "Il movimento delle scuole popolari a Verona," in *Venetica*, vol. 26, pp. 105–126.

Lynch, K. (1981) *Good City Form*, Massachusetts: Massachusetts Institute of Technology.

MacMaster, N. (2001) *Racism in Europe: 1870–2000*. Basingstoke: Palgrave.

Magagnotti, M.L. 2005. Memoria e vita quotidiana degli anziani di Veronetta. *DiPAV-QUADERNI. Quadrimestrale di psicologia ed antropologia culturale*, vol. 14 no. 3, pp. 93–116.

Marconi, F. & Testi, E. (2019) "Lega e fascisti, unioni di fatto a Verona: ecco le foto che lo dimostrano," in *L'Espresso* (22 March 2019), [accessed on 18 September 2020] available at: https://espresso.repubblica.it/attualita/2019/03/21/news/il-sindaco-di-ver ona-e-gli-amici-neofascisti-ecco-le-foto-che-dimostrano-1.332952.

Markham, A.N. (2017) "Ethnography in the Digital Internet Era: From Fields to Flows, Descriptions to Interventions," in Normal K. Denzin & Yvonne S. Lincoln (eds.) *The SAGE Handbook of Qualitative Research*, London: SAGE Publications.

Martin, D.G. (2003) "'Place-Framing' as Place-Making: Constituting a Neighborhood for Organizing and Activism," in *Annals of the Association of American Geographers*, vol. 93 no. 3, pp. 730–750.

Martin, D.G. & Miller, B. (2003), "Space and Contentious Politics," in *Mobilization: An International Quarterly*, vol. 8 no. 2, pp. 143–156.

Martiniello, M. (2017) "Visual Sociology Approaches in Migration, Ethnic and Racial Studies," in *Ethnic and Racial Studies*, vol. 40 no. 8, pp. 1184–1190.

Massey, D. (1992) "Politics and Space/Time," in *New Left Review*, vol. 196, pp. 65–84.

Massey, D. (1994) *Space, Place and Gender*, Minneapolis: University of Minnesota Press.

Massey, D. (1999) "Philosophy and Politics of Spatiality: Some Considerations. The Hettner-Lecture in Human Geography," in *Geographische Zeitschrift*, vol. 87 no.1, pp. 1–12.

Massey, D. (2004) "Geographies of Responsibility," in *Geografiska Annaler. Series B, Human Geography*, vol. 86 no. 1, pp. 5–18.

Massey, D. (2005) *For space*. London: SAGE Publications.

Massignan, G. (2020) "Verona divisa in due, a sinistra d'Adige gli austriaci a destra i francesi," in *Verona-In* (10 September 2020) [accessed on 17 September 2020] available at: https://www.verona-in.it/2020/09/10/verona-divisa-in-due-a-sinistra-dadige-gli -austriaci-a-destra-i-francesi.

Mayer, M. (1991) "Social Movement Research and Social Movement Practice: The American Pattern," in Dieter Rucht (ed.), *Research on Social Movements*, Boulder, CO: Westview.

Mayer, M. (2009) "The 'Right to the City' in the Context of Shifting Mottos of Urban Social Movements," in *City*, vol. 13 no. 2–3, pp. 362–374.

Mayer, M., Thörn, C., Thörn, H. (2016) *Urban Uprisings: Challenging Neoliberal Urbanism in Europe*, London: Palgrave Macmillan.

Mazzei, A. (2018) *Il Richiamo della Fortezza: Spazi, Sicurezza, Stranieri, e Stampa*, Verona: Smart Edizioni.

McAdam, D., McCarthy, J.D., & Zald, M.N. (1996) *Comparative Perspectives on Social Movements: Political Opportunities, Mobilizing Structures, and Cultural Framings*, Cambridge: Cambridge University Press.

McCarthy, J.D. & Zald, M.N. (1977) "Resource Mobilization and Social Movements: A Partial Theory," in *American Journal of Sociology*, vol. 82 no. 6, pp. 1212–1241.

McFarlane, C. (2009) "Translocal Assemblages: Space, Power and Social Movements," in *Geoforum*, vol. 40, pp. 561–5671.

McKittrick, K. (2007) *Demonic Grounds: Black Women and the Cartographies of Struggle*, Minneapolis: University of Minnesota Press.

Mead, G.H. (1934) *Mind, Self, and Society*, Chicago: University of Chicago Press.

Melucci, A. (1980) "The New Social Movements: A Theoretical Approach," in *Theory and Methods*, SAGE Social Science Information, vol. 19 no. 2, pp. 199–226.

Melucci, A. (1984) *Altri codici: Aree di movimento nella metropoli*, Bologna: Il Mulino.

Merrill, H. (2014) "Postcolonial Borderlands: Black Life Worlds and Relational Place in Turin, Italy." *ACME: An International E-Journal for Critical Geographies*, vol. 13 no. 2: pp. 263–294.

Meyer, D.S. & Staggenborg, S. (1996) "Movements, Countermovements, and the Structure of Political Opportunity," in *American Journal of Sociology*, vol. 101 no. 6, pp. 1628–1660.

Meyer, D.S. (2004) "Protest and Political Opportunities," in *Annual Review of Sociology*, vol. 30, pp. 125–145.

Mielke, J. (2005) "From Campanilismo to Nationhood," in Gene Brucker (ed.) *Living on the Edge in Leonardo's Florence: Selected Essays*, Berkeley: University of California Press.

Milesi, P., Chirumbolo, A. & Catellani, P. (2005) "Italy: The offspring of fascism," in Bert Klandermans and Nonna Mayer (eds.) *Extreme Right Activists in Europe: Through the Magnifying Glass*, London: Routledge.

Miller, B. (2013) "Conclusion: Spatialities of Mobilization: Building and Breaking Relationships," in Walter Nicholls, Byron Miller, and Justin Beaumont (eds.) *Spaces of Contention: Spatialities and Social Movements*, Oxon: Routledge Publishing.

Misgav, C. (2016) "Radical Activism and Autonomous Contestation 'From Within': The Gay Centre in Tel Aviv", in Gavin Brown, and Kath Browne (eds.), *The Routledge Research Companion to Geographies of Sex and Sexualities*, Oxon, Routledge.

Mitchell, J.C. (1983) "Case and Situation Analysis," in *Sociological Review*, vol. 31 no. 2, pp. 187–211.

Mitchell, K. (2000) "The Culture of Urban Space," in *Urban Geography*, vol. 21 no. 5, pp. 443–449.

Moore, N.H. (2007) "Valorizing Urban Heritage? Redevelopment in a Changing City," in Niamh Moore & Yvonne Whelan (eds.) *Heritage, Memory, and the Politics of Identity: New Perspectives on the Cultural Landscape*, Hampshire: Ashgate Publishing Company.

Morrow, E.A., & Meadowcroft, J. (2019) "The Rise and Fall of the English Defence League: Self-Governance, Marginal Members and the Far Right," in *Political Studies*, vol. 67 no. 3, pp. 539–556.

Mosca, L. (2014) "Methodological Practices in Social Movement Online Research," in Donatella Della Porta (ed.) *Methodological Practices in Social Movement Research*, Oxford: Oxford University Press.

Mudde, C. (2000) "Extreme Right Parties in Eastern Europe," in *Patterns of Prejudice*, vol. 34 no. 1, pp. 5–27.

Mudde, C. (2007) *Populist Radical Right Parties in Europe*. Cambridge: Cambridge University Press.

Mudu, P. (2004) "Resisting and Challenging Neoliberalism: The Development of Italian Social Centers," in *Antipode*, vol. 36 no. 5, pp. 917–941.

Mueller, S. & Heidelberger, A. (2020) "Should We Stay or Should We Join? 30 Years of Sovereignism and Direct Democracy in Switzerland," in *European Politics and Society*, vol. 21 no. 2, pp. 182–201.

Muis, J.C., & Immerzeel, T. (2017) "Causes and Consequences of the Rise of Populist Radical Right Parties and Movements in Europe," in *Current Sociology Review*, vol. 65 no. 6, pp. 909–930.

Murdoch, S. & Murhall, J. (2019) *From Banners to Bullets: The International Identitarian Movement*, London: HOPE not hate Charitable Trust.

Mutto, D. (2019) *Venetismo: l'invenzione identitaria e i suoi usi politici nel Veneto contemporaneo*, Masters Thesis at the University of Bologna Political Science Department.

Neal, S., Bennett, K., Cochrane, A., & Mohan, G. (2019) "Community and Conviviality? Informal Social Life in Multicultural Places," in *Sociology*, vol. 53 no.1, 69–86.

Nel·lo, O. (2016) "Seven Challenges for the Study of Urban Movements," in *City, Territory, and Architecture*, vol. 3 no. 23.

Nevola, F. (2010) "Introduction: Locating Communities in the Early Modern Italian City," in *Urban History*, vol. 37 no. 3, pp. 349–359.

Nicholls, W.J. (2008) "The Urban Question Revisited: The Importance of Cities for Social Movements," in *International Journal of Urban and Regional Research*, vol. 32 no. 4, pp. 841–859.

Nicholls, W.J., Miller, B., Beaumont, J. (2013) "Introduction: Conceptualizing Spatialities of Social Movements," in Walter Nicholls, Byron Miller, and Justin Beaumont (eds.) *Spaces of Contention: Spatialities and Social Movements*, Oxon: Routledge Publishing.

Norris, P. & R. Inglehart (2016) "Trump, Brexit and the Rise of Populism: Economic Have-Nots and Cultural Backlash." in *Harvard Kennedy School Faculty Research Working Paper Series*, (August 2016), RWP16-026.

O'Keeffe, T. (2007) "Landscape and Memory: Historiography, Theory, Methodology," in Niamh Moore & Yvonne Whelan (eds.) *Heritage, Memory, and the Politics of Identity: New Perspectives on the Cultural Landscape*, Hampshire: Ashgate Publishing Company.

Oomen, B. (2020) "Cities of Refuge: Rights, Culture and the Creation of Cosmopolitan Cityzenship," in R. Buikema, A. Buyse and A.C.G.M. Robben (eds.) *Cultures Citizenship and Human Rights*, Oxon: Routledge.

Paasi, A. (2011) "Region, Identity, and Power," in *Procedia Social and Behavioral Sciences*, vol. 14, pp. 9–16.

Pantano, A. (2016) *Verona 'Amore Sacro' nell'Opera di Ezra Pound*, Verona: Edizioni della Vitanova.

Papatzani, E. (2021) "Encountering Everyday Racist Practices: Sociospatial Negotiations of Immigrant Settlements in Athens, Greece," *in International Journal of Urban and Regional Research*, vol. 45 no. 1, pp. 61–79.

Paradiso, A. (2019) "Verona, lo spazio ideale per l'estrema destra," in *Il Manifesto* (29 March 2019), [accessed on 17 April 2019] available at: https://ilmanifesto.it/verona-lo-spazio-ideale-per-lestrema-destra.

Park, R.E., Burgess, E.W. & R. McKenzie (1967 [1926]) *The City: Suggestions for Investigation of Human Behavious in the Urban Environment*, Chicago: University of Chicago Press.

Parlato, G. (2017) "Delegitimation and Anticommunism in Italian Neofascism," in *Journal of Modern Italian Studies*, vol. 22 no. 1, pp. 43–56.

Pauwels, L. (2010) "Visual Sociology Reframed: An Analytical Synthesis and Discussion of Visual Methods in Social and Cultural Research," in *Sociological Methods & Research*, vol. 38 no. 4, pp. 545–581.

Pauwels, L. (2015) "'Participatory' Visual Research Revisited: A Critical-Constructive Assessment of Epistemological, Methodological and Social Activist Tenets," in *Ethnography*, vol. 16 no. 1, pp. 95–117.

Pauwels, L. (2016) "Visually Researching and Communicating the City: A Systematic Assessment of Methods and Resources," in *International Journal of Communication*, vol. 10, pp. 1309–1330.

Pavoni, A., Ziamakis, Y., & Campos, R. (2021) "Introduction: Political Graffiti in Critical Times," in (eds.) Ricardo Campos, Andrea Pavoni, Yiannis Ziamakis, Political Graffiti in *Critical Times: The Aesthetics of Street Politics*, New York: Berghahn Publishing.

Pickvance, C. (2003) "From Urban Social Movements to Urban Movements: A Review and Introduction to a Symposium on Urban Movements," in *International Journal of Urban and Regional Research*, no. 27 vol. 1, pp. 102–109.

Pink, S. (2011) "Images, Senses and Applications: Engaging Visual Anthropology," in *Visual Anthropology*, vol. 24, pp. 437–454.

Pirro, A.L.P. & Gattinara, P.C. (2018) "Movement Parties of the Far-Right: the Organization and Strategies of Nativist Collective Actors," in *Mobilization: An International Quarterly*, vol. 23 no. 3, pp. 367–383.

Pixova, M. & Sladek, J. (2016) "Touristification and Awakening Civil Society in Postsocialist Prague," in Colomb C and Novy J (eds) *Protest and Resistance in the Tourist City, Contemporary Geographies of Leisure, Tourism and Mobility*. London: Routledge.

Polat, D.K. (2020) "'Now the German Comes': The Ethnic Effect of Gentrification in Berlin," in *Ethnicities*, vol. 20 no. 1, pp. 155–176.

Polletta, F. & Jasper, J.M. (2001) "Collective Identity and Social Movements," in *Annual Review of Sociology*, vol. 27, pp. 283–305.

Postill, J. & Pink, S. (2012) "Social Media Ethnography: The Digital Researcher in a Messy Web," in *Media International Australia*, no. 145, pp. 123–134.

Prowe, D. (2004) "The Fascist Phantom and Anti-Immigrant Violence," in E. Weitz & A Fenner (eds.) *Fascism and Anti-fascism*, New York: Palgrave Macmillan.

Pugliese, J. (2002) "Race as Category Crisis: Whiteness and the Topical Assignation of Race," in *Social Semiotics*, vol. 12 no. 2, pp. 149–168.

Pugliese, S.G. (2004) *Fascism, Anti-Fascism, and the Resistance in Italy: 1919 to the Present*, Maryland: Rowman & Littlefield Publishers.

Pugliese, J., (2008) "Whiteness and the Blackening of Italy: La Guerra Cafona, Extracommunitari, and Provisional Street Justice," in *PORTAL, Journal of Multidisciplinary International Studies*, vol. 5 no. 2, pp.1–35.

Raffestin, C. (2012) "Space, Territory, and Territoriality," in *Environment and Planning D: Society and Space*, vol. 30, pp. 121–14.

Ravndal, J.A. & Bjorgo, T. (2018) "Investigating Terrorism from the Extreme Right: A Review of Past and Present Research," in *Perspectives on Terrorism*, vol. 12 no. 6, pp. 5–22.

Reiss, M. (2007) *The Street as the Stage: Protest Marches and Public Rallies Since the Nineteenth Century*, Oxford: Oxford University Press.

Rocca, L. (2004) "La Resistenza a Verona," in Beppe Muraro (ed.) *Sui sentieri della libertà*, Verona: Cierre Edizioni.

Romagnani, G.P. (2009) "La polemica sulle Pasque veronesi fra politica e storia," in *Venetica*, vol. 1 La Città in Fondo A Destra, Integralismo, fascismo e leghismo a Verona, pp. 17–56.

Ronzi, S., Pope, D., Orton, L. & Bruce, N. (2016) "Using photovoice methods to explore older people's perceptions of respect and social inclusion in cities: Opportunities, challenges and solutions," in *SSM – Population Health*, vol. 2, pp. 732–745.

Rose, G. (2023) *Visual methodologies: An Introduction to Research with Visual Materials (5th Edition)*, London: SAGE Publications.

Rossi, V., Perrotta, E., & De Santi, G. (2019) *I Luoghi del Ventennio: Verona, Memoria e Presente*, Verona: Scripta Edizioni.

Roversi, A. (1999) "Giovani di destra e giovani di estrema destra," in *Rassegna Italiana di Sociologia*, vol.4 October-December, pp. 605–626.

Routledge, P. (2010) "Introduction: Cities, Justice and Conflict," in *Urban Studies*, vol. 47 no. 6, 1165–1177.

Routledge, P. (2013) "Geography and Social Movements," in D.A. Snow, D. Della Porta, B. Klandermans, and D. McAdam (eds.) *The Wiley-Blackwell Encyclopedia of Social and Political Movements*, New Jersey: Blackwell Publishing.

Roth, S. (2018) "Introduction: Contemporary Counter-Movements in the Age of Brexit and Trump," in *Sociological Research Online*, vol. 23 no. 2, pp. 496–506.

Rucht, D. (2019) "Right-wing Populism in Context: A Historical and Systematic Perspective," in Gregor Fitzi, Juergen Mackert, Bryan S. Turner (eds.) *Populism and the Crisis of Democracy, Volume 2: Politics, Social Movements and Extremism*, Oxon: Routledge.

Ruzza, C. (2017) "The Populist Radical Right and Social Movements," in R.C. Heinisch, C. Holtz-Bacha, O. Mazzoleni (eds.), *Political Populism: A Handbook*. Baden-Baden: Nomos.

Rydgren, J. (2005) "Is Extreme Right-Wing Populism Contagious? Explaining the Emergence of a New Party Family," in *European Journal of Political Research*, vol. 44, pp. 413–437.

Rydgren, J. (2018) "The Radical Right: An Introduction," in Jens Rydgren (ed.) *The Oxford Handbook of the Radical Right*, New York: Oxford University Press.

Rygiel, K. & Baban, F. (2019) "Countering Right-Wing Populism: Transgressive Cosmopolitanism and Solidarity Movements in Europe," in *American Quarterly*, vol. 71 no. 4, pp. 1069–1076.

Saitta, P. (2015) *Resistenze. Pratiche e margini del conflitto nel quotidiano*. Verona: Ombre Corte.

Saitta, P. (2021) "Everyday Chauvinisms. The Making of a Mentality in the Rural and Urban Life." *Paper presented at the 8th Conference of Ethnography and Qualitative Research, University of Trento*, Unpublished Paper.

Saitta, P. (2022) *Populismo Urbano: Autoritarismo e conflitto in una città del Sud (Messina 2018–2022)*, Milano: Meltemi.

Salvini, G. (2017) "Gli anni 1969–1974 in Italia. Stragi, golpismo, risposta giudiziaria," in Carlo Fumian and Angelo Ventrone (eds.) *Il Terrorismo di Destra e di Sinistra in Italia e in Europa*, Padova: Padova University Press.

Sbicca, J. & Perdue, R.T. (2013) "Protest Through Presence: Spatial Citizenship and Identity Formation in Contestations of Neoliberal Crises," in *Social Movement Studies*, vol. 13 no. 3, pp. 309–327.

Schaeffer, R. (2014) *Social Movements and Global Social Change: The Rising Tide*, Plymouth, UK: Rowman & Littlefield Publishers, Inc.

Schwarz, A. and Streule, M. (2022) "Rendering Territory (In)visible. Approaching Urban Struggles through a Socio-territorial Lens," in Andrea M. Brighenti and Mattias Kärrholm (eds.), *Territories, Environments, Politics. Explorations in Territoriology*. Abingdon: Routledge.

Secor, A. (2004) "'There is an Istanbul That Belongs to Me: Citizenship, Space, and Identity in the City," in *Annals of the Association of American Geographers*, vol. 94 no. 2, pp. 352–368.

Semi, G., Colombo, E., Camozzi, I., & Frisina, A. (2009) "Practices of Difference: Analysing Multiculturalism in Everyday Life," in Amanda Wise & Selvaraj Velayutham (eds.) *Everyday Multiculturalism*. London: Palgrave Macmillan.

Semi, G. (2015) *Gentrification: Tutte le città come Disneyland?*, Bologna: Mulino.

Semprebon, M. (2011) "Phone Centres and the Struggle for Public Space in Italy: Between Revanchist Policies and Practices of Resistance," in *Journal of Urbanism: International Research on Placemaking and Urban Sustainability*, vol. 4 no. 3, pp. 223–237.

Sequera, J. & Nofre, J. (2018) "Debates Shaken, Not Stirred: New Debates on Touristification and the Limits of Gentrification," in *Cities*, vol. 22 no. 5–6, pp. 843–855.

Sequera, J. & Nofre, J. (2019) "Touristification, Transnational Gentrification, and Urban Change in Lisbon: The Neighbourhood of Alfama," in *Urban Studies*, vol. 57 no. 15, pp. 3169–3189.

Shoshan, N. (2019) "Spatial Configurations of Right-Wing Populism in Contemporary Germany," in *Spotlight on – Political geographies of right-wing populism. International Journal of Urban and Regional Research* (accessed on 20 November 2022]. available at: https://www.ijurr.org/spotlight-on/political-geographies-of-right-wing-popul ism/spatial-configurations-of-right-wing-populism-in-contemporary-germany.

Silver, D., Taylor, Z. & Calderón-Figueroa, F. (2020) "Populism in the City: The Case of Ford Nation," in *International Journal of Politics, Culture, and Society*, vol. 33, pp. 1–21.

Siviero, G. (2018) "Verona, dove commanda l'estrema destra," in Il Post (1 May 2018), [accessed on 26 November 2019], available at: https://www.ilpost.it/2018/05/01/estrema-destra-verona.

Smith, N. (1996) *The New Urban Frontier: Gentrification and the revanchist city*, London: Routledge.

Snow, D.A. & McAdam, D. (2000) "Identity Work Processes in the Context of Social Movements: Clarifying the Identity/Movement Nexus," in Sheldon Stryker, Timothy J. Owens, and Robert W. White (eds.) *Self, Identity, and Social Movements*, Minneapolis: University of Minnesota Press.

Snow, D.A. (2006). "Are There Really Awkward Movements or Only Awkward Research Relationship?," in *Mobilization*, vol. 11 no. 4, pp. 495–498.

Snow, D.A. & Soule, S.A. (2009) *A Primer on Social Movements*, New York: W.W. Norton & Company.

Snow, D.A. (2013) "Frames and Social Movements," in (eds.) David A. Snow, Donatella Della Porta, Bert Klandermans, Doug McAdam, *The Wiley-Blackwell Encyclopedia of Social and Political Movements*, Malden: Wiley-Blackwell.

Soja, E.W. (1971) *The Political Organization of Space*, Washington: Association of American Geographers, Commission on College Geography.

Soja, E.W. (2010) *Seeking Spatial Justice*, Minneapolis, University of Minnesota Press.

Small, M.L. (2009) "'How Many Cases Do I Need?': On Science and the Logic of Case Selection in Field-Based Research," in *Ethnography*, vol. 10 no. 1, pp. 5–38.

Stoeckl, K. (2016) "Postsecular Conflicts and the Global Struggle for Traditional Values," in *State, Religion, and Church*, vol. 3 no. 2, pp.102–116.

Sutherland, C. & Cheng, Y. (2009) "Participatory-Action Research with (Im)migrant Women in Two Small Canadian Cities: Using Photovoice in Kingston and Peterborough, Ontario," in *Journal of Immigrant & Refugee Studies*, vol. 7, pp. 290–307.

Šima, K. (2021) "From Identity Politics to the Identitarian Movement," in Jürgen Barkhoff and Joep Leerssen (eds.), *National Stereotyping, Identity Politics, European Crises*, Leiden: Brill Publishers.

Tarrow, S. (1994) *Power in Movement: Social Movements, Collective Action and Politics*, New York: Cambridge University Press.

Tarrow, S. (2011) *Power in Movements. Social Movements and Contentious Politics*, Cambridge: Cambridge University Press.

Tessadri, P. (2008) "Rom Modello Lega," in *L'Espresso* (23 July 2008), [accessed on 24 September 2020], available at: https://espresso.repubblica.it/palazzo/2008/07/23/news/rom-modello-lega-1.9349.

Tibaldi, M. (2020) *Giorgio Bertani, editore ribelle*, Milano: Milieu Edizioni.

Tilly, C. (2000) "Spaces of Contention," in *Mobilization*, vol. 5 no. 2, pp. 135–159.

Tilly, C., Castañeda, E. & Wood, L.J. (2019) *Social Movements, 1768–2018*, London: Routledge.

Torrisi, C. (2019) "How Verona Became a 'Model City' for Far-Right and Ultra-Catholic Alliances," in *openDemocracy* (19 January), [accessed on 10 May 2019] available at https://www.opendemocracy.net/en/5050/verona-model-city-far-right-ultra-catho lic-alliances.

Tosatto, F. (2007) "Resistenza, altro choc a Verona: 'Il 25 aprile per i morti di Salò'," in *La Repubblica* (24 July 2007), [accessed on 24 September 2020] available at: https: //www.repubblica.it/2007/07/sezioni/cronaca/verona-memoria-salo/verona -memoria-salo/verona-memoria-salo.html.

Trappolin, L. (2022) "Right-Wing Sexual Politics and 'Anti-Gender' Mobilization in Italy. Key Features and Latest Developments," in J. Ramme, C. Möser and J. Takàcs (eds), *Paradoxical Right Wing Sexual Politics in Europe*, Basingstoke: Palgrave Macmillan.

Tudor, L. (2014) "The Philosophy of Identity: Ethnicity, Culture, and Race in Identitarian Thought," in *The Occidental Quarterly*, vol. 14 no.3, pp. 83–112.

Turam, B. (2019) "The Contested City as a Bulwark against Populism: How Resilient is Istanbul?," in *Spotlight on – Political geographies of right-wing populism. International Journal of Urban and Regional Research* [accessed on 20 November 2022] available at: https://www.ijurr.org/spotlight-on/political-geographies-of-right-wing-popul ism/the-contested-city-as-a-bulwark-against-populism-how-resilient-is-istanbul.

Tutino, A. & Verza, R. (2013) *Verona nella strategia della tensione*, Vicenza: Caosfera Edizioni.

Urry, J. (1999) "Globalization and Citizenship," in *Journal of World-Systems Research*, vol. V no. 2, pp. 311–324.

Urry, J. (2010) "Mobile Sociology," in *The British Journal of Sociology*, vol. 61, pp. 347–366.

Valencia-Garcia, L.D. (2020) "Far-right Revisionism and the End of History," in Louise Dean Valencia-Garcia (ed.) *Far-right Revisionism and the End of History: Alt/ Histories*, New York: Routledge.

Van Stekelenburg, J. (2013) "Collective Identities," in D.A. Snow, D. Della Porta, B. Klandermans, and D. McAdam (eds.) *The Wiley-Blackwell Encyclopedia of Social and Political Movements*, New Jersey: Blackwell Publishing.

van Zeben, J. (2020) "What's the Added Value of Legalising City-zenship?," in Rainer Bauböck and Liav Orgad (eds.) *Cities vs States: Should Urban Citizenship be Emancipated from Nationality?* (EUI Working Papers), Florence: Robert Schuman Centre for Advanced Studies.

Wacquant, L. (2016) *I reietti della città: ghetto, periferia, stato*. Pisa: Eliopoli.

Ward, K, Jonas, A.E.G., Miller, B. & Wilson, D. (2018) *The Routledge Handbook on Spaces of Urban Politics*, Oxon: Routledge.

Wahlström, M. (2010) "Producing Spaces for Representation: Racist Marches, Counterdemonstrations, and Public Order Policing," in *Environment and Planning D: Society and Space*, vol. 28, pp. 811–827.

Ware C.F. (1994) *Greenwich Village, 1920–1930: A Comment on American Civilization in the Post-war Years*, Oakland: University of California Press.

Wills, J. (2013) "Place and Politics," in David Featherstone & Joe Painter (eds.), *Spatial Politics: Essays for Doreen Massey*, Oxford: John Wiley & Sons.

Winchester, H.P.M., Kong, L. and Dunn, K. (2003), *Landscapes: Ways of Imagining the World*, London: Pearson.

Yuen, S. (2018) "Contesting Middle-Class Civility: Place-Based Collective Identity in Hong Kong's Occupy Mongkok," in *Social Movement Studies*, vol. 17 no. 4, pp. 393–407.

Yuval-Davis, N. (1999) "The Multi-layered Citizen," in *International Feminist Journal of Politics*, vol. 1 no. 1, pp. 119–136.

Yuval-Davis, N. (2006) "Belonging and the Politics of Belonging," in *Patterns of Prejudice*, vol. 40 no. 3, pp. 197–214.

Yuval-Davis, N., Wemyss, G., & Cassidy, K. (2018) "Everyday Bordering, Belonging and the Reorientation of British Immigration Legislation," in *Sociology*, no. 52 vol. 2, pp. 228–244.

Zangarini, M. (1993) "Appunti sulla storia del fascismo Veronese," in Maurizio Zangarini (ed.) *Verona fascista*, Verona: Cierre Edizioni.

Zangarini, M. (2012) *Storia della Resistenza veronese*, Verona: Cierre Edizioni.

Zukin, S. (1998) "Urban Lifestyles: Diversity and Standardization in Spaces of Consumption," in *Urban Studies*, vol. 35 no. 5–6, pp. 825–839.

Zukin, S. (2015) "Presentazione: La Gentrificazione è Questa," in Semi, Giovanni, *Gentrification: Tutte le città come Disneyland?*, Bologna: Mulino.

Zúquete, J.P. (2018) *The Identitarians: The Movement against Globalism and Islam in Europe*, Indiana: University of Notre Dame Press.

Index

www.ingramcontent.com/pod-product-compliance
Lightning Source LLC
Chambersburg PA
CBHW070601270326
41926CB00013B/2386